Jewish Art and Civilization

Contributors

CHAPTER I   MUSLIM LANDS
Professor Haïm Z'ew Hirschberg
Professor at the Bar-Ilan University, Ramat-Gan

CHAPTER II   FRANCE
Dr. Moshe Catane
Librarian at the National and University Library, Jerusalem;
Senior Lecturer at Bar-Ilan University, Ramat-Gan

CHAPTER III   ITALY
Professor Shlomo Simonsohn
Rector and Professor at Tel-Aviv University

CHAPTER IV   GERMANY
Dr. Hermann Goldschmidt, D. Phil.; Author, Zurich

CHAPTER V   NETHERLANDS
Dr. Jozeph Michman-Melkman
Cultural Director, Ministry of Education and Culture, Jerusalem

CHAPTER VI   ENGLAND
Dr. Vivian D. Lipman
Former President of the Jewish Historical Society of England;
Lecturer on Anglo-Jewish History at London University

CHAPTER VII   UNITED STATES OF AMERICA
Rabbi Abraham J. Karp
Professor of History and Religious Studies University of Rochester;
President, American Jewish Historical Society

CHAPTER VIII   ISRAEL TODAY
Yaakov Tsur
Formerly Israel Ambassador to Argentina and France; Head of the Jewish National Fund,
and former Chairman of the Zionist General Council

Jewish Art and Civilization

Editor-in-Chief:

GEOFFREY WIGODER, D. Phil.

Head, Oral History Division,
Institute of Contemporary Jewry,
Hebrew University, Jerusalem;
Editor-in-Chief of the
Encyclopaedia Judaica

CHARTWELL
BOOKS, INC.

© 1972 by Office du Livre, Fribourg (Switzerland)

Reprinted with permission by William S. Konecky Associates, Inc.

ISBN 0-89009-649-X

Library of Congress Catalog Card Number: 72-80540

Printed and bound in Hong Kong

Contents

Introduction

A few years ago, the problem arose in Israel of defining a Jew. The resultant controversy engulfed the entire Jewish world and even led to the break-up of an Israel government coalition. Was a Jew one born of a Jewish mother or one who has been converted to Judaism as held in terms of Jewish Law, or was he, as the more liberal and secular definition claimed, one who regards himself as a Jew and has identified himself with the Jewish people? It was ironic that after thousands of years of existence, one of the earth's oldest peoples should suddenly find itself faced with a crisis of self-identification. Yet in a way it is not surprising inasmuch as the ineluctable exigencies of Jewish fate and history throughout the centuries had hitherto made this confrontation unnecessary. It was only the modern developments of Emancipation and secularization, coupled with the practical problems connected with revived statehood, that led the Jews even to ask the question.

When the 'Who is a Jew?' controversy was at its height, the premier of Israel of the time, David Ben-Gurion, circulated a questionnaire on the subject to a cross section of Jewish thinkers in many countries which brought back a rich variety of replies. But even more varied and wide-ranging would have been the answers had he asked another question: 'What is Judaism?'.

Although traditionally based on a unique revelation, much of the development of Judaism was empirical. It had a basic code of law but never a dogmatic creed. In the course of time, individuals endeavored to organize the accumulated code of beliefs but no formulation was officially authoritative. Heresy was essentially identified with antinomianism—a practical breaking or denial of the law rather than an inability to subscribe to a creed. It is significant that the very word 'Judaism' is of modern coinage: up till recently it was enough to speak of the Jewish religion.

An analysis of Judaism as understood in the modern world reveals a number of generally interconnected threads. The first element is the ritual and legal tradition: the Sinaitic Law as refined by the scholars and rabbis of subsequent generations, as developed and formulated in the Mishnah and Talmud and as refined by rabbinical authorities throughout the ages. This aspect today is predominant in what is called Orthodox Jewry—but this too is a modern term because until the 19th century there was no other sort of Judaism (even the major dissenting Jewish sects differed on the interpretation of the Law but not on its authority; the major abrogation of the legal tradition was initiated by Paul and became Christianity). For the Jews as a whole, there was no question as to the authenticity and relevance of the Divine Law. Subtle modifications could be introduced to account for changing needs, as they arose, but the starting point was always the word of the Bible and later the Talmud. For much of Jewish history, this was synony-mous with Judaism. Every step the Jew took was prescribed by the Law and his whole life was dictated by it.

A second element in Judaism is the ethical. Modern scholars have posited an antithesis between the priest and the prophet—the former being linked to the ritual side and the latter, sometimes by way of protest, stressing the ethical and moral angles. However, Jewish scholars in particular have found this an oversimplification. The prophet did not reject the ritual but objected to it becoming an end in itself. The priestly tradition was far from being blind to the demands of morality and indeed analysis of the Jewish ritual code, from its earliest formulation, shows it to be founded on a moral basis far in advance of any contemporary legislative code. But it is true that through the prophet's vision a greater universalism was injected into the early religion. It was through this influence that Judaism shed its parochialism. Both elements were then combined in the Pharisaic formulation.

External circumstances already, then, made introspection necessary, a turning in towards the self, which sometimes hedged in the broader vision. Throughout, the development of Judaism was the result of the interplay between internal forces and external pressures. The Jew was not a free agent and the very preservation of his values and identity often required him to withdraw into his shell and laid emphasis on particularistic tendencies. But the broader vision was always there and was able to blossom out when the Jews emerged from the ghettos. When this occurred, it was visibly obvious that humanitarianism, humanism, and humanity had been fostered and nurtured in the centuries of repression and, given the chance of expression, were a dominant motivation of the Jewish heart. Now the Jew was in the forefront of liberal causes, of struggles for justice, of fights on behalf of the underdog. Now there emerged a new trend in Judaism—Reform, which was prepared to repudiate the eternal validity of the Law and to see it as essentially a basis for an ethical tradition.

But there are further strands to be disentangled in the threads of Judaism. Here again the modern period has laid emphasis on aspects that were not considered or not required previously. This is the result of the process of secularization to which the Jew has been exposed, especially in Western lands and more recently in Israel. There are many Jews who do not subscribe to the ritual and legal demands and who feel that the ethical teachings have in the course of time become part of a universal heritage and no longer are a specifically Jewish domain and yet they remain Jews. Many of them explain this as loyalty to a Jewish culture or civilization. They feel that even setting aside the religious aspects, Judaism has evolved a worthwhile way of life with continuing cultural validity.

In certain instances, this has linked up with a further thread: the connection with the Land of Israel. Ever since the Jews had to leave their own land, they have yearned to return. This return was a natural expression of a desire for an independent Jewish existence, no longer subject to persecution or discrimination or the whim of the majority. This longing achieved concrete expressions in, for example, prayers and in periodic messianic movements. Over the past century, this aspect has been retained even where religion was rejected. It eventually engendered the Zionist movement—which itself was made up of various strands that included a political one (a home free from persecution), a demographic one (a place where Jews could again exercise all professions free of restrictions), a religious one (return to the Land promised by God), and a cultural one. For the cultural Zionist, the return to a free, majority life was necessary for Jewish creativity to express itself under natural conditions. The creations of the Diaspora were artificial, the result of circumstances over which the Jews had no control. The cultural Zionists held that only when the Jews determined their own destiny and way of life would there be any possibility of their creative genius being expressed in a natural way, free from external pressures and not through alien cultures.

There is yet a further strand in Judaism. It is noteworthy that the Hebrew term *yahadut* that has been coined for Judaism in the traditional sense can also mean 'Jewishness' in a broad sense as well as Jewish community. It is this last meaning that is being increasingly recognized as crucial. There is many a Jew today who observes no religious practices, who feels that Judaism and Jewish culture have no special message for him, who has no intention of living in Israel, and yet who is a proud Jew, completely identifying himself as such. Consciously or otherwise he feels himself included in what has been called Jewish 'Peoplehood'. Without in any way detracting from his loyalty to the country in which he lives, he feels an identification and associates himself with the Jewish people as a whole and with their fate. This is true of his attitude to Jews in all other countries—and especially with those in Israel, as was strikingly evidenced by the depth of world Jewish reaction to Israel's moment of peril in 1967. It is a feeling that has been immeasurably heightened by the trauma of the Nazi Holocaust when six million Jews perished, an experience which has left an indelible imprint on the Jewish consciousness.

Judaism—or Jewishness—today can be an expression of any one or a combination of several or all of these factors. It is often elusive and difficult to pin down, although it differs from group to group and sometimes from individual to individual. Jewish spirit and civilization mean different things to different people at different times. In fact the two terms are virtually identical; what the ancient Jew meant by 'Jewish spirit' is in modern parlance 'Jewish civilization'.

There are various yardsticks for measuring the role of Jews in world civilization, but over and above all, the inner development of their own form of civilization must be considered. This in turn has often been passed on through various channels and left its mark on its surroundings. It was central in influencing the early stages of Christianity; it was significant in the development of

Islam. The immediate impact on its surroundings has varied, often according to the extent to which intercourse was permitted. But internally the Jewish spirit proved indomitable and continued to develop according to the basic Jewish vision.

It is this vision which characterizes the spiritual history of the Jewish people and it is this vision which, communicated in various ways, has been their great contribution to the world. And remarkably it has not changed in essence since it was first experienced and formulated in Bible times. One side of the vision is man's relationship to the One God. Jews were the pioneers of pure monotheism and their vision here made possible one of civilization's greatest steps forward. Bound up with this were not only ritual observances but moral dictates. It is perhaps the special nature of the God-Israel relationship that has most disturbed other peoples and even many Jews of recent generations. The claim that the One God singled out the One People is a concept that has drawn increasing fire. Yet the concept has been progressively refined even in a Jewish context. The Jews were selected not to conquer or to dominate but to convey the Word of God, the Divine vision and its implications. Moreover, although historical circumstances compelled an exclusiveness, this is not part of the basic Jewish vision. All nations and people are free to join and participate, but participation involves obligation.

The other side of the vision is man's relationship to man which is a direct consequence of the concept of the One God. The main implication is the idea of the basic equality and dignity of all men. This has achieved expression in the deep Jewish passion for social justice, which has come to the fore even among those Jews who seem the most alienated from their sources and their people.

This vision also resulted in individual Jews playing an often disproportionate role in the cultural lives of their countries, especially since the emergence from the ghetto 150 years ago.

This book traces the history of the Jewish spirit and civilization throughout the ages. It begins where the Bible leaves off. The period and message of the Bible are too well known to require repetition. But with the return to Jerusalem from the Babylonian exile, began the history of the Jewish people; the vision had already been experienced and most of the Bible even committed to writing. The people and its ideals were now to be tried in the crucible of history. The story ends in the same place 2,500 years later—with a parallel struggle to preserve the spirit in face of both internal and external challenges.

Each chapter of this book has been written by a distinguished authority. The contributors were asked to write on the subject of Jewish spirit and civilization within their own sphere of competence, it being obvious that a cultural history cannot be entirely divorced from a political history and that a general framework was necessary inside which the spiritual life could be situated. It is indicative of the wide scope of the concept of Judaism and its various constituent strands that there should be differences of approach among the various authors. No attempts have been made to impose a rigid authority and the very contrasts are themselves revealing. Some authors have concentrated on purely cultural and religious manifestations to the virtual exclusion of any framework; others have inked the framework in heavily.

7

Some have consciously gone into details concerning the internal life of the Jewish communities, their social and economic conditions, feeling that this must be taken as a major part of their civilization. The emphasis varies from period to period, from chapter to chapter. Yet from it all, a unified picture emerges: the picture of a people intoxicated with the products of the spirit. A people that took on itself strict moral obligations but tempered them with artistic sensitivity and permeated them with its vision. History scattered it to all corners of the globe and everywhere it maintained this vision and also passed it on, not only internally but to those outside who were prepared to listen. The spirit and civilization of the Jewish people is as alive and vibrant today as it was 2,500 years ago. In this, it is unique among the peoples of the world and this explains its designation of 'a special people'.

Geoffrey Wigoder

CHAPTER I

Muslim Lands

by Professor Haïm Z'ew Hirschberg

Before Islam

Documents exist attesting the permanent settlement of Jews in the Arabian peninsula two thousand years ago. Scholars and travelers have discovered inscriptions confirming that Jews were already living in the Hijaz before the destruction of the Second Temple. It is a fact that a Judaizing movement spread among the inhabitants of South Arabia in the 5th and 6th centuries A.D., and according to Arab writers, many Yemenite (Southern Arabian) tribes embraced Judaism. The Sabean-Himyari royal family also became Jewish, and the last Jewish king, Dhu Nuwas, died fighting the Christian Ethiopians in 525.

The most important Jewish settlements in the Hijaz were Tayma, Khaybar, and Yathrib (the future Medina). These oases were regarded in pre-Islamic days as Jewish centers, where Jews developed agriculture (especially date-growing) and carried on the manufacture of tools and jewelry, which found a ready market among the South Arabian Beduin who settled nearby. The newcomers adapted themselves to Jewish society; many embraced Judaism and merged with their Jewish environment. A change occurred upon the arrival in Medina of the South Arabian Banu Aws and Banu Khazraj, who established themselves in certain districts and subdued some of the small Jewish tribes. Many historians think that the Jews—or Judaism—would ultimately have been victorious but for the arrival of Mohammed, the prophet of the new religion nurtured on Judaism and Christianity.

In the Arabian Peninsula

Mohammed's arrival in Medina in 622 led to a major change in the status of the Jews in the Arabian peninsula, and first of all in the status of all those in the Hijaz. The prophet of Islam found conditions here suitable for extensive activity. Jews had been resident in the area for centuries, and it was their influence which had predisposed their neighbors to accept Mohammed's teachings. From them, the Banu Aws and Banu Khazraj had learnt the observance of religious precepts and obedience to the word of God.

Not long after Mohammed's arrival in Medina, a pact was made between the emigrants from Mecca and the *Ansar,* the 'helpers', i.e., the Banu Aws and Banu Khazraj, including the Jewish families under their protection. This pact between Mohammed and the Jews of Medina is an interesting document which reflects the situation in Medina when Mohammed settled there, the good relations existing between Jews and Arabs, and the extent to which the Beduin tribes had assimilated with the Jews. It shows that the Jews were regarded as equal partners of the *Ansar* which is why later Arab historians were reluctant to reproduce its text in full.

The pact did not last. Mohammed hoped the Jews would eventually recognize him as their prophet and join the community of those who believed in him. But his hope was disappointed. He demanded discipline and submission of the Jews—demands not mentioned in the pact—and in return was prepared to adopt some Jewish customs, such as the holidays and the facing toward Jerusalem during prayer. However, the Jews would not give up their independence by joining the ranks of the 'believers'. Relations between Mohammed and the Jews deteriorated, particularly after his victory at Badr over the Banu Quraysh of Mecca. He then decided to tackle his enemies in Medina, from which he expelled the two large Jewish tribes.

Encouraged by this success, Mohammed soon began to besiege the third Jewish tribe settled in Mecca, the Banu Qurayza. The latter confined themselves to defensive action, and in the end, relying on Mohammed's magnanimity, surrendered unconditionally. But Mohammed ordered all the men to be put to death, and they met their fate heroically, spending their last night studying the Law. Of a total of seven hundred and fifty, only two or three converted to save their lives. The women and children were sold into slavery; some of them were later redeemed by Jews living in other oases of the northern Hijaz. There, as in Medina, only those Jews were spared who were incapable of endangering Mohammed's absolute rule. However, a not inconsiderable number of Jews remained in the Hijaz even after Mohammed's death.

In the reign of the Caliph Omar, some of the Hijazi Jews were expelled as a result of Mohammed's alleged testamentary injunction: there shall not be two religions in the Hijaz. As nobody had reported any such injunction before, it may be presumed to have been invented by Omar. Many facts suggest that the view taken by Muslims whereby Mohammed forbade Jews and Christians to live in the Hijaz is mistaken. In particular, it has no basis in the attitude of Muslim scholars, some of whom expressly permit non-Muslims to enter the Hijaz and even to visit the Kaaba, the sacred stone at Mecca.

Jews had a great share in the material and spiritual development of North Arabia. Remarkable work was done in Arabia by Jewish farmers, who turned the Hijaz into a land of gardens and cornfields, and when the Jews were forced to leave the places where they had lived free for centuries, these beautiful oases fell into neglect.

Jewish influence was conspicuous in the creation of Islam and the formation of the Koran and the *Hadith* (Oral Law). In its development after Mohammed, Islam adopted many of the ideas, views, and precepts of Judaism, a fact apparent from Arab literature, though Western scholars agree that many facts relating to the Jews are falsified in Arab historiography for the greater glory of Islam.

Under the Rule of the Caliphs

After Mohammed's death, the Arabs, under the leadership of able generals, began to expand their control over neighboring territories. Penetrating into the Byzantine and Persian kingdoms, they won great victories, and the Middle Eastern peoples, though these included a large proportion of Christians, received the conquerors with open arms.

With the 'people of the Book' *(ahl al kitab),* i.e. the Jews and Christians (later also the Parsees), the Arabs concluded treaties, similar to those concluded by Mohammed with the Jews and Christians of the Arabian peninsula, and took them under their protection. The legal term designating their status in the Arab state is *ahl al-dhimma* (protected person). The basic condition of those treaties was the payment of *jizya* (a poll-tax), by those under Arab protection and *kharaj* (a land-tax), by the owners of land and farms. The rate of *kharaj* differed according to the circumstances under which the Arabs had conquered the locality: it was high and variable in a place which had been taken by force, and comparatively low and stable where the people had accepted the conquerors peacefully.

Several versions have been preserved of the treaty concluded by Caliph Omar with the Christian inhabitants of Jerusalem (Jews had been forbidden to live in Jerusalem in the Byzantine period). According to all these versions, Omar promised the inhabitants to protect their lives and property, their churches and crosses. In particular, he agreed to the demand of the Christians that no Jews should live among them; the patriarch of Jerusalem, Sophronius, insisted on this point and asked for the Byzantine ban to be maintained. The Arab authorities, however, did not adhere strictly to this promise, and shortly afterwards, we find a Jewish community in the Holy City.

In fact, nothing is heard of persecutions of protected persons or further curtailments of their rights in the days of the four 'righteous' caliphs and the first caliphs of the Umayyad dynasty, who fully trusted them. Caliph Mu'awiya, for example, settled some Jews in Tripoli to strengthen the reliable elements there. The caliphs were tolerant by nature in their political and religious outlook, and therefore did not interfere in the internal affairs of Jews and Christians.

Intolerance toward Jews and Christians was mainly shown by those members of the two communities who had adopted Islam. Like most neophytes, they were anxious to prove their devotion to their new faith and thus became the chief persecutors of their former coreligionists.

At the time of the rise of the Abbasid dynasty, members of all three religions were to be found as important businessmen. Many Christians and Jews served in government offices, and under the Caliph al-Mamun some were court ministers. In the reign of Mu'talid (892-902), Jews held high government posts, and in 988 a Jew was governor of Siraf. There were also many Jews at the court of the Fatimid sultans in Egypt (see below).

Serious persecutions occurred in the days of the Fatimid Caliph al-Hakim bi-Amr Allah (996-1021). At first he was kind and tolerant toward the *dhimmi* but all of a sudden he changed his attitude: he ordered them to wear black; at the bathhouse Christians had to wear heavy crosses on their chests, and the Jews likenesses of a calf's head. He also ordered prayerhouses to be destroyed. According to the *Genizah* documents, synagogues were destroyed not only in Egypt, but also in Palestine and Tripoli (Syria). Many Christians, but only a few Jews, embraced Islam. The caliph eventually permitted the forced converts to return to their religion, on the grounds that a forced Muslim was not a real Muslim. He also permitted the rebuilding of prayerhouses. Later, non-Muslims were again to be found in high office at the court.

The closer we get to the end of the Mamluk period, the more we are struck by the fanaticism of Muslim clerics, which greatly harmed relations with non-Muslims. Some scholars relate this phenomenon to changes in the structure of Muslim society. The rule of mercenaries recently arrived from Central Asia, or of newly-Islamized liberated slaves, was very burdensome for the veteran inhabitants of the country and the established population gave vent to their feeling of frustration and humiliation by oppressing the *dhimmi*.

NORTH AFRICA

The army of the Caliph Mu'awiya (661-80), on reaching the northern African seaboard, found many Jewish settlements, which, according to their tradition, dated from before the destruction of the First Temple. The Berber tribes, according to Arab authors, included many Judaizers. One of these was the heroine of a war against the Arabs, called Dahia or Damiya, but she was known by the name of *Kahinah* or prophetess. She encouraged the Berbers of the Atlas Mountains to resist the conquerors and was killed fighting them, the rebellion being subsequently quelled. To prevent the spread of Judaism among the Berbers, the Arabs restricted the movement of the Jews and subjected them to many social discriminations. Nevertheless, they did not succeed in uprooting Berber Judaism, and various phenomena connected with this proselyte movement have survived to this day.

In the late 8th century, Idris, offspring of a grandson of Mohammed, wrested the region from the Abbasid caliphate, establishing an independent state. The Jews of Tunisia and Morocco were divided: some supported the Abbasids, the legitimate rulers, and others Idris. After his victory, Idris punished the pro-Abbasid Jews severely: he imposed a heavy poll-tax on them and reportedly ordered them to supply twenty-four virgins annually for his harem. The Idrisids were not the only dynasty founded in North Africa. Others likewise held large portions of this vast area. The Aghlabid emirs, and later the Fatimids developed Tunisia and in particular its principal city, Kairwan, which had been founded at the time of the Arab conquest. During the 9th and 10th centuries important and respected Jewish communities existed in the North African cities of Kairwan, Gabès, Mandiya, Tlemcen, Sijilmassa, Fez and Wadi Dara. The Babylonian *geonim* maintained regular contact with those communities, replying to their queries on matters of Law and religious practice. Kairwan, in particular, was a stopping station between Babylonia in the east and the outer Maghreb and Spain in the west, and fulfilled this role for both Judaism and Islam. The famous Kairwan rabbis, Hushiel and his son Hananel and Jacob ben Nissim and his son Nissim, founded important academies, which spread religious instruction in three continents—Africa, Asia and Europe. Parallel with these spiritual leaders, the *Nagid* (the prince) exercised his function as the political representative of the Jewish community in its relations with the authorities. The Kairwan community was not the only one to have distinguished rabbis; Fez, too, boasted some outstanding scholars.

These two important communities were struck by disaster in the 11th century. In 1032, the Fez community was caught up in a war between Berber tribes for control of the country, in the course of which the city was plundered and its inhabitants decimated. The Jews suffered most; six thousand were killed when the emir of the Banu Ifren captured Fez. The Kairwan community was also ruined. The Muslims of Kairwan, who were Sunnites, did not take easily to the rule of the Fatimid dynasty. When they rebelled, the Cairo central government sent Upper Egyptian Beduin tribesmen to restore control, who, when they entered Kairwan, wrought dreadful havoc (1057). The Jewish community never recovered from the damage sustained on that occasion.

Between the mid-11th and the mid-13th centuries, North Africa saw two successive Muslim movements of a religious-military character, both originating with Southern Moroccan Berber tribes. Both founded powerful states, which were named after them: the Almoravid state and the Almohad state.

The treatment of the Jews in the African part of the vast Almoravid realm was at first fair. One Almoravid caliph had Jewish physicians. The rise of the Almohads, however, brought disaster upon the Jews of Africa and Spain. The Almohads gave all non-Muslims the choice between conversion and emigration. Many suffered martyrdom, many apostatized, and many left for other countries. The Jewish communities in Marrakesh, Meknes, Fez, Sijilmassa, and Tlemcen were destroyed. The expansion of Almohad rule brought severe trials to the Jewries of Spain, Tunisia, and Tripolitania. Even the Jews who adopted Islam had to wear distinctive dark clothing, to make it easier to supervise them. It was at that time (1165) that Maimonides passed through Fez, where the suffering of his coreligionists and the mental anguish of the converts inspired his famous *Epistle on Forced Conversion,* in which he declared that feigned acceptance of Islam, to save one's life, was not an inexpiable sin. The tribulations continued while the Almohad state existed. Its end brought relief to the Jews, but the hatred and contempt for Jews which its rulers had instilled endured for centuries in the hearts of the people and its religious leaders, and the humiliating regulations remained in force.

MUSLIM SPAIN

In the Iberian peninsula, under the rule of the Christian Visigoths, the situation of the Jews was desperate: they had to choose between conversion and death. No wonder, therefore, that they aided the Arab conquerors, as did many of the Christian natives of Spain, who were likewise subjugated by the Visigoths. The Arabs placed some of the conquered cities under Jewish command. In accordance with their practice, the Arabs did not interfere in the internal affairs of the Jewish inhabitants, and the taxes the latter had to pay to the Muslim authorities were less burdensome than the hardships inflicted by their predecessors, the Christian kings. The situation of the Jews was incomparably better than before the conquest. They had to pay the poll-tax, but for centuries this was the only discrimination against Jews (and Christians) in Arab Spain. The number of the Jewish inhabitants increased, and in some cities

Business letter, Egypt, twelfth to thirteenth centuries. This business letter, which is from the *Genizah* (depository) at Fostat, Cairo, is in Judeo-Arabic.

they formed the majority of the population, so that Granada was called 'Jewish Granada' and the Arab geographer, Idrisi, describes Lucena as a 'Jewish' city. In the reign of 'Abd al-Rahman II (c. 825), Jewish merchants went to Spain from Christian Europe, especially from Provence, and under Mohammed I (c. 865) there were many Jewish officials in government departments. One of the most respected and influential ministers at the court of 'Abd al-Rahmän III (912-61) and his son, al-Hakam II (961-76) in Cordova, was Hasdai ibn Shaprut, a distinguished politician, scholar and physician, who knew the European literary languages of his time. On behalf of the caliph, he conducted negotiations with the Christian kings in Spain and the rulers of other Western countries and the Byzantine empire, faithfully serving the Spanish Umayyads for thirty-five years.

In the early 11th century, the Umayyad caliphate disintegrated into several small states. In the kingdom of Granada, ruled by Berbers of the Ziri dynasty (c. 1015-90), a high position was held by Samuel ha-Nagid (Samuel ibn Nagdela) (see below).

Jews also played important roles in the small principalities which were the successors to the Umayyad state. The rulers of these principalities were mostly educated men, anxious to attract Jewish scholars. In Saragossa, an Islamized Jew served as vizier under three emirs. There were Jews also at the courts of Seville, Badajoz and Valencia whose ability and knowledge enabled them to act as officials and interpreters in dealings with the Christian Spanish kings, just as there were Jews at the courts of the latter whose task it was to negotiate with the Arabs.

In the late 11th century, Spain came under the rule of the Almoravids. They did not persecute the Jews, and their leader, Yusuf ibn Tashfin, even ordered the return of the property stolen from Granada Jewry in the 1066 riots. It is true that he demanded that the Jews of Lucena should adopt Islam, but this was merely a pretext to replenish his exchequer; he left them in peace once they had paid a large sum of money. Hard times came when the fanatical Muslim sect of the Almohads defeated the Almoravids and gained control of Africa and later also of Spain (1147). Their Jewish and Christian subjects were forced to choose between conversion and emigration. Disaster befell the magnificent communities of Seville, Cordova, Lucena, and Malaga; many Jews were killed and their synagogues destroyed. Many fled to the Christian Spanish kingdoms, others went to Italy or the East. Some outwardly adopted Islam and waited for an opportunity to return to Judaism.

More than half a century later, the Almohads lost their grip and were expelled from Spain (1212). But by that time, Muslim rule was collapsing. The struggle of the Christians for the reconquest of Spain *(Reconquista)*, which began in the north as early as the 10th century, spread to areas of the center and the south.

REBIRTH OF THE HEBREW LANGUAGE

Jews exerted decisive influence upon their neighbors, especially in a number of countries on the fringe of the new centers then emerging. In these regions, entire tribes, or at any rate large portions of them, assimilated to Judaism to the point of adopting various Jewish customs, or even actually converting. Examples are the conversion of members of a royal family in Southern Arabia and the Judaization of whole tribes, in Yemen, and the royal Khazars in Khazaristan (south-eastern Europe), and the adoption of Jewish customs by Berber tribes in north and west Africa.

As in the Byzantine empire, Hebrew revived in areas under Arab rule. The languages used in synagogues—Greek, Aramaic, and to some extent Latin (in epitaphs)—were completely superseded by Hebrew, which for centuries had ceased to be in everyday or even literary use. Biblical personal names began to reappear. All this was before the period that Palestinian Jews had begun to compose liturgical poetry in Hebrew. The change of attitude toward the Hebrew language stemmed from various factors, but it would certainly be wrong to describe them, collectively, as a national revival. One of the factors operating in the Diaspora was the need to revive the language common to the whole Diaspora and to eliminate the languages current in the different centers, that is, Aramaic and Greek. True, the removal of the Aramaic translation (Targum) from the reading of the Law on the Sabbath was considered almost a transgression of rabbinic injunction. The *gaon* Hai (d. 1038) stated: 'It is obligatory to translate at the synagogue: the reader of the Law must translate the

Rosewater bottle or spicebox, Near East, nineteenth century. Silver. Jerusalem, Israel Museum.

13

Page found in Cairo Genizah, Egypt, 1098. Page from a record book of the rabbinical court in Fostat (Old Cairo), summarizing two sessions dealing with a dispute arising from a business venture to Upper Egypt (March 1098). Thousands of deeds, records and letters between the communities in Africa and Spain and the academies in Babylonia, court-decisions, responsa and so on were found in the *Genizah* (depository) of the old synagogue of Fostat in the 1890s and sold to libraries and museums all over the world. This page is in mixed Hebrew and Judeo-Arabic. The Isaac ben Samuel mentioned in the document was *dayyan* (judge) at Fostat. Cambridge, Westminster College, Fragm. Can. 50 v.

portion from the Law and the reader of the prophetical portion the section from the prophets; this rule has come down to us from the times of the prophets.' But it is significant to note the assertion by the people of Fez, not later than the beginning of the 10th century (or about one hundred and fifty years before Hai Gaon), that they were able to follow the weekly portion in the original and could thus dispense with the Aramaic translation. The testimony of the people of Fez concerning Hebrew antedates by at least fifty years what is known about the spread of the language in Spain.

KARAISM

Whereas the messianic sectarian movements were transitory phenomena, greater importance must be attached to Karaism.

This rebellion against the domination of the rabbis and the Oral Law expounded by them wished to base Judaism solely on the Written Mosaic Law, as they understood it. The originator of Karaism was Anan ben David (d. between 790 and 800), who belonged to the family of the exilarchs. Anan took advantage of trends opposed to Oral tradition that were still in existence—centuries after the disappearance of the Sadducees—and were causing a split in Judaism. His views found response especially in regions remote from the Babylonian academies; and from there came the leaders of the new sect, Benjamin Nahavendi and Daniel al-Kumisi, who called themselves *Bnai Mikra* (Karaites). Abu Yusef Karkasani, himself a Karaite, speaks at length about differences between Anan's teachings and those of later heads of the sect, stressing especially extreme divergences in practical outlook which resulted from the freedom granted each individual to interpret the Law according to his lights. The differences between Karaism and Rabbinism were essentially ritual. Karaite Halakhah was stricter (for example in its Sabbath and its purity laws). The sole doctrinal difference concerned the attitude to the Oral Law. But it may have been precisely because of the differences that Karaism gained wide support, spreading to all countries of the Middle East, to the farthest corners of North Africa, and to Spain. In its heyday (9th to 11th centuries), it constituted a grave danger to Rabbinite Judaism. An important center of a Karaite subgroup, which styled itself 'Mourners for Zion', was Jerusalem. That center disappeared with the general decline of Palestine in the second half of the 11th century and the destruction of the Jewish population of Jerusalem by the Crusaders, and the Gaon Saadyah's persistent struggle against Karaism diminished the latter's influence in Iraq. Apart from the Byzantine empire, sizable Karaite communities continued to exist in Egypt, Syria, Iraq and even Spain. But they ceased to constitute a danger to Rabbinite Judaism and the tension which prevailed during the first centuries after the split lessened considerably.

THE ACADEMIES IN BABYLONIA AND PALESTINE

We must now evaluate the role of the two great centers of the period, Babylonia and Palestine, in consolidating Jewish society into a single entity. In both countries, the most active and fertile brains gathered in the academies from where their influence spread near and far. The main function of the academies was the teaching of the Law. The role of the Babylonian was greater than that of the Palestinian academy. Palestine, however, was more important in the domains of religious feeling, faith, and other factors concerning the irrational. The Babylonian academies were attended by hosts of students—scholars, not beginners—for intensive study of the Talmud; they included men from the Byzantine empire, Egypt, Africa, Italy, and Spain. Palestine attracted a flow of pilgrims from all countries who wished to fulfill the religious duty of 'going up' to Jerusalem. On returning to the Diaspora, they would bring with them something of the sanctity and poetry of the Holy Land and of the yearning of its people for Redemption.

Twice a year, in the 'months of assembly', *(yarhai kalla)*, i.e., *Adar* and *Elul,* a great number of rabbis would meet at the Babylonian academies to refresh their learning and take part in the debates of the *geonim* and other distinguished scholars. During the Festival of Tabernacles, on the other hand, pilgrims would convene on the Mount of Olives, opposite the site of the Jerusalem Temple, to pray and receive the blessings of the Palestinian *gaon* and to hear his announcements on matters of religious Law and the festivals of the coming year, as well as anathemas against the Karaites.

RESPONSA

The teaching of the Law by the Babylonian Jews was not confined to oral instruction; much greater significance, in fact, was attached to the guidance they provided in writing, by replies to questions submitted to their heads, the *geonim.* Judging by the material largely addressed to North Africa and numbering (together with the questions, only fragments of which have been preserved) tens of thousands of items, this mode of teaching was highly developed and took in all aspects of religious and intellectual life. Beside practical questions concerning halakhic rules for the multiple activities of daily life with regard to the individual and the community, the relationship between man and his fellow, and between man and God, there are many theoretical questions concerning the interpretation of biblical passages, the explanation of obscure words and terms in the Talmud, and abstract problems of belief and religion. In view of the state of transport and communications, several questions were usually submitted at a time, and manuscripts often contain grouped answers, which were sent simultaneously to a particular locality. The questions would be sent to one of the two academies, either to Sura or to Pumbedita. It was against established custom to submit the same question to both academies and when this was once done the *gaon* reprimanded the questioners. The questions were addressed to the *gaon,* the head of the academy, and he discussed them with rabbis who either lived permanently at the seat of the academy or stayed there during fixed periods. After the discussion, the *gaon* would dictate the answers to the clerk of the academy, add greetings at the beginning and end of the missive, and affix his signature. The academies maintained archives where texts of the questions and answers were kept, which greatly facilitated the work of the *geonim.*

An important aspect of the Babylonian academies was the formulation of ordinances *(takkanot)* in response to current requirements. As already stated, the source of livelihood of a majority of the Jewish people changed in those days. Agriculture was abandoned, Jews moved to the cities (some of them newly founded), and many laws and customs, based on the economic and social system of the preceding period, became outdated, so that an adjustment of legal norms to the new realities had become imperative. As this was not always possible by a reinterpretation of the existing Halakhah, it became necessary to issue regulations, a method already adopted in the days of the Mishnah and Gemara.

Thus the Babylonian academies enacted a number of regulations, some of which were accepted throughout the Jewish world and are in force to this day, while others were of a temporary nature. The responsa and ordinances constitute in effect a continuation of the work of the talmudic rabbis. They served as a vehicle for updating and—within the given framework—adapting Judaism to new situations.

RABBINICAL COURTS AND JUDGES

The *geonim,* as well as the exilarch, were competent to appoint *dayyanim* (rabbinical judges) in their districts and to see to the proper administration of justice. Each of the two Babylonian academies had a *bet-din gadol* (high court) attached to it, headed by an *av bet-din* (presiding judge), who served as deputy to the *gaon* and sometimes succeeded him. While the *bet-din gadol* could not be appealed to from the judgment of a lower court, it was possible to apply directly to it from the outset. A similar court was attached to the exilarch's office, but its decisions were subject to the approval of the *geonim.*

In Palestine, appeals against judgments of the lower courts were lodged with the *geonim.* The jurisdiction of the head of the Palestinian academy comprised also the Jews of Egypt. Court decisions show that at least seven or eight religious courts existed in the communities west of Egypt during the *geonic* period, viz. in Tripoli and Kairwan and, after the latter's destruction, in Mahdiya, which took the place of Kairwan as a trading center. Presumably religious courts existed in other important communities, such as Tahert, Tlemcen, and Fez, as well.

The *geonim* were only competent to appoint communal judges within their areas of jurisdiction; cases from other countries could not be submitted to them unless both parties consented. At the same time, they exerted considerable influence upon the organization, procedure, and course of decisions of the religious courts by their responsa concerning these matters.

END OF THE GAONIC PERIOD

The *geonim* were not all people of great worth. Some are only known by name, and others, we are expressly told, did not have any special qualities and were dominated by the exilarchs. The twelfth-century historian Abraham Ibn Daud describes Hai Gaon as 'the last of the *Geonim*' (Hai died in 1038), but this is a biased view. Ibn Daud is correct, however, in his appraisal of Hai's work: 'He taught the Law in Israel more than any other *gaon,* and students of the Law from east to west walked by his light'. In fact, the responsa of Hai and his father and predecessor Sherira make up about half of the responsa that have survived. Hai also wrote commentaries on the Talmud and treatises on civil and ritual law. All these were originally written in Arabic, then translated into Hebrew and circulated in the Jewish world. Sherira is also noted as the author of an historical treatise. Hai's father-in-law was Samuel bar Hofni, a *gaon* of Sura (d. 1013). Like Saadyah, (see below), he dealt with linguistics, exegesis, the establishment of halakhic rules on matters of civil and religious law, the composition of responsa, and philosophy. Almost all his books were written in Arabic and, although numerous, are neither as original nor as profound as those of Saadyah or Hai. After the deaths of Hai and of Rabbi Israel, Samuel bar Hofni's son, no scholars capable of heading the academies could be found. The members of Hai's academy thereupon made the exilarch Hezekiah their chief and had him occupy the chair vacated by Hai. By his learning he deserved this honor, but he did not bear the title of *gaon*.

This combination of the two functions, the academic and the administrative, was frequent in the later period, that is, in the days of Maimonides and his descendants (for five generations, until the end of the 14th century). They were *negidim* (secular heads of Jewry) in Egypt and its dependencies, and at the same time spiritual leaders, to whom questions of religious Law were submitted. The Palestinian *geonim* continued to maintain their academies in Jerusalem until the Seljuk invasion (1071), and moved to nearby Tyre when distress reigned in Palestine, and used to travel to Haifa to proclaim the intercalary month. Until recently nothing was known about contemporary events in Palestine, whose history was only revealed upon the discovery of the *Genizah* material. Like the exilarchate, academies continued to exist in Babylonia, Syria, and Egypt.

Letter of Appointment of an Academy Head

The only extant text relating to the appointment of a chief of Jews by the Muslim authorities in Baghdad concerns the academy head *(ra's matiba)* Daniel ben Eleazar, *gaon* of the Baghdad academy and noted halakhic scholar, who was appointed in 1209 by the Caliph al-Nasir. Here is an extract from that text: 'At the request of Daniel ben Eleazar ben Hibbat Allah to appoint him academy head...al-Nasir al-Din...has ordered that he be appointed academy head ... and that he be respected in the area of his appointment in the same places in which the preceding *gaon* used to exercise control. And he shall be distinguished from his colleagues (the rabbis) by the vestments granted to the holders of similar offices (the heads of other religions). And it is the duty of the communities and *dayyanim* of the Jews in the City of Peace (Baghdad) and the confines of Iraq to obey his command and listen to his voice in arranging their affairs, and to do as he bids them. And they shall pay him the fees which according to custom were due to his predecessor from the places ruled by him, and they shall not oppose him in this matter. (These rights are coupled) with the obligation to fulfill the conditions of protection (*dhimma*, granted to Jews and Christians) in everything he does and orders, and he shall, moreover, strictly comply with the ordinances and directions of the Authority and the Glory [the caliph] ...')[1].

This text shows that the authority of the academy head was considerably extended at that period: he acted as the official

representative of the Jews in its relations with the government, a function formerly carried out by the exilarch. The text also rehearses the duties of the head of the academy toward the Muslim authorities. This obviously implies a material change in the functions of the *gaon*, who was originally an internal religious authority. The line of *geonim* who were heads of the Baghdad Academy continued until the end of the 13th century.

Background to the Cultural Relations Between Judaism and Islam

Definite parallels exist between the concepts, tenets, and institutions of Judaism and those of Islam. This is primarily due to influences exerted upon Mohammed by a Jewish environment—especially during his residence in Yathrib—and are clearly discernible in the Koran and the *Hadith*. It would be wrong, however, to attribute these parallels wholly to Jewish influence and thus regard them as 'borrowings'. Much is accounted for by similarities in the spiritual make-up of the two peoples, Jews and Arabs. Thus, for instance, what certainly cannot be explained as a borrowing from Judaism is the division of the sources of Islamic Law—the *shari'a*—into two main complexes: 1) the Koran, which was handed down from Heaven, just as the Jewish Written Law was given at Mount Sinai; 2) the *Hadith* (Oral Tradition) containing the *sunna* (Law based on teachings and practices of Mohammed) similar to the Jewish Oral Law. Nor can other sources of the *shari'a*, such as the *ijma'* (the consensus of the community), the *ijtihad* (independent decisions of authoritative religious scholars) and others be traced back to Jewish influences, though similar concepts exist in Jewish literature.

In any event, the affinity between the concepts and institutions of Judaism and of Islam—especially their common belief in the unity and uniqueness of the Creator and their complete repudiation of the Trinity—was the main reason for the development of a special relationship and fruitful interaction between the two religions. This reason, in conjunction with others, prevented the adoption of mutually hostile attitudes: the rejection of Islam as idolatry on the one hand, and the persecution of the Jews as deicides, stamped with the mark of Cain, on the other.

On this basis, a satisfactory cultural relationship could develop. Particularly significant in this connection was the role of Arabic, the sacred tongue of Islam. The text of the Koran was traditionally communicated to Mohammed in visions by the archangel Gabriel, and Orthodox Islam, therefore, does not usually admit the possibility of translating it into another language or of praying in a language other than Arabic.

We know the negative attitude of Judaism toward Greek and Latin from the moment they became the language of the Christian Church. No Jew subsequently wrote any work on a Jewish religious subject in either of these languages, or at any rate no such work has come down to us. A different attitude prevailed with regard to Arabic which was the channel through which many cultural values flowed in both directions: from the Jews to the Muslims and vice versa. The Jews acquired Arabic from the outset

[1] The Arabic text was published by S. Poznański, *Babylonische Geonim im nachgaonäischen Zeitalter*, pp. 37 and 38.

with ease. Those who lived in Arabia in the pre-Islamic period and were later exiled to other areas used Arabic and knew it remarkably well. Jews in Babylonia, Syria, Egypt, and north-west Africa adopted it within a short time and to such an extent that it was felt necessary to translate the Bible for them into Arabic. Some think that such translations already existed in the early days of Islam, but the first translation preserved in its entirety is by the *gaon* Saadyah, who was also the first who used Arabic in halakhic writings. It may be due to his example that Jewish philosophic and religious treatises, as well as many Bible and Talmud commentaries, were written in Arabic; they were later translated into Hebrew to make them accessible to Jews in Christian Europe.

THE GAON SAADYAH

Arab culture, in every sphere of religion, language, literature, science and scholarship made a major impact upon the Jews living within the Muslim realm. The golden age of this influence and of Jewish-Arab creativeness was the 9th to 11th centuries in the East and the 11th and 12th centuries in Muslim Spain. Many instances could be given of the great Jewish writers and scholars, but as an outstanding instance of this aspect of Judeo-Arab cooperation—a phenomenon unparalleled in Jewish history—we should first mention figure of the *gaon* Saadyah.

Saadyah (d. 942) represents a complete fusion of Judaism and Arab culture. A spiritual leader of the Jewish people in difficult days and a pillar of rabbinic wisdom, his many-sided activities defended Rabbinite Judaism against the Karaite secession and other heresies, strengthened its position, and secured its victory. At the same time, he was imbued with the culture of his environment and wrote his works in Arabic. For all his attachment to the Written and Oral Law and his loyalty to Jewish tradition, his philosophic treatise *Kitab al-Amanat wal-I'tiqadat* (Beliefs and Opinions) is tinged with Greek thinking, as embodied in the writings of rationalist Muslim philosophers and theologians. This was a pioneer work of medieval Jewish philosophy and like most of its successors was written to reconcile traditional Judaism with contemporary rationalism. That book, like earlier and later Jewish-Arab literature, is written in Arabic in Hebrew characters. Saadyah translated the Bible into Arabic in two versions: a short version (which was available also in Arabic characters) and a larger version accompanied by explanations (this version, existing only in Hebrew script, is called *Tafsir*). He also engaged on research into the Hebrew language, influencing the development of Hebrew grammatical studies and philology and was active in various fields of rabbinic teaching. He also prepared a prayer-book with instructions in Arabic (the text of the prayers is in Hebrew).

JEWISH TRANSLATORS

Jews played an important part in the general development of sciences and scholarship. Contemporary Muslim authors of biographical and bibliographical dictionaries mention a number of

Court decision, Jerusalem, 1537. Decision given by the *Shari'a* court (the religious court) of Jerusalem in 1537 in matters concerning a purchase deed of the Sephardi community in Jerusalem during the Ottoman rule there.

Jews who distinguished themselves in various branches of natural science, astronomy and medicine. The most outstanding of them was certainly Maimonides, and we shall comment later upon his work and that of many other Jewish savants and writers. One aspect of the activity of Jewish scholars which proved of international significance was translating. In the 11th to 13th centuries, Spain, Sicily, and Southern France produced a school of Jewish translators which communicated the achievements of Arab science to Europe through excellent translations of a number of works from Arabic into Hebrew, from which they were subsequently translated into Latin. The linguistic knowledge and skill of the Jews enabled them to translate the best of Arabic literature on philosophy, medicine, astronomy, and natural science. The further translations into Latin (and Spanish) were sometimes done by Jewish converts to Christianity. Most of the originals of these works have been lost and they are preserved only in translation. Where the original Arabic text has come down it is sometimes written in Hebrew square script, which indicates that the copyists were Jews.

From the second millennium A.D., intellectual activity slackened. Stagnation set in, which in some areas degenerated into paralysis. The decline was particularly marked in Palestine as a result of several factors: the devastation of the country by frequent invasions in the 11th century, the extermination of the Jewish population by the Crusaders and the degradation of the country under the Mamluks, to whom it was a mere trouble spot, an obstacle to normal communications between Egypt and Syria. A reawakening took place only in the late 15th century, upon the advent of a new wave of settlers in the region, who were, in fact, Jews expelled from Spain and Portugal.

Autonomous Administration

In the unanimous view of Jewish sources, the first caliphs, Omar and Ali, were well disposed toward the representatives of the supreme bodies of Babylonian Jewry: the exilarch and the head of the academy at Firuz Shabur, to which the rabbis of Pumbedita had moved when Jewish religious and administrative institutions were affected by social upheavals. The position of the Jews had at that time been upset in every way, but a period of renewed prosperity began with the stabilization of Arab rule, which did not interfere in the internal organization of the non-Muslims. Under these circumstances, the Jews, after a period of depression and humiliation, were able to recover a remarkable degree of self-government.

There were different religious trends among the Jews but even the Karaite split did not impair the organizational functions of the majority institutions. The leaders of Iraqi Jewry—both elected and hereditary—were charged with the collection of all taxes imposed on the Jews, their representation in their relations with the Muslim rulers, the administration of justice, the enactment of regulations for the welfare and security of the community and, last but not least, the supervision of rabbinic studies.

The 'secular' autonomous administration in Persia was headed by the exilarch, whose office originated in the days of the Parthians and continued under the Sassanid dynasty. The exilarch was a descendant of David; his position was hereditary in the Davidic family. After a period of instability prior to the Arab conquest, Bostanai (d. 670) was recognized as exilarch and subsequently passed on the office to his sons by a Jewish wife and by a wife who was a daughter of the king of Persia. The sons of the Jewish wife challenged the eligibility of the sons of the Persian one; they contended that she had been a captive and had not been properly converted to Judaism and that her sons, therefore, were slaves and disqualified for the exilarchate. The rabbis eventually decided in favor of the 'Persian' branch, and from then onward there were two lines of the Bostanai dynasty, both of which produced exilarchs and *nesi'im* (princes).

The Karaite dispute may have been the cause of a curtailment of the power of the exilarch in the reign of the Caliph al-Mamun (813-33). Some think that it was in answer to pleas by the Karaites, who wished to be independent of the exilarch, that the caliph issued a decree permitting any ten Jews, Christians, or Zoroastrians to form a separate community and elect a leader for themselves. However, this decree may have been prompted by other complaints. According to the *Gaon* Sherira's historical treatise, the exilarchs sometimes behaved high-handedly, deposing and appointing academy heads at will.

The decline of the Abbasid caliphate entailed a waning of the influence of the Babylonian *Geonim* over the Jewish communities. In territories not controlled by the Baghdad caliphs, that is, Egypt, North Africa, and Spain, independent Jewish authorities emerged, not subordinate to those in Babylonia. In the shrunken Abbasid domain, however, the powers of the exilarch subsisted and were used by the caliphs to extort money from the Jewish community. The Muslim authorities also made use of the heads of the communities for the enforcement of discriminatory regulations.

Nesi'im (princes) of Davidic stock continued in Baghdad until the days of Tamerlane (1401). At the time of the decline of the Abbasid caliphate in the 11th century, when power passed to the Seljuks, small-scale governments emerged in Mosul, Damascus, and Aleppo. Members of the exilarch families, who had settled in these cities, had risen to important posts in which they were confirmed by the governments. The memory of the Davidic kingdom was so prized by the people that descendants of the king were held in high esteem everywhere. Their title was *nasi* (prince). Because of their descent, they were placed, as a matter of course, at the head of the community as its recognized representatives. The *nesi'im* collected tithes, poll-tax, and other duties, appointed officials and communal judges, and administered justice.

Information on developments in Palestine during the first centuries following the Arab conquest is scanty. From what is known about Mar Zutra, who, because of the political situation in Persia, fled to Palestine in 520, the Palestinian tradition of the unity of political and spiritual leadership appears to have been revived about that time. Mar Zutra became *rosh ha-perek* (head of the Academy) and *rosh ha-Sanhedrin* (head of the Religious High Court). It seems that his descendants also held both offices, and

Synagogue doors, Egypt, twelfth century. Doors of the Ibn Ezra synagogue in Cairo. The carved wood panels are from the thirteenth century. Jerusalem, Israel Museum.

that this unity was preserved when members of other families became heads of the Palestinian academy. Thus, for instance, Aaron ben Meir (early 10th century), the first Palestinian *gaon* of whose life anything is known, traveled to Baghdad on community business, while the *gaon* Solomon ben Judah, who held office about a century later, maintained a ramified correspondence with Jews in Egypt, the center of Fatimid rule, and went to Fostat himself on behalf of Palestine Jewry.

THE NEGIDIM IN EGYPT AND NORTH AFRICA

More details are known of the forms of organization of the Jews of Egypt and North Africa. For political reasons, it did not seem desirable to the Fatimid caliphs in Egypt that the Jewish communities within their realm, which extended as far as what is now

Morocco, should be subject to Jewish authorities outside it so that they—like the Umayyads in Spain and part of Morocco—encouraged the severance of local Jewry from the Babylonian center.

When the Fatimids set out to conquer Egypt (969) an Italian Jew, Paltiel, headed the Jewish community in North Africa, which was already under Fatimid rule. Allegedly he was the first holder of the office of *nagid* in Egypt and was followed by a line of *negidim* extending over centuries. About the same time, the Umayyad caliph in Spain appointed Jacob ben Jau head of the Jews of Spain and the Outer Maghreb. He issued a document to him setting him 'over all the Jewish communities from Sijilmassa to the Duero, which is the boundary of his realm...' The caliph or emir would appoint a man acceptable to him to be *nagid,* or representative of the Jews, responsible to him for the fulfillment of the latter's obligations toward the government (payment of

19

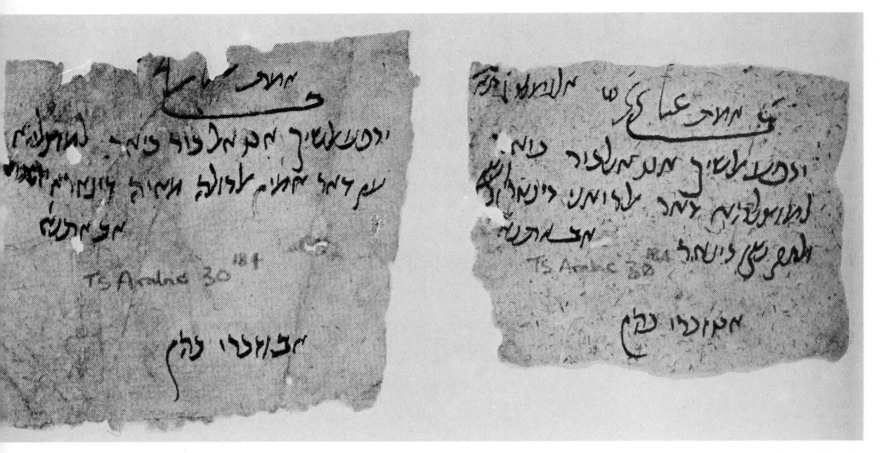

Payment orders, 1140. Two payment orders issued by Abu Zikri Kohen in summer 1140. The one on the left is for 100 dinars. Cambridge, University Library, TS Arabic Box 30, f. 184.

taxes and the like). The *nagid* was accordingly empowered to collect taxes from the members of his community, appoint various officials (perhaps also religious judges), and so on. His tenure was usually based on designation by the ruler of the country, and not on election by the community or approval by Jewish authorities abroad, such as the exilarchs and *geonim* in Babylonia or the heads of the Academy in Palestine. The *nagid* generally occupied an important position at the court of the ruler, being his secretary (in one instance perhaps even vizier), his physician or his banker and treasurer. Devoted service won him the confidence of his master, which made it easier for him to fulfill the task of intercessor on behalf of his coreligionists.

Paltiel's jurisdiction extended over all the Jews in the Fatimid state; as Ahimaaz[1], his ancestor, put it in his *Scroll of Descent,* he was *nagid* of the communities of the people of God living in Egypt, Palestine, Palmyra, Africa or anywhere else in the Arab realm.

Texts have been discovered of the letters of appointment of several Egyptian *negidim,* which show that the functions of the *nagid* were similar to those of the exilarch: he represented all the Jews, gave halakhic decisions, administered justice according to rabbinic law, drew up marriage deeds and decrees of divorce, and saw to it that people said their prayers facing in the right direction, that is toward Jerusalem; it was his duty to enforce the

[1] See chapter II.

special regulations applying to the *dhimmi.* Although the *nagid* was a Rabbinite Jew, he was competent to tryy Karaites and Samaritans as well.

The office of *nagid* existed in Egypt until some years after the Turkish conquest in 1517. It was revived in Morocco in the 16th century, while holders of similar offices in Algeria and in Tunisia and Tripolitania were called *muqaddam* and *qa'id* respectively.

THE MAINTENANCE OF COMMUNAL INSTITUTIONS AND LEADERS

We know that pilgrims to Jerusalem contributed to the maintenance of the Palestinian academy. It should be noted, however, that the official recognition of Jewish institutions by the Muslim authorities enabled the former to levy taxes and fees from the people under their jurisdiction. According to a Palestinian *gaon* of the early 11th century, the first Fatimids in Egypt went even further: the scholars 'were supported by the authorities and we were thus not a burden' on the community. The Fostat academy likewise received assistance from the authorities.

The situation was different in Babylonia. The country was divided into three areas of taxation. In the area under the direct control of the exilarch, he collected—directly or through a judge sent by him—taxes and fees for public purposes and for his own household.

The academies of Sura and Pumbedita each had their own area of taxation. In addition, they shared the gifts sent them from other Diaspora countries. All these revenues were used for the maintenance of the academies and their scholars and students. A scholar received a fixed grant *(hok)*, but if he distinguished himself he got an extra allowance, and if he was negligent or lazy he got less and was warned that unless he mended his ways he would get nothing.

In normal times, the academies subsisted comfortably on these revenues. But in times of political upheavals, or when the flow of assistance from abroad ceased for any reason, most of the scholars and students were badly off, and the *geonim* had to issue calls for aid. In the 11th century, the Palestinian academy was almost always in need of foreign help, and most of the letters of the *gaon* Solomon ben Judah deal with this subject.

The economic decline of Middle Eastern Jewry, as well as the slackening and, at the time of the Crusades, temporary severance of its ties with the Occident, destroyed the material foundations of its religious and administrative institutions. This was another cause of the decline of the academies and the loss of status of the exilarch (or *nasi* or *nagid*) and all the autonomous bodies.

ECONOMIC LIFE

Much information—comparatively—has reached us concerning the role of the Jews in the economic life of the Muslim East, but this information has only recently received due attention. Arab geographical literature, which began to develop in the middle of the 8th century, provides the background for an understanding of many phenomena in the economic field; the data it supplies about the Jews, though sketchy, is of considerable importance. Late aggadic *midrashim,* responsa of Babylonian *geonim,* court decisions, and various *Genizah* documents, most of which were written in the 10th to 12th centuries, permit a closer study of details. It should be noted in particular that the *Genizah* documents confirm in a striking way the statements of the Arab geographers and the conclusions drawn from *gaonic* literature concerning the role of Jews in various branches of the economy: handicrafts, retail and petty commerce, wholesale and maritime trading. Records in Christian European royal archives, responsa of African rabbis, reports of Jewish travelers and accounts of Arab historians, which take over at about the point where the above-mentioned sources dry up, complete the picture up to the end of the Middle Ages.

The sources are not evenly distributed over the different areas and periods. Still, the politico-social and cultural uniformity of the Middle Eastern Muslim countries during most of this time—a uniformity which existed to an even greater degree in Jewish society, especially in the economic field—enables us to draw an accurate picture.

The Arab campaign of conquest tore down the barriers separating Persia from Byzantium and the latter from Visigoth Spain, and all the subjects of the caliph had an equal chance to display their initiative and abilities. The spoils of war and the taxes imposed on the non-Muslims brought fabulous riches to the Arab tribesmen who took part in the fighting and to their heirs, but being relatively few in number, they had to leave free scope to the initiative of non-Arabs and non-Muslims.

Capital cities and major administrative centers sprang up. They included (from east to west) Ahwaz, Tustar, al-Kufa, Baghdad, Ramle, Fostat, Cairo, Mahdiya, Kairwan, Asir, Tahert, and Tlemcen. In the course of time, these cities also became trading centers and seats of religious and secular learning. There was a recurrence of the phenomena of rival twin cities, well known in antiquity, as, for instance, Jerusalem and Caesarea. New cities developed as a result of the decline of the old (Lydda—Ramle; Ctesiphon—Baghdad; Fostat—Cairo). The Mediterranean became an Arab sea; the Byzantine fleet ceased to play an effective part in Mediterranean trade. North Africa was now an important link in east-west and north-south maritime trading.

Changes in the distribution and economic structure of the general population brought about far-reaching shifts in Jewish society. It would seem that at the beginning of Arab rule there were still a not inconsiderable number of Jews in the villages of Palestine (and of Babylonia). Contrary to the prevailing view that the Arab conquest ruined Palestinian agriculture, reliable witnesses report at the end of the first millennium A.D. that the country was still remarkably fertile and that its agricultural products, especially oil and various fruits, were major items of export.

Extant information thus indicates that a rural Jewish population still existed in Palestine in Arab times, but like the general Jewish population, it was evidently dwindling. Villagers moved to the newly built cities, and many city-dwellers migrated to areas where life was easier, such as Egypt, North Africa, and Spain.

The sources suggest that Jews engaged in agriculture, horticulture, fruit-growing and cattle-raising in North Africa and in Spain. Some of the questions addressed to the Babylonian *geonim* refer to fields irrigated by water-courses, the lands belonging to orphans, and the sowing of garden-beds. Some of the stories in *Hibbur Yafeh me-ha-Yeshu'ah*[1] show that Jews engaged in sheep- and cattle-rearing. A rural or semi-rural landscape is the background to several of these stories. The images used by the author must have been familiar to his readers and are therefore evidence that the Jews in those countries engaged in agriculture and fruit-growing.

HANDICRAFTS AND PETTY COMMERCE

It nevertheless appears that most Jews in those days made a living from handicrafts and in petty commerce. Such is the view of Arab sources, which note that most Jews in Syria were dyers, tanners, barbers, cooks, or *jahabidha* (see below). On the other hand, most physicians and government officials were Christians. An order of the caliph al-Muqtadir (908-32) limited the employment of Jews and Christians in government service to physicians and *jahabidha,*

[1] A collection of *midrashim* and stories in Arabic by Nissim ben Jacob, a distinguished Kairwan rabbi of the middle of the 11th century.

21

but this order was not strictly adhered to, so that they are also found in other functions. The fact that *gaonic* responsa do not contain much material concerning crafts and craftsmen is not surprising, since special halakhic or legal problems, requiring instructions or guidance by the Babylonian academies, did not generally arise in these occupations. The silence of these sources would not therefore permit any conclusions to be drawn even if important material contained in other types of literature were not available. In fact, it is inconceivable that precisely during that particular period the Jews should have withdrawn from occupations that they had practiced since olden times, such as spinning, weaving, dyeing, and especially the fashioning of precious metals.

Islamic Law forbids the faithful to exercise the trade of a gold- or silversmith. It regards as usury the remuneration received by a craftsman for shaping precious metal and lays down that no Muslim may charge more for gold and silver articles than the value of the material, without any payment for the work and without compensation for wastage. Muslims, in consequence, avoided working in precious metals in any way that might be said to involve the charging of interest. This was why in Muslim countries—especially during the early stages of economic development—occupations connected with the handling of gold and silver were monopolies of non-Muslims. These were the occupations of a gold- and silversmith and of a *jahbadh* (plural *jahabidha*), that is, an examiner of precious metals, a money-changer (initially including money-lender and banker), a collector of taxes and customs, who not only had to be familiar with different kinds of coinage, able to calculate its value according to its precious metal content, denomination, and weight, but also to keep proper accounts, an art common among Beduin.

The fact that Muslims refrained from gold and silver work was, moreover, the reason why mints in Muslim countries were in Christian and later also Jewish hands. Though we lack precise information as to the early period, we know, for instance, that at one time the mint in Egypt was in Jewish hands, and Jews also minted coins in Yemen and North Africa.

The *Genizah* has preserved lists of payers of taxes and dues and of recipients of alms, as well as many business letters and documents providing interesting information on people of different occupations and livelihood. The conclusions to be drawn from them are no doubt valid not only for Egyptian Jewry, but for Jewish society in general. Researchers into the *Genizah* have compiled a list of hundreds of crafts and other professions pursued by Jews in Muslim countries. In the light of this, there appears to be no truth in the statements of Muslim writers limiting the occupations of the Jews to a small number of despised trades: moneychanging, tanning, shoemaking, dyeing, weaving, and masonry. Jews carried on trading in cloth, silk, perfumes, corals and pearls, highly respected occupations that Muslims also engaged in.

The high proportion of dyers is remarkable. They are followed by moneychangers, coin examiners, gold- and silversmiths and dealers in gold and silver, cooks and manufacturers (or sellers) of beverages. Also mentioned are millers, tailors, bakers and manufacturers (or sellers) of oil. Many are dealers in textiles, pharmacists,

or sellers of chemicals. Occasionally someone is described by the Persian term *nakhodad*, which originally denoted a ship-owner and was later used in the sense of a pilot or helmsman. Jews owned ships in the Mediterranean both within the Christian sphere of influence and in Muslim areas. We know of Jewish-owned Indiamen as well.

There were Jewish ironsmiths and armorers in the Arabian peninsula in the pre-Islamic period. Leo Africanus[1] reports the presence of Jewish ironsmiths in the mountains of Morocco as late as the beginning of the 16th century. In fact, Jews were the only craftsmen (blacksmiths, carpenters, goldsmiths) in certain parts of the Atlas Mountains until not very long ago.

TRADE

Jewish economic activity was not confined to retailing: it comprised business extending over the whole of the inhabited world of those days. A first intimation of this occurs in a book by the geographer Ibn Khurdadhbeh (d. 912) telling of the travels of the Radhanites, or Jewish traders, in Europe, Africa, and Asia. They spoke all the languages then current: Arabic, Persian, Greek, Frankish (presumably French), Spanish, and Slavonic. Their activities were most varied. They imported eunuchs, female slaves, young boys, brocade, furs, hides and swords from Europe to the East. They brought musk, incense, spices, and perfumes, which were in great demand in Europe. Ibn Kurdadhbeh mentions the principal stages of their journeys from Europe to China. One route led via the port of Farama (ancient Pelusium), Qulzum (ancient Klysma, modern Suez) and Sind (in southern Persia). Another passed through Antioch, al-Jabiya (in northern Syria), the Euphrates and Tigris, and the city of Ubulla at the outlet of these rivers into the Persian Gulf.

Some of the Radhanites crossed from Spain to the western tip of North Africa (Sus al-Aqsa) and from there proceeded via Tangiers, Kairwan, Fostat, Ramle, Damascus, al-Kufa, Baghdad, Basra, Ahwaz, Faris, Karaman, Sind, and Hind. This means that they passed through the countries in which the majority of the Jews were then concentrated: Spain, North Africa, Egypt, Palestine, Iraq, and Persia. Presumably they came into contact with the inhabitants of the countries through which they passed and let the local Jews take part in their business in one form or another.

JEWS IN LEADING ADMINISTRATIVE AND ECONOMIC POSITIONS

In the second half of the 10th century, mention is made for the first time of a Baghdad merchant who became vizier in Fatimid

[1] Author of a famous description of Africa.

See illustration page 33.

Torah Ark, Egypt, thirteenth century. Coming from Cairo in the 13th century, this reconstruction of the Torah Ark is 119″ high, 76½″ wide and with a diameter of 20½″. The reconstruction of the socle and shrine was carried out in 1902. New York, Jewish Museum, S. 727.

Egypt. This was Jacob ben Killis, a native of Baghdad, who occupied at first the position of merchants' representative at Ramle, that is, the official agent of the Jewish merchants in that important administrative and political center. He enjoyed the confidence of Kafur, the Ikhshidi ruler of Egypt, who placed him in charge of the revenues of the *Diwan* (Finance Ministry) in Egypt and Syria. However, he aroused the jealousy of the Muslim vizier, and after Kafur's death he was forced to flee Egypt and sought refuge in Kairwan. It is said that with the help of Jews at the court of the Fatimid caliph al-Mu'izz, he was received into the service of that ruler, who was just then preparing to march against Egypt. According to Arab writers, Jacob proved of great assistance to al-Mu'izz's army commander during that campaign. At the Fatimid court in Egypt, he rose to ever higher rank and

was eventually appointed vizier, laying the foundations for public administration and tax collection in that country, where he died in 991. Although he converted to Islam, he maintained friendly relations with the Jews and employed some of them as his representatives in Egypt and Syria for purposes of tax collection and intelligence. One of these was Manasseh al-Qazzaz (or the 'silk merchant'), who represented the Fatimid regime in Syria and continued in this function even when a Copt was appointed vizier. A poem in honor of his son, 'Adiya, says about Manasseh: 'He was feared in Aleppo, Tyre, Sidon, and Ramle... and he humbled the Beduin.' 'Adiya served as scribe (government secretary) and his sons were *Negidim* and *Sarim.*

After the convulsions afflicting Egypt during the reign of the caliph al-Hākim bi-Amr Illah (996-1021), Jews were again to be found at the court of the Fatimid caliphs in administrative-economic posts. Especially prominent were the descendants of the merchant Sahl al-Tustari, i.e., members of a family originating from southern Persia (Tustar in the 10th century was an important commercial center, and Jews had a considerable share in its prosperity). A wealth of material exists concerning the firm of Banu Sahl. The sources especially stress their trade in precious stones, but they also supplied other goods to the court. Trading in precious stones led to their participation in international commerce, and they carried on correspondense with many countries. It is not surprising that their economic activities made an impact on affairs of state, and Muslim writers vividly describe their wealth. But the Banu Sahl were not the only Jewish trading firm in Egypt during that period. The tolerant attitude of the Fatimids attracted many Jewish merchants to Fostat, especially upon the decline of Kairwan. Ties between the latter and Fostat were very close as long as the Fatimids ruled over both Tunisia and Egypt. Fostat was then the natural meeting-place of traders from the Maghreb, Sicily, and eastern countries, as far as China. In addition to Babylonian and Palestinian-Syrian Jews ('Iraqis' and 'Shamis', respectively) there was a considerable number of Jews from the Maghreb, who had either settled in Fostat or were there for a long time on business. The flow of immigrants to Egypt increased in the second half of the 11th century following political upheavals in both east and west.

TRADE WITH INDIA

The first half of the 12th century saw a marked increase in Jewish trade between Egypt and India by a land-sea route passing via southern Arabia or via the African Red Sea port of 'Aidhab, Egypt's southern customs-station. The particular effort of North Africans in this field is understandable. In addition to general factors (the Crusades, in particular), there was a decisive local reason: the decline of the Maghreb, which compelled Maghrebi merchants to seek new sources of livelihood. *Genizah* documents present a very lively, personal picture of these traders and their way of life, problems, connections, and activities.

In the 12th century, the *Genizah* letters contain many names of travelers to India, some occurring frequently, others mentioned only once or twice. It is well known that Moses Maimonides' brother, David, was drowned on the way to India.

The dimensions of international trade called for new methods to overcome technical and legal difficulties. Traders were organized in family partnerships and maintained a division of functions among themselves. Not all of them were always traveling, nor could the supply of goods and their preparation for sale be left to chance. But even the members of a ramified family could not conduct business in different parts of the world, sell, buy, barter, and undertake trips lasting months and sometimes years, without using agents, factors, and partners acting under special contracts. The *Genizah* yields a wealth of material concerning the organization of Mediterranean and Indian trade in the 11th and 12th centuries.

THE PERIOD OF DECLINE

Important political and economic events—the Crusades, the Almohad conquests in Spain and North Africa and the attendant oppressive policies, the rise of the port cities of Venice, Pisa, Genoa, and Marseilles, and the Mongol campaigns—began to affect the Muslim East and its trade. They impaired the livelihood of the Jews, who were compelled to adjust to new conditions of life. Even those living in Egypt, then the richest country in the Middle East, became impoverished, and although they were still the best off among the Jews, they barely managed to make a living. State monopolies on various branches of trade reduced the share of the Jews in them. Trade with India declined owing to European competition, which took the new routes. Religious fanaticism debarred the Jews from the civil service, although some Jews, as well as some Christians, managed to get in. The number of Jewish doctors, on the other hand, seems to have been still relatively large and included famous specialists who continued the tradition of Maimonides.

On the whole, it may be said that the nearer we get to the end of the Middle Ages the smaller the number of skilled Jewish craftsmen becomes and the larger the quantity of poverty-stricken peddlers. We also note a decline in the merchant class, that suffered from the economic instability of the Mamluk state, which then extended right into the center of Asia Minor.

ECONOMIC RECOVERY IN THE MAGHREB

In the countries west of Egypt, the Jewish populations had suffered at the hands of the Almohads. The decline of the Almohad dynasty in the middle of the 13th century was the signal for the reconstitution of Jewish communities in cities from which Jews had been expelled a century before. This new trend was caused, among other things, by the economic needs of the dynasties that took over the Almohad areas. The economic recovery of the Jews is attested by the fact that the kings of Spain used Jews for diplomatic and commercial missions to North African countries. During the same period, we hear of Jews as experts in the cultivation of dates and industrial crops (on the island of Djerba), and especially of Maghrebi Jews as wealthy merchants (in Tlemcen, Fez and elsewhere).

The peace treaty concluded in 1360 between the sultan of Tunis and the king of Aragon repeatedly made mention of the Jews of Catalonia and those of Tunis. They, like the other subjects of the two states, were promised safety on the roads and protection against robbers. One article provides that no Muslim or Jewish Tunisian shall be held prisoner in Aragon after the conclusion of the treaty, and that if any such is in prison he shall be released; a corresponding provision relates to Aragonese subjects in Africa. Lastly, the sultan promised the king an annual payment of 2,000 great gold dinars out of the customs duties on goods imported by Christian and Jewish Aragonese subjects.

This explains why, following the catastrophe of 1391 in Castile, Aragon, Catalonia, and Mallorca, refugees from these areas sought shelter in the cities of the central Maghreb, the region now called Algeria. Many of them settled in the city of Algiers, which from then on experienced economic prosperity and developed as an administrative center. Others went to Tlemcen and Honain, cities in the kingdom of the Banu Ziyan which then knew a short period of prosperity. A similar distribution took place upon the arrival in Morocco of those expelled from Spain in 1492.

SPANISH JEWRY: A RETROSPECTIVE VIEW

The Jews who lived under Arab and Berber caliphs and emirs in Spain for about four hundred years, from 711 to about the middle of the 12th century, were an entity unto themselves. From the cultural point of view, they can hardly be placed in the Muslim East, nor can they be included within Christian Europe. During the first three hundred years, Muslim Spain was politically united, either as part of the Umayyad caliphate or as an independent state. In the early 11th century, it split into small principalities under Berber or Arab rulers, some of which were independent, others tributary to the kings of Castile or Aragon, who had begun their *Reconquista* campaigns. In the late 11th century, the Muslim principalities were aided by Yusuf ibn Tashfin, the leader of the Almoravids. He defeated the king of Castile in 1086, and a few years later made himself master of the more important principalities. His victory ushered in a period of trial for the Jews in the areas concerned. In the middle of the 12th century, the Almohads, another fanatical religious movement of similar origin, took over

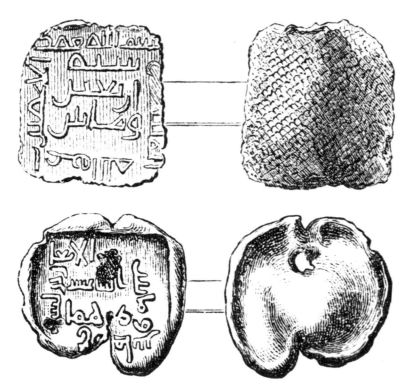

Leaden tags, North Africa, ninth century. Jews and Christians had to wear leaden tags (or seals) around their necks and wrists as proof that the poll tax *(jizya)* for the financial year had been paid. Photo Harris.

from the Almoravids in Africa and Spain. They subjugated and regimented the entire population, Jews and Christians being the chief sufferers. Their rule lasted for two generations. In 1212, they sustained a crushing defeat at the hands of Christian Spain and were forced to evacuate the country. The *Reconquista* had by then been going on for over a hundred years, and about fifty years after the defeat of the Almohads all the Muslim principalities were in the hands of the Christian kings, except little Granada, which was in fact a vassal of the kings of Castile, but only surrendered to them absolutely in 1492. When this happened, the Muslims of Granada were immediately expelled and the Jews were expelled from the whole of Spain some months afterward.

This political background, which is only one facet of the varied life of the population of Muslim Spain—Muslims, Jews, and Christians—explains many features in the life of the Jews, who could be classified in three main groups, differing in their past history and socio-religious traditions:

a) Remnants of the community of Visigoth days, which had been decimated by the anti-Jewish measures of the Councils of Toledo. They were mostly farmers, craftsmen, and shopkeepers.

b) Immigrants from North Africa and Asia. They brought with them a tradition of the Jewries of the Arab Muslim East: a deep respect for the Babylonian Talmud and the teachings of the *geonim.* They belonged to the merchant class and contributed to the strengthening of ties between the Muslim East and the Maghreb. They included an important, though not—so far as is known—large group of intellectuals: grammarians, philologists, liturgical poets, and religious and religious-legal scholars. These Jews were attracted by the centers of intellectual life: Cordova, Lucena, and Granada. Their departure had impoverished Jewish life in Morocco in the 11th century

c) The above-mentioned political and social conditions, and especially the ties between the Jews of the two regions (Muslim and Christian), and also between them and the Jews of Provence and Italy, encouraged Jewish immigration from the Christian West to Muslim Spain. The immigrants included not only merchants, but also intellectuals, and the twelfth-century historian Abraham Ibn Daud mentions, for instance, R. Paregoros, an eminent scholar from France, who settled in Cordova about 1055 and instructed one of the local rabbis in various branches of learning. R. Moses ben Enoch, a captive who was redeemed from a Muslim admiral and settled in Cordova in the 10th century, was in all probability of Italian origin; he furthered rabbinic studies in that city.

The amalgamation of those three groups, which used different languages—Romance Arabic, Hebrew, and Latin—both in everyday life and in literature, produced a society open to all intellectual influences and trends then prevailing in the eastern and western worlds.

In the religious sphere, Spanish Jewry was linked to the eastern centers, Sura and Pumbedita in Babylonia. According to a tradition preserved among eleventh-century Spanish rabbis, the deposed eighth-century exilarch Natronai wrote down the text of the Babylonian Talmud for the Jews of Spain. Amram, ninth-century *gaon* of Sura, prepared an order of prayers for the whole

25

year at the request of the Barcelona community. In fact, the Spanish rite was similar to the Babylonian, while the Italian and Ashkenazi-French rites were influenced by the Palestinian. R. Sherira and R. Hai, the last heads of the academy of Pumbedita, tried hard to strengthen the ties with Spanish Jewry, and Samuel ha-Nagid (see below) corresponded regularly with R. Hai.

However, Spanish Jewry did not neglect its relations with Palestine, whose academy was the object of its care. At the same time, the separate centers in Italy and Provence, which had already emerged in the 10th century, also made their influence felt.

We must note further factors which made their impact upon the development of Jewish society in Spain. Arab-Muslim culture reached a climax in Spain in poetry, speculative thought, science, and scholarship, as well as in material civilization, architecture, and the arts. The Jews, who had a perfect command of Arabic, easily acquired the intellectual and esthetic values offered, and their taste became refined as a result. They acted as intermediaries between Muslim culture and that of Christian Europe. Odd as it may seem, the *Reconquista* induced a favorable, tolerant attitude toward the Jews, both those who were subjects of the Christian states and those who lived in the conquered cities of Muslim Spain or sought refuge from Almoravid or Almohad persecution in Christian-controlled territory. The Christian kings found it expedient to enlist the help of the Jews in fighting the Muslims. This situation, certainly, coupled with the influence of the rationalistic Aristotelian philosophy, led to religious indifference, and even defection, in some Jewish circles.

Under the circumstances outlined above, the Jews of Muslim Spain developed features distinguishing them from their brethren in both the Muslim East and the Christian West. The most salient of these, which earned them a particularly high reputation, was the many-sided brilliance reflected in the achievements of their most prominent representatives. R. Saadyah and R. Hai in the east, Rabbenu Gershom and Rashi in the west, each made a unique contribution to Judaism. But Moses Maimonides was unique in his own way. A native of Cordova, he was compelled in his youth to flee Spain because of the Almohad persecutions. He stayed for a time in Fez and eventually settled in Cairo in 1166, where he died in 1205. Maimonides started as a youth to compose a commentary on the Mishnah in Arabic. He finished its first version in 1168, but never stopped correcting and revising the text. The intention of his commentary was to explain each law in the Mishnah. The purpose of his *Book of Commandments* was to give a summary of the Commandments, selected and arranged according to fourteen principles he laid down. This attempt met with considerable opposition.

Maimonides' biggest and most impressive work is the *Mishneh Torah,* a great code of the whole of Jewish Law, on which he worked for many years. The first draft of it was completed in 1175-6, but he worked continuously on it to the end of his life. The Code is known under the title *Yad Ḥazakah* (Strong Hand) because it is divided into fourteen books (the letters of *yad* = 'fourteen') in which all laws (those in use and those not in use in the Exile and after the destruction of the Temple) are summarized. But Maimonides' assertion in the Introduction that the study of his Code would be sufficient to learn the entire Oral Law, dispensing with the need to go back to the sources, aroused the anger of many scholars.

The Code served as target for attacks from Samuel ben 'Ali, the head of the Baghdad academy and R. Abraham ben David of Posquières who wrote very sharp objections—especially concerning its method. But in later generations the Code had a tremendous influence on the theory and practice of Jewish Law and Maimonides is one of the greatest authorities on the subject.

Not less important was Maimonides' influence as a philosopher, as author of the *Guide of the Perplexed*. The *Guide* is written in the spirit of Aristotelian philosophy which Maimonides seeks to reconcile with Judaism (although where he discerns a conflict between the two, the religious approach is indicated). The *Guide* was a complete survey of Jewish faith—a fitting companion to the *Yad* which was a comprehensive survey of Jewish practice. It became the outstanding work of Jewish philosophy and was influential beyond Jewish circles, being quoted by scholars such as Thomas Aquinas. However, the insistence that Judaism can only be properly understood in terms of Aristotelian thought aroused widespread criticism in the Jewish world where the book was the subject of prolonged controversy. Maimonides, who was physician to the sultan, was also a medical authority and his books on medicine were widely used in Jewish and Arab circles.

POETS AND PHILOSOPHERS

Research into the Hebrew language did not originate in Spain, but it reached its peak in the works of scholars who lived there, especially Judah Hayyuj, a native of Fez, and Jonah Ibn Janah (called R. Merinus in Jewish sources) who both wrote in Arabic and whose works were translated into Hebrew. Their studies served as a basis for grammatical research and lexicography, as well as biblical exegesis, in the 19th century.

It is difficult today to appreciate the importance of poetry in those times. It played a vital role in various spheres of life, holding a key position in society and politics. It was considered an integral part of education, and everyone who had any pretention to good breeding tried to become adept at it. The Hebrew poetry of Spanish Jewry, therefore, reflects that community as it really was, with all its contrasting facets. When comparing the religious and secular poems and the philosophical treatises of certain authors, it is sometimes hard to believe that they were written by the same person. The gulf between the two forms may have been a characteristic of the mind of the Spanish Jew.

Of the many distinguished Hebrew poets, we will mention only the three most famous: Solomon Ibn Gabirol (11th century), Moses Ibn Ezra and Judah Ha-Levi (contemporaries and friends, 12th century).

Ibn Gabirol, though he died young, wrote many secular and religious poems, and at the same time was a profound philosopher. His *Fons Vitae,* which contains neo-Platonic ideas—including a detailed plan of creation by emanation—made a great impression in Catholic monastic circles and later with Spinoza. Until the 19th century, it was known only in Latin translation and was ascribed to an Arab author—which was due in no small measure to the total absence of Jewish content. Only then was a Hebrew summary discovered which proved that Ibn Gabirol was the real author. Two other philosophical works by him exist in Hebrew translations, but they, too, betray scarcely any Jewish inspiration.

Moses Ibn Ezra, a native of Granada, of noble lineage, was also called ha-Sallah, or writer of *selihot* (penitential hymns). His *selihot* display a remarkably rich and fertile imagination. His secular poetry, however, contains descriptions of sensual abandon unparalleled in medieval Hebrew poetry. Ibn Ezra is the author of a work on Hebrew poetry entitled *Book of Discussion and Remembrance,* which incorporates answers to questions he had been asked on the subject. Of particular historical interest is the answer to the fifth question: 'Why are the Jews of Spain superior to the other exiles in Hebrew poetry, rhetoric and epistolography?' The answer gives an extensive survey of the development and practitioners of Hebrew poetry in Spain. Ibn Ezra also wrote a philosophical treatise, *The Bed of Balsam,* at the instigation of Christian intellectuals.

The most celebrated of the Spanish-Jewish poets, especially in recent generations because of his *Sons of Zion,* is Judah Ha-Levi. In his poems and in *The Kuzari* (see below), he expresses his longing for the Land of Israel, and his laments over its devastation have become part of the liturgy of the Fast of the Ninth of *Av.* He also wrote many penitential hymns and poetic prayers. But even he did not shun the anacreontic genre.

Judah Ha-Levi's fame as a thinker rests on a philosophical treatise in Arabic, *Book of the Demonstration and Proof about the Victory of the Despised Creed,* known under the title *The Kuzari,* which was given it in the Hebrew translation. The Kuzari is a king of the Khazars, a people in Russia who had adopted Judaism about four hundred years before the composition of the book, in which the Kuzari is the central figure. His counterpart in the book is a Jewish sage who explains to him the principles of Judaism, and especially the ideas of Exile and Redemption and the role of the Holy Land in the process of Redemption. Unlike the other classics of medieval Jewish philosophy, Judah Ha-Levi does not undertake an overall reconstruction of theology and current rationalism. Judaism, he holds, is based on a divine revelation which does not require philosophical proof to be bolstered up. The Jews, he held, are the heart of all the nations and the sufferings of the Diaspora are a period of trial and preparation for the eventual return to the Land of Israel. Judah Ha-Levi regarded settlement in the Land of Israel as likely to bring Redemption nearer. He therefore bade farewell to his family and friends and boarded a ship bound for Egypt, to go on from there to the Holy Land. He reached Alexandria and reluctantly took up an invitation to visit Cairo, but while preparing to set out for Palestine, he died at the beginning of 1141. Legend has it that he died a martyr's death at the gates of Jerusalem, trampled by the horse of an Arab while reciting his lament, 'Zion, dost thou not ask the welfare of thy captives?'

These remarks about a few aspects of the intellectual and religious life of Jewry in Muslim Spain are very far from exhausting

that vast subject; we catch another glimpse of some aspects in the following chapter on Christian Spain. Much could be said about their many achievements in the sciences, as astronomy, mathematics, geodesy (Abraham bar Hiyya), medicine, and so on.

JEWS AT THE COURTS OF SPANISH MUSLIM RULERS AND IN THE GOVERNMENT

In the middle of the 10th century, Hisdai Ibn Shaprut, physician and tax-collector, was at the court of Caliph Abder-Rahman III in Cordova. Though not a religious scholar himself, he patronized rabbis and showed interest in the study of the Hebrew language. He translated a Greek book on medicine into Arabic. He was conversant with the languages of Christian Europe and was therefore entrusted with missions to neighboring countries and negotiations with foreign delegations.

Hisdai used his position at court to help Jews in distress in Christian countries. He made great efforts to verify the rumors concerning the Judaized Khazars on the distant Volga; he eventually established contact with their king and entered into correspondence with him.

A completely different sort of person was Samuel ha-Nagid (Samuel Ibn Nagdela, 993?-1056?), the vizier of Habus and his son Badis, Berber emirs of the Banu Ziri dynasty, who ruled Granada in the 11th century. He was an educated man and had access to the emiral court thanks to his beautiful Arabic script and polished Arabic style. He was at first appointed *katib* (secretary), but his intelligence and good sense ensured his advancement, until he became vizier, a post not usually entrusted to a non-Muslim. He was also the commander of Badis' armed forces, and in his numerous poems he describes his victories over hostile neighbors, as well as the dangers threatening him through their intrigues and through those of his rivals at the emir's court.

Samuel ha-Nagid was also an outstanding rabbinic scholar. Not content with merely assisting rabbis and buying them books to facilitate their studies, he wrote talmudic treatises himself. In 1027, he was appointed *nagid* for the Jewish communities, and thereupon, in the words of the historian Ibn Daud, took care of them 'in Spain, the Maghreb, Ifriqiya, Egypt, Sicily, indeed as far as the academy in Babylonia and the Holy City'.

When not occupied at court, on the battlefield or in the Jewish communal sphere, he was active as a writer and poet. By his intelligence and prudence he was able to avoid the pitfalls of his exalted position. However, his son, Joseph, who was appointed his successor in office, although endowed with the same abilities as his father, lacked the wisdom to appreciate his position as a Jew. He was assassinated toward the end of 1066 and his death had dire consequences for the Jews of Granada.

The three men mentioned were not the only Jews at the courts of Muslim emirs. There were still the Ibn Ezras in Granada, the Ibn Albalias in Cordova and Seville and others. Even at the court of the Almoravid ruler, 'Ali Ibn Yusuf ibn Tashfin, in Marrakesh (Morocco), there were two Jewish physicians who had great influence upon the emir and his family.

The characteristic feature of the Jewish communities in Middle Eastern countries at the end of the Middle Ages was a general decline—religious (in piety and learning), social, economic as well as numerical. This process had already started by the time of the fall of the Abbasid caliphate, but from the 14th century on, signs of this decline were unmistakable. The Oriental lands from Persia, Mesopotamia, Syria, Palestine, and Egypt to the outermost Maghreb were partially emptied of their Jewish communities.

In the middle of the 12th century a small return movement to the East began, giving new energy, fresh impetus, and new religious ideas to the communities there. Individuals and groups from the Maghreb settled in Egypt and Palestine as a result of the policy of the Almohads. A large group of rabbis from France immigrated to Palestine in the 13th century. From the 14th century on, immigration from Christian-dominated countries spread over the whole Muslim East. At first merely symbolical, in time it became a real movement and in the late 15th and early 16th centuries assumed significant proportions. It never ceased from then on. Most of the immigrants were 'returnees' (sometimes after centuries) from countries where they had been persecuted (Spain, Hungary, Ukraine), but many came from countries where their lives had not been in danger (Italy, Western Europe).

Apart from settling in Algeria, many Jews who left the Iberian peninsula continued eastwards to Egypt and Palestine since there were no favorable conditions for settling in Morocco, while the other Berber countries were in danger of being invaded by Spain. Those who reached Egypt joined the once-famous communities of Cairo and Alexandria, which had declined in Mamluk days. The Cairo community, however, being in the capital of the state, was still very important since the *negidim,* the recognized leaders of all Jews in the vast Mamluk realm, resided in the city. On the capture of Cairo by Sultan Selim in 1517, Egypt became a part of the Ottoman empire, and from then onward, the Cairo community was controlled from Constantinople. In the 16th century, it included a number of eminent rabbis and scholars, and as was natural, the Cairo sages maintained close relations with those of Palestine.

Spanish Jews settled in Palestine even prior to expulsion from Spain at the end of the 15th century; we find them in both Jerusalem and Safed. Upon the conquest of the country by the Turks in 1516, the stream of immigrants turned especially to Safed, where they established the clothing industry.

A further wave of emigrants reached the countries of North Africa (except for Morocco) from the late 16th century onward. They were the *Gornim* (the people from Leghorn), mostly descendants of refugees from Spain, but including also Italian Jews and North Africans. Long after they were given the right to settle in that port city, they struck out for the southern shores of the Mediterranean. They are first attested in Tunis and Tripoli and later also in Algeria.

Prominent among the earliest refugees were a few men who had a decisive influence upon the life of the Jews both from an organizational and a spiritual and religious point of view. R. Isaac

Torah case, Damascus, 1565. This cylindrical Torah case, of inlaid copper with silver arabesque ornaments, is 32″ high and 7″ in diameter. It is of Samaritan manufacture, signed Joseph, and comes from Damascus (1565). The scroll inscriptions are in Samaritan, with Bible quotations praising the Lord. New York, Jewish Museum. S. 21.

Hanukkah lamp, North Africa, nineteenth century. Silver. Height: 10½″; width: 8″. Jerusalem, Sir Isaac and Lady Edith Wolfson Museum, Hechal Shlomo ref. 1738-26-89.

Bag for prayer shawl, North Africa, nineteenth century. Bag of velvet and gold thread. A prayer shawl is worn by adult Jews at the morning prayer service. When not in use, it is kept in a special bag. Jerusalem, Israel Museum.

ben Sheshet Barfat, and his younger colleague, R. Simeon ben Tzemah Duran, both came to Algiers, were active leaders of the community, and may be said to have shaped the character of the North African Diaspora in modern times. R. Isaac ben Sheshet was about sixty-five when he settled in Algiers in 1391, after serving as a rabbi in large Spanish cities for a long time. R. Simeon was of distinguished parentage, wealthy, and an expert surgeon. In Majorca (which he had fled with his family following the persecutions) he had practiced medicine rather then teaching as a source of livelihood. During one of the riots, his property had been looted and, on arrival in Algiers, he and his family were threatened with starvation. Having no choice, he accepted the position of a salaried rabbi, religious judge, and teacher.

A third personality deserving mention, because of the peculiar role he played even up to the present day in the life of North African Jewry, is R. Ephraim Enkaua. Son of an illustrious family of rabbis, he, too, came as a refugee from Spain. After some wandering, R. Ephraim was for an unknown length of time rabbi at Honain; from there he moved to Tlemcen, which had developed as a center for refugees. He gained honor and influence at the court of the emirs, and after his death, a wreath of legends was woven around his personality. He was called simply 'the Rabbi' and is still famous throughout the area among members

of all three communities. Pilgrimages are made to his grave and, especially on *Lag Ba-Omer,* thousands gather in the cemetery where he is buried.

THE OTTOMAN EMPIRE

We now turn our attention to the eastern part of the Middle East where a shift in the balance of forces had already set in by the second half of the 14th century. From then on, the military might of the Ottoman Turks increased and Ottoman expansion reached its peak in the days of Suleiman the Lawgiver and Selim II. These conquests brought many Jewish communities under Turkish sway, both in hitherto Christian-controlled areas and in Muslim countries threatened by Spanish invasion; they could then breathe freely.

In the 15th and 16th centuries, there were Ashkenazi and Italian communities in several cities of the empire: Constantinople, Adrianople, Salonika, Sofia, Fleven, Vidin, Trikkala, and Arta. The Ashkenazim came from Germany, France, and Hungary, the Italians from Sicily (then under Spanish rule), Apulia, Otranto, and Calabria.

But those expelled from Spain and Portugal in the years 1492-7

29

played the decisive role in shaping the character of the Jewish communities in the Ottoman empire. Although they do not seem to have numbered more than 7-8,000, in time they left their mark on all the other Jews, both the veteran residents in the Arab and Byzantine areas (the latter called Romaniots) and the Ashkenazi and Italian immigrants. They arrived in the days of Sultan Bayezid II (1481-1512), who opened wide the gates of his country to the Jews. The newcomers naturally preferred places with a

Jewish population which had mostly settled earlier than the ruling majority groups (Turks, Mamluks, Arabs).

The impression which the first refugees from the affluent European countries received upon meeting the 'residents' was dismal in every respect. Their material and spiritual conditions were poor. Books were then very expensive, and even Torah scrolls for use in the synagogues were lacking. The persecutions during the Almohad era and the ensuing curtailment of relations

Pair of Torah finials, Algeria, 1895. The finials are ornaments placed on the staves of the Scroll of the Law. Here the names are possibly those of the donors. Silver. Height: 1′ 5″; width: 3 ⅞″. Jerusalem, Sir Isaac and Lady Edith Wolfson Museum, Hechal Shlomo, ref. 1867-4-38.

Torah scroll mantle, North Africa, nineteenth century. Velvet with gold-embroidered thread. Unlike the usual Oriental Jewish practice, the mantle is here placed over the scroll in the typical Western manner. Length: 2′4″; width: 1′ 5 ½″. Jerusalem, Sir Isaac and Lady Edith Wolfson Museum, Hechal Shlomo, ref. KT 12-34.

Complaints were voiced against the immigrants from Spain by R. David Cohen, a Romaniot rabbi who lived in Constantinople about the time of the Expulsion. He accused them of ignorance in religious matters, the reading of apocryphal books, and of neglect of the Torah and deplored the fact that they were not Godfearing. All, he said, thought themselves very clever, and as they did not recognize the ordination of rabbis (which had then been introduced with the Ashkenazim in Italy and with the Romaniots) every one of them regarded himself as competent to make decisions and issue instructions in matters of Jewish Law.

Looking at and trying to assess the characteristics of the new immigrants, it must be admitted that their sense of intellectual preeminence and superior economic ability was justified. At the same time we cannot overlook their conceit and vanity which may have been the result of their close contact with the Arabs and Spaniards, two peoples particularly noted for their lofty pride.

As a result, the immigrants from Spain and Portugal organized themselves everywhere into separate communities, called *kehalim*. They had synagogues of their own with rabbis, religious educational establishments (such as talmudic schools), charitable institu-

Portrait of Mohammed II by Bellini, 1480. Mohammed II's conquest of Constantinople represented the deathblow to Byzantium. After his conquest, the sultan settled new inhabitants there, among them many Jews. London, National Gallery.

with communities elsewhere had arrested their development. Maimonides' great treatise was the only halakhic work in their possession. In the opinion of refugee scholars ignorance was rife among the masses and the religious leaders.

Obadiah of Bertinoro, who immigrated to Palestine in 1488 and settled in Jerusalem, describes the utterly wretched condition of the inhabitants of that city. He found there some conversos who had returned to Judaism—certainly immigrants from Spain. R. Obadiah preached in the synagogue twice a month in Hebrew. He had two Spanish disciples who studied regularly with him. His efforts led to a great improvement of the situation a few years later.

Jewish woman courtier, Turkey, eighteenth century. Engraving of the eighteenth century. Some Jewish women played a part in Turkish court life, as for instance Esther Chiera (c. 1520-93) who exercised considerable influence over state affairs until she was murdered in a court intrigue. Jerusalem, Israel Museum.

tions, and separate taxation. The *kehalim* were not transitory institutions, gradually losing importance or being superseded as time went by, as was the case in the Maghreb. Although the differences in languages, culture, economic circumstances, and religious customs which justified the existence of a separate organization of the immigrants immediately after their arrival grew less acute, the original divisions did not disappear, owing to a tendency toward sectionalism and fragmentation among the Sephardim. Evidence of this is the formation of separate communities according to region, even city, or origin, and subdivisions within these communities as a result of debilitating internal squabbles. Things went so far that regulations had to be issued forbidding the withdrawal of members from their communities, accession to other communities, or communities combining together to form new ones.

LEGAL AND SOCIAL STATUS

Until the mid-19th century no change occurred in the legal position of the non-Muslim subjects of Muslim rulers. The special tax laws and the restrictions regarding the erection of new synagogues and altering the shape of the existing ones (those decrees forming the hallowed tradition based on Omar's regulations) remained in force. The sympathetic attitude of the rulers toward the immigrants from Christian Europe did not exempt them from the application of Omar's regulations, nor give them a status on a par with that of the Muslims. The Jewish sources ignored personal discriminations and restrictions providing they did not go beyond accepted custom. The immigrants from Christian Europe for their part saw nothing unusual in them, since they were accustomed to similar restrictions in their countries of origin.

The situation of the Jews and the legal status of the Jewish religion in the Ottoman empire were generally not different from those of Christians and Christianity, although the veteran Jewish residents could not claim the protection of the European powers who regarded it as their sacred political and religious duty to assist Christians and Christianity in Muslim countries.

Non-Muslims knew how to circumvent the regulation forbidding them to construct new buildings for religious worship, which, if followed, would have restricted them to the use of those built prior to the Arab conquest. In actual fact, many hundreds of houses of worship were erected in cities founded under Islam such as Kairwan, Baghdad, Fez, and Cairo; they included large and sumptuous ones, as may be concluded from a letter describing the destruction of the Jewish community of Kairwan. Naturally things were not the same all the time. According to Obadiah of Bertinoro, the Jew of his period (late 15th century) was forbidden to rebuild his home and yard (in Jerusalem) without permission, even if they were falling down, and the permit was sometimes more costly than the rebuilding itself.

At approximately the same time the Ottoman sultan Mehmed al-Fatih forbade the construction of new synagogues, but permitted the use and repair of old ones. A generation or two later R. Jacob Ibn Haviv, a scholar of the first generation of refugees from Spain, describes conditions in Turkey: 'We are not permitted

Parokhet (Ark curtain), Turkey, eighteenth century. A decorative Turkish carpet like a Turkish prayer carpet with a Hebrew quotation from Psalm 118:20 which often appears over the entrance of synagogues. The carpet measures 6' 6¼" × 4' 10". Jerusalem, Sir Isaac and Lady Edith Wolfson Museum, Hechal Shlomo.

to obtain permanent quarters for a synagogue, let alone build one, we are compelled to hide underground, and our prayers must not be heard because of the danger.'

The special dress *(ghiyar)* of non-Muslims in the East is described in detail by European tourists. The refugees from Spain in Algiers were distinguished by the *capos* or *caperon* (a cloak) and thereby differed from the veteran residents whose headdress was the cap *(shashiyya)*. In the late 15th century the chief rabbi of Constantinople forbade the wearing of the *caperon*, the cloak of the Sephardi sages, but the difference in dress between veteran residents and descendants of immigrants from Europe long continued.

The archives in Constantinople contain a number of orders, issued in the years 1568-1837 concerning the headgear and clothes of Jews and Christians. These orders lay the emphasis on the headgear, as did the clothing regulations for Jews in Persia in the 17th and 18th centuries. The headgear of the non-Muslim became such an established characteristic that its replacement by the turban of the Turks was deemed evidence of a change of religion.

The Jews generally had to wear dark clothes. Light or colored clothes were only permitted on Sabbaths and religious festivals

Necklace, North Africa. The necklace has small amulets against the evil eye. Jerusalem, Sir Isaac and Lady Edith Wolfson Museum, Hechal Shlomo.

Torah Group, North Africa, nineteenth century. The Torah Scroll is covered with a *meil* or mantle that is velvet with gold and silver thread embroidery, leatherbacked with morocco. The finials are minarets in miniature and are of silver, with gilt and enamel. Jerusalem, Isreal Museum.

Ketubbah, Persia, nineteenth century. This *Ketubbah* is in Arabic script and the Persian language and comes from Meshed (Persia). In 1839, the Jews of Meshed were forced to embrace Islam. Although the community had to pose as Muslims, they secretly observed the Jewish laws, until they could openly return to Judaism. Berkeley, Dr. Fischel Collection.

Ketubbah, Yemen, 1795. Marriage c[on]tract containing the settlement of [the] amount due to the wife on the death [of] her husband or on divorce. These c[on]tracts are usually illuminated and [are] sometimes very attractive specimen[s of] folk art, of great historical inte[rest.] Jerusalem, Israel Museum. Photo H[...]

Jewish woman, Algeria, c. 1840. Married Jewish woman from Algiers. According to Jewish law married women are forbidden to go out bareheaded or be seen by anyone other than their husband without a head-covering. Colored engraving. Jerusalem, Israel Museum.

Gargush Merassaf headdress, Yemen, end of nineteenth century. Yemenite headdress for the married woman of San'a. The coins are the Maria Theresa thaler, a currency still used in the Persian Gulf. Brocade, silver and gold thread embroidery, gold filigree ornaments. Jerusalem, Israel Museum.

within their own districts. The authorities seem to have been particularly strict about the prohibition of green (a green headgear was a sign of descent from the prophet Mohammed) and purple. But there is evidence that these Ottoman decrees were not rigidly applied; according to eighteenth-century sources many Jews in Constantinople wore green turbans and the same type of shoes as the Turks. The strict prohibition to wear green and purple clothes issued in Morocco by Mawlay Yazid in 1790-2 (and revoked by his successor Mawlay Suleiman), shows that the prohibitive decrees were not rigorously implemented in the Maghreb either.

The *ghiyar* are mentioned in official Turkish sources until almost the mid-19th century. A decree of 1837 says that Jews and

Christians permitted to wear the tarbush must provide it with special marks so as to be distinguished from Muslims. The *berat* issued to the first chief rabbi of Jerusalem in 1841 says that his official emissaries are exempt from the *ghiyar* so that they may travel unmolested. They were also permitted to carry arms in order to defend themselves if attacked. Only a small section of the population was involved in this emancipation of the outer appearance by the shedding of the *ghiyar*. The overwhelming majority of the Jews of Morocco, Tunisia, and Tripolitania, of the 'Old *Yishuv*' (community) in Palestine and of the Jews of Yemen, Kurdistan, Persia, and Afghanistan retained their traditional garb until quite recently.

Plan of Constantinople, c. 1520. Plan of the town of Constantinople by Giovanni Vavassore of about 1520. The inscription 'Sepulture de Giudei' which figures above that of Pera indicates the site of the Jewish cemetery just beyond the Golden Horn. It was in use for several centuries.

THE JEWISH QUARTER

The residence of non-Muslims in separate streets and quarters has been a prominent feature of the Muslim city ever since the Arab conquest in the 7th century. Owing to certain historical, ethnic, religious, and economic factors, the Jewish quarter is the most conspicuous of all the non-Muslim quarters, and has been the object of much attention by European travelers since the 16th century. Their descriptions give the impression that the Jewish quarter was from the outset a ghetto, like that established in Christian environments from the 16th century. Yet their sometimes unfavorable accounts are not always sufficiently objective.

In reality, the territorial concentration of the Jews in separate quarters in or near eastern cities preceded the Arab conquest and was caused by the need for every Jew to be able to live in accordance with religious law. The inhabitants of the separate quarter regarded it as the citadel of their independence, enabling them to live and organize their lives in accordance with their traditional customs. Here they could establish, without hindrance, places of worship and other religious institutions and set up endowments managed by their own people; here they could preserve their own language or dialect. The quarter was not hermetically sealed to the inhabitants of other quarters, who were able to rent property (plots of land and shops) in it for the conduct of their business.

These quarters are called *mellah* in Morocco, *hara* (also *shara*) or *zanqa* in Algeria, Tunisia, and Tripolitania, *qaʿa sharba* or *masbata* in Yemen, *mahalla* in Turkish and Persian environments. There is nothing derogatory in any of these terms. Most of them are used for Muslim and Christian localities and also mean 'quarter', 'lane', 'place', or 'camp'. Much research has been devoted to the explanation of the term *mellah,* which means 'saltmine' in literary Arabic. All that is known for certain is that it was the name of the first Jewish quarter in Morocco, established near the royal palace in New Fez in the 13th century. In the 16th century Fez had also a Muslim *mellah*. The name was subsequently applied to Jewish settlements in Morocco generally, and today designates any such settlement, whether part of a town or village or some distance away from one. *Mashata* means a quarter where the Sabbath is observed; this name is not offensive either.

The influx of immigrants from Europe caused far-reaching changes in the administration of the Jewish quarters in Muslim countries. The immigrants brought with them the democratic features of resolutions and ordinances adopted at meetings of all the franchise-holding members of the congregation. In the Ottoman empire—at first in Rumelia and afterward also in Anatolia—the fragmentation of the community into congregations, each of which formed a self-contained jurisdictional unit, independent of any other congregation within the quarter, reached its climax.

Developments in the Maghrebi countries, where some of the earliest refugees settled, were not uniform. The Jewish quarter in the Moroccan capital, that is Fez and afterwards Meknes, was headed by a *nagid* appointed by the ruler; beside him there were congregations, each of which made its own bylaws. A different situation prevailed in Algeria: in the 17th century control was still in the hands of three *mukkadems* (wardens, selected members of the board, *adelantados*), but in the 18th century and until 1835 there was only one *mukkadem,* appointed by the *dey* (governor). The common feature of all the Jewish quarters in North Africa was that they turned in time into ghettoes, so that the terms *mellah* and *hara*, which designate respectively the Jewish quarters in Morocco and in the rest of North Africa, became synonymous with 'ghetto'. The degradation of the Jewish quarter in North Africa to the status of ghetto was not accidental. The same process occurred in the other countries where the Jews were the only remaining non-Muslim community, as in Yemen, Afghanistan, and Persia.

RELIGIOUS AND INTELLECTUAL LIFE

The profound changes occurring at the end of the Middle Ages, on the threshold of the modern era, were more evident and conspicuous in the religious and intellectual spheres than in other fields. For many generations the religious life of the well-established communities in the areas of Muslim rule followed a fixed pattern. Reverence for the sages of earlier generations and their teachings hindered the quest for new ways of studying Torah, and scholars were content to rehearse the decisions embodied in ancient literature. Once the storm over Maimonides' philosophical writings had abated, no fresh impulse came to develop or carry forward religious thought. The great merit of the immigrants from Spain, Italy, and other European countries was to have injected some new ideas into this slightly ossified atmosphere. The successive blows that shook occidental Jewry from the Crusades onward (and even before) and the numerous crises and disasters which befell the Jews of Spain and Portugal set in motion religious and intellectual activity that had hitherto hardly found expression in official religious literature.

A few years after the Ottoman conquest of Palestine, Safed, a city without any Jewish antecedents, became an important religious center that drew a large number of eminent scholars. The *bet midrash* of R. Jacob Berab, a refugee from Spain who settled there after some wanderings in North Africa, was founded soon after the Ottoman conquest, and it was as his place of residence that Safed first became famous. His great learning drew many students to the city and, in addition to Safed's record as an administrative center in Mamluk days, attracted many refugees and members of other Diasporas. In their wake came practically minded people who took advantage of the existing favorable conditions for the development of the clothing industry that became the basis for Safed's economic progress.

The school founded by Berab comprised all Safed's scholars, some of whom were the colleagues of the school's founder. They dealt with all matters collectively, wrote responsa, and issued decisions. Here the idea of the revival of ordination *(semikhah)* arose, whereby qualified rabbis would be invested with some of the powers of the Sanhedrin, the central religious and legal body that had existed in Palestine at the time of the Second Temple and was abolished during the first centuries of Roman rule. R. Levi Ibn Haviv, rabbi of Jerusalem and Berab's fierce opponent, accused him of secretly planning to establish a Sanhedrin in Safed, and regarded Berab's attempt to revive the ordination of the Safed scholars as a first step in that direction. R. Levi also charged Berab with coveting the office of president of the Sanhedrin. In 1538 Berab ordained some of his companions. Although the first holders of ordination in turn ordained their disciples, the idea was doomed to failure through the vigorous opposition of R. Levi Ibn Haviv and was ultimately abandoned.

Berab's most renowned colleague was R. Joseph Caro, also a refugee from Spain who settled in Nikopoli after a period of wanderings and tribulations in Europe, but who moved to Adrianople on the instruction of the mentor angel *(maggid)* which he believed appeared to him. Here he began to write his outstanding commentary on Jacob ben Asher's *Arbaah Turim* (The Four Columns), a digest of accepted rules of the Oral Law. In this commentary *Beth Yoseph,* Joseph Caro traces every legal provision from its roots in the Bible through all the stages of its development down to his time. Caro continued to work on his commentary during his stay in Greece and subsequently in Safed where he joined Berab's *yeshivah* (school) and though certainly not inferior to him in learning and wisdom, called him 'our great teacher'. The huge task was completed after thirty years' research and careful consideration of all the sources. Shortly afterward Caro wrote the *Shulhan Arukh* (The Prepared Table), first printed in Venice (1564-5). The author intended to provide observant Jewry with a practical religious code, comprising all spheres of life. This code, with the glosses and commentaries of later rabbis, has remained binding for Orthodox Jews to this day.

Despite Safed's importance as a halakhic center for sixteenth-century Jewry, especially in the Ottoman empire, another feature

Left: *Hanukkah lamp,* Syria, beginning of twentieth century. The inscription refers to the concept of light and probably depicts the Wall of Jerusalem. Brass set in silver. Height: 2′ 9¾″; Width: 1′ 6¾″. Jerusalem, Sir Isaac and Lady Edith Wolfson Museum, Hechal Shlomo, 1610-26-103. Right: *Synagogue lamp,* Morocco, end of nineteenth century. With small amulet hands echoing the hand above. Brass and glass. Jerusalem, Israel Museum.

in its religious life had a significant impact on future generations: the revival of the Kabbalah, the mystical stream in Judaism (for its earlier history, see the chapter on Spain).

Joseph Caro himself had mystical leanings, as is evidenced by his book *Maggid Mesharim* (Declarer of Things That Are Right). Joseph Caro's disciples included some like R. Moses Cordovero and R. Solomon Alkabetz who devoted themselves to the mysteries of the Kabbalah. These three initiated the pre-Lurianic Kabbalah (see below) in Safed. The most notable in the field of theoretical Kabbalah was Cordovero who first tried to describe the process by which the ten spheres emanate from God's hidden abode. He interpreted the emanations as degrees of divine existence, and his book *Ha-Pardes* attempts to give the Kabbalah a logical explanation.

ISAAC LURIA

The Kabbalah reached its peak with R. Isaac Luria Ashkenazi. Born in Jerusalem in 1534, he died in Safed at the age of thirty-eight. Luria, surnamed ARI (an acronym of the Hebrew words Ashkenazi [or *elohi* 'divine'] Rabbi Isaac), was the exact opposite of his teacher, R. Moses Cordovero. Of all the books and tracts known as the *Writings of ARI,* only one, a commentary on the Book of Concealment, was written by him. His system was founded on a belief in the unity of God and creation. God is originally all-encompassing but by a continuous process of contraction forms a vacuum in which He can create. Evil is described as the result of the breaking of the holy vessels containing light: the sparks descended to the depths of darkness and man must repair the damage by descending to the depths to rescue the divine sparks. This mystical doctrine was to play a major role in Sabbetaianism and was used to justify Shabbetai Tzevi's conversion to Islam (see below). Luria's personality made a very deep impression on his disciples. His teachings are known from tracts and commentaries written by his disciples, the most famous of whom was Hayyim Vital Calabrese.

Luria's activity in Safed lasted no more than three or four years (1569-72). Shortly after his death, people began to tell stories—some true, some embroidered—around his impressive personality, and in the following generation these stories were collected in *Shivhei ha-Ari* (Praises of Ari).

The people were especially captivated by the messianic element in Luria's teachings. Here was the mystical outlet for a yearning whose beginnings in the Middle Ages can be found in Arabia before the appearance of Mohammed and which expressed itself in a succession of 'Messiahs' and announcers of the Messiah in the Islamic East. The expectation of an early coming of the Messiah merged with the earnest desire for the *tikkun* of the individual, or, in other words, the moral regeneration of man. This phenomenon to some extent explains the events of the time of Shabbetai Tzevi.

Halakhic and kabbalistic writings also spread in the Islamic East by means of printed editions. Striking proof of this intellectual alertness of the Spanish refugees is that only two years after the

Expulsion, *Arbaah Turim* was printed in Constantinople. During the subsequent centuries (16th to 18th), printing presses in Constantinople, Salonika, Smyrna, Safed, and Fez (only in the 16th century) turned out a series of important halakhic, aggadic, historical, and kabbalistic works. The first polyglot Jewish Bible was printed in Constantinople in 1546. When these printing presses ceased to operate, others were established in Baghdad, Calcutta, Poona, and eventually also on the island of Djerba (off Tunisia), in Tunis, Sousse, Algiers, Oran, and, in the 20th century, in Casablanca. It should be noted that a large proportion of the works published during the past hundred years are kabbalistic books, especially popular prayer-books, Bible commentaries, *midrashim*, and various tracts dealing with practical Kabbalah. They were printed in Ladino (the Spanish dialect of the Sephardi Jews) or in the Jewish-Arabic dialect, as were various folk-stories, abridgements of French novels and periodicals written in North Africa. The names of the authors and titles of the books printed are further proof that rarely did any clash occur between the two trends, the nomistic on the one hand, and the mystical and messianic on the other.

Crown for Torah scroll, Morocco, nineteenth century. Silver crown for Torah scroll. Height: 7½"; Diameter: 9". Jerusalem, Sir Isaac and Lady Edith Wolfson Museum, Hechal Shlomo, 1767-3-10.

SHABBETAI TZEVI

This harmony was disturbed in the middle of the 17th century by the rise in the Muslim East of Sabbetaianism, a religious movement sparked off by the ideas of the Lurianic Kabbalah and especially by its messianic hopes.

Shabbetai Tzevi (1625-76), a native of Smyrna, was from his

Shabbetai Tzevi, eighteenth century. Pseudo-Messiah who appeared in the Ottoman empire in the middle of the 17th century and later converted to Islam. Illustration from a travel-book of the 18th century. Jerusalem, T. Kollek Collection.

youth subject to psychic conditions bordering on mental illness. He studied Jewish Law in the traditional manner as well as the books of the Lurianic Kabbalah. He had morbid fantasies of being the Messiah who would redeem his people from exile. His 'prophet' was Nathan ben Elijah ha-Ashkenazi (1644-80), usually called Nathan of Gaza. The latter studied Jewish Law in Jerusalem and later settled in Gaza. Here he began to occupy himself with the Kabbalah. He read the Zohar and the writings of Luria and his disciples. He engaged in *tikkunim* (moral purification exercises and meditations) and asceticism. Once after a spell of fasting he felt imbued with the spirit of prophecy and had a vision of the Messiah. About that time (1665) Shabbetai Tzevi, after spending some time in Egypt, arrived in Gaza and there proclaimed himself openly the Messiah. Nathan became his 'prophet' and devoted all his ability, energy, and fervor to stirring up propaganda for him. Shabbetai's fame spread throughout the East from Morocco to Persia. Hopes were kindled everywhere for the ingathering of the exiles and rumors were abroad of imminent redemption and of the rediscovery of the Ten Tribes who were said to be preparing to join their brethren in the return to Zion.

Shabbetai meanwhile went back to his native Smyrna where he began to rally 'believers', who were ready to do whatever he told them. He made a show of royal pomp and solemn ceremonial as befitted the King Messiah. At the same time he engaged in strange practices: he publicly contravened Jewish Law, both Written and Oral. He desecrated the Sabbath, ate forbidden food, changed the liturgy and abolished fasts commemorating the destruction of the Temple and Jerusalem; his behavior with women was also talked about. Moreover, he became interested in the figure of Jesus. Shabbetai assured his supporters that all his doings were aimed at overcoming the hosts of Satan, and they believed him. Some scholars, headed by R. Aaron Lepapa, one of the local *dayyanim,* tried to stop his activities, but R. Aaron was swept from office, and R. Hayyim Benveniste, a prominent halakhist who was thereupon appointed sole *dayyan,* became a Sabbetaian.

Trading and industry in Smyrna, which had developed into an important commercial center, were suspended. All the local Jews celebrated and held mass processions shouting 'Long live the King Messiah! Long live the Sultan Tzevi!'. At the same time, by order of the 'king' they held penitential exercises. When the news of these events reached Constantinople, the Ottoman authorities—anticipating civil disorders—sent appropriate instructions to the local administrations. This seems to have been one of the reasons why Shabbetai and some of his followers left Smyrna late in 1665 for Constantinople. The Jewish population of the capital city was divided in its attitude. Many feared that Shabbetai's appearance would provoke the central government into punitive action against all Jews. Others were carried away by the upsurge of messianic enthusiasm. Shabbetai was arrested by the authorities before he set foot in Constantinople. He was detained at the fortress of Gelibolu (Gallipoli) where he continued to hold court because his guards had been bribed into permitting his followers to visit him. When Sultan Mehmed IV, then in Adrianople, heard of these goings-on, he ordered Shabbetai to be

Lamp for a synagogue, India, eighteenth century. Bronze lamp for a synagogue from Cochin, India. Notwithstanding their isolation, the Jews of Cochin maintained a vigorous intellectual and artistic life. Jerusalem, Israel Museum.

Torah finials, Hebron, nineteenth century. Silver. Jerusalem, Israel Museum.

brought before him. In Adrianople, Shabbetai and several of his followers converted to Islam in September 1666.

This step dumbfounded the Jewish world. Shabbetai's opponents warned of the danger threatening Judaism should others follow his example, but many of his adherents regarded his conversion as the acceptance of suffering in order to hasten redemption. They were particularly numerous in Morocco where the assertion that Shabbetai's apostasy held a profound mystery was widely believed. Here Abraham Cardozo was most active in offering this explanation, spreading it also in Turkey and the Balkans. He, as a Marrano who had left Madrid, developed the theory that all Jews had been doomed to forced conversion and a Marrano life, but that Shabbetai had taken upon himself the suffering of the people, and that this proved his messianic mission.

Shabbetai's opponents were likewise deeply perturbed and were not sure how to react to the propaganda of the movement. The first to raise his voice against the movement was R. Jacob

Sasportas, a native of Oran, successively a *dayyan* in Tlemcen and Sale, who was in Hamburg at the time. Sasportas' utterances against the Sabbetaians collected in his *Tzitzat Novel Tzevi* (A Fading Flower is Beauty) are our principal source of information on the Sabbetaian propaganda in the Maghreb.

Manifestations occurred in Morocco of belief in a second appearance of Shabbetai as Messiah a few years after his conversion. Similar phenomena occurred at the other end of the Islamic world: scholars in Kurdistan composed songs in honor of Isaac Luria and Hayyim Vital and tracts and poems on Sabbetaian themes.

Shabbetai Tzevi died in 1677—almost exactly ten years after his conversion—in the fortress of Dulcigno (Ulcinj) at the southern end of the Dalmatian coast where he had been deported four years previously from Adrianople. After his death Sabbetaian legend and propaganda initiated traditions that he did not die, but merely vanished. A myth was created concerning the deification of the Messiah and the incarnation of the Godhead in him.

Torah scroll case, India, 1875. This case for a Torah scroll is of wood with silver platelets. Among Oriental Jews, the tradition is to place the Torah in a stand which is set on the reading desk and from which the Torah is read. Height: 3′2½″; perimeter: 3′½″. It was made in 1875 in Calcutta, India. Jerusalem, Sir Isaac and Lady Edith Wolfson Museum, Hechal Shlomo, ref. 417-2-2.

There developed the Dönmeh sect, descendants of the three hundred Sabbetaians who had converted to Islam in Salonika in 1667. They subsequently split into three sub-sects, differing in customs and beliefs. They maintained their (secret) racial and religious identity until World War II, although their strictness as regards custom and endogamy began to relax after World War I. Some of their poems and songs, which are almost all in Ladino, were published.

IRAQ AND INDIA

As a result of increasing interest in Middle Eastern affairs and of the changes occurring in that region, the Jewish communities in Iraq and the Persian-speaking territories emerged from the oblivion into which they had sunk. Centuries of the history of these areas are known, it at all, only by vague and fragmentary reports. From the middle of the 13th century Iraq had a checkered history. Baghdad, once the capital of a world power, became the seat of the pasha of a remote province impoverished by frequent wars and even more by its severance from the great international trade routes. The lack of competent Jewish scholars in Baghdad forced the community to address questions on religious matters to the rabbis of Aleppo, some Aleppine scholars even settling in Baghdad.

Particular importance lies in the commercial activities of Baghdadi and Basran Jewish traders who began to emigrate to India in the late 18th century. A sizable British-protected Jewish colony came into being in Surat, which traded with cities in Iraq and on the Persian Gulf. From the early 19th century onward the importance of Surat decreased, and the Baghdadi merchants thereupon moved to Calcutta, Bombay, and Poona. Among the founders of these communities the Sassoon family deserves special mention because it had a large share in their religious and intellectual development. These Iraqi Jewish colonies maintained close contact with Far Eastern markets and with London, the commercial and political metropolis. Relationships formed in India between erstwhile Baghdadi Jews and the British trading companies, which also performed governmental functions, had considerable influence on relations and contacts within Iraq itself during the British Mandate.

In India, the Iraqi immigrants came upon two groups of communities whose origin and historical past are still not clear. The members of the larger group call themselves Bene Israel. In the mid-19th century they were estimated at 5-6,000 persons. They claim descent from the Ten Tribes, but there is reason to assume that they are the remnant of immigrants who came to India from one of the Arab countries, perhaps from Southern Arabia. The center of the Bene Israel was in Bombay and the villages of the Bombay District, and here the Baghdadis met them. They speak Marathi and English. Their neighbors call them *shanwar tellis*, or 'Sabbath-observing oil pressers', as they refrain from work on that day. They keep the holy days and the commandments of the Written Law, but it seems that until the arrival of the Iraqis they had never heard of the Oral Law or of the customs and rules which spread after the conclusion of the canon of the Hebrew Bible. The Bene Israel have always preserved their religious identity and kept apart from the Indian population. There is also a small group of 'Black Bene Israel', apparently the offspring of intermarriage with the Indians.

The other—smaller—group which never exceeded 2,000 was concentrated in the south of the Peninsula in the city of Cochin and the cities of the Malabar coast. This congregation, called the 'White Jews' of Cochin, has in its possession to this day two copper plates on which are engraved in the ancient Tamil language certain privileges granted many centuries ago by the Hindu ruler of Malabar. These plates, cherished by the congregation as their most precious documents, and their original settlement deed, are deposited in the Paradesi Synagogue of the 'White Jews' and carefully guarded by its Elders.

The Paradesi Synagogue was built in 1568 and after its partial destruction by the Portuguese in 1662 was renovated in 1664. The synagogue is one of the most impressive houses of worship in all of India, remarkable for its magnificent structure, its internal and external architecture, its Dutch-style clock-tower (built in 1761), and other elements.

The past of the 'White Jews' is controversial. In any event, it is certain that Jews have been settled in Cochin province for at least 1,500 years. A decree, apparently from the 5th century, engraved on the copper tablets indicated that the ruler of the state of Cranganore granted them various rights, such as exemption from taxes and recognition of their leaders who had the rank of high dignitaries. The Portuguese dislodged the Jews from the coast and forced them to concentrate in the city of Cochin, but here, too, they suffered at the hands of the conquerors. During that period new immigrants, refugees from Spain, and former inhabitants of Germany, joined the communities. From then onward there were two strata: 'white' Jews and the dark-skinned veteran settlers, augmented by the 'freedmen' who had been the slaves of 'whites' or veterans. All these spoke Tamil or Malayalam, but at the same time they had poems and ditties in Hebrew. Their ties with Jewish customs and tradition were incomparably stronger than those of the Bene Israel, no doubt owing to their contact with Middle Eastern Jewry and immigrants from Europe. In recent years, the numbers of Indian Jews—both Bene Israel and in Cochin—has dwindled considerably as a result of migration, mostly to Israel.

PERSIA

Our knowledge of Persian Jewry shows a gap which for Persia proper extends up to the 16th century and for the areas under Persia's political and cultural influence, Transcaucasia, Georgia, and Armenia, up till the 19th century.

A Christian traveler reports the existence of Jewish communities in the days of Shah Abbas I (1587-1621). He puts the number of Jews at 8-10,000 families (about 50,000 persons) scattered all over the country. Jewish communities extended in the northern region from Qazvin in the west to Khurasan in the

Hanukkah lamp, Iraq, eighteenth century. *Hanukkah* lamp from Baghdad of the eighteenth century. The hand against the evil eye, the star and fertile crescent show the influence of the surroundings. Jerusalem, Israel Museum.

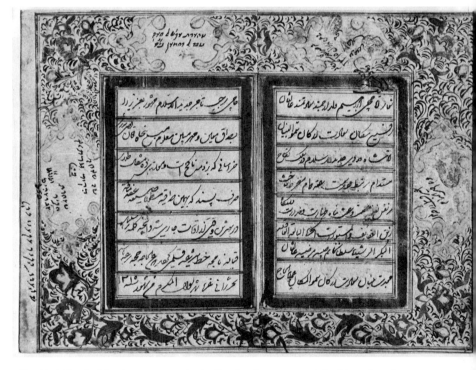

Ketubbah, Persia. Marriage contract in the Persian language and Arabic script of forced conversos from Meshed. Berkeley, Dr. Fischel Collection.

east and Jewish settlements straggled south as far as Lar and Kerman. We also find Jews in the southern seaports of Bender 'Abbas and Hormuz. Jews engaged in all crafts and in commerce. Many made a living by the manufacture and sale of alcoholic liquors; there was no lack, either, of moneylenders. There were

Torah headpieces, Iran, nineteenth century. These headpieces decorate the top of the Torah case. The quotation is what the congregation say when the Scroll is raised before it: 'This is the Law that Moses placed before the Children of Israel'. Silver and precious stones. Manuscript on parchment. Jerusalem, Israel Museum.

Amulet, Iran, eighteenth century. Amulet from Iran made of silver, glass and paper with inscription against the evil eye. On it stand the names of the twelve tribes, with the name of God repeated twice and a biblical verse. Jerusalem, Israel Museum, 103/70.

also a great many witch-doctors and soothsayers and women mixers of love-potions.

Persian Jewry's belief in witchcraft prompted a Jewish renegade to allege that they used the formulae of the books of the practical Kabbalah in order to harm the shah, whereupon a decree was issued in 1620 for the confiscation and destruction of these and many sacred books. The opposition of the Isfahani community to the destruction of the books led to an order for the forced conversion of the heads of the community, subsequently extended to all its members. This measure remained in force until 1628. Further persecutions occurred under Abbas II (1642-66). They began with expulsion from Isfahan and eventually all Jews in the country were ordered to adopt Islam (1656).

The forced converts were called *jadid al-Islam* (neo-Muslims). They were freed from the poll-tax and duty to wear special dress and received gifts of money. Nevertheless, they remained Jews in their hearts, and five years later they were permitted to revert openly to Judaism on condition that they returned the gifts of money, paid the poll-tax for the time they had been exempt from it, and again wore distinctive clothing.

The persecution of Persian Jewry reached another peak in 1839 with the forced conversion of the community of Meshed, the capital of the district and one of the holy cities of the Persian Shi'ite sect, only this time without their being able to return to Judaism. For three generations the community had to pose as Muslims while secretly observing the Jewish laws. Many of them, indeed, succeeded in crossing into neighboring countries, especially Afghanistan, thus strengthening the small communities in Kabul, Herat, and Balkh, which to some extent had been constituted by refugees or emigrants from Persia who had arrived in the preceding centuries. It is noteworthy that the Meshed Marranos established a community of their own in Jerusalem, which still maintains two synagogues.

The religious life of Persian Jewry was indelibly marked by a number of factors: isolation from the communities outside the Persian-speaking area, recurrent persecution, the hostility of the Shi'ite population, and fanatical clergy, but perhaps most of all the abandonment of the communities by their spiritual leaders. Biblical learning fell into oblivion as did Hebrew—the language of the ancient prayers—and Aramaic—the language of the Zohar and

Left: *Illumination from manuscript,* Persia, seventeenth century. Moses and Aaron in the battle against the Amalekites. Illumination from a Judeo-Persian seventeenth-century manuscript. There exists an extensive Judeo-Persian literature. Berlin, Staatsbibl. Preussischer Kulturbesitz, Orient. Abteilung, Ms. or. oct. 2885. Right: *Judeo-Persian manuscript,* Teheran, seventeenth century. Scene from the Persian epic of Chosroe and Shirin. New York, Jewish Theological Seminary Library.

other kabbalistic books, extracts from which were still recited by rote. The link with the spiritual treasures of Judaism was preserved through a translation of the Bible into the Persian-Jewish dialect, liturgical poetry *(piyyutim)*, popular literature, and ritual observances. Conditions thus created were favorable to the influence of various religious trends, such as the Bahai movement which won adherents among the Jews, and to Jews joining Sufi orders.

To complete the picture we must mention the Persian-speaking communities in Uzbek territory: Bukhara, Tashkent, Samarkand, and Kokand. In the first half of the 19th century Bukharian Jewry is said to have numbered over 5,000. In the second half of the 19th century these communities came under tsarist rule. They all preserved strong ties with Persian Jewry through a common language and literature.

EPILOGUE

The society in which the Jewish communities lived was stagnant and no longer able to exert any influence, and this determined the situation of the established Jewish population in Oriental countries. Jewish-Arab cooperation in the sphere of the sciences and the humanities, which existed in the Middle Ages, came to a complete halt. The Jews continued to use their special Arabic (or Persian-Jewish) dialect which developed in the Middle Ages and which was sufficient for everyday conversation and commercial or professional dealings, but nothing more. The successive waves of refugees and emigrants from Europe moved away from its spiritual domain as well. Moreover, a small class of merchants and agents in the coastal cities cultivated a knowledge of Western European languages enabling them to carry on foreign trade or

Synagogue inscription, Iran, eighteenth century. This detail of an inscription for a synagogue reads: 'This is the House of the Lord'. Of glazed ceramic tiles, it comes probably from Isfahan. Jerusalem, Israel Museum.

to act as interpreters to Muslim rulers, or as the diplomatic agents of European countries. But the knowledge of these languages entailed no contact with European intellectual life.

Changes in this sphere first became noticeable in the second half of the 19th century. The outstanding Jewish philanthropists in Europe such as the Rothschilds, Sir Moses Montefiore, Baron Maurice de Hirsch, and Abraham Camondo in Constantinople, anxious to better the condition of Middle Eastern Jewry, regarded the raising of their general educational standard as a lever to help them attain their goal. Although utilitarian considerations were foremost in the establishment of schools with instruction in French and many general subjects—with the addition of several hours for religious education—we should not overlook the ideals of enlightenment which inspired the work of principals and teachers. The tendencies then prevalent in Western Europe particularly affected the French organization, the Alliance Israélite Universelle which adopted the spread of European education as one of its main objectives. The first school was opened in Tetuan in 1861.

Fifty years after the establishment of the Alliance Israélite Universelle, the network of schools maintained by it—sometimes in partnership with the Anglo-Jewish Association—covered all the eastern countries where Jews lived, from Morocco to Persia, including the Balkans. The only such country where the Alliance did not succeed in establishing a single school was Yemen.

We still lack the necessary perspective to allow us to make an objective evaluation of the events that have occurred in the Middle East during the present generation. At the same time it is obvious that since the 1920s the population of the entire region has been in a fast-growing state of ferment and tension and the crystallization of a new society is still far off.

The traditional cosmopolitan Muslim state assigned definite spheres and duties to the non-Muslim communities. The new Muslim states, even those claiming to be secular and socialist, show little understanding toward their non-Muslim citizens. The

concept of the *millet,* the separate non-Muslim community, is ineradicably fixed in the consciousness of the Muslim public.

There is no reason to suspect the various national governments of harboring any pronounced anti-Christian or anti-Jewish feelings. It is only natural, however, that they should care for their own coreligionists first. They are bound to devote themselves to rehabilitating the backward Muslim citizen before turning their attention to those who are much better off economically and educationally.

Communal consciousness exists in the new Arab states; even the Christian Arabs in Lebanon, Syria, and Egypt feel the social cleavage between themselves and the Muslim population. Obviously, communal segregation in Arab states was practiced especially with regard to the Jews. While in Arab states with an Arabic-speaking Christian minority, the majority is prepared, with certain reservations, to accept the former as Christian-Arabs, the term Jewish-Arab, that is, Arab of the Jewish persuasion, does not exist. Arabic-speaking Jews in Arab countries are described as Iraqi or Syrian Jews or in some other way. The feeling that the Jew is not an Arab, although his ancestors lived in the country even before its conquest by the Arabs, is old. The Alliance education, especially the *présence française* in the Maghreb and its influence in Egypt, widened the extent of the existing economic and political gap.

This gap has certainly acquired a most negative connotation in the national states which tend toward total uniformity. In the struggle for independence and sovereignty, Jews and Christians and naturally all foreigners were suspected of aiding international—French, British, American—imperialism, and incited

Marriage contract, Jerusalem, 1844. *Ketubbah* marriage contract in Aramaic. ▶ Paper with colored illustrations. Length: 3′2″; width: 2′5″. The *ketubbah* is read out under the marriage canopy, as part of the ceremony. Here it has the signs of the zodiac. Jerusalem, Sir Isaac and Lady Edith Wolfson Museum, Hechal Shlomo, ref. 1983-54-46.

Glass bottle, Syria, seventeenth century. Opaque glass wine bottle with Hebrew inscription. London, Victoria and Albert Museum, No. C 674-1936.

mobs drew the practical conclusions by resorting to violence. At the same time laws and regulations were enacted to better the condition of the population, whose immediate—though sometimes unintentional—effect was to harm the Jews.

It is impossible to make any final pronouncement upon this period of the history of Asia and Africa before all the forces at work in the area have been traced. However, it is certainly quite feasible—and even necessary—to point out the practical conclusions drawn by the Jews there. The number of Jews in Asia (except for Israel) and north-west Africa dropped from between 950,000 and 1,000,000 at the end of World War II to about a sixth of that number in 1970. The others left the countries where their forefathers had lived for hundreds or even thousands of years. The rich and the well-to-do mostly succeeded in transferring their property or a great part of it before they themselves left. The poor—who were the overwhelming majority—carried their paltry belongings with them.

Only two-thirds (about half a million) of those who left their countries of residence migrated to Israel while one-third scattered all over the world, the great majority of them settling in France. Several thousand Moroccan Jews settled in Spain, chiefly in Madrid and Barcelona; there were no Jews in Spain from the Expulsion in 1492 until the establishment of a small community in Barcelona in the early 20th century and the arrival of a number of refugees from Central Europe during World War II.

Clearly the political changes and developments in intercommunal relations provided solid grounds for the exodus. But in addition we may be faced here with irrational impulses which it is hard to explain. Oriental Jewry became aware that it was no longer able to exist in Muslim lands either as a separate group or as Jewish individuals, and most of them drew the only possible conclusion. Part of them felt that, as a group, they were deprived of their legal status, stripped of the framework to which they were accustomed, and that the right to react like any other group was forbidden them. Some, again, realized that if they remained, they would never be accepted as equals in Arab society; besides, they had been taught to regard the cultural and social level of that society as lower than theirs.

Objective expert observers, far removed from Jewish national ideologies, predict that a great part of those still remaining in comparatively large concentrations in Morocco, Turkey, and Iran, will emigrate to countries willing to admit them, leaving behind only those who for various reasons are unable to go. Several tens of thousands of Jews will doubtless continue to live among hundreds of millions of Muslims, but the time of organized, autonomous Jewish communities in Muslim countries is drawing to a close. On the other hand we should note the fact that, with the completion of one cycle in the life of Middle Eastern Jewry, a new cycle has opened with the State of Israel which seeks its place and way among the peoples of Asia and Africa.

CHAPTER II

France

by Dr. Moshe Catane

Although the first actual evidence of the presence of Jews in ancient Gaul dates back to the 4th century, it is very probable that Jews had settled there a long time before.

The most plausible hypothesis is that Jews came to Gaul in the wake of the Roman armies. At the time of the conquest of Gaul, the famous Jewish community of Rome was well-developed, particularly in the field of foreign trade, and it would seem that its merchants had attained a considerable level of sophistication. It is therefore very likely that they should have followed the conquering Roman armies. This might account for the finding of numerous traces of Jewish communities near the sites of Roman garrisons; but it does not account for the subsequent proliferation of *juiveries* (Jewries) on the territory of Gaul. To explain this, we must bear in mind a historical fact which is all too often ignored: the persistence of Jewish proselytism. This proselytic trend probably made it possible for relatively small nuclei of Jewish settlers to become the basis of large communities of native converts. French Jewry might thus largely be of local origin.

It would also be wrong to imagine that the early Jews had the same complexes as many of their descendants and to evoke the traditional image of the timid and furtive Jew, bent on leading a quiet, self-effacing life, or the converse image of the Jew who engages in public life but thinks it wise to conceal his Jewish origin. No matter how justifiable such clichés might be regarding Jewry in later centuries, they are certainly false as far as the early stages of French Judaism are concerned. At that time, the Jewish faith was one among many philosophies from the Orient that opened new horizons to the 'Romanized' populations. The Church had not yet repudiated a number of Jewish customs (among them, the fixing of Easter according to the Jewish calendar, which prevailed until the end of the 8th century) and a number of Christian communities practiced Jewish customs. Another fact to note is that the Jews had not a long history of martyrdom behind them: they were close to their glorious past. They could boast of having long resisted their conquerors, militarily as well as spiritually. As a result of all these factors, the condition of the dispersed Jews was then different from what was to characterize them after further centuries of tragic sufferings. As a rule, the surrounding populations were friendly toward the Jews, though this attitude was fiercely opposed by the hierarchy of the Church. From the 5th to the 7th century, conciliar decisions repeatedly warned Christians against imitating Jewish customs, like observing the Sabbath on Saturday instead of Sunday, or adopting Jewish customs of keeping the Sabbath rest. They also warned against associating with Jews or working for them. The fact that such warnings had to be repeated again and again shows that the population of Gaul tended to disregard the official attitude of the Church.

The commoners, as well as the nobility, seem to have looked upon disputes between priests and rabbis with amused curiosity and without taking the side of either party. This is well illustrated by the famous dispute between Gregory of Tours and the Jew Priscus. Gregory tells how Chilperic, the Frankish king of Neustria, engaged in a theological discussion with his Jewish purveyor and how he himself was summoned to the court in order to help the king in arguing on behalf of the Christian faith.

Later, Chilperic decided to expel the Jews from his kingdom. This step was occasioned by the assassination of Priscus, who was murdered on Sabbath day (because on that day he went out unarmed) by a new convert. The assassin in his turn was killed in revenge by one of Priscus' family. This banishment of the Jews (582), as well as the later deportation of the community attributed to King Dagobert (600-39) by the pseudo-Fredegaire, even if they really did take place (which is doubtful), probably remained without practical effect.

The reign of the Carolingian kings approximately coincided with the end of the general influence of Jewish beliefs on the masses of the Frankish kingdom. Still, Jews continued to occupy important positions and enjoyed great credit with certain lords and princes. The conversion of the deacon noble Bodo in 839, attested by historical documents, is typical of the period. This deacon, who was a chaplain in the Imperial palace, took the name of Eleazar, married a Jewess, and went to live in Muslim Spain where he is said to have engaged in anti-Christian propaganda.

Progressively, the situation changed, although the Jews continued to be tolerated and their functions in society remained diversified. But through prolonged catechizing, the priests succeeded in instilling into their congregations contempt and hatred for the 'deicide' people. Confronted by this new development, the Jewish community of France gave itself a structure which was to remain unchanged during the subsequent period, its so-called 'Golden Age'. At that time, the number of Jews kept growing and they were living more and more in towns. This fact is attested by toponymy as well as by the indication of the dwelling places of rabbis of that time whose commentaries and decisions have come down to us. The Jews were active in all kinds of professions—including manual work and agriculture—for they had not yet been compelled to restrict themselves to mercantile activities and moneylending. Unlike during the preceding period, however, they were forced to separate themselves from their neighbors who obeyed the directions of the Church and rejected them. This withdrawal into themselves probably explains why, from then on, the Jews devoted themselves exclusively to their own culture and heritage.

THE GOLDEN AGE OF MEDIEVAL JUDAISM

The period of glory of Oriental Jewry, described in earlier chapters, had scarcely faded before a Jewish cultural renaissance began to emerge in western regions of the Mediterranean. We have already heard of developments in Spain and Italy; we now turn our attention to the French rabbis, the *Hakhmei Tzarfat*.

Though northern France was the center of intense activity in Torah studies, the *juiveries* of southern France did not remain

Hanukkah lamp, Avignon, probably twelfth century. The lamp has eight compartments for the oilwicks. The inscription reads: 'For the Commandment is a Lamp; and the Law is Light' (Prov. 6:23) and is often used on *Hanukkah* lamps. Commemorating the victory of Judah the Maccabee over the Syrians (in 165-4 B.C.) the Jews celebrate for eight days the *Hanukkah* festival. Of marble from the Pyrenees. Paris, Klagsbald Collection.

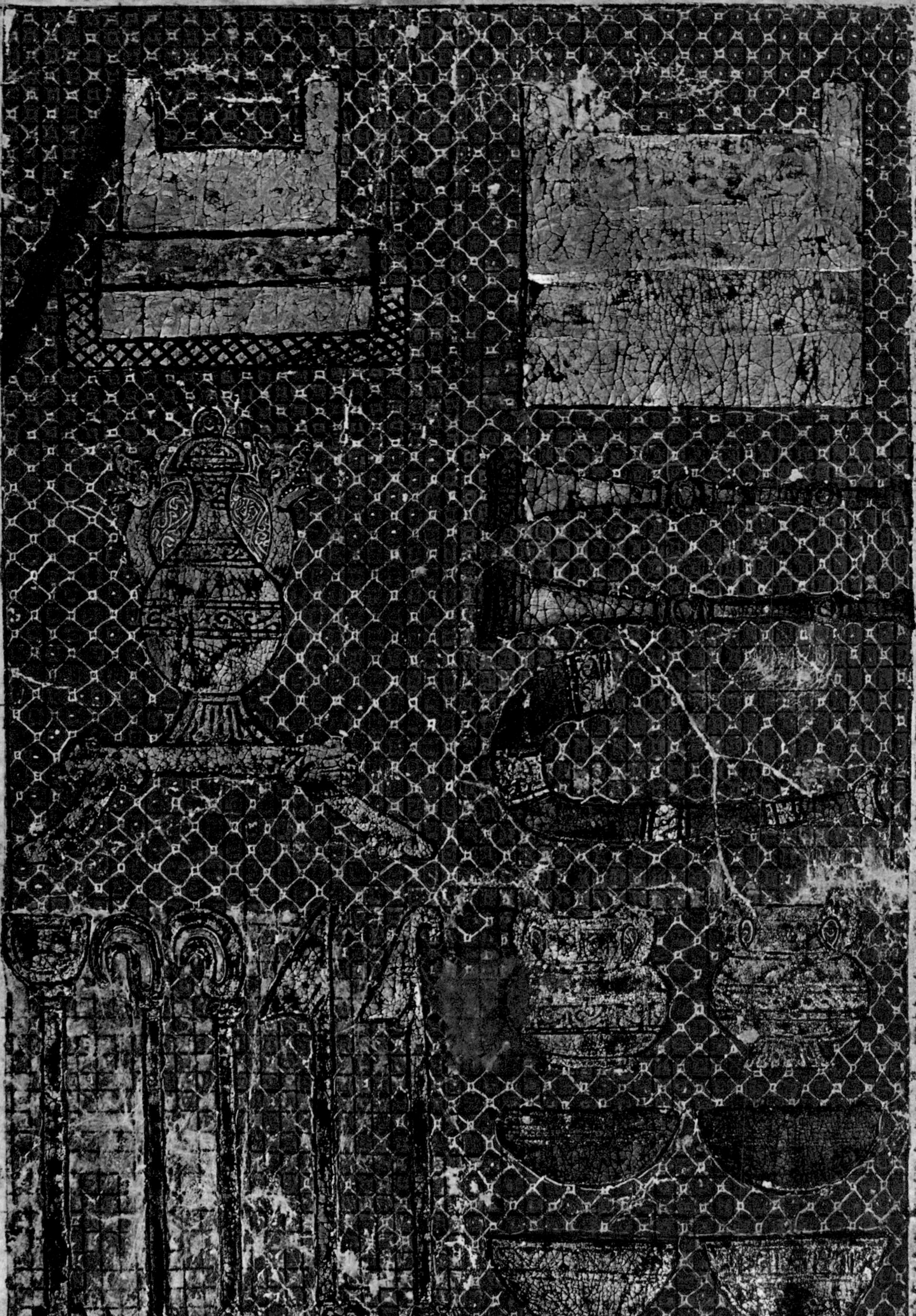

Facing:

Illuminated page from a Hebrew Bible, Provence, 1301. On this page of an illuminated manuscript, all cult vessels of the temple are shown. The text, in verse form, expresses the longing for the return to Zion. This Bible was written by the scribe (or by him and his family) in 1301 in Provence. Copenhagen, Royal Library, Cod. Hebrew II.

Page from illuminated Hebrew Pentateuch, Pontarlier, 1300. This page shows the high-priest lighting the *menorah* (seven branch candlestick from the Temple), and several scenes from the Bible, such as the Sacrifice of Isaac, the Judgment of Solomon and others. The text on the other side of the page is visible through the thin parchment. Paris, Bibliotheque Nationale, CAb. des Manus., Hebreu 36.

Over:

Illuminated page from a Bible, Perpignan, 1299. Illustration of some of the cult objects in the Tabernacle including the *menorah* and the tablets with the Ten Commandments. The text quotes the regulations concerning the making of the *menorah*. Paris, Bibliotheque Nationale, Cab. des Manus., Hebreu VII.

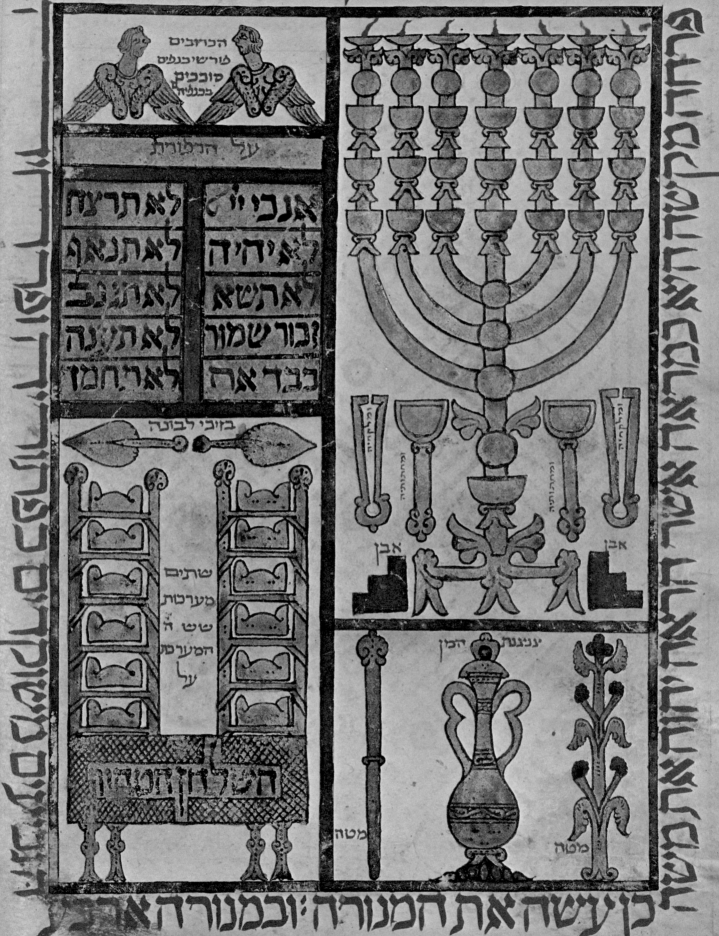

inactive. It was from there that the first great figure of French Jewry emerged. This rabbi, Moshe ha-Darshan (Moses the Preacher), was the head of the Narbonne school, c. 1000. His family had probably been long in the city, one of the cradles of southern French Jewry. Not much is known about him and there is no first-hand knowledge of his work which was possibly called *Yesod* (Basis). His writings are only known from quotations contained in the books of subsequent authors. From them, it is possible to infer that his *Yesod* was an ethical commentary on the Pentateuch, probably in allegorical or apologetic form, considering philosophical problems such as the existence of God, the creation of the world, and the promulgation of the Decalogue.

But northern France was the region where French Jewry was to reach its greatest achievements. This was mainly in Lotharingia (the future Lorraine) which stretched from Champagne to the Rhineland, a vast expanse of land populated by groups who, like today, spoke French dialects in the west and Germanic ones in the east. However, it can be surmised that all the Jews who lived there spoke French (which explains why this survey deals also with the communities living on the banks of the Rhine).

The first known scholar from Lorraine—Master Leontin (Lion) or Judah—was from Mainz, and it was perhaps he who in the 10th century founded the talmudic academy of the city. More famous still was his disciple, Gerson (Gershom) ben Judah (c. 960-1030) who later came to be known as 'Meor ha-Golah' (Light of the Diaspora). He was born in Metz though he is said to have lived in Mainz for the greater part of his life.

A synagogue inscription in stone, S. of France, end of seventh or early eighth century. The Latin-Hebraic text reads: 'In the Holy Name of God, may God deal favorably with those who come here; may hostile eyes perish. Jonah has dedicated this gift.' This is followed by the word 'Shalom' (peace) in Hebrew and by the drawing of a seven-branched candlestick. Musée de St-Germain-en-Laye, No. 20380.

At this same time, Hai Gaon was still living in Pumbedita in Babylonia. It was customary then to send for authoritative advice to the Babylonian academies whenever an important decision was to be made. However, Babylonian supremacy was on the wane and Gershom ben Judah of Metz, as a talmudic scholar of international fame, guided the Jews in Christian lands in Jewish law without having to resort to the decisions of Asian authorities.

Tradition has it that these *takkanot* (ordinances), twenty-five in number, were issued at Worms by a synod of three hundred rabbis. Since then, Western Jews have adhered to them as compulsory rules of behavior. An interesting fact is that one of the purposes of these rules was to raise the level of morality in the community (within the frame of Jewish ritual tradition), so that non-Jews could not accuse their neighbors of being a barbaric people. If Gershom ben Judah was the actual promoter of this unprecedented step, he deserves indeed to be considered the initiator of the civilizing role played by French-speaking Jewry.

The first *takkanah,* which is also the most widely known, forbids polygamy. In actual fact, the habit of marrying several wives had been a very rare occurrence as early as the talmudic period, and only survived as a theoretical right (except in those countries where the Jews were surrounded by a polygamous population and were infected by the example). It must also be borne in mind that the Merovingian kings, including Charlemagne, were not monogamists, at least in the sense that they had official favorites. Other ordinances made marriage legislation more flexible and forbade the automatic carrying out of the levirate (attribution of a childless widow to one of the brothers of the deceased husband), the repudiation of a wife without mutual agreement, and the abandoning of the family even for a short period. Certain of these steps were intended to consolidate the structure of the community by strengthening the feelings of solidarity among its members. It was, for example, considered despicable to indict a fellow Jew before a secular court of justice or to take advantage of Jews who were struck by oppressive measures. Rules of honesty complete the list of ordinances in this code. It is compulsory to declare the finding of lost property; the confiscation of pledges is strictly forbidden; it is an offense to violate the privacy of correspondence, and other such exhortations. One of the major preoccupations of the *takkanot* was to enforce strict order inside the synagogues. They forbade the unlawful removal of books or ritual objects without explicit authorization, just as they condemned the tearing out of pages in order to use their margins as writing paper. They also considered it an offense to prevent a man from building a synagogue or from taking part in a religious service. Fights inside the synagogue were severely punished and those who disturbed regular services were publicly punished. Charitable contributions had to be made voluntarily. In the same way, the procedure of rabbinical courts was simplified. Another highly moral rule was that which forbade holding the past crimes of a repented sinner against him.

The activities of Gershom who, throughout the Diaspora, became known as 'Rabbenu' (our Master) Gershom, were mani-

fold. He was a great exegete of the Talmud, but most of his books have been lost and those known are of dubious authenticity. Certainly of his authorship are a body of twenty decisions concerning ritual matters as well as a number of elegies that have become part of the liturgy and which contain his name in the acrostic. Here is one of these which belongs to the liturgy of the Day of Atonement and is also read in other ceremonies of repentance:

'From one Exile to another Exile
The nation of Israel wanders.
How cruel are its sufferings
And no one intercedes in its favor...'

All this reveals an extraordinarily harmonious personality, in which science, wisdom, and moral qualities excelled. His sole motivation was love for his fellow man, a love which dominated all contingencies. Unfortunately, only legends have come down to us concerning the life of the 'Light of the Diaspora', and these seem inspired by the spirit of his teachings rather than by historical reality. However, the history of Jewish culture in France began in an aura of elegance of thought and purity of faith.

RASHI

The achievements of Gershom were continued by Rashi and his disciples. R. Shelomo (Solomon) Yitzhaki (son of Isaac), generally known by his Hebrew acronym 'Rashi', is to this day regarded by cultivated Jews as the greatest exegete of the Bible and the Talmud, while even modern critics acknowledge that he throws light on many problems and that, in the historical perspective of the Middle Ages, it would have been difficult to improve on what he achieved. There can be no doubt that he belonged to French Jewry. Though he studied in Worms, he was born, worked and died in Troyes in Champagne (1040-1105). Another unmistakable evidence of his French origin is the presence of French words in his writings. His punctilious way of interpreting the sacred texts compelled him to resort constantly to his environment for parables or similes, so that his work seems a mirror held up to everyday life. To describe this he transcribed thousands of French terms into Hebrew.

With the emergence of Rashi, the center of talmudic studies shifted to Champagne. There, he founded and headed a school, and was succeeded by his sons-in-law and later by his grandchildren. This school acquired considerable fame throughout northern France and south-western Germany. Later, his commentaries became household works in the whole Jewish world, as the inseparable complement to the Bible and Talmud. It is significant that the very first book printed in Hebrew was Rashi's commentary on the Pentateuch (in Italy in 1475).

Though a multitude of legends surrounds his biography, Rashi emerges as an industrious and modest man who devoted himself totally to explaining the Scriptures and the Talmud and trained many scholars. The rest of his personality is concealed behind his work. Besides his thorough knowledge of the sacred texts that he commentated, he knew most of the scholarly works published at that time within the Jewish world. His grammar tends to be empirical rather than theoretical and his approach to his subject is far from being that of a philosopher: he relies on his common sense and does not like mysteries. This attitude accounts for the wonderful clarity and inimitable concision of his explanations.

His commentary on the Talmud is almost totally concerned with the various tractates. Those treatises he did not succeed in annotating were completed after his death by his disciples on the lines he had laid down, though with notably less talent. Without him, numerous passages of this monumental work of Judaism would have remained a dead letter. His approach to talmudic problems was dual: either he followed the tradition of the *geonim,* or he himself clarified confused discussions and elucidated rare terms. His biblical commentaries, especially those on the Prophets and the Hagiographa, are less dense but his authorship is not always attested. In any case, both works have become so basic to the education of pious Jews that no biblical or talmudic studies can be conceived without them. The Pentateuch commentary is actually much more than a mere commentary and goes further than elucidating meanings (although Rashi reiterates that his sole purpose is to explain the general meaning). He frequently indulges in the association of ideas that are suggested to him by riddles in style, and derives from the texts moral lessons or justification for rituals in addition to their simple meaning.

Rashi did not hesitate to evoke his environment when this facilitated his explanations. He frequently used words from the vernacular to define technical terms or a specific occupation. Very few French texts from the 11th century have come down and those that have seldom describe everyday life. Consequently Rashi is often the only attested source of numerous old French words. He also introduces terms the existence of which had been unsuspected. Finally, he provides an invaluable indication of medieval French pronunciation.

When describing the objects or the various trades which the Talmud mentions, Rashi often gives important information about such matters in the 11th century, throwing light not only on Jewish life, but also on the lives of the non-Jewish inhabitants of Champagne, for at that time there was no great difference between the ways of life of both groups. Further still, his works reflect the intellectual climate of his epoch. Though Rashi generally avoided expressing his personal opinion, his personal conceptions emerge despite his conscious intention.

Like Rabbenu Gershom, he does not approve of people who pitilessly reject those Jews forced into converting from Judaism: 'One must be careful not to take against these unfortunate people some extreme measure that might isolate or humiliate them,' he writes to a correspondent who asked his advice about this specific point. 'They have strayed only because they were threatened by the sword. But they yearn to retrieve this act of a moment of confusion. Their heart is still longing for the Lord and they will defect from the new religion into which they have been forcibly converted the moment they have the opportunity to do so.'

THE TOSAPHISTS

Rashi must have been a peerless educator and it is no wonder that he should have produced a generation of famous talmudists. Over the next years, throughout northern France and southern Germany, a multitude of rabbis derived their teachings from the 'Master of Troyes'. They were called the *tosaphists* (*Baale Tosaphot*) after the name of their works which were actually 'appendices' (*tosaphot*) to Rashi's commentaries. These rabbis kept dissecting the work of their great master, until the end of the 14th century, when the expulsion of Jews brought the Golden Age of French Jewry to a close.

Rashi's grandson, R. Samuel ben Meir of Ramerupt, usually called 'Rashbam' (1085-1174) tried to emulate his grandfather in commentating the classics. He carried his method still further and submitted the primary meanings of words to a still more punctilious analysis. But, as a result, he oversimplified the meaning of the Pentateuch which Rashi had enriched through the many-sidedness of his approach.

In the field of talmudic studies, a new method was discovered and led to some original results. Unlike Rashi who followed his text word for word and explored the meaning of each term, sentence or argumentation, the *tosaphot* appear as notes of unequal length and without connection with each other. Except in rare instances, they assume that the reader is perfectly acquainted with his subject. Their approach consists in pointing out the contradictions which appear in the passages of the Talmud dealing with a common subject, or between the plausible meaning of the text and the interpretations of the various commentators (among whom Rashi, as could be expected, holds the first rank). Actually their work constitutes more than a mere commentary and is a kind of super-Talmud.

At the time of the *tosaphot,* that is to say, during the 12th, 13th, and 14th centuries, medieval Christianity created its masterpieces; and yet it was already decadent. The structures which had come into existence after the fall of the Roman empire to meet the requirements of the new era—the feudal system and the Church—were no longer adjusted to the new social conditions. They continued to work through their inherent momentum and to obey their own impetus. When institutions start functioning in this way, in a sort of vacuum, they must justify the continuation of their own existence by creating new objectives, even artificial ones if need be. It was probably this feeling of decadence that drove the nobility of Western Europe into the mad adventure of the Crusades. Large-scale Jew-hunting, which began at

See illustration page 54.

that time, was also probably due to the same cause: barons and bishops no longer had to protect their peoples against the barbaric hordes (Germans, Normans, and Moors) who had been assimilated or defeated; they felt the need to discover a new enemy of mankind. No group was easier to strike than the Jews who had remained unassimilated amid the nations. The literature of the *tosaphot* period includes many elegies for the victims of the massacres perpetrated by the Christians. It also contains numerous polemics which develop the arguments used in the controversies between Jews and Christians. The arguments of the Jews had no chance of being heard, for the monarchs who were supposed to arbitrate such disputes could hardly decide in favor of the Jews (who were considered renegades and deicides) against the priests of their own faith. Yet, these fiery 'apologies' of the Jewish faith had a more practical effect: they encouraged the Jews to resist conversion and baptism, even if they had to pay with their lives for their stubbornness.

The area in which the *tosaphists* pursued their activities was almost completely included between the Rhine and the Loire.

The eastern part of this area was ancient Lotharingia which had been reduced to a conglomerate of territories without fixed borders and was torn between French and German influences. In the west, the scholars were concentrated in provinces which all spoke the 'langue d'oil'. The main nucleus, however, was constituted by Champagne (Troyes, Dampierre, Ramerupt, in the department of Aube), Joinville (Haute-Marne), Vitry (Marne), and Coucy-le-Château (Aisne). It was flanked by the Jewish centers of Burgundy: Saulieu (Côte d'Or), Joigny, and Sens (Yonne). Then came Paris with its numerous rabbis (like the famous Jehiel) followed by Ile-de-France (Corbeil, Pontoise, Melun) and the region around Chartres (Dreux). The area along the Loire was also very active (Chinon, Bourgueil, Orleans) although less so than Normandy which was second only to Champagne for the number and fame of its masters (especially Falaise, Touques in Calvados, and Evreux). In the northeast, the main centers of Jewish activity seem to have been the towns of the Three Dioceses (Metz, Toul, and Verdun) as well as the cities on the Rhine.

Circumcision knife, France, end of seventeenth century. Copper, gilt and enamel. The circumcision ceremony is performed on male children on the eighth day after birth. Circumcision knives, as this one from France, were often beautifully fashioned to emphasize the importance and intimate significance of the ceremony. Hanover, Kestner-Museum, Inv. No. 1913/36.

These communities formed a dense and thickly populated network all over northern France. They had an intense activity, both on the level of internal organization and studies and on the level of their contacts with the outside world, which often extended beyond the borders of France. They maintained contacts with Spain, Germany, England and even with the Holy Land where some famous scholars went to end their lives.

At least until the Crusades, French Jews lived among the Christian population. When they concentrated in certain specific quarters of the cities, they did it of their own accord and in so doing retained their close relationship with their non-Jewish fellow townsmen. Tolerance, though no longer general as in the preceding period, was still frequent and feelings of contempt and hatred between Jews and Gentiles were not very common— unlike the situation to emerge during the following period.

The Provencal Center

We have spoken at length about Rashi and *tosaphists* because they were an essential element of Jewish thinking in France. It is they who were mainly responsible for the fame of the French scholars (*Hakhmei Tzarfat*). Yet they did not represent the whole of French Jewry, even taking into account the many secondary activities which concentrated in their centers of supremacy.

As early as the 11th century, Limoges produced a famous rabbi, Joseph ben Samuel Bonfils (Tov Elem), the author of commentaries and liturgical poems. And Limoges was only one of the numerous French cities that acquired fame all over the Jewish world through the excellence of its scholars.

But the real rival of Champagne, Lorraine, and Normandy, though in a different sphere of thought and action, was Provence. Like the Jews, the Christians of Provence were proud of their ancient civilization and often turned toward Italy and Spain for inspiration, rather than to the misty provinces of the north. In the same way, Provençal Jews, although they kept up contacts with Troyes, Paris, and Touques and were influenced by these cities, lived as an independent community. It was in Provence, as well as in Italy and Spain, that philosophy and the codification of religious customs was developed. These matters were not familiar to the northern scholars. Moreover, the rabbis of Provence became specialists in mathematical, astronomical, and medical studies. They translated from Arabic secular works by the great scientists of ancient times. From the very beginning, the Narbonne school achieved considerable fame. Other towns, like Arles and Lunel, were centers for the study of the Law. As in the north, the Talmud was the almost exclusive occupation of rabbis. This lasted until they came into contact with the Jewish civilization of Spain. The first works of the new current were actually composed by Spanish immigrants, though the introduction of new ideas did not come about without serious conflict. The Provençal Jews were inordinately proud of their achievements and traditions and resented the intrusion of 'foreigners'.

Each foreign work of some stature was the occasion of a struggle between those rabbis who accepted it and those who could not bear the mere idea of innovation. Of course, the battlefields of these disputes were normally the parchments and manuscripts in the pages of which scholars exchanged their arguments. Yet, more serious enmities sometimes arose.

Such was the case of Alfasi's abstract and of Maimonides' legal code. The latter, *Mishneh Torah,* was harshly criticized by Abraham ben David of Posquières (1120-98), a genial talmudist. This rabbi was so completely engrossed in traditional studies that nothing outside his field had any reality for him. He found fault with Maimonides for doing away with the traditional exposition of contrary arguments and replacing it with a summation from which a single opinion emerged—namely that which the writer preferred.

However, Spanish influence did help to produce genuine Provençal Jewish science. Joseph Kimhi (d. *c.* 1170) and his son David (1160-1235), Judah Ibn Tibbon (1120-90) and his son Samuel (1150-1230), both Spanish families that had settled in Provence, headed this movement. The former were preeminently grammarians and introduced methodical linguistics into France, where empiricism had, until then, reigned supreme. The Ibn Tibbons (or Tibbonides, as they are sometimes called) set themselves the task of translating the Arabic works of Jewish scholars. The father produced Hebrew translations of Saadyah, Ibn Gabirol, Bahya, and Judah Ha-Levi, while his son translated the philosophical works of Maimonides.

It was precisely Maimonides' *Guide of the Perplexed* which first aroused the ire of the French rabbis. The Montpellier chief rabbi, Solomon ben Abraham, who was shocked at the 'audacity' of certain thoughts contained in the book, won the consent of the rabbis of northern France to whom all philosophy was alien, and had the work publicly condemned. The communities of Lunel, Béziers, and Narbonne reacted together and cast the anathema over R. Solomon. This dramatic struggle lasted for years. The 'Orthodox' communities even appealed to the Church to burn publicly the books of their great opponent (through a historical coincidence, the Church was at that time waging a fierce war in the same region of France against the Albigenses, whose heresy it sought to eradicate).

Undoubtedly, the presence in southern France of many Jewish physicians of Spanish origin who were thoroughly acquainted with Arab literature helped to create the university of Montpellier (around 1220) which at first was exclusively a medical faculty. Montpellier remained the center of French medical knowledge for many centuries after those to whom it owed its creation had been expelled from the country.

The great number of Hebrew manuscripts that survived represent only a tiny part of what was actually written or copied by the Jews in this epoch, for there was intense intellectual activity in the fields of philosophy, medicine, mathematics, and astronomy. The works most frequently translated were those of Averroës and of Galen, and at a later period, those of Arnaud de Villeneuve.

In the following years, Provençal Judaism produced a philosophical genius in Levi (Leon) ben Gershon, of Bagnols (a village which no longer exists but was located in the present *département* of Gard). This philosopher (1288-1344) was also called Gersonides. Like all the great thinkers of medieval Judaism, he was primarily a talmudic scholar and beside his philosophical works, he wrote a biblical and a talmudic commentary, and set about compiling a code of traditional customs. He was also an eminent scientist, especially in the fields of mathematics and astronomy, developing the camera obscura and inventing a nautical instrument called 'Jacob's Staff'. In our own time a plain on the moon has been named after him. The most original of his contributions was his theological treatise *Milhamot Adonai* (The Wars of the Lord) in which he proposes a theory of world harmony based on the principles of Aristotle but in keeping with the concept of Judaism.

EXPULSIONS

From the 11th century, however, the situation of the Jews had become almost unbearable. The first explosion of hate seems to have occurred around 1096, at the time of the First Crusade, when the general population found it absurd to go on an expedition to kill distant heretics when a large group was living in their midst. They therefore proceeded to massacre the Jews, especially in the provinces which border on the Rhine. The eminent contribution of French Jews to Jewish religious tradition was thus interrupted by violence. Nevertheless, the literary and philosophical activities continued after the 11th century. As the central authority of the king was not strongly rooted, the Jews were able to escape from the province in which they were persecuted into another where they could live in peace. The king himself sometimes sought to appear as their protector if he could make a financial profit by it. After announcing his intention to expel them, he would sometimes agree to cancel his decision in exchange for a large sum of money (for the king was frequently poorer than his vassals). These arrangements enabled life to continue, although in a disturbed fashion, in the *juiveries,* and the Jews could devote themselves to study. The consolidation of the monarchy, however, forced the Jews into final exile. The first expulsion was ordered by Philip Augustus, probably as a financial operation (this theory is supported by the fact that, previous to this expulsion, the king had created a series of new taxes).

In 1182, the Jews were driven from the provinces where they had found shelter, as the authority of the king now extended to these. In 1198, however, they were permitted to return. Louis IX, the pious Christian king, did not show the same ruthlessness. He was content to apply the measures recommended by the Holy See, which were mainly restrictions in the economic field, but there were also 'spiritual' pressures. France was the scene of many disputes between rabbis and apostates. The first and best-known occurred in Paris in 1240, after which the Church publicly burnt editions of the Talmud.

Philip the Fair was not a man who could be satisfied with such ineffective measures. On July 21 1306, he ordered a round-up of the Jews and expelled them to foreign countries, while canceling the debts he owed them. Later, he again admitted the Jews into France in order to borrow new sums from them. Then he expelled them again. Public opinion might well have been reflected in the *Chronicles* of Geoffrey of Paris, however, who laments the expulsion of the Jews saying that they were more amenable than Christians:

Car Juifs furent debonere	For Jews were obliging people
Que ne sont ores Crestiens	Unlike the Christians of today
... Mes se li Juif demoure	Had they remained in the Kingdom
Fussent au reaume de France	of France
Crestien mainte grande aidance	Christian could now rely on their help
Eussent eu que il n'ont pas	Which they sorely need...

After the death of Philip the Fair (1315) the Jews were recalled to France. They could not, however, regain their former wealth and many failed to return. In the end, Charles VI ordered their final banishment in 1394. Even in regions more hospitable to them, like Franche-Comté, Dauphiné, Provence, and Roussillon, the Jews had eventually to leave for a new exile. In the last years of the 16th century, there was not a single overtly religious Jew in the whole kingdom of France. This was to have serious repercussions on the intellectual activity of the communities and their scholars. The Golden Age of French Judaism was over. From now on, for nearly three centuries, France remained an exclusively Christian kingdom.

THE 'MARGINAL' COMMUNITIES

Originally, the king's law only applied to the territories directly under his control. Now, his power extended over regions that had never belonged to his domain proper. There were only three exceptions: the Comtat Venaissin, the county of Nice, and Alsace, which at that time were foreign territories. There, Jewish communities were allowed to live. They also absorbed large numbers of refugees from France.

Alsace and a large section of the Rhine valley had been peopled by Jews from the Roman period, although very few documents concerning their existence previous to the 12th century have been discovered. From the 12th century onward, a lot of information is available concerning almost all the Alsatian localities. The Alsace Jews had the status of protégés of the emperor and mainly lived by moneylending.

Now and then, their protector decided to cancel a certain amount of the debts owed them. From the 12th century onward, he let the local dignitaries of the Church increasingly apply their own laws to the 'deicide people'. Persecutions became more frequent. The persecutions against the Jews were usually based on the accusation of 'ritual murder'. There were also retaliatory expeditions organized by religious fanatics who accused the Jews of being the cause of the general poverty. In 1348, during the epidemic of the Black Death that took such a terrible toll among the population of the provinces, Jews were burned at the stake in many Alsatian towns, a persecution which is still commemorated in the name of certain streets, especially in Strasbourg. During these massacres, the most heroic among the Jews committed collective suicide while others converted. The Alsatians Jews,

Bronze Hanukkah lamp, Lyons, fourteenth century. One of the oldest known *Hanukkah* lamps, found during the excavations in the old Jewish quarter of Lyons. The decoration is reminiscent of the windows of Gothic cathedrals. Paris, Musée de Cluny, Strauss-Rothschild Collection, Inv. No. 12248.

however, never faced mass deportation. When they were driven away from a town, they usually found shelter in the next one. They vanished from the larger cities and concentrated in villages. As they were not allowed to make a living by tilling the soil, they had to live close to mercantile cities. They therefore concentrated in the suburbs. At night when the sound of the horn signaled them to leave the city, they only had to cross the walls and return to their nearby homes. Thus, a dense suburban population grew up. These communities led thrifty and industrious lives and did not produce famous scholars or create prestigious schools, though they scrupulously practiced their religion.

The renaissance of talmudic study stemmed directly from the imprisonment of the outstanding rabbinic authority, R. Meier of Rothenburg, in the Ensisheim prison (1286-99). This caused a number of his disciples to gather in this city where they created a school for talmudic studies. There were also a number of *yeshivot* in villages, but these were of mediocre standard and did not produce any important work. When printing presses were introduced, the only locality where Hebrew books were published was the imperial city of Haguenau.

It is also significant that the most famous authority of Alsatian (and of German) Jewry should not have been a rabbi or a philosopher but a *shtadlan* or an 'interceder' in favor of the Jews at the court of potentates. This man was Joselman (from Joseph) Louhans of Rosheim who was active between 1510 and 1554 and his status as intermediary was part go-between, part ambassador. He managed to be recognized as the commander (*Befehlshaber*) of all the 'Jewries' in the empire of Charles V.

Joselman was ready to resort to every expediency if this could save a fellow-Jew.

After the Thirty Years' War, when Jews suffered more than the other inhabitants of this province, Alsace was progressively annexed to France. The 18th century promised to be an era of real progress. From then on, the communities of Alsace and Lorraine were politically separated from the area to which they continued to belong culturally: the region known in Jewish tradition as Ashkenaz, that extends from Holland through the Rhine valley to the village of Endingen and to Lengnau in the Swiss canton of Aargau.

The king of France accepted the Jews together with the rest of the population of Alsace. As there had been no Jewish problem in France since the deportation of the 14th century, no government official sought to torment them. It was also easier to suppress acts of hostility and meant that, for a while, Alsatian Jewry prospered. A few Jews became very rich and many of them were appointed to the post of purveyors of the king's armies. The most famous of these purveyors was Cerfbeer (Herz Medelsheim). Relying on the permission of the king, he entered the city of Strasbourg where he settled despite the interdict of the Council of the Fifteen. Respectful of tradition, he founded several pious institutions. In Bischheim, he created a talmudic academy, at the head of which he appointed his brother-in-law, David Joseph Sinzheim.

But the most prosperous and prestigious community of all was that of Metz. This became one of the most sought-after rabbinical posts in all Europe. Outstanding talmudists left German, Bohemian, or Polish centers in order to teach there.

Among the most famous were Jonathan Eibeschütz who worked in Metz between 1745 and 1750, and Aryeh Leib ben Asher (or Loew Ginsburg) author of the halakhic responsa *Shaagat Aryeh* who died there in 1785 after twenty years' teaching. These masters only came to Metz because they knew that Jewish intellectual life was flourishing there and they contributed to the development of its many *yeshivot.*

A few Jewish communities lived in the Roman enclave constituted by the Avignon territory, in the Rhone valley, to which the Pope had been exiled in the 14th century. These communities were located in Avignon, Carpentras, Cavaillon, and L'Isle-sur-Sorgue. Despite the protests of the natives, these communities increased in number after the expulsion of 1394, and especially in the 15th century, when the Jews who had until then been allowed to stay in Dauphiné and Provence were driven from their last shelter. They were denied the right to extend their dwelling area and had to develop their quarters (their *carrières* as they were called) along vertical lines. A specific culture was engendered in this enclave which was facilitated by the extreme density of the Jewish population. Usually the authorities

See illustration page 56.

Carpentras synagogue, South France, eighteenth century. The synagogue at Carpentras was rebuilt in 1741 in the place of an older building dating from 1367. This beautiful building was erected by a community of only 750 families, and until 1789, irritated the successive bishops of the town, who were upset that it should be taller than the cathedral tower. Photo Franck, Paris.

let the Jews administer their own affairs, share among themselves the heavy burden of the taxes they had to pay, and have their own courts of law (except when the offense was a capital one). The vernacular of the Jews was Provençal. It pervaded the liturgy to the extent that many of the hymns that were sung during certain ceremonies were based on alternating Hebrew and Provencal folklore.

The Jewry of the Comtat Venaissin has also left a precious legacy of a kind not found in Alsace and Lorraine: its ancient synagogues, the architectural gems of Provencal Jewry. As one can see them now, most of these synagogues were restored during the 18th century. They are the testimony of a way of life more than six centuries old. In 1791, the annexation of this territory to France, which gave the Jews equal rights, precipitated the decline of these picturesque communities whose members became assimilated and scattered throughout the whole country.

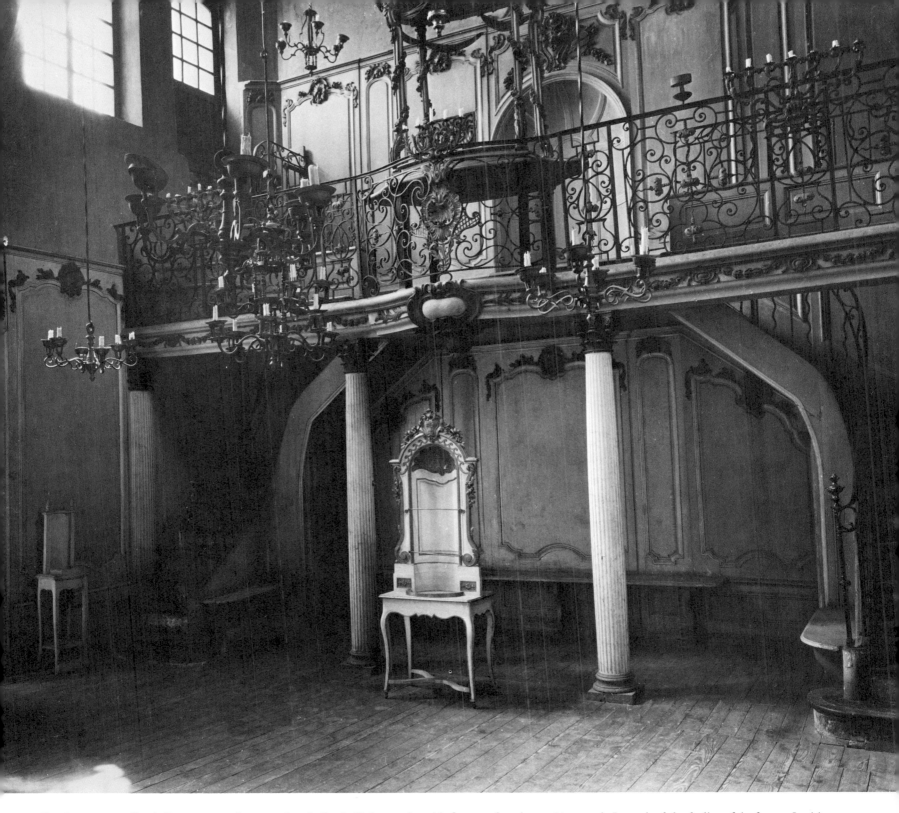

Cavaillon synagogue, South France, 1774. A masterpiece in Louis Quinze style, with fine woodcarving and ironwork. It survived the decline of the former Jewish community of this town and was brought again into active daily use with the immigration of Algerian Jews to France, mainly Southern France, in the early 1960s. Photo Franck, Paris.

THE 'NEW JEWS' AND THE PROBLEM OF EMANCIPATION

Outside these two enclaves—Alsace-Lorraine and Comtat Venaissin—the year 1394 marked the almost complete disappearance of the Jews from French territory. Officially, the French realm remained without Jews for over three hundred years. And yet, the infiltration of the conversos, considered Christian but who secretly clung to their original faith, was particularly important in south-west France and the Atlantic harbors (see chapter on Conversos).

The French Renaissance was characterized by an atmosphere of tolerance. This tolerance continued despite the Wars of Religion and the Revocation of the Edict of Nantes that was more a political than a confessional move. Nothing, in fact, prevented the Jews, both those who were overtly religious or those who concealed their faith, from passing through France or even settling

65

Handwritten Scroll of Esther, Provence or Italy, c. 1600. Handwritten *Megillah* or Scroll of Esther. The initial illustration depicts here the story of Adam and Eve. Every Jewish family had a Scroll of Esther, often decorated in a spirit of gaiety. Paris, Musée de Cluny, Strauss-Rothschild Collection, Inv. No. Cl 12263.

there. From time to time, the king reminded his subjects of the anti-Jewish decrees. These warnings were usually caused by the too manifest presence of many Jewish immigrants and generally resulted in an increase in the taxes which the Jews had to pay. What is certain is that during the period of humanism, many practicing and converted Jews participated in the biblical and Hebrew researches initiated by Christian scholars.

From the 18th century onward, a new type of Jew emerged: the Jewish financier who was often the official purveyor of the army. As a rule, this characteristic type came from Alsace and Lorraine. His trade, however, compelled him to reside for long periods in Paris. Though business transactions did not usually do credit to those who carried them out, the honesty and skill of the Jewish businessmen won the appreciation of their clients and acquaintances. The consideration which certain Jews enjoyed in Christian society, as well as in Jewish circles, fostered among the Jews the idea that they could become the equals of Christians with the same status as other subjects of the kingdom.

At the outbreak of the French Revolution, the Jews were ready for their emancipation. Those who favored this emancipation pointed out insistently that the lowly position of the Jews in society was the result of historical circumstances that had been forcibly imposed upon them by Christian society. They felt confident that once the Jews were granted equality, they would soon rid themselves of the feelings of inferiority they had acquired when they were at the bottom of the social scale. These generous views had to overcome many obstacles. First there were local particularities: the Bordeaux Jews, who had attained a high social status, spurned the Jews from Comtat Venaissin who clung to their old ways and customs. Yet both groups agreed that they would not mix with the Alsatian Jews whose poverty and narrow-minded piety they despised, as if the Alsatians were beings from another world. As a matter of fact, the Jews from Alsace were chiefly peddlers, pawnbrokers and beggars, ignorant of the customs and refinements of Christian society. There was one problem to which no quick solution could be given:

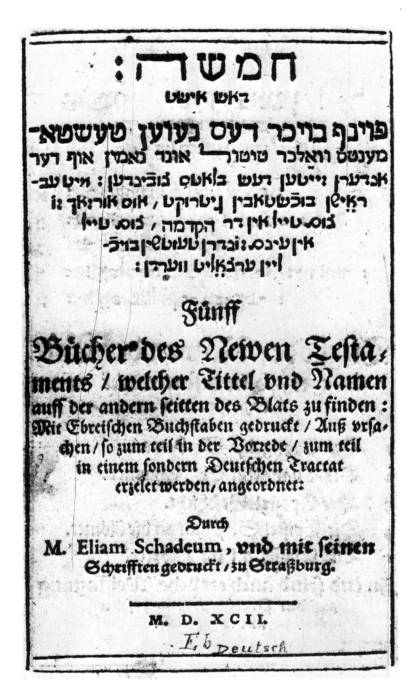

New Testament in Yiddish, Strasbourg, 1592. Title Page. The Five Books of the New Testament in a Yiddish translation with German annotations by E. Schad. The existence of this work shows the interest of the Strasbourg humanists in Jewish studies as well as indicating the desire to use the New Testament text to convert Jews to Christianity. Strasbourg, Bibliothèque Nationale et Universitaire, No. R 102038.

usury, which owing to external circumstances, had become an essentially Jewish occupation. Too many interests were bound up with usury for this problem to be solved without painful conflicts. Jews and Christians also had deeply rooted habits in this connection which could not be easily eradicated. To adjust to the new style of life the Jews needed spiritual guides.

Unfortunately, confronted by the new conditions most of the rabbis of the old school were not capable of original thinking. Some of the younger rabbis found in the Scripture passages imbued with the generosity of revolutionary doctrines. These

discoveries, however, did not influence religious life which remained unaffected by the new outlook. In the following century, scholars like Samson Raphael Hirsch in Germany or Samuel David Luzzatto in Italy developed new conceptions of Torah studies, which could be proudly held up to the promoters of modern philosophy. But thinkers of a similar stature did not appear in France, either at the end of the 18th or in the

Collection bag, Strasbourg, 1778. Bag for the collection of contributions on the occasion of marriages and other joyful ceremonies. The inscription wishes 'Good Luck' and gives the name of the donor, Wolf, son of Gabriel May of Alsace. Painted wood and leather. Strasbourg, Musée Alsacien, Dépôt permanent de la Société pour l'Histoire des Israélites d'Alsace et de Lorraine.

Shield of David, Jungholtz (Haut-Rhin), 1770. Carved wood, painted. A piece of unleavened bread was inserted and kept until the following Passover for legal religious reasons. Strasbourg, Musée Alsacien, Dépôt permanent de la Société pour l'Histoire des Israélites d'Alsace et de Lorraine.

of France. This eventually turned into a process of de-Judaization. It is a sad but characteristic fact that the formulation of a new attitude had to come from outside and was actually imposed on the Jewish leaders by the reformatory and unifying will of Napoleon Bonaparte.

It is well-known that the emperor had inherited from his Catholic education many prejudices against the Jews and a complete ignorance of their actual life. He shared his admiration for biblical heroes, who were glorified by the Church, with contempt for their descendants which Christian theology impressed into young men. It seem, however, that he sincerely intended to 'regenerate' the Jewish people (if possible with their cooperation, but if need be, against their will). Above all, he meant to carry out his work of stabilization in revolutionary France by endowing his new regime with institutions capable of ensuring a smooth running of the state machinery.

The decree of May 30 1806, canceling the debts which the farmers of the eastern provinces owed to the Jews and calling for the constitution of an assembly of rabbis and notables, was the result of a compromise between a repressive and a liberal tendency. The exponents of the former trend, however, were entrusted with enforcing these laws. On the other hand, the attitude of the Jewish delegates who met in Paris on July 15 1806 and came from all the departments containing a Jewish population

19th century, when enlightened rabbis became the proponents of a spineless religion.

As the result, the only solution left to those who could no longer adhere to the medieval modes of thought of their spiritual leaders was total adherence to the views of their Christian contemporaries. This process sometimes led to conversion. Whole families broke away from Judaism and, through apostasy and mixed marriages (a process which had begun in the salons of intelligent German Jewesses and continued until the end of the 19th century), joined the ranks of the Christian population. These elements were sometimes devoutly Christian but were often indifferent toward religion. Without a constant stream of fresh blood from communities outside the borders, especially from Alsace and abroad, French Jewry would probably have died out through assimilation.

As individuals, the 'French citizens of the Jewish religion' found the doors of French society opened to them. Those who availed themselves from the first of this opportunity were a small minority. They were the sons of ancient families from Bordeaux, Nancy, Metz, and Strasbourg, who had matriculated in the Écoles Centrales, entered the universities, or had engaged upon a career in the army, in literature, science or the arts. For the Jewish masses, such a metamorphosis was not so easy. They had to go through an intermediary stage when the sons of the poorer classes went to study in elementary and professional Jewish schools in which they received the basic elements of secular culture. The second generation was then able to enter directly the state schools

Purim plate, Les Islettes (Meuse), end of eighteenth century. Faience plate used for the sending of presents (usually sweetmeats etc.) on Purim. The source of this custom is indicated in the text on the rim of the plate, taken from the Book of Esther (9:22): '...and of sending portions one to another and gifts to the poor'. The inner inscription and the illustration refer to the humiliation of Haman by Mordecai (Esther 6:11). Paris, Musée de Cluny, Strauss-Rothschild Collection, Inv. No. 21113.

The Napoleonic Sanhedrin in session, Feb. 9 1807. In 1806 Napoleon summoned an assembly of Jewish notables to clarify the Jewish attitude on the subject of the relations between Church and State. The following year a Sanhedrin was convened in Paris to ratify the recommendations of the Notables. Engraving by Damame de Martrait. Paris, Bibliothèque Nationale, Cabinet des Estampes.

(including Belgium, Rhineland, the annexed regions in the Alps, and the Italian kingdom) was dictated to them by the omnipotent administration of the empire. This administration knew exactly what its objectives were. On the contrary, the Jews had no central organization to which their local synagogues were responsible and the variety of their origins seemed to make the creation of a unifying program very problematical.

Most of them only asked to be allowed to remain faithful to their Law within the framework of the new order. But all of them were convinced that the Jews had to reach some kind of a compromise with the new regime. This manifested itself in the adulatory declaration (in an epoch that was still very close to the monarchic period and had retained its habits of speech)

of allegiance toward Napoleon made by the Great Sanhedrin (the institution which emerged, in 1807, from the Assembly of the Notables). Here is an excerpt from the preamble to its decisions:

'Blessed in all eternity be the Lord, the God of Israel, who put on the throne of France and Italy a prince according to His heart. God saw the misery of the descendants of Jacob and chose Napoleon the Great to be the instrument of their redemption...'

It was easy for the Notables of the Sanhedrin to reject polygamy for it had not been in practice in their communities at least since the Middle Ages. In the same way, they agreed to let divorces and marriages be preceded by a civil ceremony. Yet

Passover plate, Strasbourg, end of eighteenth century. Passover plate with a scene of the *Seder* (Passover) meal being celebrated in a family. The father is reading the *Haggadah* and has raised his cup for the *Kiddush* (sanctification prayer). The engraved words indicate the different stages of the *Seder* ceremony. Pewter, engraved by Johann Isenheim, Strasbourg. Hamburg, Altonaer Museum, Inv. No. 1954/206.

Chair of Elijah, Alsace, end of eighteenth century. Double seat, the so-called Chair of Elijah, used at circumcision ceremonies, with cushions. The prophet Elijah is traditionally believed to be present at the ceremonies to protect the newborn child from any dangers. Walnut and deal. Strasbourg, Musée Alsacien, Dépôt permanent de la Société pour l'Histoire des Israélites d'Alsace et de Lorraine, Inv. No. 85.

they obstinately refused to declare interconfessional marriages legitimate or desirable, as the emperor wanted them to.

Concerning usury, the delegates explained that the Pentateuch had never permitted the taking of exorbitant rates even if the sums were lent to non-Jews. According to the Law, it was even an obligation to lend money without any interest to those Jews who needed it in order to survive. They went on to say that now that they could consider other Frenchmen as their brothers, this Law would become an obligation to the Jews in their dealings with Frenchmen. Universal brotherhood was advocated by the Bible and the Talmud and was offered to all who wanted to reciprocate it. Patriotism was also an obligation which Judaism imposed on its believers toward any state who considered them as equal citizens. There had never been before such a clear formulation of the new obligations which met the requirements of the new conditions. The Great Sanhedrin did not hesitate to obey the intimations of the authorities and asked 'all Israelites, especially in France and in the Italian kingdom, who now enjoyed civil and political rights, to devote their efforts to inspiring youth with the love of work and direct their youth toward the engineering and the liberal professions.' The Great Sanhedrin further advised the Jews to 'try and acquire landed property as a means of setting up a stronger link with their homeland, give up those occupations that expose a man to the hatred and contempt of his fellow-citizens, and strive to be worthy of their consideration and good will.'

The only concrete step that was taken by the Assembly was that 'all Jews who are called to military service are exempted by the Law from all religious observances that are incompatible with it.' This exemption was the utmost concession which the rabbis were prepared to make. Going beyond this would have made them renegades in their own eyes.

The official character of these decisions made French Jewry an institution of the French state. It was organized in Consistories responsible for a *département* or a whole province, which controlled the local communities. At the head was the Central Consistory of French Jews, an organization which today is still the semi-official structure of the Jewish religious institutions in France.

At the time of the Restoration and during the first half of the 19th century, the prestige of the Catholic Church caused a great number of Jews to become Christians, especially among rich and cultured circles who felt closer to their Christian neighbors than to their own coreligionists. The best Jewish families were thus decimated. Other Jews became alienated from Judaism and married Christian women, this latter process becoming more general at the end of the century.

This progressive loss of contact was accentuated by the slow move toward the towns of the Jews from villages who

The French Jews receive definitive civic status, 1808. Page from a register of the Strasbourg municipality of the year 1808. One of the decrees made by Napoleon was that Jews should settle on fixed surnames. In this case the Jew, who was of small stature, took the name of Klein (small). His first name—Naphtali—was the classical form of Hirtz (stag), emblem of the Naphtali tribe. Archives départementales du Bas-Rhin.

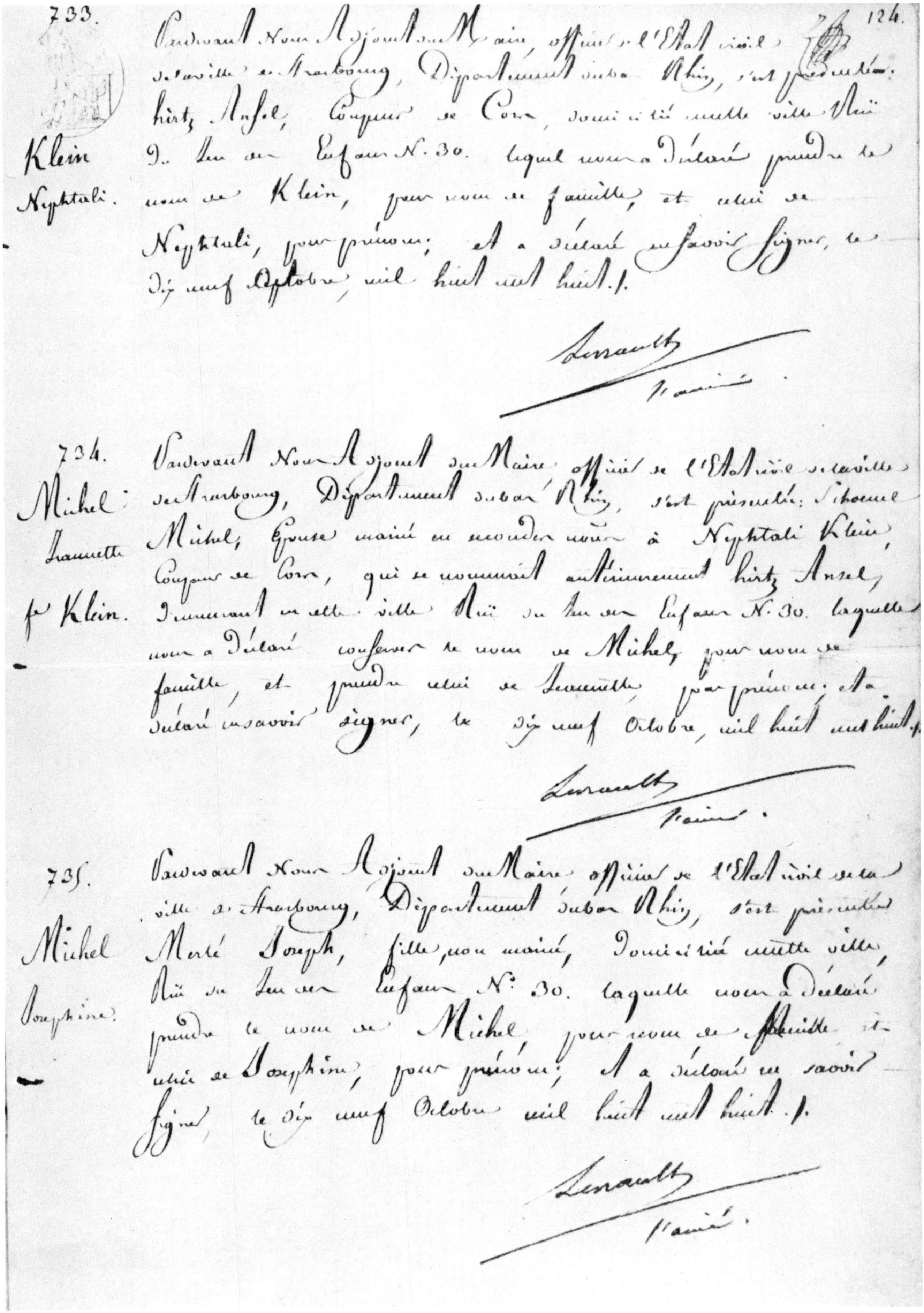

733.

Klein
Nephtali.

Par devant Nous Adjoint au Maire, officier de l'État civil de la ville de Strasbourg, Département du bas Rhin, s'est présenté: Hirtz Ansel, Coupeur de Cors, domicilié en cette ville Rue du Feu au Enfant N. 30. lequel nous a Déclaré prendre le nom de Klein, pour nom de famille, et celui de Nephtali, pour prénom; Et a déclaré ne savoir Signer, le Dix neuf Octobre, mil huit cent huit.

Lerault
Maire.

734.

Michel
Jeannette

fe Klein.

Par devant Nous Adjoint au Maire, officier de l'État civil de la ville de Strasbourg, Département du bas Rhin, s'est présentée: Jeanne Michel, Épouse mariée en seconde noce à Nephtali Klein, Coupeur de Cors, qui se nommait antérieurement Hirtz Ansel, Demeurant en cette ville Rue du Feu au Enfant N. 30. laquelle nous a Déclaré conserver le nom de Michel, pour nom de famille, et prendre celui de Jeannette, pour prénom; Et a déclaré ne savoir signer, le Dix neuf Octobre, mil huit cent huit.

Lerault
Maire.

735.

Michel
Joséphine.

Par devant Nous Adjoint au Maire officier de l'État civil de la ville de Strasbourg, Département du bas Rhin, s'est présentée Marie Joseph, fille, non mariée, Domiciliée en cette ville, Rue du Feu au Enfant N. 30. laquelle nous a Déclaré prendre le nom de Michel, pour nom de famille et celui de Joséphine, pour prénom; Et a déclaré ne savoir Signer, le Dix neuf Octobre mil huit cent huit.

Lerault
Maire.

had not yet been touched by the new outlook. Then in their towns, these Jews assimilated and were replaced by elements from foreign countries. Assimilation was a disaster for the Jews. Yet it was an inevitable process, given the overwhelming differences in power and numbers between the Jewish and the Christian communities.

France was then the main European power and was considered the hub of the civilized world. French Jews were not very numerous (about forty thousand at the outbreak of the Revolution) but there were great differences in character between one community and another: three-quarters of the community (the Jews from Alsace and Lorraine) were drawn to the German nation whose language they spoke and wrote. The remaining quarter had nearly as many different liturgies as there were towns. Yet they had neither the material strength of German Jewry nor the spiritual powers of Polish Jewry. In the first half of the 19th century, therefore, French Jewry had a defensive attitude toward the more prestigious culture which confronted it and into the midst of which they had been so abruptly admitted.

Havdalah spicebox, Alsace, end of eighteenth century. Pewter spicebox for *Havdalah* made for an Alsatian Jew probably named J. Storch (judging from the initial J. Sch and the simple drawing of a stork). Nancy, Musée Historique Lorrain, Inv. Zone D.

SCIENCE AND WELFARE

It would be completely arbitrary to regard any one year as the date when scientific and welfare institutions were created by French Jewry. Yet the fact that two decisive events took place within one year may have been more than a mere coincidence. In 1859 the rabbinical school of France was transferred to Paris and in 1860, the Alliance Israélite Universelle came into being.

As a matter of fact, the maturing of the new Jewish society born of the French Revolution was over. Those who had known the *Ancien Régime* were now dead and all the members of the community had been raised in an environment where the Jews enjoyed equality of rights.

Havdalah candleholder, France, late eighteenth century. *Havdalah* (end-of-Sabbath service) candleholder combined with drawer for the spices used in the course of the service. On the large rounded foot, a medallion with the tablets of the Law, on which each Commandment is represented by a number in Roman figures. Nancy, Musée Historique Lorrain, Inv. No. 1069.

Fromental Halévy (1799-1862). The famous composer was the first Jew to be elected a member of the Institut de France in 1846. His most famous work is the opera *La Juive,* composed in 1835. He taught at the Paris conservatoire from 1827, his pupils including Gounod and Bizet. Paris, Bibliothèque Nationale, Cabinet des Estampes.

Adolphe Crémieux (1796-1880). A well-known lawyer, Crémieux was twice Minister of Justice, once at the end of the Second Republic, and once during the Third Republic. An ardent advocate of equal civic rights for the Jews, his name was given to the 'Loi Crémieux' which accorded such rights to the Jews of Algeria, and had an end put to the humiliating oath *more judaico*. Paris, Bibliothèque Nationale, Cabinet des Estampes.

The last vestige of the special status of the Jews was the swearing by Jewish witnesses *'more judaico'*, or 'in the Jewish manner'. Certain courts of law used to have Jews take the oath in a synagogue over the Torah scrolls (which were supposed to replace the cross on which Christian oaths were sworn in secular courts of law). The outstanding lawyer and politician, Adolphe Crémieux, was resolved to do away with this proceeding and told the rabbis to refuse to participate in this ceremony. A rabbi from Phalsbourg, Lazare Isidor, who had been particularly adamant in resisting the legal authorities was himself summoned before a tribunal. Crémieux acted as his counsel and succeeded in getting his acquittal, an acquittal which implied the final rejection of this special form of oath (1846).

As equality of rights was now total, the France of Guizot and of Napoleon III became the paradise of cosmopolitan millionaires. German and Russian Jews whose enterprising minds were capable of taking immediate advantage of the possibilities offered by modern technology and science set up prosperous financial institutions and succeeded in winning their way into the new society by their generosity as philanthropists and patrons of

the arts, a generosity which was more beneficial to the country where they were active than to their own brethren.

Endowed with titles granted by the monarchs they had saved from bankruptcy, the bankers De Hirsch, De Poliakoff, and Fould-Oppenheim ruled the stock exchange, the salons, and sometimes the Cabinet. The archetype of these dynasties of bankers was the Rothschild family with its numerous branches active in different countries. In France, as elsewhere, their name became the symbol of wealth, and also of generosity. This family remained faithful to its religion, at first because they were pious, then because of their personal pride. For a long period all the presidents of the Central Consistory of France and of the Paris Consistory came from this family. The Rothschilds also took care of the budgets of these organizations. The Rothschild family served the French nation when Bismarck demanded the payment of an enormous war indemnity after the defeat of 1870, and the Rothschilds supplied a great part of the sum and took upon themselves a burden that would have crippled the economy of France.

At the same time, the Jews assimilated into French culture

and gave it many famous authors, scientists, and composers. Jews particularly distinguished themselves in the musical field. Meyerbeer and Offenbach came from Germany but found Paris more receptive to their talents. Unlike them, Fromental Halévy represents total assimilation to French musical culture. The composer of *La Juive* was a man who led an austere and dignified life. He was the son of the cantor Elie Halévy who was born in Bavaria and had become one of the best Hebrew poets of his time. By a strange coincidence, Fromental Halévy was born on the site of the future Paris opera where his works were later performed. He entered the Académie des Beaux-Arts in 1836 and became its permanent secretary in 1857. He was probably the first Jew to become a member of the French Institute. Later, Adolphe Franck (1809-93) from Lorraine followed him there. He was professor of philosophy at the Collège de France and vice-president of the Central Consistory. His book *The Kabbalah or the Religious Philosophy of the Jews* (1843) won him a seat in the Académie des Sciences Morales et Politiques. Another member of the French Academy was Solomon Munk (1803-67),

Kiddush goblet, France, first half of nineteenth century. Goblet for the *Kiddush* with engraved blessing, used for the wine blessing and other joyful ceremonies. Cut glass. Nancy, Musée Historique Lorrain, Inv. No. 1129.

a former secretary to the Central Consistory, who in 1858, was elected to the Académie des Inscriptions et Belles-Lettres. Joseph Derenbourg and his son Hartwig, who came from the Rhineland and were specialists in Judeo-Arabic literature, were also admitted to this Academy in 1871 and 1900 respectively. This was equally the case of Assyriologist Jules Oppert (1825-1905), also born in Germany, who entered the Academy in 1881.

The Académie des Sciences also opened its gates to a number of Jewish scientists: in 1873, to the astronomer Maurice Loewy and in 1883 to the physicist Maurice Lévy. In 1880 the economist Maurice Block was elected into the Académie des Sciences Morales et Politiques. Young Jewish scientists knew that they could make a scientific career in France without being hindered by racial obstacles.

The field of politics had also been the dream of many young Jews who wanted to prove to themselves and to the world that they really enjoyed all the civic rights of the other citizens, by attaining the highest positions in the administrative bodies of the State. Yet it was not until the first cabinet of the Second Republic, a humanitarian and ephemeral regime, that two Jews

The Wandering Jew, engraving, nineteenth century. Engraving by G. Doré. The legend of the 'Wandering Jew' was developed by Christians from the idea that Israel had been cursed and condemned to eternal wandering because of the Jews' refusal to recognize Jesus as the son of God. According to Jewish belief, the wandering of the Jews was a punishment for their unfaithfulness to the Laws of the Bible. Paris, Bibliothèque Nationale.

who had participated in the struggle against the Orléans family were chosen as ministers. They were Michel Goudchaux, the Finance Minister, and Adolphe Crémieux, the Minister of Justice. The latter was to become a minister again, in the government of National Defense in 1870-1. He signed the famous Crémieux Decree with Gambetta, Glais-Bizoin, and Fourichon on October 24 1870, which proclaimed that 'all Jews born in the *département* of Algeria were French citizens'.

The consequence of this promotion into modern civilization was that the Algerian Jews finally renounced their social particularism. But the rules set up by the Great Sanhedrin remained valid. Only the religious laws of the Pentateuch were to be enforced. Traditional laws governing the political and legal organization of the Jewish people were to be set aside until the advent of messianic times in the very dim and distant future. The rabbinical courts that were still extant in some places and dealt with legal matters had to be replaced by the national institutions and the national law.

The same considerations gave rise to the Alliance Israélite Universelle. Though it was created by a few individuals, it was built within the framework of the civic evolution of the French Jewish community. During the month of May 1860, a declaration called on world Jewry to unite under the ancient Hebrew motto: *Kol Israel Haverim* ('All Jews are Comrades') in order to fight prejudice and racial discrimination. This appeal was intended to draw the attention of the world to the political and social conditions which prevailed in Oriental countries and hindered progress among the Jews. It noted the dangers still facing the Jews and the partial character of Emancipation in the countries where this had already been achieved. At the same time it expressed complete faith in the future of Mankind which it saw as dominated by Science and Liberty.

At first, the Alliance concentrated its efforts on political and diplomatic action. Its successes on the diplomatic front were chiefly due to the activity of Crémieux who acted as president of the Alliance between 1863 and 1880. Later, this type of

Passover dishes, Alsace, beginning of nineteenth century. The strict ban on having leavened bread in the house at Passover generally led also to a complete change in crockery. To avoid any mistakes, a special set of Passover dishes was brought out and used during the week. As in this set, they were often clearly marked with the word '*Pesach*' (Passover). Strasbourg, Musée Alsacien, Dépôt permanent de la Société pour l'Histoire des Israélites d'Alsace et de Lorraine.

Sheet with prayers for Sabbath eve, Alsace (?), first half of nineteenth century. Decorated prayer-sheet for Sabbath eve. Watercolor on paper with wooden frame. Signed: 'Meir Segal (=Mayer Levi) from Haigerloch (near Sigmaringen), now teacher in Mittersholz (Bas-Rhin)'. Both are small towns in Alsace. Strasbourg, Musée Alsacien, Dépôt permanent de la Société pour l'Histoire des Israélites d'Alsace et de Lorraine.

activity, although never completely discarded, never had the same importance in the work of the great Parisian institution.

From the first, the leaders of the Alliance founded an educational network. In 1860, its first school opened in Tetuan. Later, other schools were set up in all the Islamic countries, from the Atlantic Ocean to the Persian Gulf: in Morocco, Tunisia, Libya, Egypt, Palestine, Syria and Lebanon, Persia, Turkey (including the province of the Ottoman empire that was to become Iraq), Bulgaria, Greece, Serbia, Rumania, and elsewhere. These schools were to function until they were integrated into the governmental network of these countries.

Indeed, the fundamental problem of the Jewish communities was the school problem: how could a young Jew achieve pro-

fessional promotion or attain a more dignified position without education? This aspiration toward education was also in keeping with the Jewish tradition which considered ignorance a serious sin. Yet, as the Alliance emphasized universal education based on the teaching of the French language, it declared war not only on

Amulet for woman in childbirth, Alsace, nineteenth century. These amulets summoned both God and the mysterious dark forces lurking in the world. Various combinations of magical texts were invoked to pacify Satan and Lilith. Here the verse: 'Thou shall not suffer a witch to live' (Exod. 22:17) is repeated in three different word-combinations. Watercolor. Strasbourg, Musée Alsacien, Dépôt permanent de la Société pour l'Histoire des Israélites d'Alsace et de Lorraine.

Hanukkah lamp, Alsace, beginning of nineteenth century. The Hebrew inscription consists of the latter part of the blessing recited while lighting the lights. Basle, Judisches Museum der Schweiz, 97.

struction of the Land of Israel. It now overlooks the buildings of Tel Aviv which sprawl over the plain to its very front door.

Without being directly linked to the institutions of the Alliance, the initiative of Baron Edmond de Rothschild for the development of Jewish agriculture and industry in Palestine was based on similar principles. This man, who became known in the Holy Land as *Ha-nadiv ha-yadua* ('the famous philanthropist'), always rejected the theories of official Zionism, whose settlement activities developed only twenty years after the beginnings of his own creative work on Palestinian ground. He advocated rather a total merging into French society, as befitted an adherent of the 'Consistory'. Despite this difference of opinion, his religious tendencies, the deep love he bore his persecuted people, and the awareness of the role he could play thanks to his fortune made him ready to cooperate with the Zionists in reconstructing the Land of Israel.

He organized the cultivation of grapes and created a large-scale wine industry at a time when vineyards had in fact

the ignorance of the children who sprawled in the dirt of the *mellahs*: it also intended to do away with the primitive forms of education which consisted in having children of all ages and all aptitudes chant automatically the basic texts of the prayer-book, the Pentateuch, and the Talmud under the direction of a master whom no one respected.

In 1866, the problem of Palestine was submitted to the Alliance by the Hungarian rabbi Joseph Natonek (1813-92). This rabbi appeared before the Central Committee of the organization together with the author of *Rome and Jérusalem,* the utopian socialist Moses Hess. He exposed the situation of the Jewish communities in the Holy Land that lived on charity and recommended the promotion in the Holy Land of an enlightened network of schools and of agricultural colonies. His proposal was approved and its promoter was sent on a mission to Constantinople. Although this mission bore no fruit, the leaders of the Alliance created in the Land of Israel the Mikveh-Israel school, the first important institution which was to help the Jews in Palestine return to agricultural work.

The Alsatian businessman, Charles Netter, became the enthusiastic patron of this 'utopia'. In 1869, in the outskirts of Jaffa, in the middle of a sandy plain bristling with cacti, an agricultural school sponsored by the Alliance Israélite Universelle was created. It taught the modern conceptions of agriculture. Its very name, 'Hope of Israel', revealed the objective of its founders. This school, which still functions today as a semi-national institution, was one of the chief instruments of the peaceful recon-

Brass Havdalah candleholder, France, first half of nineteenth century. Combination of *Havdalah* candleholder and spicebox shaped like a stove, complete with stovepipe to hold the candle. Strasbourg, Musée Alsacien, Dépôt permanent de la Société pour l'Histoire des Israélites d'Alsace et de Lorraine.

Hanukkah lamp, Alsace, c. 1800. Glazed earthenware; the work of an amateur. Strasbourg, Musée Alsacien, Dépôt permanent de la Société pour l'Histoire des Israélites d'Alsace et de Lorraine.

Passover plate, probably Les Islettes (Meuse), c. 1800. Simple Passover plate mentioning only 'Pesach' and the first names of the owners: 'Meir' and 'Kela'. Faience. Strasbourg, Musée Alsacien, Dépôt permanent de la Société pour l'Histoire des Israélites d'Alsace et de Lorraine, Inv. No. 42.

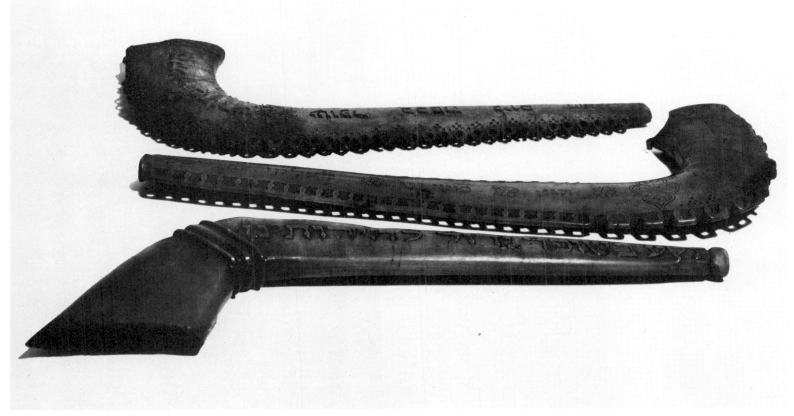

Shophars, Alsace, c. 1800. The *shophar* (which is blown during the New Year service) bears the inscription: 'Blow the great horn for our freedom'. The sound of the horn, with a certain number of tones, blown in a precise way, calls the worshiper to repentance on the New Year. Strasbourg, Société pour l'Histoire des Israélites d'Alsace et de Lorraine, Inv. No. 9.

Goblet, France, first half of nineteenth century. Cut-glass goblet engraved with two words in Hebrew meaning 'He chose' (i.e. Israel) and 'they will be blessed' (i.e., all the peoples of the world thanks to Israel). Nancy, Musée Historique Lorrain, Inv. Zone C.

We have described the main activities carried on or organized by French Jewry outside the borders of its country. They were generally efficient and generous although the organizers tended to regard the ideal of assimilation as a panacea and did not adhere to the basic impulse of the Jewish people toward a national renaissance.

A similar attitude suffused the development of Jewish studies in France. The young Jews who had been educated in *lycées* and universities (where the only power which resisted clericalism was the rationalist thought of the Encyclopedists, Revolutionaries, and ideologists) rejected mysticism and, when they did not become total atheists, adhered to a rationalized Judaism. All these young Jews, who were the future spiritual leaders either as rabbis or as professors, engaged in a pitiless critique of their sources. As we have already mentioned, the transfer of the

fully disappeared from Arab Palestine. Other enterprises were less successful (silkworms, preparation of glass, creation of Tantura harbor). Yet they gave a new impulse to private and collective initiative and this was to prove decisive in later periods. It has been estimated that Baron Edmond spent fifty million gold francs on the Holy Land during his lifetime. This helps to understand why the Zionist leader Nahum Sokolow declared in his funeral speech:

'He was our uncrowned king; not a king who receives tributes from the people, but a king who paid his own tribute to the people.'

French Jews also made efforts to help the victims of the Russian pogroms which took place after the assassination of Tsar Alexander II. The representatives of the Alliance Israélite Universelle, among them Charles Netter, went to the rescue of the refugees who flooded into Brody (Galicia). Emergency convoys were organized. However, a long-term solution was needed. A small group of immigrants was thus directed toward the Holy Land (although at that time immigration into that part of the world was a delicate matter), and others to South America, more particularly to Argentina, to the villages founded by Baron Maurice de Hirsch.

Mizrah, Alsace, middle of nineteenth century. Watercolor on paper in a wooden frame, showing a vase with roses and tulips, and the initials, probably of the owner rather than the artist, in Latin letters. Strasbourg, Musée Alsacien, Dépôt permanent de la Société pour l'Histoire des Israélites d'Alsace et de Lorraine.

Mizrah, Alsace, second half of nineteenth century. The *Mizrah* (East) is the sign placed on the eastern wall of a synagogue or house to indicate the direction to turn during prayer. (Jews, wherever they are, face Jerusalem at time of prayer.) Silk, embroidered. Strasbourg, Musée Alsacien, Dépôt permanent de la Société pour l'Histoire des Israélites d'Alsace et de Lorraine.

rabbinical school to Paris was the starting point of this evolution. The Jewish leaders no longer wanted pious scholars of the ancient type but enlightened scholars who could influence their environment and preach civic virtues and moderate piety.

In 1880, the Society of Jewish Studies was founded under the sponsorship of the Paris chief rabbi, Zadoc Kahn, and with the material assistance of the Rothschilds and other patrons. This society was open to all and some of its members were non-Jewish orientalists. It organized lectures, symposiums, and published invaluable scientific works (such as the historical survey of French Jewish commentaries *Gallia Judaica* by Heinrich Gross and *Greek and Roman Texts concerning Judaism* by Theodore Reinach). Its chief activity was the editing of the *Revue des Études Juives.* This periodical, which was the work of a brilliant staff, gave a tremendous impulse to research into Jewish studies.

POLITICANS AND POETS

The two spheres of activity which seemed to be characteristic of the contribution of French Jewry during the second half of the 19th century were based on an optimistic view of the future of the Jewish people, seen in a perspective of scientific and social progress. By devoting their energies to fighting poverty and ignorance in foreign countries and concentrating on the study of history, they implied that there was no longer any problem for Jewish existence. The events which occurred at the end of the century were to prove them wrong.

The mere fact that the French people did not rise against the metics after the Panama Affair (in which a number of Jewish crooks had participated) or when the 'betrayal' of Captain Alfred Dreyfus was noisily announced, was firm proof of the final

HISTOIRE D'UN TRAITRE

PRIX : 0 Fr. 10

IMAGE FRANÇAISE

La Complainte de l'Ile du Diable

Air de *FUALDÈS*

'Story of a Traitor', contemporary with the Dreyfus Affair. French 'comic strip' issued at the time of the Dreyfus Affair. It contains all the classical themes and stereotypes of anti-Semitism (his physical repulsiveness, domination through money, his amorality) and also vilifies as traitors all the supporters of Dreyfus, notably Émile Zola. Jerusalem, National and University Library, A. Ludvipol Collection.

Leaflet supporting Dreyfus and his defenders, Sceaux. Every effort has been made in this leaflet to stress that the supporters of Dreyfus came from the right and center parties and not only from the left, and the slogan 'Long Live the Army' is prominently displayed.

83

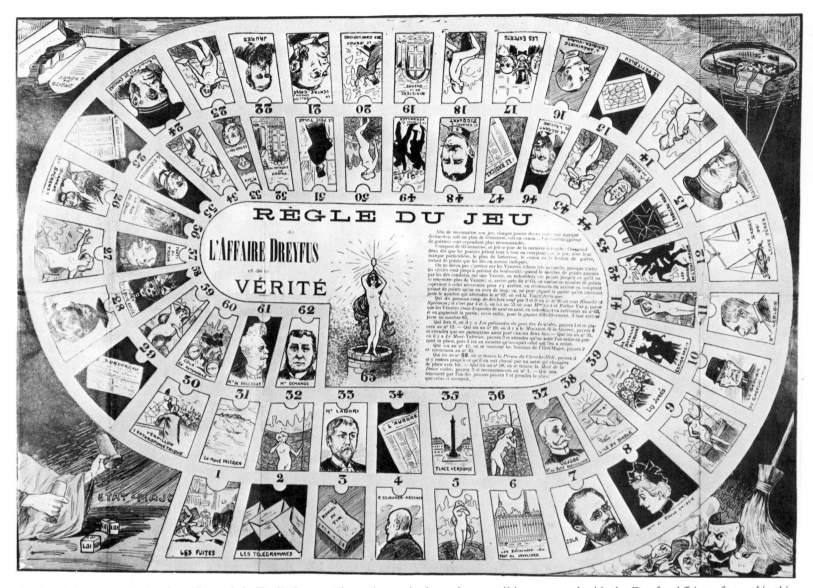

Dreyfusard dice game 'The Dreyfus Affair and the Truth', Sceaux. The various episodes and personalities connected with the Dreyfus Affair are featured in this game and the winner was the first to reach the Naked Truth in the center. Jerusalem, National and University Library, Collection A. Ludvipol, 296.25.

rejection of anti-Semitism by the French. Despite the agitators who tried to exploit the emotion caused by 'the Affair', no official measure was ever taken against the Jews.

Yet, the more sensitive and those who were endowed with a more vivid imagination could not be satisfied with the comfortable sophisms with which their brethren tried to set their minds at rest. A great part of the Jewish élite emerged from this ordeal with a different attitude toward its environment. They were men who launched themselves into politics to change the society whose iniquity had humiliated them. Others wrote books in which they gave vent to the sufferings of their tormented minds. These two trends meet in the personality of an extraordinary character: Bernard Lazare (1865-1903). He was the son of an ancient family of Nimes (his real name was actually Lazare Bernard) and he made his first steps in life as a young bourgeois. He could have made a career in French society like his brothers, for instance, and have become a famous university professor. Later, when he engaged upon literary works, he could have made a reputation as a decadent poet (decadent poetry was the

fashion at that time) like his contemporary, Gustave Kahn, or his older colleague Catulle Mendes. Yet something in him drove him to be absolute, sincere, and intense. This aristocratic and generous anarchist began his career by fighting for Dreyfus because this officer had been the victim of racial prejudice. But he also wanted to save Jews who suffered all over the world. At first, Bernard Lazare was drawn to Herzl's doctrine. But the author of *The Jewish State* was a politician and a diplomat and the revolutionary prophet Bernard Lazare was never able to understand him. He started traveling all over Europe and tried to obtain real emancipation for his brothers. Lazare became the friend of Péguy. He shared his hatred of the political exploitations which follow the victories of the spirit. After the premature death of his friend, Charles Péguy wrote a moving eulogy on him.

In the following generation we shall mention one figure of comparable stature: Léon Blum (1872-1950) the descendant of a pure Judeo-Alsatian family and the most remarkable personality in French politics during the first half of the 20th century. He was admirable not only because he was courageous enough to

Torah pointer, Alsace, nineteenth century. Torah pointer used during the reading of the Law, decorated with the usual hand on one side and a Torah crown on the other. Wood. Nancy, Musée Historique Lorrain, Inv. No. 1050.

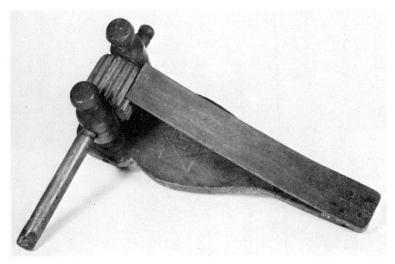

Purim rattle, Alsace, nineteenth century. This rattle is a noisemaker sounded by children during the reading of the Scroll of Esther to blot out the name of 'Haman' during the reading. Wood. Nancy, Musée Historique Lorrain, Inv. No. 1195.

Chair of Elijah, possibly from Bischwiller (Bas-Rhin), c. 1800. Circumcision bench or Chair of Elijah in walnut wood, with two Hebrew inscriptions, one stating: 'This is the Chair of Elijah' and the other from the biblical account of the Divine command to circumcise (Gen. 17:10). Strasbourg, Musée Alsacien, Dépôt permanent de la Société pour l'Histoire des Israélites d'Alsace et de Lorraine.

Torah breastplate, France, nineteenth century. Breastplate for the Torah Scroll. Breastplates usually bear an inscription indicating the holiday for which this particular Torah Scroll is used. In this case it reads: 'Day of Remembrance' i.e. New Year. Silver. Nancy, Musée Historique Lorrain, Inv. No. 1039.

remain in the Opposition (until 1936) and reject the temptations of a system which obstinately resisted progress. Neither did he owe his glory to his having been several times the prime minister of his country. He was admirable in the last analysis for the new style which he gave to political life without compromising any of his principles. Because of a man like Blum, the world could think that France had a special vocation and was endowed with a kind of patriotism that was not narrow-minded but expressed

Linen tablecloth, Alsace or Germany, mid-nineteenth century. Imprinted with the Ten Commandments, prayers and blessings. These were used on Sabbath days and holidays so that the family would have the prayer text in front of them. Basle, Jüdisches Museum der Schweiz, No. 42.

Left: Mizrah, France, early nineteenth century. *Mizrah* with a primitive representation of Jerusalem and above it the high-priest at the altar. Many signs are similar to French patriotic emblems and the pontiffs' miters and their types of beard are also very characteristic of the place and period. Watercolor. Nancy, Musée Historique Lorrain, Inv. Zone L.

Right: Sabbath prayer tablet, Alsace, mid-nineteenth century. One of the hymns on the tablet *'Lekhah dodi'* was introduced into the Friday evening service by the Safed Kabbalists in the 16th century and only later in the Western communities. There, these supplementary texts were recited by the reader not from his usual desk but from the platform in the center of the synagogue. This tablet was therefore placed there so he would have the text before him. Strasbourg, Société pour l'Histoire des Israélites d'Alsace et de Lorraine.

Torah shields, Alsace and Germany, nineteenth century. Torah shields were hung around the Scroll of the Law to indicate in which order they should be used in the service. Strasbourg, Musée Alsacien, Dépôt permanent de la Société pour l'Histoire des Israélites d'Alsace et de Lorraine, Inv. No. 77 and 78.

INAUGURATION D'UN PANTATEUQUE

fête Israelite de Reichshoffen Célébrée le 7 November 1857.

Inauguration ceremony of Scroll of the Law, Reichshoffen (Bas-Rhin), 1857. Watercolor, signed Stern, 1857. Inauguration ceremony of a new Scroll of the Law at the synagogue at Reichshoffen (Bas-Rhin) in the presence of the leading local figures and population on November 7 1857. Strasbourg, Musée Alsacien, Dépôt permanent de la Société pour l'Histoire des Israélites d'Alsace et de Lorraine, Inv. No. 53.3.

its faith in social renewal and in a socialism that was not a rootless nihilism. One was justified in thinking that the French people took Mankind as its highest value.

The fact that the emergence of Crémieux and of Blum was possible implied that the Jews had overcome their complexes. The Jewish poets who made their names around 1900 expressed

the pathetic character of this struggle. It is a fact that the readers of André Spire (1868-1966) and Edmond Fleg (1874-1963) are not very numerous outside the borders of France, yet one can always hope that their message will be heard in other parts of the world, as long as French Jewry retains its dynamism.

Both writers are fairly typical of French Jewry which admires

Léon Blum (1872-1950). Léon Blum addressing the Chamber of Deputies on August 8 1936. Blum was France's first Jewish premier, and came to office after the electoral victory of the Popular Front in 1936. Paris, Bibliothèque Nationale, Cabinet des Estampes.

university and administrative careers. The fact that one of them was born in Nancy while the other came from Geneva does not change this basic characteristic. The most important fact is that both writers adhered to the ideas of Zionism while remaining ardent French patriots. With Spire, this adherence was more militant and extreme whereas Fleg showed a greater indulgence

and a more pluralistic attitude. In any case, both poets represent a sincere and intelligent confrontation between the modern world and Jewish consciousness.

In more recent times, younger writers have made their impact in France. These include a group—mainly survivors of the Nazi concentration camps who have made their homes in France—

such as André Schwarz-Bart (author of *The Last of the Just*), Anna Langfus, Elie Wiesel (who now lives in New York but still writes in French), Piotr Rawicz, and others. Then there are the poet Yves Bonnefoy, Albert Memmi (one of the outstanding intellectual representatives of the North African Jews who largely moved to France in the 1950s and 1960s), and the critic Raymond Aron.

The French experience, particularly with the emergence of the State of Israel, has added to the self-definition of the Jew. Now that the Jews have regained their place among the nations, the problem of the relationship between a particularistic and a universalist attitude has re-emerged in an acute form. In this respect, valuable lessons can be learned from the history and experience of French Jewry.

The yellow badge (1941-5). This square yellow patch with the word 'Jew' printed in black letters had to be worn by all Jews in almost every country occupied by Nazi Germany, for them to be readily identifiable. The concept was based on the 'Badge of Shame' which had to be worn by Jews in Christian countries in the Middle Ages.

CHAPTER III

Italy

by Professor Shlomo Simonsohn

Italian Jewry is the oldest Jewish community of the European Diaspora; its origins go back to the days of the Roman republic. From then on Jewish connections with Italy and especially with Rome have been virtually uninterrupted to the present day. The Jewish population in the Peninsula probably reached its peak in early Imperial times—immediately after the destruction of Jerusalem and its Temple. Large numbers of prisoners of war, brought back to Italy by the victorious Romans, eventually regained their liberty, and settled in the country. According to a medieval tradition, Titus brought to Rome four noble families from Jerusalem: De' Rossi (Min Ha'adumim), De' Pomi (Min Hatapuhim), Delli Mansi or Piatelli (Min Ha'anavim), and De' Vecchi (Min Hazekenim). These families figure prominently in Italian Jewish life through the ages.

In Roman, as in later, times, Rome was the largest Jewish center in Italy. Chief evidence of Jewish life in antiquity in Rome and elsewhere throughout the Peninsula are the epitaphs from catacombs and other burial sites. The inscriptions are mostly in Greek, which was the language of Diaspora Jewry at the time. In the Imperial capital there existed upwards of ten synagogues,

Synagogue at Trapani, Sicily, c. 1200. There is evidence of Jewish settlement in Sicily from the 1st century B.C. The Arab occupation (9th–11th centuries) profoundly influenced the culture of Sicilian Jewry but the Jews reached the height of their prosperity under the Normans. As Sicily came under the Aragonese crown the history of Sicilian Jewry parallels that of Spanish Jewry, with massacres and expulsion in 1492.

Homage paid by Roman Jewry to Emperor Henry VII, Rome, 1312. An inscription at the bottom reads: 'Imperator dans Judeis legem Moysis in rotulo' (the emperor hands the Jews the Laws of Moses in a scroll). The hats are typical of those worn by the Jews. Berlin, Codex Balduini Trevirensis, publ. 1881, tavola 24.

and recently the ruins of the ancient synagogues at Ostia and Aquilaea have come to light. The communities employed the titles of Greek city and corporate organizations, and may have modeled themselves, at least partly, on their structures, though in due course Latin rather than Greek became the preponderant language among Italian Jewry. In pagan Rome, Jewish life was for the most part peaceful. The status and situation of the Jews began, however, seriously to deteriorate toward the end of the Roman era, after Christianity had become the dominant religion.

Throughout the Middle Ages the Jews of Italy continued to live mainly in Rome and the south, including Sicily. Migrations and the expulsions of the 13th, 15th, 16th centuries shifted the demographic center to the north. From the 16th century the Jews of Italy were confined to ghettos, a type of Jewish quarter set up for the first time in Venice in 1516, which derived its name from the Venetian foundry located there. From Venice the term spread throughout Italy and abroad. The French revolutionary armies broke down the Italian ghetto walls, some of which were later

restored, so that the last ghetto, that of Rome, was abolished as late as 1870.

The life of Italian Jews in the Middle Ages was subject to the special conditions of Jewry prevailing in Europe at that time. They were deprived of most civic liberties, but enjoyed religious freedom, though with limitations dictated by the Church. For the most part they enjoyed considerable latitude in their economic activities. During the Middle Ages most of them engaged in trade, crafts and agriculture, but toward the close of the Middle Ages and especially in central and northern Italy, loan banking became a major activity. The ghetto period witnessed an almost universal economic decline of Italian Jewry.

The beginnings of Jewish communal organization in Italy are rather obscure, yet by the end of the High Middle Ages they emerge as fully fledged corporate organizations. They probably anticipated by a couple of generations or so similar institutions in Christian society, and may have had some influence on the early development of the latter. The 'Universitas Judaeorum' achieved increasing autonomy, and was recognized by the authorities as the representative body of local Jewry. In time its status, privileges, and obligations approximated those of Christian guilds. By a process of mutual influence a considerable degree of similarity came eventually to exist between the corporate institutions of Christian and Jewish society in Italy.

JEWS AND GENTILES

Early encounters between Jews and the Roman environment tended to emphasize the differences between the two civilizations. At first garbled accounts of Jewish rites and customs found their way into Roman literature. For instance the resting on the Sabbath was regarded as wasting every seventh day, and was thought to be a day of fasting. Serious writers, such as Tacitus, present fantastic versions of Jewish history and religion. To Seneca was ascribed the saying: 'The vanquished have given laws to the victors'. This complaint is thought to have been directed against the success of Jewish missionary activities among the Romans.

The Jews of Italy and elsewhere continued to be energetic proselytizers after the victory of Christianity, a process that continued well into the Middle Ages, even in the face of repressive measures. However, with the advent of the new religion, closely related to Judaism, much of the latter's strangeness to Gentiles disappeared.

The relations between Church and Synagogue were fraught throughout with conflict. Yet, for a variety of reasons, at times there existed a modicum of mutual tolerance between the two religions. This was particularly true at the center of Christendom—Rome. All through the Middle Ages the popes attempted to mitigate somewhat the rigors of oppression and persecution of Jews and Judaism in Christian Europe. In pursuance of the psalmist's 'Slay them not, lest my people forget', the Papacy, in most cases, tried to shield the Jews from acts of physical violence. Admittedly, this protection, more often than not, remained ineffective. Yet the Jews of Rome and other papal territories enjoyed a degree of safety rarely paralleled by other medieval Jewries. No other European city harbored a Jewish community for so long a continuous period as did Rome.

There were a few turning points, mostly for the worse, in the attitude of the Papacy to the Jews and Judaism. On two occasions the hegemony of the Roman Church over Western European Christendom was seriously threatened by reform movements: in the 13th and in the 16th centuries. In both instances the Catholic Church's reaction was directed partly against the Jews. The Church felt that the heterodoxy of Albigensians and Waldensians, and later the revolt of Lutherans and their fellows against the authority of Rome, were due in part to Jewish influence on Christian heretics. The resolutions of the Fourth Lateran Council of 1215, presided over by Pope Innocent III, included several provisions concerned with the status of the Jews in Christian Europe. Those included the imposition of the Jewish 'badge', which became the symbol of the social ostracism of Jews. The Bull entitled '*Cum nimis absurdum*' published by Pope Paul IV in 1555, incorporated the provision instituting the ghetto. This document is a landmark in the relations between the Papacy and the Jews. The introduction to the Bull is eloquent enough:

'For as much as it is highly absurd and improper that the Jews, condemned by God to eternal slavery because of their guilt, should, on the pretext that they are cherished by Christian love and are permitted to dwell in our midst, show such ingratitude to Christians as to insult them for their mercy and presume to mastery instead of the subjection that beseems them ... and considering that the Roman Church tolerates the Jews in witness of the true Christian faith ... We do therefore order the following measures...'

Henceforth, though the Papacy as a rule still did not tolerate physical violence, it became identified with the severest oppression of Jews. Ecclesiastical restrictions on the intercourse between Jews and Christians impeded but did not sever relations between them. Even express prohibitions often enough were violated by the Papacy itself. A case in point is the employment of Jewish medicine and practitioners in Italy throughout the Middle Ages.

MEDICINE AND SCIENCE

The early appearance of Jewish doctors in southern Italy has already been mentioned (see Chapter II). Jewish physicians figure prominently in Rome and elsewhere throughout the Middle Ages. Many of them were in attendance on popes and on princes. This became particularly marked from the 13th century on. Hardly a pope did without the services of a personal Jewish medical attendant. Many Italian rulers emulated the example set by the pontiff. There were even Jewish women among the medical practitioners of Italy. Some Jews served with the armies in the field as military physicians. Others were specialists, such as oculists and dentists.

The list of famous Jewish physicians in medieval and Renaissance Italy is a long one. Many belonged to veritable dynasties of physicians. One such dynasty is that of the Delli Mansi or Piatelli (Anau, Min Ha'anavim), one of the four famous families mentioned, said to have been brought to Italy by Titus. The genealogical tree of the family goes back to the 10th century. Many of its members made outstanding contributions to scholarship and to medicine.

Another famous family of physicians was that of the Portaleone which derived its name from a Roman quarter. The doctors Portaleone became noted from the 15th century on. The first outstanding physician of the Portaleone was Guglielmo Mizolo (Benjamin) who served as body physician to some of the most famous Italian rulers of his day. These included King Ferdinand I of Naples, who knighted him. Later the king sent him to serve his kinsman, Duke Galeazzo Maria Sforza of Milan. On the latter's death, Portaleone went to Mantua and there served, until his death in 1500, three rulers of the house of Gonzaga: Lodovico, Federico and Francesco.

Page from Avicenna's Canon, fifteenth century. The introductory text from ▶ the Hebrew translation of Avicenna's *Canon*. Bologna, University Library, Cod. 2197, fol. 2r.

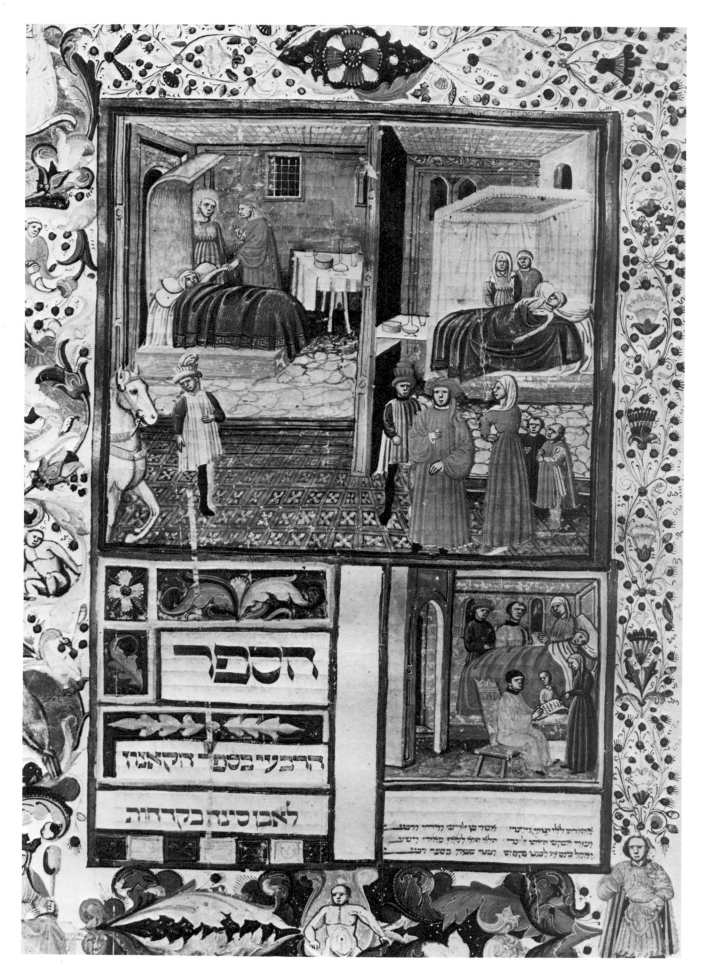

His son Abraham continued in the medical service of the Gonzaga, and also attended for some time on the duke of Urbino, Guidubaldo di Montefeltro. Abraham Portaleone became very famous indeed. One of his most prominent patients was the celebrated condottiere Giovanni delle Bande Nere. Portaleone treated him for a wound received shortly before the battle of Pavia (1525). Giovanni's cousin, Pope Clement VII, expressed his appreciation of the successful cure. When, however, the condottiere was again and more severely wounded in the following year, he was left unattended for too long. The Jewish doctor's treatment was of no avail; the patient succumbed to his wounds, and Portaleone was accused of having poisoned him.

The most eminent member of the Portaleone family was another Abraham, who served the Mantuan dukes Guglielmo and Vincenzo I. At the behest of the former he wrote a book on the employment of gold in medicine (*De auro dialogi tres,* Venice, 1584); and another on medical practice in general *(Consilia medica).*

An outstanding medical figure of the Renaissance was Master Elijah ben Sabbatai Beer da Fermo. He was one of the first Italian Jews to attain the title of 'artium et medicinae doctor', and one of the first to be knighted for his skill. In 1405, together with two other Jewish physicians, he had the privileges of a Roman citizen conferred on him. Master Elijah was physician to the popes Martin V and Eugenius IV, and an official lecturer in medicine at the university of Pavia. Master Elijah's fame even spread abroad. In 1410 King Henry IV of England invited him from Bologna to London to try and cure the sovereign of a long-standing illness. At that time Jews had long been forbidden to set foot on English soil.

Another Italian physician whose fame spread to England was Jacob Mantino. A native of Spain, he studied medicine and philosophy at Italian universities, and was appointed professor of medicine by Pope Leo X. He practiced his art also in other Italian cities, Bologna, Venice, and Verona among others. At Venice he treated the aristocracy and members of the diplomatic corps. At the request of one of his patients, Teodoro Trivulzio, marshal of France and governor of Genoa, Mantino was exempted from wearing the Jewish badge. When the pope requested Mantino to add his opinion on the legality according to biblical law of England's King Henry VIII's marriage to Catherine of Aragon, the physician supported the pontiff's stand against the English viewpoint.

Another exile from the Iberian peninsula was the Marrano physician Amatus Lusitanus. A native of Castello Branco in Portugal, he took his medical degree at Salamanca University, and sometime afterward left the Peninsula for Italy. He practiced medicine at Ferrara, Venice, and in other Italian cities. He is said to have been invited by Duke Ercole II d'Este to occupy a chair of medicine in Ferrara. Here Amatus lectured on Hippocrates and

◄ *Page from Avicenna's Canon,* fifteenth century. Illuminated page from manuscript of Hebrew translation (15th century) of Avicenna's *Canon,* showing stages of illness (fever). The *Canon,* the chief medical work of the great Muslim philosopher and physician, enjoyed considerable fame in the Middle Ages and was translated into Hebrew and Latin. Bologna, University Library, Cod. 2197, fol. 402r.

Galen. But even in Italy the long arm of the Inquisition almost lay hold of him. When Pope Paul IV started his infamous persecution of the Marranos at Ancona (1555-6), that ended in the burning at the stake of twenty-four men and one woman, the henchmen of the Inquisition broke into the house of Amatus. All his valuables were taken, including his books and manuscripts, and he only managed to save himself by fleeing. Eventually he settled in Salonika. Among those manuscripts was the fifth volume of his *Centuria.* The medical works of Amatus appeared in seven volumes, each containing one hundred case histories with commentaries. He quite often mentions the names of his patients, many of them distinguished Jews and Christians, and his writings are interspersed with interesting references, literary and personal. The medical discoveries of Amatus included the valves of the veins and their function in blood circulation, and a variety of diagnoses and treatments covering a wide range of illnesses. His *Centuria* enjoyed considerable popularity as clinical handbooks throughout the 16th and 17th centuries.

One more eminent Jewish physician of the Renaissance was David De' Pomi, medical attendant to the Sforza and others. In his *Apology for the Jewish Physician,* he defended Jewish medicine and its practitioners, especially with reference to the false accusations leveled against them by way of justification for the restrictions placed on them by the authorities during the Counter-Reformation.

Though the Jewish contribution was notable chiefly to medicine rather than to science (as indeed was that of the Christian efforts in the Middle Ages), some Jewish Italian scientists are worthy of mention. One or two of them became quite famous during the Renaissance, such as Bonetto de Lattes, physician to the popes Alexander VI, Julius II, and Leo X. His invention was an astronomical ring-dial, an astrolabe worn on the finger. Its purpose was to determine the time by day and by night by measuring the altitude of the sun and the stars. He dabbled in the medieval 'science' of astrology, and published an annual astronomical calendar, and that for 1498 was dedicated to Cesare Borgia. Among other prognoses the calendar included the announcement of the Messiah's coming in 1505.

The most outstanding figure in this field among the Jews of Italy was Abraham Colorni. A native of Mantua, he started his career as architect in the service of Duke Alfonso II of Ferrara. He assisted in the planning and designing of Ferrara's fortifications, and of the ducal villa. He was also in the service of the duke of Mantua. In 1588 he was invited to Prague by Emperor Rudolph II. Colorni claimed to be an expert on escapes from prison, and the emperor wanted to employ him to set free his imprisoned brother, the Archduke Maximilian. Later he was in the service of Duke Frederick I of Wurttemberg. Colorni undertook to develop a cheap process for the production of saltpeter, the chief constituent of gunpowder. The duke became dissatisfied with Colorni's efforts and put him in jail. Colorni made good his claim, and escaped from the duke's prison. He returned to his native city, where he died shortly afterward. Colorni was chiefly interested in military engineering, and he claimed to have invented an automatic gun. He also invented prefabricated bridges, boats, and folding ladders for assaults on fortified positions. He improved the firing of artillery, and the production of mines and of other arms and ammunition. Colorni wrote on applied mathematics and on mechanics, on secret writing, and against the superstitions of physiognomology and chiromancy.

CULTURAL MEDIATION

If one had to single out the most noteworthy Jewish contribution to medieval culture the role played by Jewish translators would probably be a fair choice. The philosophical and scientific heritage of ancient Greece was almost forgotten in medieval Christian Europe. Meanwhile, however, this heritage had been adopted by the conquering Arabs, and had become the basis of Islamic medieval culture.

The revival of learning which took place in Christian Europe in the 12th century was accompanied by the rediscovery of the Greek heritage. However, it was not readily available to the scholars of Latin Christendom, owing chiefly to the language barrier. The Jews of southern Europe, including those of Italy, played a major role in bridging the gulf which separated the two civilizations. Jews were physically and intellectually at home on both sides of the frontier. Moreover, they were the only element that maintained constant personal relations across the border. It was therefore only natural that the job of cultural intermediaries and interpreters should fall to them.

The translators and scholars often enjoyed the patronage of kings and princes, particularly in southern Italy and Sicily. Here

Hanukkah lamp, Italy, fifteenth century. Lamp used at the Feast of Lights to commemorate the rededication of the Temple in Jerusalem by the Maccabees. Bronze. Jerusalem, Israel Museum, 188/606 Feuchtwanger Collection.

the process of returning its ancient cultural patrimony to Europe was encouraged by the rulers of the cosmopolitan courts of Palermo and Naples. It reached its peak at the time of Emperor Frederick II Hohenstaufen, who spent much of his time at his Italian court, and no mean scholar himself, was named 'the world's wonder' by his contemporaries. Frederick's benevolent attitude toward his Jewish subjects was suitably expressed in his *Liber Augustalis,* issued at Melfi in 1231. He set up a state monopoly over the manufacture of silk and the dyeing industry, and entrusted the administration exclusively to Jewish agents. The Jews of southern Italy and Sicily had been associated with these handicrafts from time immemorial. Frederick had reinforced Jewish manpower engaged in these crafts by bringing immigrants from Africa to Sicily, and giving them land to develop plantations for the extraction of raw materials required for dyes.

Frederick II employed a number of Jewish scholars as translators and was in constant and close personal contact with them. The most outstanding among them was Jacob ben Abba Mari Anatoli, physician, homilist and translator. A native of Marseilles, he went to live at Naples, where he was employed by the emperor as physician and translator. He was on friendly terms with another scholar employed by the emperor at Naples, Michael Scotus. Anatoli cites him and their royal patron with due respect. Anatoli's translations into Hebrew were chiefly the major philosophical works of Averroës—the greatest Aristotelian Muslim philosopher—and several Arabic writings on astronomy. The intellectual diversity of men like Anatoli, probably enhanced by intercourse with their Christian peers, found suitable expression in their own original scholarly contributions. Anatoli's collection of homilies *Malmad ha-Talmidim* did much to propagate the study of philosophy, especially that of Maimonides, among the Jews of Italy.

Emperor Frederick II is said to have commissioned a Latin translation of Moses Maimonides' famous philosophical treatise *The Guide of the Perplexed* and to have discussed a passage of the treatise with its translator. This Latin version was studied jointly by a Christian and a Jewish scholar, namely Niccolò Paglia di Giovenazzo, founder of the Dominican convent at Trani, and Moses ben Solomon of Salerno. The latter wrote a commentary to Maimonides' treatise, including an Italian glossary. The emperor also corresponded with another Jewish scholar, Judah ben Solomon Mosca of Toledo, who served Alfonso X of Castile as translator from Arabic to Spanish, and eventually came to Frederick's court in Italy.

The Angevin rulers who succeeded the Hohenstaufen in southern Italy and in Sicily continued and even intensified their patronage of translators and scholars. This was especially true of Charles I and Charles II lo Zoppo. The outstanding scholar in the employ of Charles I was Faraj (Moses) ben Salem of Girgenti (Sicily), physician and translator. He was a 'member of the royal household', and in receipt of a royal salary. His major contribution was the translation of *Al-Hawi* by Abu Bakr Mohammed Al-Razi (Rhazes), one of the most famous medical treatises of the Middle Ages. The illustrations of the manuscript, which was illuminated by Fra Giovanni (1282), are said to portray him at work on his translation, and presenting the opus to his patron. Faraj also

Manuscript, Sicily. Miniature from a manuscript showing Faraj of Girgenti (Sicily) and his royal employer Charles of Naples. Here he is depicted engaged in rendering the medical work of Rhazes (Al-Razi) known as *Liber Continens,* and handing the king the finished product of his labors. Paris, Bibliothèque Nationale, Ms. Latin 6912.

did other translations of medical texts. His colleague and compatriot, Moses (Musa) of Palermo, was instructed in Latin by Master Matteo Sciliaco (Sylvaticus?) on the king's orders, 'so that books may be translated by him'. Several converted Jews belonged to this group of translators, among them John of Capua, who did the Latin version of the famous Oriental fables *Qalila wa-Dimna.* He used the Hebrew version then current among European Jewry. This is considered a major element in the development of the European fairy tale.

These peaceful activities contrasted strangely with the cruel persecutions of the Jews in southern Italy, organized by the Angevin kings at the end of the 13th century. Solomon Usque, a sixteenth-century Jewish chronicler of Ferrara, records a strange anecdote in this connection. As Charles I was approaching the end of his life he instructed his son to repay the Jews for the services they had rendered him. Charles II decided that he 'ought to pay the Jews spiritually by saving their souls and making them all Christians'. When the Jews refused the gift, the king 'made a proclamation throughout his kingdom, stating that from the moment of its publication until the time it took a taper to burn out, all Jews were to become Christians or face death.' The only authentic part of the anecdote is its ending.

Nevertheless the Angevin kings continued their interest in Hebrew scholarship. Thus King Robert the Wise (il Saggio) brought to Italy Kalonymos ben Kalonymos of Arles, a translator and author in his own right. At the same time Robert of Anjou employed other scholars and translators, such as Shemariah Ikriti of Rome, who dedicated his commentary on the Bible to the king.

The work of the Jewish translators in Italy continued apace through the 14th century and on well into the 16th century. However, by the close of the 14th century, a large part of the translations made were for Jewish consumption only. By then, most of the important texts had been made available to Latin scholars, and the decadence of Muslim culture eliminated the need for further efforts. At the same time Jewish scholars felt the need to make available to those Jews who knew too little Latin, the product of medieval European culture. Nevertheless the translations from Hebrew into Latin continued, though on a somewhat diminished scale. Once again the main effort was directed to medical and philosophical texts. In one way the latter-day translators had a wider reading public than their predecessors, since many of the texts were now published in print. Some even became almost scientific bestsellers, and enjoyed numerous editions.

Noteworthy among the later group of cultural mediators were several physician-philosophers, who included Jacob Mantino, Abraham de Balmes, and Moses Alatino. Their interests centered on Aristotelian philosophy and its Arab commentators. It would appear that the Jews played a big part in reconstituting the Aristotelian texts used in the Renaissance. The great and famous Venetian edition of Aristotle in Latin with commentaries and additional texts, published in the middle of the 16th century in eleven volumes, is reckoned to have been based directly or indirectly largely on the work of Jewish translators and scholars.

'JAPHETH IN THE TENTS OF SHEM'

The so-called Latin Renaissance has been placed in the 12th century, and from then on until the 16th century there took place a revival of one or more branches of the arts and literature. In addition the 15th and 16th centuries were the age of humanism, which was accompanied by a growing interest on the part of Christians in Hebrew and Jewish literature.

Admittedly this was not entirely new. But before the Renaissance revival, Christian interest in Hebrew had at best been

Circumcision knife, Italy, seventeenth century. The carving depicts the Sacrifice of Isaac. The group consists of Abraham, Isaac, the ram and the angel. Tel Aviv, Joseph Stieglitz Private Collection.

sporadic, and even then had been mainly for theological reasons. Thus Hebrew and rabbinical literature were studied by the Dominicans to support their polemical and missionary activities. King Robert of Naples was taught Hebrew by the philosopher Judah Romano. The king is said to have read through the entire Hebrew Bible with his teacher. These were isolated cases, as were the early attempts at studying Hebrew in the first half of the 15th century. Scholars like the Apostolic secretary Poggio Bracciolini, the diplomat Marco Lippomani, or the general of the Camaldolensian Order, Ambrogio Traversari, had no more than a smattering of Hebrew, and do not deserve to be named Hebraists. However, these early amateurs prepared the ground for more serious and widespread interest and study.

The first Italian Christian Hebraist worthy of the name was Traversari's pupil Gianozzo Manetti, the Florentine scholar-statesman. His interest in Hebrew was due to a mixture of intellectual curiosity and theological fervor. Christian scholars wished to check the version of the Vulgate against the Hebrew original. At the same time, some, like Manetti, desired to use the knowledge thus acquired for missionary purposes among the infidels, especially the Jews. Manetti's biographer, Vespasiano da Bisticci, tells how he stipulated of his first Hebrew teacher that they converse in Hebrew only. While Manetti studied Hebrew he managed to convert his teacher, known thereafter by the name of his patron, at the baptismal font. Some time later Manetti came to an arrangement with one of the richest and most erudite Jewish bankers of Florence, Immanuel ben Abraham da San Miniato, whereby the banker undertook to improve Manetti's Hebrew, while the latter pledged himself to perfect the banker's knowledge of natural and moral philosophy. Manetti employed the Hebrew proficiency he had gained for the two purposes he had had in mind from the outset. He wrote a polemical treatise against the Jews, and prepared a new translation of the Psalms. His library of Hebrew manuscripts eventually passed into the Vatican library.

The circle of Christian Hebraists in Italy grew considerably in size, and the knowledge gained by its members widened and deepened. One outstanding member of this group, whose Hebrew studies carried him much further than those of his predecessors, was Marsilio Ficino, the master and leader of Florentine neo-Platonism. Ficino was attracted to Hebrew literature and Jewish thought by his attachment to Platonic philosophy and his devotion to the Christian faith. He was particularly interested in Jewish mysticism, which had much in common with the mysticism of neo-Platonism. Ficino, like many of his friends, was drawn toward the main current of Jewish neo-Platonism as expressed in the *Fons Vitae* of Solomon Ibn Gabirol, though he and his contemporaries were not aware that the author was a Jew. Ficino's erudition in Jewish sources and knowledge was vast, though faulty in detail. This is particularly evident in his *On Christian Religion,* written and published in 1474. He quotes ancient and medieval Jewish literature, and appears relatively well informed on various aspects of Jewish life.

Ficino's interest in Kabbalah was not an isolated case. Some Christian scholars were convinced that Jewish mysticism contained the key to true religion or to philosophy, or both, although the Catholic Church considered most of these views stark heresies. Yet some churchmen, even pontiffs, shared to a certain extent the beliefs put forward by the Christian champions of the Kabbalah. When, at the beginning of the Counter-Reformation, the Church burnt some Jewish books, and had others expurgated, the printing of the Zohar and other mystical works was permitted, or even encouraged. This special treatment of Kabbalah soon came to an end, but while it lasted it was due to that earlier Christian attitude to Jewish mysticism.

It is perhaps only fitting that the person who was largely instrumental in propagating Jewish esoteric lore among Christians

Giovanni Pico della Mirandola, Florence, fifteenth century. Behind the distinguished humanist della Mirandola is a Jew (with the beard) said to be one of his teachers. The Count della Mirandola was an outstanding Christian Hebraist and pupil of Elijah Delmedigo, Johann Alemanno and others. Detail of a fifteenth-century fresco by Cosimo Rosselli. Florence, Church of San' Ambrogio. Photo Alinari.

has become himself something of a mystery. This is due at least in part to his propensity for assuming a large variety of aliases, carrying somewhat too far the fashion of the period of adopting classical pen-names. Flavius Mithridates (as he was often called) was the son of an educated Jew of Girgenti in Sicily. He became a convert to Christianity, and for some time subsisted on the forcibly extracted contributions of Sicilian Jewry. Later he taught Hebrew and other Oriental languages in Italy, Germany, and France. He was a professor of theology in the 'Sapienza' at Rome, and did many translations from Hebrew and Arabic, including the Koran (for the duke of Urbino), and various kabbalistic treatises, as well as writing on Hebrew grammar. On Good Friday of 1481

he preached the sermon on the Passion before Pope Sixtus IV and his cardinals in the Vatican. In a way Mithridates was a typical product of his age. While no doubt a man of vast erudition, he also creates the impression of being something of an adventurer. Mithridates is perhaps best known as the instructor of Pico della Mirandola in Hebrew and Jewish literature, especially Kabbalah.

The greatest Italian Christian Hebraist of them all was Count Giovanni Pico della Mirandola, the precocious scholar prodigy of Italian humanism. His first contact with Jewish studies took place in his third year of university studies, at the age of eighteen. He met Elijah Delmedigo at Padua University in 1480, and from then for several years the two studied together when in each other's

Fresco, Florence, fifteenth century. Fresco by Benozzo Gozzoli representing the journey of the Three Kings to do homage to the infant Jesus. The setting is the hill-country around Florence, and the artist introduces all the notable personalities of contemporary Florence. The bearded figure riding in the procession (bottom), has been identified as the scholar Elijah Delmedigo (see also chapter on Byzantium). Florence, Palazzo Riccardi. Photo Alinari.

company, or corresponded when separated. Delmedigo was a philosopher in his own right (see chapter on Byzantium). When Pico and Delmedigo first met, the latter was lecturing at Padua. Delmedigo continued these lectures at Pico's invitation at Florence. The stay of the two philosophers at Florence has been commemorated in a famous fresco by Benozzo Gozzoli, portraying the Three Kings on their way to the infant Jesus. It covers one of the walls in the chapel of Palazzo Riccardi at Florence. Among the contemporary personalities introduced into the scene by Gozzoli are Pico and his teacher, who has been identified as Delmedigo. The two separated after 1486, and sometime later Delmedigo returned to his native Crete. The influence he had on the great Italian humanist is thought to have been decisive.

From Mithridates, Pico obtained most of his early knowledge of the Kabbalah. Pico became one of the greatest Christian enthusiasts of Jewish mysticism. He was convinced that the Kabbalah contained the tenets of Christian faith, and of Greek philosophy. Like many Christian Hebraists he was sure that the Kabbalah supported the Christian viewpoint in the age-long debate with Judaism. In Pico's own words: 'There is no science that can more firmly convince us of the divinity of Christ than magic and the Kabbalah'. These views Pico included in the nine hundred theses he presented at Rome, which were so badly received that he had to flee the country. Despite this official antagonism to the results of his Jewish and philosophical studies Pico would not give up. He returned to Florence at the invitation of Duke Lorenzo the Magnificent, who put a villa at his disposal. There Pico conducted what has been described as his third and last stage of Jewish studies, biblical exegesis. His mentor was another Jewish scholar, Johanan ben Isaac Alemanno, who had grown up in the household of the wealthiest and most cultured Florentine Jewish banker Jehiel (Vitale) da Pisa. The banker, very much in the manner of his affluent contemporaries, Jews and Christians, maintained Alemanno in his household as teacher and scholar. Alemanno wrote a commentary on the Song of Songs. His chief opus is *Hai ha-Olamim* (The Immortal), a philosophical treatise based on this commentary.

Pico's Hebrew studies are said to have had far-reaching repercussions. In 1490 he was visited by Johannes Reuchlin. The two are said to have discussed Jewish subjects, and especially Kabbalah. Reuchlin too thought he had discovered the truth of the Christian religion in Jewish mysticism. He had studied Hebrew with R. Obadiah Sforno, the noted Bible commentator. He, too, had met the notorious Mithridates and quotes him on Hebrew grammar. Eventually Reuchlin took up the cudgels in defense of Hebrew literature, especially against the vicious attacks of the 'obscurants'. One of the long-term results of this polemic was the beginning of the Reformation in Germany. The popes of the Counter-Reformation were not entirely at fault when attributing some of the responsibility for the defections from Rome to the 'insidious' influence that Jewish studies were having on Christian scholars.

Another Jewish scholar who belonged to this circle of Italian humanists was Leone Ebreo or rather Don Judah Abrabanel, elder son of the scholar-statesman Don Isaac Abrabanel (see chapter on Spain). Don Judah was one of the victims of the 1492 Expulsion from Spain, and settled, like most members of his family, in Italy. He was a physician and philosopher, and practiced his art in many Italian cities. Among other occupations he was body physician to the Spanish viceroy of Naples, and taught medicine and astrology at the local university. Amatus Lusitanus reports in one of his case histories that Don Judah wrote a philosophical treatise *About the Harmony of the Heavens* at the request of Pico della Mirandola. The question of whether the two scholars ever met in person, and if so, where, is still debated. At any event there can be no doubt that they were in touch with each other, at least by correspondence. Leone Ebreo's magnum opus is his *Dialoghi d'Amore* (Dialogues of Love) which deals with the philosophical aspect of love, a favorite subject in Italy at that time. Many members of the humanist circle, including Ficino, Pietro Bembo, Mario Equicola and others dealt at length with this subject. Don Judah's *Dialogues* enjoyed great popularity, and were translated into many languages. Their influence on contemporary philosophical thought, and even on that of later generations, has been placed very high. It has been traced in the *Cortigiano* of Baldassare Castiglione, in the writings of Giordano Bruno, and of Benedict Spinoza, Michel de Montaigne, and others.

Toward the end of the Renaissance, Jewish studies, especially Hebrew, became fairly popular among scholars and princes. Soon chairs of Hebrew were established at Italian universities, as at Bologna in 1488, and a little later at Pavia, Rome, and so forth. Long lists of distinguished Italians who knew at least a little Hebrew have been drawn up. They include condottieri, prelates of the Catholic Church, princes, and other dignitaries. For a while the study of Hebrew became part of the liberal education of the Italian upper classes. While some Christians managed to persuade their Jewish mentors to embrace their pupils' religion, one or two cases of the opposite process are known to have occurred at that time. For instance there was the Franciscan Cornelio da Montalcino, who became converted to Judaism after prolonged studies of Hebrew and Jewish literature. He paid for his misconduct by being burnt at the stake in 1553. The Jewish chronicler Benjamin Nehemiah ben Elnathan tells of having met in the Roman prison of the Inquisition two Christians who spoke Hebrew and said their daily prayers in Hebrew. They have been tentatively identified as Bartholomeus Spatafora, a nobleman and scholar from Messina, and Onorato Fascitelli, a scholar and writer of some distinction. At that time (1559) they had spent five years in prison.

Finally mention should be made of the Hebrew studies of Cardinal Egidio da Viterbo, general of the Augustinian order. He too became an enthusiastic student of the Kabbalah and especially of the Zohar. His chief mentor was the famous Elias Levita (Elijah Bahur), whom the cardinal maintained in his Roman palace for over a dozen years. Levita's halcyon Roman days came to an abrupt end with the sack of Rome (1527), when the palace was plundered and several of Levita's writings disappeared. In Renaissance Italy, as we have seen, there were many such relationships between Jewish and Christian scholars, of which the last mentioned was perhaps the most ideal.

No incident better illustrates the extent to which Jewish ideas had penetrated even the highest circles in the Church than the adventures of the messianic impostors, David Reuveni and Solomon Molkho, in Italy. The story itself is one of the most fantastic in Jewish history, and one of its rather remarkable features is the credence the impostors were given by personages such as Cardinal Egidio da Viterbo and Pope Clement VII.

David Reuveni appeared suddenly one day in the Near East on his way from the mythical independent Jewish state in the 'desert of Habor' to Europe. In 1524 he arrived in Italy aboard a Venetian vessel. He claimed to be the son of Solomon, late king of the lost tribes of Gad, Reuben, and the half tribe of Manasseh, and younger brother of the reigning monarch Joseph. He described himself as a warrior and commander-in-chief of his nation's army. Reuveni pretended to be on a diplomatic mission from his royal brother to the leader of Christendom, the pope. Reuveni set foot on Italian soil at Venice. His first supporter there was Moses da Castellazzo the painter, in whose house he stayed before leaving for Rome. There he acted like an Oriental potentate, proud and short-tempered. He rode to the Vatican on a white horse, and was received in audience by Cardinal Egidio da Viterbo. The cardinal was soon convinced of Reuveni's authenticity, and became the chief champion of his cause in Rome. He introduced Reuveni to Pope Clement VII and other prelates. Reuveni claimed ignorance of all languages but Hebrew and a little Arabic, and the cardinal consented to act as interpreter between him and the pope. The audience with the pope must have been a singular spectacle, even in those extraordinary days: the spiritual ruler of Western Christendom in conversation with the colorfully bedecked Jewish 'ambassador' on affairs of state, with a Hebrew-Italian interpreter in attendance. Reuveni thus defined his mission to the pope:

'King Joseph and his elders instructed me to tell you that you should make peace between the emperor and the king of France, that being to your and to their advantage, and that you give me letters (addressed) to these two rulers, (asking them) to support us and (telling them that) we shall aid them, and that you write on my behalf also to Presbyter John (or Prester John, the semi-legendary title of the Ethiopian ruler in medieval Europe)...'

Reuveni's plan called for Christian Europe to unite in a new Crusade. His strategy was to have the European army attack the Turks from the west, while the Ethiopians and the (lost) ten tribes were to attack from the east. His idea was to effect thus the liberation of Palestine, and to bring about the Redemption of the Jews and the coming of the Messiah. Clement was quite unable to interfere effectively with the policies of the two great European powers, at war with each other over the mastery of Europe, especially in Italy. Instead, he gave Reuveni a letter of recommendation to John III, king of Portugal.

Reuveni's mission to Portugal was a failure. Its only effective result was the return to Judaism of several Marranos (which was the chief factor contributing to the Portuguese fiasco), including a promising young government official, Diogo Pires, who became famous as the pseudo-Messiah Solomon Molkho. Reuveni, after two years of captivity in France, reappeared in Italy at the end of 1529. He went to see Charles V and Clement VII at Bologna, shortly after the two had ostensibly made up their differences, and the pope had crowned Charles. This should have afforded a golden opportunity to Reuveni, had it not been for the fact that shortly before this event he had exploded the myth he was trying to create around himself. During his captivity in France his documents had been taken from him. These he had refabricated at Mantua, while staying early in 1530 as an honored guest in the house of Abraham Portaleone the physician. He was found out, and Portaleone informed Federico Gonzaga, who earlier had given an interview to Reuveni. The marquess instructed Francesco Gonzaga, his ambassador at the papal court, to inform the pope and the emperor discreetly of the impending hoax. This he did successfully, and without discrediting the pope for his earlier credulity. Later that year Reuveni again turned up in Venice. The Venetian senate instructed Giovambattista Ramusio, the noted traveler and geographer, to interrogate Reuveni. Ramusio was not impressed by Reuveni's antics, probably having seen worse during his travels. He furthermore warned the senate in his report (quoted verbatim by Marin Sanudo in his *Diaries*) that Reuveni was on the verge of lunacy. The last stage in the drama took place after Molkho and Reuveni had joined forces in northern Italy.

In the six years between his reconversion to Judaism and the reunion with Reuveni, Molkho had led a rather hectic life. He immersed himself in the study of the Kabbalah in Safed and Salonika, and soon became convinced that he was the Messiah. He then came to Italy, and fascinated audiences in the synagogues with his preaching. He went to Rome, and sat at the city's gates among the beggars and the sick, to fulfill a talmudical legend about the Messiah. In Rome he predicted the flooding of the Tiber, an earthquake in Portugal, and the appearance of a comet. All three prophecies came true. Clement VII was much impressed by him, and entertained him for quite some time in the Vatican. When Jacob Mantino the physician (for reasons of his own) told the Inquisition of Molkho's true antecedents, and the Holy Office condemned him to death, the pope had a substitute burnt at the stake. The supreme pontiff concealed the Jewish pseudo-Messiah in his palace, and eventually aided his escape from Rome.

Later Reuveni and Molkho joined forces and went to see Charles V at Regensburg. Reuveni repeated his military plans for the conquest of the Holy Land, this time with the aid of a Jewish army to be recruited in Europe. Molkho, on the other hand, is said to have suggested to the emperor that he embrace Judaism. The leader of German Jewry, Josel von Rosheim, advised the two adventurers against their attempt, but to no avail. The emperor had them arrested and carried in chains to Italy. Molkho was condemned by a tribunal of the Inquisition and executed in Mantua (1532). Reuveni was sent to a Spanish prison, and is said

See illustration page 121.

Spice (besamim) boxes, Italy, mid-seventeenth century. Spicebox ornamented with birds, flowers, and human figures. Silver. London, Victoria and Albert Museum, Inv. No. M. 427-1956.

to have been identical with another victim of the Inquisition burnt at the stake a few years later.

It is, of course, no mere chance that some of the actors in this drama were in the forefront of Jewish-Christian relations in Italy. The question often has been put: did Clement VII really believe the tales told him by either Reuveni or Molkho? Clement, born Giulio de' Medici, was one of the most learned and enlightened men of his age. Admittedly, at that time there were still large areas on the globe which to Europeans were no more than mythical abstractions. On the other hand, there was little to recommend either the pseudo-ambassador or the false Messiah. Attempts have been made to explain away the obvious, and to find overt or covert hints of the pope's skepticism. Others try to explain the pontiff's enthusiasm for Reuveni by the desperate political straits in which the papacy found itself at this juncture. Even if he was not really taken in by Reuveni—they argue—he grasped at a straw, in the hope of starting a political plot, which eventually would involve the great European powers, and divert their attention. Clement was indeed sitting on a powder keg which finally exploded in 1527,

accompanied by the sack of the Eternal City. But there was more to it than mere political intrigue. Furthermore, Molkho appeared at the Vatican after the pope's return from the peace meeting of Bologna in 1530. The key to the pope's attitude, therefore, is at least partially to be found in the atmosphere created by two generations of Christian Hebraists and enthusiasts of Jewish mystical lore. They prepared the ground for the messianic delusion, which took hold of official Rome at the beginning of the 16th century.

HEBREW POETRY AND PROSE

Some of the Hebrew literature we have spoken of was produced in Italy in the course of the Middle Ages and the Renaissance. The renaissance of the Hebrew language in Southern Italy and some of its literary products have already been mentioned (see chapter on Byzantium). There was a fair sprinkling of poets among Italian Jewry during the High Middle Ages, but only a little of their poetry has survived which is practically all of the *piyyut* type, i.e., religious poetry. The most noted poets of that period were members of one single family, in which the art was handed down from generation to generation, over a period of some two hundred and fifty years. Amittai the Elder, the first identifiable figure of that family, lived in the 9th century, probably in its first half. He is the first synagogal poet in Europe known by name.

The contribution of medieval Italian Jewry to rabbinical literature, strictly speaking, was comparatively negligible. The most noteworthy halakhic works (Jewish religious law) were the talmudical commentaries and compendia of Isaiah of Trani (13th century), and of his grandson and namesake (14th century). The elder Isaiah's pupil, Zedekiah ben Abraham Anau wrote *Shibbole ha-Leket* (Gleanings), an extensive collection of religious usages. None of these, not to mention their inferiors, left a really important mark on this branch of Hebrew literature. This lack of important original contributions was somewhat made up for by the great diffusion of Jewish culture among Italian Jewry throughout the Middle Ages.

Hebrew poetry, on the other hand, continued to be the forte of Italian Jewry. The greatest Hebrew poet in medieval Italy was Immanuel ben Solomon of Rome (Manoello Giudeo). He was a contemporary of Dante, and was a native of Rome or its province. His life was rather unsettled, and at various stages of his career he has been traced in half a dozen Italian cities. He is said to have studied medicine, but his known occupations are those of official scribe to the Jewish communities, and especially tutor in the houses of the rich. He was one of the first in a long series of Jewish scholars and writers to make a living in this fashion. Immanuel's literary output was considerable and included a philosophical commentary on the Bible, although his chief claim to fame is as a poet.

Jewish-Italian court of law, fifteenth century. In the miniature various types of ▶ law court are shown, with, in front, the litigants pleading their case. From Jacob ben Asher's Legal Code, copied in 1435 by Isaac ben Obadiah in Mantua. Vatican Library, Codex Rossiana 555, 293 v.

Toward the end of his life, in about 1328, while at Fermo near Ancona, Immanuel's patron at this time suggested that he should collect his poems in a single volume. This was sound advice, and went a long way toward preserving all of Immanuel's poetry. He did it by linking the poems in the pattern of the *maqama* (assembly) of Arab poetry, introduced into Hebrew literature by Judah Al-Harizi of Spain. Immanuel collected his poems into the *mahberot* (Compositions). They are of a curious variety, and were set together rather incongruously. Immanuel assembled into the *mahberot* his entire poetical and semi-poetical compositions of every imaginable description. Elegies rub shoulders with satires and religious poems are placed next to love rhymes. Though the influence of Hebrew poetry of the Spanish Golden Age on Immanuel is undeniable, the Italian influence is quite pronounced, especially that of the *dolce stil novo* of Dante and his circle. He was the first to introduce the form of the Italian sonnet into Hebrew literature, and in accordance with the formal scheme defined by Immanuel's contemporary Guittone d'Arezzo. One of Immanuel's poems is an imitation of the *Serventese del maestro di tutte l'arti* (Serventese of the jack-of-all-trades). The twenty-eighth *mahberet,* which is also the last, contains the poet's vision of Heaven and Hell (The Composition of Topheth and Eden), an imitation of Dante's *Divine Comedy.*

The relationship, on the literary, or even personal level, between Dante and Manoello has been the subject of much research and considerable controversy. While it has been established with near certainty that the two never met, many points of contact have been traced, including several friends they had in common. Immanuel is thought to have set down his vision under similar circumstances to those of Dante when creating his comedy—in exile. While Dante's predicament was the result of the political strife in his native Florence, Immanuel had to leave Rome in 1321, owing to a papal expulsion order, directed against the Jews of the city. Though the expulsion was both unusual and short-lived, the poet left Rome, apparently never to return. Immanuel settled temporarily in Gubbio, an Umbrian hill-city, in the home of his friend, the wealthy loan-banker Daniel. Unfortunately his patron died shortly after the poet's arrival. Some consolation lay in store for the poet, coming from an unexpected quarter. There were at that time at Gubbio the poets Bosone and Cino da Pistoia, jurist and poet, both close friends of Dante, and prominent members of the poet's circle. Immanuel met them, and became rather friendly with them, especially with Bosone. Several of Immanuel's Italian

See illustration page 123.

sonnets, written at that juncture, have been preserved (though most of them have been lost), probably thanks to one or both of his friends. The arrival at Gubbio of the news that Dante had died in September of 1321 apparently coincided with the death of Immanuel's patron. Bosone addressed a consolatory sonnet to Immanuel, in which he mourned the deaths of the two as similar losses to the world. Immanuel replied in kind. The incidents of that year are believed to have inspired Immanuel to imitate Dante's *Divine Comedy*.

The story of Immanuel's vision joins the events of that fateful year. The death of his friend Daniel turned his thoughts to the future world. In response to his call, there appeared to him his friend's namesake, the prophet Daniel, who guides the poet through the 'Topheth and Eden.' Immanuel's hell is populated with some of the Greek philosophers and scientists, chiefly for their views, as well as some two dozen classes of the damned. Paradise, on the other hand, is peopled by most famous characters in Jewish history. It has been pointed out that the Jewish poet showed considerably more tolerance than his great contemporary, by 'allotting' a section in Paradise to the 'pious of the nations of the world'. Christian theology at that time would not allow such forbearance to Dante. When the Hebrew poet died (between 1328

Madonna della Vittoria, Mantua, fifteenth century. Painting by an anonymous pupil of Montegna depicting the Madonna della Vittoria with a model of the church constructed on the site of Daniel Norsa's confiscated house in Mantua. Daniel Norsa and his family are shown at the bottom of the picture (see next illustration). Mantua, Church of S. Andrea. Photo Giovetti, Mantova.

and 1336), Cino da Pistoia addressed a sonnet to Bosone da Gubbio. In it he presumed that Immanuel had now joined Dante in the Inferno, both being punished for their attitude toward women. Bosone, not quite so intolerant, suggested in his answering poem that eventually both would be redeemed.

A lesser poet, but a much closer imitator of Dante, was Moses ben Isaac di Rieti, born in that city in 1388. He was a physician of a commune in Umbria and in the service of Pope Pius II. He wrote on medicine, philosophy and theology, and defended his faith in disputations with Christians. One such debate in which he participated was the famous banquet and polemical discussion, which took place in 1448 in Rimini. It was organized by Sigismondo Pandolfo Malatesta, the local tyrant, who has been described as 'almost a pagan ... though nevertheless interested in religious discussion'. The Christian side is said to have been represented by the Hebraist Gianozzo Manetti.

Moses di Rieti's imitatory effort is entitled *Mikdash Me'at* (The Lesser Sanctuary). It is divided into two parts, the first being a survey of theological and philosophical knowledge, and the second, which describes a visit to Paradise, is closely related to the Dantean model. In addition to other matter, it contains a description of Jewish literature, and an enumeration of those who dwell in the City of God: scholars, pious heroes, and so forth. Among those whom the poet excludes from Paradise is (of all people) Immanuel of Rome, whom he rejects 'because of his wantonness'. The poet employs throughout the terza rima (inter-rhyming tercets) of the *Divine Comedy,* and is the first to do so in Jewish literature. Parts of Rieti's *Sanctuary* were translated into Italian. The most noted translation is that by the Jewish poet Deborah Ascarelli who lived in sixteenth-century Rome, her husband being the head of the Catalan synagogue. Her translation and some original verses of her own were published at Venice in 1602. Italian-Jewish poets produced two more Hebrew imitations of Dante's comedy as late as the 17th and 18th centuries.

Manoello Giudeo was not the only Jewish poet to employ the medium of Italian. He himself mentions a Jewish poet of Rome who was a member of the delegation sent to Pope John XXII at Avignon, to bring about the withdrawal of the edict for the expulsion of Roman Jewry. He is described as a jongleur and troubadour in 'Hebrew, Arabic, and Christian' (i.e., Italian), who excelled in sword-play and was a skilled lancer. At the same time he was a pious Jew, visited the Holy Land, and conducted religious debates with Christians. Unfortunately none of his verses has come down to us, and his very identity is still obscure.

Other Jewish Italian poets were more fortunate, though none equaled Immanuel in ability. Among them was Sarah Coppio Sullam, who lived in Venice at the end of the 16th and the beginning of the 17th century. The range of her education was exceptional. At fifteen she was fluent in Latin, Greek, Spanish, Italian, and Hebrew. Her contemporaries considered her a great beauty, and praised her for her character, sweet voice, and accomplishments as a poet. Her home in the Venetian ghetto has been described as 'something of a literary salon'. It was frequented by Jews and Christians, rabbis and priests, who came to visit her and to listen to her verses. Ansaldo Seba, monk and poet, sent

The Norsa family (detail of previous illustration). The family originally came from Nurcia in Umbria, hence the Hebrew form 'Norzi'. Many were rabbis in Mantua where the family had its own synagogue. Mantua, Church of S. Andrea. Photo Giovetti, Mantova.

Sarah a copy of his epic poem on Esther, and she informed him that she slept with it under her pillow. That started a long correspondence between the two, punctuated by the monk's efforts to obtain her conversion to Christianity. While she consented to read the New Testament and Christian theological writings, she remained steadfast in her ancestral faith. On his deathbed he commended her to the prayers of his fellows. Baldassare Bonifaccio, who was to become bishop of Capo d'Istria, accused Sarah in a pamphlet of denying the immortality of the soul. She defended herself energetically and successfully.

Women are more often the subject matter of poetry than its authors. Jewish medieval poets, especially in southern Europe, took an active part in the poetical controversy over the merits of

women and of marriage. Immanuel of Rome was the first Italian poet to take sides over this issue. In addition to love sonnets, some of which have been described as rather lascivious, he wrote several poems on women, in which he heaps ridicule and even abuse on the fair sex. Later generations continued to take up poetical arms for or against women, depending on the personal taste and inclination of the poet.

The battle raged on intermittently for centuries and reached a fresh pitch in the 1490s. Abraham of Sarteano (in Tuscany) reopened hostilities by attacking womanhood in his merry *Woman Hater*. Avigdor Fano rushed to the defense of the maligned sex. From then on the fight continued unabated and became rather heated in the middle of the 16th century. Until then most Hebrew-

Norsa

Modigliani

Montalbotti

Montefiore

Pomis de

Portaleone

Porto Coen Rapa

Coats of arms of Jewish-Italian families. Many Italian-Jewish families had distinctive badges from the sixteenth century on. Later they were to be found among certain Jewish families who were ennobled. In a number of cases, such as the Montefiores and Sassoons, a Hebrew motto was incorporated.

Italian contributions to this branch of poetry had been written in the style introduced by Moses di Rieti, the terza rima. Then, at that moment the style changed. One of the most popular forms adopted by Jewish poets in Italy at this time was the bilingual poem—a mixture of Hebrew and Italian. It became so perfected—technically of course rather than artistically—that its alternating verses or stanzas, though written in different languages, meant and sounded the same. The rather artificial result was called the 'echo-poem'. Some of the poems on women written then were of the multilingual type (a game enjoyed also by some contemporary non-Jewish poets). A noted example is the poem called *The Shield of Women* by the dramaturgist Leone de' Sommi. This rather confused the modern editor of the text, who published the Hebrew lines in one article and the Italian ones in another. It took several decades before it was realized that the two parts did not make sense separately. The most famous Hebrew-Italian echo-poem is an elegy by Leone da Modena in memory of his teacher, written in 1584, at the age of thirteen. Needless to say, these macaronic manipulations, in which Hebrew was used instead of Latin, were not conducive to great or even mediocre poetry.

Some Renaissance Men of Letters

No less marked than the influence of the Jewish spirit on some Christian humanists and men of the Renaissance was the effect on Italian Jews of the spirit of the environment. It was not limited to the style and meter of Italian poetry, adapted for use in Hebrew from the days of Manoello Giudeo. The reciprocal influence of the Renaissance spirit expressed itself in most branches of Jewish-Italian thought and literature, among others in a revival of interest in history. Some of the resulting compositions are of the medieval chronicle type, while others are more closely related to either the literary style or critical attitude of the Renaissance.

So far no satisfactory explanation has been offered for the comparatively poor contribution from medieval Jewry to historiography. There is no lack of indication of the interest in historical literature shown by European Jews at that time. Those very few histories available to medieval Jews enjoyed great popularity, and yet, apparently, this did not encourage further efforts along these lines. Sixteenth-century Italy produced more Jewish contributions to this branch of literature than the combined efforts of European Jewry throughout the Middle Ages.

One very popular work was Solomon Ibn Verga's *Shevet Yehudah* (Judah's Rod) which went through several editions from 1550 on. The central theme of the chronicle is the Expulsion of the Jews from Spain, and the events which led up to it. This was the major national disaster to befall European Jewry at the end of the Middle Ages, and became the object of much soul-searching on the part of Jewish contemporaries. Ibn Verga was one of the few Jews to inquire into the political and social aspects of the disaster. Although he clothed his narrative in the style of the Italian novelette, the influence of the new Italian attitude to history is discernible. Incidentally both Machiavelli and Guicciardini praise the Catholic Monarchs for their statesmanship in

ridding the country of the Jews. Even Pico della Mirandola, disciple and friend of Jewish scholars, welcomed the Expulsion for having thus confounded the predictions of Jewish astrologers. Little wonder, then, that most Jewish contemporaries looked for religious and moral explanations.

Samuel Usque wrote in a similar vein. He was a former Marrano who settled in Ferrara, and was author of *Consolaçam às Tribulaçoens de Israel* (Consolation in the Tribulations of Israel), published in 1553, in the printing house of his brother Abraham. The *Consolation* is written in the form of a 'pastoral dialogue' in three parts. The first and second parts deal with ancient Jewish history to the destruction of the Second Commonwealth. The third dialogue contains thirty-seven chapters of events in medieval Jewish history, crowned by the recent calamity of Spain and Portugal. The last part has some merit as an historical source, though rather unreliable.

Undoubtedly the greatest chronicler of this age was Joseph ben Joshua ha-Cohen. A native of Avignon, he and his family settled in Italy. Joseph studied medicine, and became a practitioner in various places in southern Italy. He translated into Hebrew the medical treatise of Meir Alguades, and added a list of medicines of his own, including a cure for the 'French disease'. Next to medicine his chief interest was history. He translated J. Behaim's *Omnium gentium mores leges et ritus,* and Lopez de Gomoras' *La Historia General de las Indias.* Joseph's original contributions to historiography were his *History of the Kings of France and of the Ottoman Turks* and his *Vale of Tears.* He has been described as the most 'responsible' Jewish historian of his time. Though his critical acumen is faulty at times, he attempts to check his facts, and to steer clear of fiction and fancy. Joseph's historical writings are of especial value as a source for contemporary Italian history, both Jewish and non-Jewish. He was the first Jew to attempt a general history covering nearly a millennium.

Other Jewish histories of that period are greatly inferior to the last mentioned. Nevertheless, one should mention the *Chain of Tradition* by Gedaliah ibn Yahya of Imola; *The History of Pope Paul IV* by Benjamin Nehemiah ben Elnathan; the anonymous *Story of the Tribulations that Came to Pass in Italy;* and there are others space will not allow us to dwell upon. There was also at that time an incipient Jewish interest in biography. Baruch Uziel Forti (Hasachetto) wrote a biography of the scholar-statesman Isaac Abrabanel, by way of introduction to the Ferrara edition of Abrabanel's messianic treatise *The Wells of Salvation,* and Leone da Modena wrote a detailed autobiography *Hayye Yehudah* (Judah's Life). In the 15th century, the physician and scholar Judah Messer Leon in his work on logic *Nofet Zufim* (The Honeycomb) included a chapter, which, it has been suggested, 'may be considered the earliest Jewish experiment in the field of political science'.

There also was a growing interest among the Jews of Italy in geography—in line with the general curiosity aroused by the great discoveries. This was in addition to the traditional accounts of travel to the Holy Land, which were avidly collected and edited. Some were translated into European languages for non-Jewish readers. The outstanding writer on geography among the Jews of Italy at that time was Abraham ben Mordecai Farissol of Ferrara. Like many other Jewish scholars he took part in a theological disputation—this one at the court of Duke Ercole I d'Este. The result was his apology of Judaism *Magen Avraham* (The Shield of Abraham). In addition Farissol was a Bible commentator and a musician. His geographical work is entitled *Iggeret Orhot Olam* (Treatise on the Paths of the World), also published in Latin as *Tractatus itinerum mundi*. This contained all the information Farissol was able to glean on geographical subjects and was the first Jewish book to mention the discovery of the New World by Christopher Columbus.

AZARIAH DE' ROSSI

The most outstanding Jewish contribution to Renaissance literature is the *Meor Enayim* (Enlightenment of the Eyes), by Azariah de' Rossi. Born in 1514 in Mantua he lived subsequently also in Bologna, Venice, Ancona, and Ferrara. He was on friendly terms with many contemporary scholars, Jews and non-Jews. Azariah was one of Amatus Lusitanus' patients. The famous physician describes in detail the physique and the complaints of the scholar, as well as the cure prescribed for him. The physician flattered himself on the success of the treatment, which consisted principally of a diet. On November 18 1571, a colossal earthquake shook the city of Ferrara. Azariah, whose house had been damaged, escaped into the countryside, along with the entire population. At this juncture he met another fugitive, a Christian scholar, who was whiling away the time reading the *Letter of Aristeas*. This product of Jewish-Hellenistic literature describes rather extravagantly the wonders of the Temple in Jerusalem, and tells at length the legend concerning the origin of the Septuagint translation of the Bible. Having come up against a textual difficulty, he asked Azariah for the Hebrew version. Azariah then became aware that no such version existed, and was pained to admit as much, and that the *Letter,* though Jewish in origin, was hardly known at all among Jews. The incident decided Azariah to write his book.

Meor Enayim contains a description of the earthquake and of the author's consequent experiences; a Hebrew translation of the *Letter of Aristeas*; and a series of essays, divided into four parts, on various aspects of ancient Jewish history, examined with the aid of classical literature, guided by Renaissance principles of critical historical enquiry. The essays form the main body of the work. The author's purpose was to draw the attention of contemporary Jewish scholarship to the records in Latin and especially in Greek which have a bearing on Jewish antiquity, and to compare them to parallel Hebrew sources. The extent to which such a procedure required defense even at that time in Italy becomes evident in the light of the author's lengthy apology on the subject. Azariah then reintroduces to Jewish scholarship the writings of Philo of Alexandria, totally neglected by Jews since antiquity. Among the subjects treated in *Meor Enayim* is the genesis of the Septuagint in relation to the story told in the *Letter,* and the variant readings in the Hebrew original and the Greek trans-

Meor Enayim, Mantua, 1574. Title page of *Meor Enayim* (Enlightenment of the Eyes) by Azariah de' Rossi, the first attempt to apply to Jewish studies the standards established during the Renaissance for the study of Classical texts and antiquities. New York, Jewish Theological Seminary of America.

lation. Another subject treated by him are various episodes shortly before and after the destruction of the Second Temple. One entire part of the *Meor Enayim* deals with Jewish chronology. The fourth and last part is devoted to Jewish archaeology.

Azariah's achievement lies less in the discoveries of his inquiries into Jewish history than in the spirit in which they were conducted and in the questions he posed. He introduced into Jewish studies some of the principles recently formulated by Christian scholars for the study of Greek and Roman antiquities. The range of his erudition was enormous. His treatises abound in quotations from nearly all important classical authors, poets, philosophers, scientists, physicians, historians, jurists, and so on. He was familiar with and quoted at length the writings of the Church Fathers. In addition he quotes Christian medieval writers, including theologians, as well as, of course, Dante and Petrarch. Furthermore he was acquainted with many contemporary writings, Italian, Spanish, German, and so forth. Needless to say, he was at home in all branches of Jewish literature, ancient, medieval, and contemporary.

The *Enlightenment of the Eyes* was printed immediately on its completion in 1573, and became controversial on publication. Even some Italian Jews, rather more tolerant at that time than Jews in other countries, criticized the book, though mostly from a scholarly point of view. Moses Provenzali, rabbi and scholar, and Azariah's friend, objected to his critical treatment of Philo and to his amendments to the accepted Jewish chronology. On the latter subject a stinging criticism was printed by R. Isaac Finzi of Pesaro. Some of his peers took an even graver view of the matter. They believed Azariah's work to be dangerous reading matter, and forbade its perusal except by special dispensation. They objected not so much to the author's views, at variance with many deep-rooted tenets, but rather to the author having nothing to offer but nonconformity. This happened at a moment when the Counter-Reformation was starting to take a hand in the suppression of unwanted opinions among humanists, both Christians and Jews.

In 1553 an auto-da-fé had been held on the Campo de' Fiori in Rome, at which large quantities of Hebrew books were burned on the pretext that they contained blasphemies against Christianity and its founder. Following this, a self-imposed Jewish censorship was set up, soon to be followed in its turn by an official one of the Catholic Church. Not surprisingly, the censors abused the authority vested in them to suppress not only real but imaginary insults to Christianity. Some of the objectors to Azariah's treatise felt that the qualified prohibition imposed upon the work was insufficient. They consulted the aged Joseph Caro, considered by his contemporaries the greatest rabbinical authority then living. Caro ordered *Meor Enayim* to be burned, but died before any such drastic step could be carried out. In the end the book was not suppressed, but its study was permitted only to those aged at least twenty-five.

Though some Jewish-Italian scholars joined the ranks of the 'obscurants', others kept faith with the spirit of the Renaissance, sometimes for as long as a generation or more after the onset of the new reactionary age. Azariah de' Rossi's difficulties did not deter some of his younger contemporaries from immersing themselves in the study of ancient and medieval non-Jewish literature. One such scholar was Abraham Portaleone, whose medical treatises have been mentioned earlier. His claim to fame in Jewish literature is his *Shilte ha-Gibborim* (The Shields of the Heroes). Written in the author's old age, it was completed in 1607. It is the most

Shir ha-Shirim Asher li-Shlomo, Venice, 1623. Title page of *Shir ha-Shirim Asher li-Shlomo* (The Songs that are Solomon's), canto by Salomone de' Rossi; the first synagogue music. De' Rossi was the outstanding Jewish composer of the Renaissance in Italy, and a musician in his own right in the service of the Gonzaga. He collaborated with Monteverdi.

extensive archaeological treatise published in Hebrew before modern times. Portaleone's motivation has been described as 'a pious obsession with the former service of the Temple in Jerusalem'. This led him to attempt a complete literary reconstruction of the Temple and its service. The effort was as mighty as the subject, and was further increased by the author's proclivity to digress at length from the main topics under discussion. The themes thus introduced by Portaleone include among others a discussion of ancient Jewish architecture, a treatise on music, and an essay on military science. Other subjects dealt with in the *Shields of the Heroes* are a monograph on precious stones, their medical use, the current price of diamonds, and the method for the detection of paste; and chapters on zoology and botany, chemistry and pharmacology, including a section on gunpowder. Portaleone's erudition did not fall short of de' Rossi's, and he too quotes from every possible source, ancient and contemporary, Jewish and non-Jewish. He expressed great enthusiasm for classical studies, and advocated their dissemination among the Jews.

Portaleone's work aroused no known opposition. On the other hand one of the author's fellow-Mantuans, Eliezer David del Bene (Mehatov), a preacher of some renown in a Mantuan synagogue, let his enthusiasm for classical culture get the better of him. In one of his sermons he went as far as to sanctify the Roman goddess of hunting, by describing her as 'that Holy Diana'. This created quite a stir among the zealots, and del Bene had to retire from the pulpit (1598).

LEONE DA MODENA

The most typical son of the Renaissance among the Jews of Italy, who personified in many ways the spirit it had evoked, was Leone (Judah) da Modena. He was born too late, as it were, and eventually became something of an anachronism during his lifetime. Da Modena was born in 1571 in Venice, to which his parents had escaped from Ferrara, recently destroyed by an earthquake. He enjoyed the benefits of that liberal education which the Jewish upper class, especially the bankers, afforded their children in Renaissance Italy. That included all branches of Jewish studies, and Italian language and literature, Latin, music, and dance. He became one of the most versatile men of this by no means staid age. In a way he was the embodiment of the environment in which he lived, especially during his youth. From his early years he began to display unusual talents, and soon turned into a child prodigy. At the age of two and a half, he publicly recited the weekly lesson from the Prophets in the synagogue. This was the usual initiation into Hebrew studies and Divine service, though not as a rule quite so early in life.

We have already mentioned that Leone da Modena never succeeded in making full use of his potentialities. His failure was due to a variety of causes, including financial difficulties, personal misfortunes, and an overdose of versatility and consequent inability to concentrate. He himself lists twenty-six professions and occupations, which he describes as the means whereby he attempted—unsuccessfully—to make a living. These included teaching, various literary pursuits, book printing, theatrical and musical ventures, and even matchmaking. In addition he acted as rabbi and communal judge of Venetian Jewry. Modena's literary output was formidable. He wrote his first printed opus at the age of thirteen: *Sur Mera* (Depart from Evil), a tractate directed against gambling and games of chance. It is a rather revealing trait of Modena that he was a passionate gambler all his life—though a constant loser. He has been described as the most articulate Jewish writer in Italy to put a pen to paper. Like so many men of his age, he was torn between extremes. He was an opponent of the Kabbalah, and attacked its devotees with the arguments of critical rationalism. At the same time he believed in astrology, and attached great importance to dreams, signs, portents, and amulets. Modena closely followed the latest scientific developments of his age, yet took part in alchemical hocus-pocus. He wrote a spirited anti-Christian polemical treatise, directed chiefly against the writings of Petrus Galatinus, yet was on intimate terms with members of the clergy. He was an active rabbi, yet was considered rather lax in the observance of certain Jewish precepts. To say the least, he was imbued with more than the normal share of human inconsistency.

Leone da Modena's writings are as varied as his character and his interests. He was a poet and a rhymester who cut his verses to suit every occasion: births, weddings, deaths and so forth. These verses were produced on demand and against payment. His prose writings, in addition to those already mentioned, include a collection of some of the sermons he had delivered on various occasions. Many of those had been attended by Venetian and foreign Christian notables, in defiance of the express ecclesiastical prohibition. Modena wrote several dictionaries, as, for instance, a Hebrew-Italian one of the Bible. Then there is his pamphlet on mnemonics; another directed against the belief in metempsychosis; one on chess; and a series of commentaries on the Bible. His treatise *Historia de' riti Hebraici* (History of the Jewish Rites) made him famous among non-Jews in Italy and abroad. It ran to numerous editions, and was translated into several languages. In it Modena attempted to describe and explain Jewish rites and ceremonies to Gentiles. It was one of the few Jewish literary efforts before modern times produced solely for non-Jewish consumption. Several volumes of Modena's letters and responsa have survived, as well as a number of lesser writings.

Modena's literary production of greatest interest to the modern reader is his autobiography. In it the author vividly expressed his versatile character, and colorfully described the ups and downs of his variegated career. With his death in 1648 there disappeared from the Italian scene the last Jewish man of letters of the Renaissance—and perhaps the most complete—who had outlived his times by at least half a century.

HEBREW PRINTING

The history of the book of course antedates that of the printed volume. Yet there exists a fundamental difference between the manuscript and the printed book. The invention of printing not only gave the book an additional dimension; it greatly extended the diffusion of knowledge and learning, and in consequence increased literary and scientific activities. In due course it became a major element in communication, chiefly in spreading information abroad. At the time of its invention the printed book was instrumental in popularizing humanist and Renaissance studies.

Jewish participation in early European printing apparently goes back to a much earlier date than has been assumed. The Gutenberg Bible, generally taken to be the first printed book, was produced in or about 1455. But there were earlier attempts, and one of those was carried out some ten years before that date, by a

עוד בחכמות אמתיות ומושכלות נקיות בעבורם ידרוש
להס בראשונה גס חכס ונבון ושאחרין וזאת   בכבר ל
מעבה טבע עונותיהס בין האור העהי וביגס   כמעצ
גרעך עליהס קיכת מסבתירות התשגחה להעוב   אל
המקרי המאריי והיתה אריכם לשמה ולחרפה   וחלשה
בהס ידיעת אמיתית התורה וסתריה והסתתרה חכמת'
ובינתס ריחוק להס העונש עד טימאסס   וישנאוה
בזוריהס בארצות הגריס אש   כעתכו מש אחר כן בסה
שיבא מהזמן תסובבנה הסגלות כלס   אל עטמוטס
הקרומה ישוב המולכו ותצמח החכמה ותחזק ההשגח'
וווררו עיע הלבכות בחדרי הסתרי התנרי בטוב ﾑ
שיב שמן ועיענו תחזינה ותכלי כל הטורבן הזמעו חיצ'
מי ישריט בגריתס ונפשותס התאשונכו להתהות בהס
מת מעשי ﾏ כי כוראח הוח   סוף דבר תשמיל
לבבי מו תאמין תאמין בכל כל סיהאמין בו אחדון
הקדמועס בזמן ראשס בחטיבות המורה הגריל רבי'
משה עב אטר מטר אין עדון תלין בכל חכמי ישריע ﾎ אתר
חתימס התלמור בזאת אע בוטח אשר בכל חרדי'
החכמה וה נורה את ﾏ עהיך תירא
חזן
אנכי אשטרלינה אשת ארע איטי הנכבר כסר' מברהס
כונת יוויא כתבתי זאת האגרת בחינת עולס עס עזר
ביטעיר ייע זב לוי מארץ פרוונ:כה מטרשיטון יחי חמן

Colophon of Behinat Olam, Mantua, 1475. The colophon of the work *Behinat Olam* (Examination of the World), an ethical poem by Jedaiah of Béziers, a very well-known book, reprinted over eighty times. Shown here is one of the first Hebrew incunabula, printed by Estellina, wife of Abraham Conat, assisted by Jacob Levi of Tarascon. Jerusalem, Jewish National and University Library.

Jewish dyer in southern France. He had the Hebrew types cut for him, and is said to have experimented with them—with what results we do not know. The significance of the invention was recognized almost immediately, and one of the first Jewish printers predicted that owing to his work 'the earth shall be full of knowledge'. There was, of course, also some opposition to printing Hebrew, especially on the part of professional copyists, who rightly expected to go out of business. Their attitude was similar to that of the copyist-monks, who described printing as the 'devil's handiwork'. Some rabbinical authorities were worried about the religious implications of printing the divine name, and the like. But all these initial difficulties were swiftly overweighed by the great advantages derived from printing.

In 1464 the first printed book appeared in Italy. Some ten years later Abraham ben Garton published in a remote southern town (Reggio di Calabria) Rashi's commentary on the Pentateuch. It is the first dated Hebrew printed book, though some undated

volumes may have preceded it. A few months later, at the other end of Italy (Piove di Sacco), the physician Meshullam Cusi printed Jacob Ben Asher's ritual code *Arbaah Turim* (see chapter on Spain and Portugal). These two were soon followed by another physician-printer, Abraham Conat of Mantua, who printed another edition of Jacob Ben Asher's *Code*. Shortly after that the first non-Jewish book published by a Jewish printer appeared in Naples. Fittingly it was Dante's *Divine Comedy*.

The most famous family of Jewish printers of incunabula, in Hebrew and in Latin characters, were the Soncino. Of some one hundred and fifty Hebrew incunabula identified so far, about two thirds were printed in Italy, and out of these more than half were printed by the Soncino. Israel Nathan Ben Samuel (he too was a physician) immigrated from Germany to Italy and settled in Soncino, situated in the plain of Cremona, and from it the family derived its name. In association with his son Joshua Solomon he founded in 1483 a Hebrew printing-shop at Soncino. The son carried the business to various places, including Naples and Casalmaggiore. His editions comprise various parts of the Talmud, some prayer-books, the Bible and commentaries, a philosophical treatise, and a ritual compendium. Altogether he printed some forty Hebrew incunabula.

Even more prolific was Joshua Solomon's nephew, Gershom (Geronimo) Ben Moses. He was a typical wandering printer, that is to say, a traveling journeyman, carrying along a complete printer's outfit. Some of the famous early European printers belonged to this class. Gershom Soncino traveled all over Italy, and wherever he went he set up his printing shop and started production. His various editions are a guide to his itinerary, which included in Italy: Ancona, Barco, Brescia, Cesena, Fano, Pesaro, Ortona, and Rimini. Gershom's claim to fame as a printer is not limited to the annals of the Hebrew book, and includes those of the Latin and the Italian book. In all he printed about a hundred Hebrew volumes, and a similar number of non-Hebrew ones. Soncino had to contend with the ever-increasing competition of Christian printers—first over non-Hebrew printing, and later even over Hebrew printing. In the end he was practically forced out of business. At the end of the 1520s he surrendered and emigrated to Turkey. There he set up his presses, and after his death was succeeded by his son.

Gershom Soncino's chief competitors were the great Aldo Manuzio and Daniel Bomberg. The conflict with the first-named started over the letters cut by Francesco Griffo da Bologna and an edition of Petrarch, published by Soncino at Fano and dedicated to Cesare Borgia. Master Francesco had been in the service of Aldo, and had cut for him a type known as 'Cursive' or 'Chancery' (i.e., italics). The artist and Aldo apparently fell out over the commercial exploitation of the new letters. The artist then cut a revised version of the type, and offered them to Gershom who used it in his edition of Petrarch. As if that were not enough, Aldo had only recently put on the market a Petrarch of his own. It is thought that the enmity between the two printers was intensified through the official exclusion of Soncino from the city of Venice. Aldo was chiefly responsible for this measure, or Soncino at least thought so.

The non-Jewish publications of Gershom Soncino included city statutes, as those of Rimini, Fano, and of Iesi; classical literature (Virgil); contemporary Italian literature, such as works of Lodovico Ariosto and Lorenzo de' Medici; and even Christian theological tracts and treatises. He even did an edition of Petrus Galatinus' anti-Jewish work *De Arcanis Catholicae Veritatis*. Soncino must have been aware of the nature and object of the volume, not really mitigated by the author's defense of Reuchlin.

Soncino's Hebrew printing also covered a wide range of subjects. His chief competitor in this branch of printing was the other Venetian printer mentioned—Bomberg. Some very limited attempts to print Hebrew had been made in Venice before Bomberg. But even of Aldo's plan to publish a polyglot Bible

מגדל עוז שם יי

בו ירוץ צדיק ונשגב

Printer's flag of Gershom Soncino, fifteenth and early sixteenth centuries. Gershom Soncino was the most famous printer of Hebrew books in Italy, producer of some seventeen incunabula before 1500 and another hundred volumes after that date. His imprint is associated with: Soncino, Brescia, Barco, Fano, Pesaro, Ortona, Rimini, Salonika and Constantinople. Jerusalem, Jewish National and University Library.

nothing more came than the issue of a prospectus. In fact, it has been suggested that the Venetian government looked with disfavor on the idea of regular Hebrew publishing activities in the city. Daniel Bomberg, a rich patrician of Antwerp, founded in 1521 at Venice the first non-Jewish Hebrew printing house, which soon became the largest publisher of Hebrew literature to date. From then on until the middle of the century some two hundred Hebrew editions issued forth from the press. Daniel Bomberg belonged to that large circle of Christian Hebraists, whose motives were a mixture of humanist curiosity and Christian religious zeal.

Bomberg's motives for printing the largest systematical edition of practically all Hebrew standard works have been variously estimated. Some attributed the mainspring of his activity to commercial considerations. Others describe him as a 'noble-hearted Christian enthusiast'. A third evaluation by a contemporary of the famous printer suggests yet another explanation. A Jewish convert to Christianity named Gerardus Veltvyck, the emperor Charles V's ambassador at Constantinople, wrote a virulently anti-Jewish tract, attacking most branches of Jewish learning, with the exception of the Kabbalah. The book was published in 1536 by Bomberg's press, and the writer, in the manner of many a grateful author, praised the publisher in the introduction. According to Gerardus, Bomberg was motivated in his enterprise by the desire to reveal the secret weapons of Judaism, and to uncover the evil contained therein. Be that as it may, Bomberg became a central figure in the annals of Hebrew printing, and the diffusion of the Hebrew book in the Renaissance is said to owe more to him than to any single individual.

Bomberg's press was succeeded in Venice by that of Marcantonio Giustiniani. His virtual monopoly of the Hebrew book market in Venice was challenged by another Venetian patrician, Alvise Bragadini. A conflict broke out between the two Christian printers over an edition of Maimonides' *Code (Mishneh Torah)*. Giustiniani denounced his rival's edition to the Roman Inquisition, as containing passages offensive to the Christian faith. Bragadini replied in kind, and accused his competitor of committing similar offenses. This resulted in the previously mentioned auto-da-fé of Jewish literature in 1553, but it did not put an end to Hebrew printing in Venice and elsewhere in Italy. Admittedly activities were hampered, chiefly by censorship, but the Hebrew printing presses of Venice, Mantua, Ferrara, Sabbioneta, Cremona, and others, continued to put out a steady flow of Hebrew books.

ART

The biblical injunction against representational art rather impeded Jewish participation in artistic creation, though it did not completely suppress it. Recent discoveries have confirmed this to be true also in Italy. The synagogue at Ostia, dating back to Roman times, is decorated with the same ornaments employed at that time in Oriental Jewish places of worship. Though most of the paintings and decorations in the Roman and other Italian Jewish catacombs portray the stereotype symbols of ancient Judaism, there are quite a few examples of artistic representations to which no ritual

Synagogue, Mantua, fifteenth century. Interior of a synagogue in the fifteenth century during prayers. The Ark of the Law is open and a member of the congregation is shown holding the Scroll of the Law. The style of the building is late Gothic to early Renaissance. From Jacob ben Asher's Legal Code, copied in 1435 by Isaac ben Obadiah in Mantua. Vatican Library, Codex Rossiana 555, 12 v.

symbolism can be attached. These come carved or painted on the arcosolia, on the walls or ceilings of the catacombs, and on sarcophagi. Some have been described as 'carefully executed representations of no slight artistic merit'. There are not only birds and quadrupeds, but also human figures, including even a nude youth, and one or two instances of pagan representations, such as a winged Victory and the goddess Fortuna.

If there were ever any pictorial works of art by the Jews of Italy during the Middle Ages prior to the Renaissance, none has come down to us. Those few surviving buildings of medieval synagogues in southern Italy, as at Trani, for instance (now the Church of S. Anna), and at Naples (Church of S. Caterina Spinacorona, later S. Maria della Purificazione), are in no way exceptional artistically or architecturally. But the paucity of the material at our disposal prevents any appraisal. Practically all surviving synagogues date from the 16th century on. Those built before the Emancipation have the inconspicuous exterior—usually a blank wall—in common, chiefly for security reasons. Some of

these buildings, though, have magnificent interiors, and one or two were designed by famous non-Jewish architects. Needless to say, medieval and early modern synagogues were largely devoid of any pictorial or sculptural ornaments.

Outside the synagogue, too, there was little scope for the Jewish painter or sculptor. Most representational art of that time was intended for the Church, which automatically excluded the Jewish artist. There is, in fact, only one Jewish painter in Renaissance Italy who has been identified with any degree of certainty. This is Moses da Castellazzo, the painter who received Reuveni, and who lived at the end of the 15th century and the beginning of the 16th, at Venice, Mantua, and Ferrara. He has been identified as an intimate friend of Pietro Bembo and of one of his mistresses, Maria Savorgnan. Not one of his creations has survived. He is known to have done a medallion of Duke Ercole I d'Este, and he and his sons received a copyright for illustrations to an edition of the Bible. This was granted him by the Venetian Council of Ten, and by Marquess Federico of Mantua. In his petition Moses describes himself as an artist who 'for many years ... has been making portraits of gentlemen and other famous men...' We are similarly unfortunate with regard to the creations of a few other Jewish painters at this period. These include Angelo di Elia and Giacobbe di Vitale, members of the painters' guild at Perugia. A post-Renaissance Italian Jewish painter is Shalom d'Italia, a native of Mantua who went to live in Amsterdam, and did, among others, a portrait of Manasseh Ben Israel.

There is some disagreement over the question of to what extent the decorations of Hebrew manuscripts written in Italy were the handiwork of Jewish or Christian artists. While some such Jewish illuminators in Germany, France and Spain have been identified by name, the illustrators of Hebrew manuscripts in Italy have remained anonymous throughout. The miniatures adorning some of these manuscripts belong to the finest examples of this branch of decorative contemporary art. Some portray Jewish types, as is the case in a few paintings and miniatures done by non-Jews. In addition decorations of the miniature kind were also introduced into the *Ketubbah* (the Jewish marriage contract), and the *Megillah* (the Book of Esther recited on Purim).

While Jewish participation in painting was negligible, there was one handicraft, very popular with Jews ever since antiquity, which allowed for considerable artistic scope. This was the gold and silversmith's craft. In Renaissance Italy it became a veritable Jewish industry. In Mantua, for example, a group of Jews put up in 1527 a workshop employing forty jewelers and goldsmiths. An entire street in that town was named after the Jewish artisans 'Via degli orefici ebrei'. Again we come up against the difficulty arising out of the anonymity of the artists. Nevertheless it has been estimated that 'a relatively large number of the anonymous specimens of the goldsmith's craft in the Renaissance period are of Jewish workmanship.' This is in all probability true with objects

Vittorio Veneto synagogue, Vittorio Veneto, c. 1701. A very small house of prayer that combines the Baroque and neo-Classical styles. The women's gallery is above, behind the lattice screen. Wood, gilt, brass and silver. Today incorporated into the Israel Museum, Jerusalem.

אִילּוּ נָתַן לָנוּ אֶת הַשַּׁבָּת

וְלֹא קֵרְבָנוּ לִפְנֵי הַר סִינַי דַּיֵּנוּ

אִילּוּ קֵרְבָנוּ לִפְנֵי הַר סִינַי

וְלֹא נָתַן לָנוּ אֶת הַתּוֹרָה דַּיֵּנוּ

אִילּוּ נָתַן לָנוּ אֶת הַתּוֹרָה

וְלֹא הִכְנִיסָנוּ לְאֶרֶץ יִשְׂרָ דַּיֵּנוּ

אִילּוּ הִכְנִיסָנוּ לְאֶרֶץ יִשְׂרָ

וְלֹא בָּנָה לָנוּ אֶת בֵּית הַבְּחִירָה

דַּיֵּנוּ

עַל אַחַת כַּמָּה וְכַמָּה טוֹבָה
כְּפוּלָה וּמְכֻפֶּלֶת לַ־
לַמָּקוֹם עָלֵינוּ שֶׁהוֹצִיאָנוּ מִמִּצְרַיִם

Illuminated page of Bible, Ferrara, 1397. Illuminated page of a Bible manuscript with commentaries by Rashi, Abraham Ibn Ezra, David Kimhi and Levi ben Gerson. Copied by Solomon ben Hisdai in Ferrara in 1397 at the behest of Menahem Corinaldi. Florence, Bibl. Mediceo-Laurenziana, Pluteo 2/1.

Illuminated page from Passover Haggadah, ascribed to Italy, fifteenth century. The scene depicted shows the roasting of the Passover lamb. The accompanying text contains the conclusion of the *Dayyenu* poem recited in the course of the *Seder* Passover service. Washington, Library of Congress.

destined for use by Jews, especially for ritual purposes, e.g., wedding rings, silver and gold plate, ornaments of the 'Scrolls of the Law' and the like. One or two Jewish artisan-artists have been identified by name. There is, for instance, the Jew Graziadio, mentioned by Benvenuto Cellini as his mentor in the goldsmith's art during his formative years in Bologna.

Another similar handicraft with which the Jews of Italy were associated was ceramics. There are several Jewish majolica workers known by name, though in this case too most productions were unsigned. Here again some objects were intended for Jewish ceremonial use, such as Passover plates. The same applies to embroidery, lace-making and other needlecrafts.

THE THEATER, MUSIC AND DANCE

The medieval European theater, Christian and Jewish alike, was limited to religious drama. Christians presented chiefly Passion plays, while the Jews did Purim plays. In addition there were the carnival burlesques and buffooneries, in which Jews figured, often against their will. Toward the end of the Middle Ages, there was a revival of the secular theater. From the very beginning the Jews of Italy participated actively, as actors, producers and dramaturgists.

The first surviving record of Jewish secular acting in Italy dates from 1489 In that year the Jewish community at Pesaro staged a

Ketubbah, Rome, 1771. Marriage contract between Jedidiah Hayyim ben (son of) David Bon Dei and Regina bat (daughter of) Mordecai Samuel Veneziani. The scene depicts the Queen of Sheba visiting Solomon, with all the different virtues round the edges. The text begins: 'Here in Rome, on the banks of the Tiber...' Jerusalem, National and University Library.

Ketubbah, Venice, 1650. Richly ornamented marriage contract. The bridegroom was Abraham, son of Jacob Munion, the bride Juditta, daughter of Daniel Valensin. Jerusalem, Jewish National and University Library, Ketubbot Collection 118.

dramatic performance based on the story of Judith and Holophernes. It formed part of the wedding celebrations of Giovanni Sforza and Maddalena Gonzaga. The bride was the sister of Marquess Francesco Gonzaga, ruler of Mantua. There, in the 16th century, developed the main center of Jewish histrionic activity in Renaissance Italy.

The record starts in the 1520s with a performance conducted by two Jewish actors on the occasion of Marquess Federico's accession celebrations. A few years later the Jewish community presented an original play, written by its members. Unfortunately no further details have survived. From then on to the middle of the 17th century a regular theatrical company (though consisting chiefly of amateurs) was maintained, manned, equipped, and managed by the Jewish community of Mantua. Most performances were carried out for the benefit of the dukes and their court, especially during carnival-tide, or on other festive occasions,

though the Jewish company was summoned for a performance whenever the Mantuan ruler's whim commanded. Some performances became rather popular, and enjoyed frequent repetitions. The first mention of the staging of a contemporary drama by the Mantuan company occurs in 1563 (there may have been earlier unrecorded instances), when the play put on was Lodovico Ariosto's *I Suppositi*, in honor of a visit by the Austrian archdukes, Rudolph and Ernest.

Other plays performed by the Jewish actors included *Gli Ingiusti Sdegni* by Bernardino Pino da Cagli; several dramas by Leone de' Sommi Portaleone; *Delli Intreghi de Amor* by Torquato Tasso; and many others, some known only by their titles. The Mantuan company's heyday occurred in the reign of Duke Vincenzo I, at the turn of the 16th century. There took place some magnificent presentations, sometimes more in the nature of a pageant than of a regular theater performance. Tasso's play was

Wedding rings, Italy, sixteenth century. Wedding rings used only for the ceremony. On two of the rings the initials M.T., standing for *Maazal Tov* (Good Luck), are engraved. Another is adorned with the text of the marriage benediction. Paris, Musée de Cluny, Strauss-Rothschild Collection, Inv. No. 12280; Pforzheim, Schmuckmuseum, 2009/405, 416, 413.

presented in 1606 by a body of sixty-odd men, as was the comedy put on in the preceding year. The company then numbered among its members a rabbi, several prominent and rich members of the Jewish community, one or two professional actors, a professional musician, a singer, and a dancer. Performances continued right up to the war of the Mantuan Succession and the 'Sack of Mantua' in 1630. The revival of the Jewish theater's activities after the war is something of a marvel, considering that the Renaissance had long since come to an end, and the ghetto regime had become universal in Italy. For about five years (1644-9) the Jews of Mantua continued to put on performances.

The central figure of Jewish dramatic activity in Italy is Leone ben Isaac de' Sommi. He belonged to a branch of the Portaleone

Cofranetto, Ferrara, second half of fifteenth century. Housewife's casket for jewels and keys. The three main duties of a Jewish wife are shown: the symbolic separation of the dough, taking the ritual bath, and the lighting of the Sabbath candles Silver, partly gilt, and niello work. Jerusalem, Israel Museum. Photo Kneller, Jerusalem.

family of physicians and scholars, and was born in 1526, probably in Mantua. Leone was a poet, playwright, impresario, actor, and author of *Dialogues* on scenic production. He was a prolific writer, though unfortunately most of his literary output was lost in the great fire of 1904, when the Turin Library and most of its contents were destroyed. Formerly there were at that library sixteen manuscript volumes, containing the major part of Leone's Italian works. They included four volumes of poetry, ten of plays, and two of prose. Copies of some plays, a few poems, and the *Dialogues* are extant, as are his scattered Hebrew compositions.

Leone de' Sommi wrote twelve Italian plays, a prologue and intermezzi to da Cagli's play, and a Hebrew drama. Most of his plays were put on the stage at the courts of Mantua and Turin. His Hebrew play *Zahut Bedihuta de Kiddushin* (A Fine Comedy of Betrothal) was performed on the Mantuan stage. It consists of five acts, and deals with the complications arising out of irregular practices of engagements and marriage contracts, prevalent among contemporary Italian Jewry. Leone's most important effort in the matter of dramatic art is his *Dialoghi in materia di rappresentazioni sceniche,* or *Trattato sull'arte rappresentativa* (Dialogues, or Treatise on the Theater). It has been judged 'perhaps the most memorable contribution by a professing Jew to general literature in the age of the Renaissance, after Judah Abrabanel's *Dialogues of Love.*' It consists of four dialogues, and deals with stagecraft in all its aspects, and is the first treatise of its kind ever produced, as well as a valuable source on contemporary scenic production. Side by side with important information and sound advice on theatrical ways and means, the author, in the fashion of his age, introduces much incidental and superfluous matter. Thus he traces the origins of the theater to Moses, for being (according to tradition) the author of the Book of Job—that being the earliest example of a colloquy. The dialogues deal with the origin of comedies and other types of plays; the division of the comedy into five acts; the proper ways of recital, dress, and acting; and the setting of the stage.

Leone de' Sommi's histrionic activities enjoyed considerable popularity among contemporary Jews and Christians. His plays were applauded, and his talents as an impresario were in great demand. The dukes of Mantua and of Savoy vied with each other for his services. His particular patron was Cesare Gonzaga, Lord of Guastalla, who formed in 1562 the Mantuan Academy 'degli Invaghiti' (The Charmed). This was one of many academies founded in Italy at that time. Some were especially interested in classical learning, others in drama and poetry. Many obtained special privileges, and conferred the title of knight on their members. Those of the Mantuan academy were granted it by Pope Pius V in 1566. Cesare Gonzaga was a great enthusiast of dramatic art and the theater. He therefore proposed Leone de' Sommi's membership, but other members objected, especially the writer Bernardino Marliani. The Jewish playwright had to be content with an appointment as '*scrittore*', or the academy's official playwright. After all, the badge which the academy's knights wore incorporated the papal arms!

Though he undoubtedly was the greatest, de' Sommi was by no means the only Jewish Italian playwright. There are the (largely anonymous) plays produced by Jewish actors in Mantua

and elsewhere, which centered chiefly on the Purim story. Leone da Modena wrote a pastoral comedy *Rachel and Jacob*. He edited another pastoral play by his friend Angelo Alatrini. Benedetto Luzzatto, Modena's pupil, wrote and published in 1631 a pastoral fable, *l'Amor possente* (Powerful Love), dedicated to a member of the ducal house of Modena. Joseph Sarfatti (Giuseppe Gallo) the physician, scholar and poet, composed a Hebrew adaptation of the Spanish comedy *Celestina*. The ghetto period did not entirely suppress Jewish interest in plays and their presentation, though it tended to revert to the religious theme of pre-Renaissance days.

Dancing and music were closely linked to the theater, and music too had its origins in the ritual. Only fragments of medieval Jewish synagogue music have survived. An example is a leaf of neumes, ascribed to Obadiah, the Norman proselyte of the 12th century. Obadiah was a native of Oppido in southern Italy, who embraced Judaism and migrated to the East. There being no Jewish musical notation available, he employed the Lombardic system he had learned in his native Italy, and which was used by the Church at that time.

Secular music came into its own during the Renaissance, and was no longer limited to medieval ballads and the like. Dancing and music soon became part of the education accorded the children of the Christian and Jewish upper class in Italy. Jewish masters were to be found in these arts not only in the households of their coreligionists; in fact, many of the music and dancing teachers of the Italian aristocracy were Jews. The first known case is of the beginning of the 15th century, when the Lord of Pesaro employed Musetto the Jew as dancing master for his children. From then

on there is a steady flow of information in evidence of an increasing Jewish activity in this realm.

From the 15th century on Jewish musicians, chiefly instrumentalists and vocalists who often were composers at the same time, became increasingly famous in Italy. One of these was a lute-player of German origin, who came to Florence and was converted to Christianity. His patron was Giovanni de' Medici, later Pope Leo X, and he was named after him Giovanni Maria. Strangely enough the convert continued to be known by his nickname 'Jew'. When he had been elected pope, his patron conferred on him the revenues of a small town and the title of count. Later Giovanni Maria became the Venetian doge's fife-player. Eventually he went to Mantua, and then returned to papal service in Rome. His compositions became famous in Italy and abroad, including Germany and England.

As with the theater Mantua became the main center of Jewish musical activity. Abramo dell'Arpa ('of the harp') and his nephew Abramino were especially esteemed at the court of the Gonzaga. Abraham's fame spread abroad, and for a while he acted as music teacher to the children of Emperor Ferdinand I in Vienna. Abramino entertained the dying Duke Guglielmo, and cheered his last hours with music. Isacchino Massarano was a versatile musician in the service of the Gonzaga. He composed music, sang, played the lute, was an expert on choreography, and taught music and dancing. He was on intimate terms with Duke Vincenzo I, before and after his accession. When the Jewish community undertook to stage *Gli Ingiusti Sdegni,* Massarano provided the dances. He did the same for a number of other plays, including Guarini's *Pastor Fido.*

The greatest Jewish composer in Renaissance Italy was Solomon ben Azariah de' Rossi, probably born in Mantua in the second half of the 16th century. He became known at first as a viol-player and as a singer. He too entered the service of the Gonzaga—together with his sister, also a singer. Later he conducted a company of musicians, which gave concerts at Mantua and elsewhere. De' Rossi's chief claim to fame is as a composer of original music, though in addition he and his brother Menahem were members of the Jewish community's theatrical company. De' Rossi was a contemporary of Monteverdi, who also served the Mantuan court. In 1608, at the celebrations of the wedding of Francesco Gonzaga to the Infanta Margherita of Savoy, Monteverdi's *L'Arianna* was performed for the first time and Battista Guarini's *L'Idropica* was also put on. Monteverdi and de' Rossi collaborated in the composition of the music for the intermezzi of the play. The spectacle was one of the most magnificent ever presented at the resplendent court of the Gonzaga. De' Rossi's sister took part in it. She sang in Monteverdi's opera and took the role of Europa in Guarini's play. This part brought her the sobriquet 'Madame Europa', by which she became known.

De' Rossi's major musical compositions were his five collections of madrigals, two of *madrigaletti,* and four of '*sinfonie e gagliardi*'. The former were vocal and the latter instrumental music. His volumes went through repeated editions which were dedicated to various members of the ducal house of the Gonzaga, the duke of Modena, and various other princes. In addition to this, de' Rossi

קדוש

יום הַשִּׁשִּׁי נַיְכֻלּוּ הַשָּׁמַיִם וְהָאָרֶץ וְכָל צְבָאָם: וַיְכַל אֱלֹהִים בַּיּוֹם הַשְּׁבִיעִי מְלַאכְתּוֹ אֲשֶׁר עָשָׂה וַיִּשְׁבֹּת בַּיּוֹם הַשְּׁבִיעִי מִכָּל מְלַאכְתּוֹ אֲשֶׁר עָשָׂה: וַיְבָרֶךְ אֱלֹהִים אֶת יוֹם הַשְּׁבִיעִי וַיְקַדֵּשׁ אֹתוֹ כִּי בוֹ שָׁבַת מִכָּל מְלַאכְתּוֹ אֲשֶׁר בָּרָא אֱלֹהִים לַעֲשׂוֹת: סַבְרִי מָרָנָן: בָּרוּךְ אַתָּה יְיָ אֱלֹהֵינוּ מֶלֶךְ הָעוֹלָם בּוֹרֵא פְּרִי הַגָּפֶן: בָּרוּךְ אַתָּה יְיָ אֱלֹהֵינוּ מֶלֶךְ הָעוֹלָם אֲשֶׁר בָּחַר בָּנוּ מִכָּל עָם וְרוֹמְמָנוּ מִכָּל לָשׁוֹן וְקִדְּשָׁנוּ בְּמִצְוֹתָיו וַתִּתֶּן לָנוּ יְיָ אֱלֹהֵינוּ בְּאַהֲבָה (שַׁבָּתוֹת לִמְנוּחָה וּ) מוֹעֲדִים לְשִׂמְחָה חַגִּים וּזְמַנִּים לְשָׂשׂוֹן אֶת יוֹם (הַשַּׁבָּת הַזֶּה וְאֶת יוֹם) חַג הַמַּצּוֹת הַזֶּה וּזְמַן חֵרוּתֵנוּ בְּאַהֲבָה מִקְרָא קֹדֶשׁ זֵכֶר לִיצִיאַת מִצְרָיִם כִּי בָנוּ בָחַרְתָּ וְאוֹתָנוּ קִדַּשְׁתָּ מִכָּל הָעַמִּים (וְשַׁבָּתוֹת) וּמוֹעֲדֵי קָדְשֶׁךָ (בְּאַהֲבָה וּבְרָצוֹן) בְּשִׂמְחָה וּבְשָׂשׂוֹן הִנְחַלְתָּנוּ בָּרוּךְ אַתָּה יְיָ מְקַדֵּשׁ (הַשַּׁבָּת וְ) יִשְׂרָאֵל וְהַזְּמַנִּים: בָּרוּךְ אַתָּה יְיָ אֱלֹהֵינוּ מֶלֶךְ הָעוֹלָם בּוֹרֵא מְאוֹרֵי הָאֵשׁ: בָּרוּךְ אַתָּה יְיָ אֱלֹהֵינוּ מֶלֶךְ הָעוֹלָם שֶׁהֶחֱיָנוּ וְקִיְּמָנוּ וְהִגִּיעָנוּ לַזְּמַן הַזֶּה:

קַדֵּשׁ . וּרְחַץ . כַּרְפַּס . יַחַץ . מַגִּיד .
רָחְצָה . מוֹצִיא מַצָּה . מָרוֹר .
כּוֹרֵךְ . שֻׁלְחָן עוֹרֵךְ . צָפוּן .
בָּרֵךְ . הַלֵּל . נִרְצָה .

Majolica plate, Padua, 1673. Majolica plate in use in the *Seder* (Passover) service, showing the various objects and scenes from the Passover ceremonial. The center of the plate is inscribed with the text for the benediction over the wine *(Kiddush)*. Diameter: 16½". Jerusalem, Israel Museum.

Preceding page:

Page from the Rothschild Miscellany, Northern Italy (Ferrara?), 1470. This very richly illuminated manuscript contains over fifty religious and secular books, copied in both main and border texts, with some 300 text illustrations to the various books. Jerusalem, Israel Museum, Ms 180/51.

Jewish-Italian wedding, Mantua, fifteenth century. Jewish-Italian wedding showing (a) bride and bridegroom (b) wedding ceremony with the bridal cou[ple] under the traditional canopy as the bridegroom puts a ring on the brid[e's] finger. The officiating rabbi is depicted in the middle. The clothes worn a[re] typical of those of the upper class in the fifteenth century. From Jacob b[en] Asher's Legal Code, copied in 1435 by Isaac ben Obadiah in Mantua. Vatic[an] Library, Codex Rossiana 555.

Treatise on dancing by Guglielmo da Pesaro, c. 1463. Guglielmo da Pesaro, Jewish dancing master of the Renaissance and two of his pupils with the lute player in the background. The illustration is taken from his *Trattato dell'arte del ballo* (Treatise on the Art of Ballet). The miniature portrays the dancers with their fingers interlocked, performing a *bassa danza*, the 'Queen of Measures'. Bibliothèque Nationale, Paris, Fonds Ital. 973.0.

Facing page:

Moses, tapestry by Chagall. Part of the tapestry triptych by Marc Chagall (1887-) in the main hall of the Knesset (Israel's parliament), Jerusalem. Chagall left Russia in 1922 and settled in Paris but his work nevertheless has drawn much inspiration from scenes of life among the East European Hasidim and village communities near his native Vitebsk. Photo Harris, Jerusalem.

Rimmonim ornaments, Venice, eighteenth century. *Rimmonim* literally means 'pomegranates', and was the name given originally by the Sephardim, and now most Jews, to the finials, the ornaments on the Scroll of the Law. They were formerly shaped like pomegranates, though later took on the form of towers. Amsterdam, Portuguees Israelietische Gemeente.

Torah crown and finials, Italy, eighteenth century. This particular arrangement whereby the crown was combined with the finials to decorate the Scroll was often used in Italy. Silver. Height: 15½". Goldsmith's mark: Rodvigo. Jerusalem, Israel Museum.

was the 'father' of modern Jewish music. His contribution to synagogal music, the first ever to be published, is entitled: 'The Songs that are Solomon's, hymns, songs, and praises, created according to the science of playing and music, for three, four, five, six, seven and eight voices, by Master Solomon de' Rossi, of the Mantuan Jewish community, to thank the Lord and to sing hymns to His Mighty Name in all manner of holiness, (that being) a new thing on earth.' The volume was seen through the Venetian press by the author's friend Leone da Modena. The latter wrote an introduction in which he defended the practice of using music in synagogal services against those who objected to it. *The Songs that are Solomon's* consists of thirty-seven compositions, all of which are said to have been performed in the synagogues of Mantua and elsewhere. They are Renaissance music, without a trace of the traditional Oriental elements of synagogal music.

'Madame Europa's' sons and grandsons continued the musical tradition of the family. Her son Mordecai (Angelo) and his two sons Joseph (Giuseppe) and Azariah (Bonaiuto) entered the service of the dukes of Savoy. They taught music and dancing at court, composed ballets, and played the lute and the guitar.

The outstanding Jewish contribution to the dance in the Italian Renaissance is Guglielmo da Pesaro's *Trattato dell'arte del ballo* (Treatise on the Art of Dancing). He was a pupil of Domenico da Piacenza, the inventor of the *balletto* (the precursor of the modern ballet). Guglielmo apparently was in touch with the court of the Medici in Florence. In his treatise he included two dances composed by the youthful Lorenzo the Magnificent. Guglielmo was responsible for the famous show organized at the Pesaro wedding of Costanzo Sforza to Camilla d'Aragona (1475). The entire spectacle was organized by Guglielmo and enacted by the Jews of Pesaro. Later he became dancing master to the children of the heir to the Neapolitan throne. He was last heard of as dancing master at the court of Ferrara.

These are some details of the artistic activities of Italian Jews in the Renaissance which were not limited to a few individuals, but enjoyed widespread popularity. There is a long list of Jewish artists, of musicians, dancers, actors, and so forth. Leone da Modena founded a musical academy in the Venetian ghetto, which called itself in the fashion of the age *L'Accademia degli Imperiti* (Academy of the Unskilled). Among its members were composers,

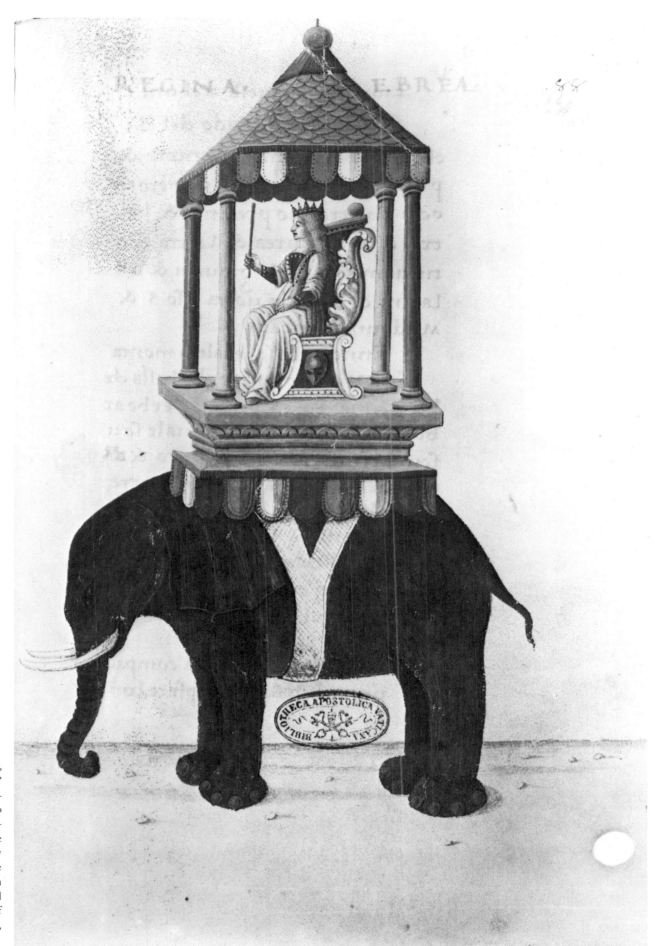

'Jewish Queen' at pageant, Pesaro, 1475. 'Jewish Queen' (Queen of Sheba) at the wedding pageant of Costanzo Sforza with Camilla d'Aragona at Pesaro in 1475. The pageant was organized by Guglielmo da Pesaro. The queen rode on a wooden elephant, sitting on a gold throne under a canopy of silver. Vatican Library, Codex Urbino Lat 899.

vocalists and instrumentalists, and it exchanged the usual courtesies with sister academies in the Christian quarters of Venice. Though artistic activities rather diminished in the Italian ghetto of the 17th and 18th century, they did not cease altogether. Recently much information has come to light, showing that the musical tradition never really died out among Italian Jews.

JEWISH LIFE IN ITALY

The Jews of Italy, except during the Roman era, were numerically among the smaller European Jewries. Their contribution to Jewish culture and civilization, and to those of their environment, was sometimes much larger than was justified by their numbers. This was particularly true during the Renaissance, which was the heyday of Italian Jewry, especially in the center and the north. For a while, during the 15th and 16th centuries, Italian Jewry became the melting pot of Jewish culture from all parts of Europe. Furthermore, nowhere else, before modern times, did the Jews of the European Diaspora assimilate so much of the spirit of their surroundings, and participate so actively in the life of their non-Jewish neighbors. This is even more noteworthy in view of the comparatively limited impact this participation in general life had on their Jewish loyalties. Of course there was the odd convert to Christianity among the physicians, scientists, artists, and others of the Renaissance, but the majority remained faithful to Judaism. They studied simultaneously rabbinical lore and the writings of classical antiquity, and taught the Bible and dancing, Hebrew grammar and Italian poetry, all in complete harmony. Many incidents illustrate the extent to which this was achieved in daily life.

It has been pointed out that personal relations between Jews and Gentiles 'were more intimate in the Renaissance period than was ever again to be the case in any land in Europe until the 19th century.' These cordial relations extended to the nobility and some of the outstanding rulers of the time: the Medici, Sforza, Gonzaga, Este and many other famous Italian names, including even in some instances the pope and other prelates of the Roman Catholic Church.

Symbolical, as it were, in this context, was the carrying of arms by Jews, and the skill they attained in their use. In most European countries Jews were not permitted to do this and it was one of the indications of their status. There are several examples of Jews taking part in fighting in Renaissance Italy, as during the siege of Siena in 1552. Some recently published documents indicate that Jews were engaged in raising troops for the armies of the condottieri.

Italian Jews of the Renaissance assumed many of the habits and pastimes of their Christian neighbors. Gambling was rampant everywhere in Italy. Ecclesiastical, city, and Jewish communal

◄ *Jewish wedding,* Italy, eighteenth century. Wedding showing the bridal couple under wedding canopy. One man is holding the *Ketubbah* and another holding the winecup with the wine to be drunk under the canopy. Copper engraving. Jerusalem, Israel Museum.

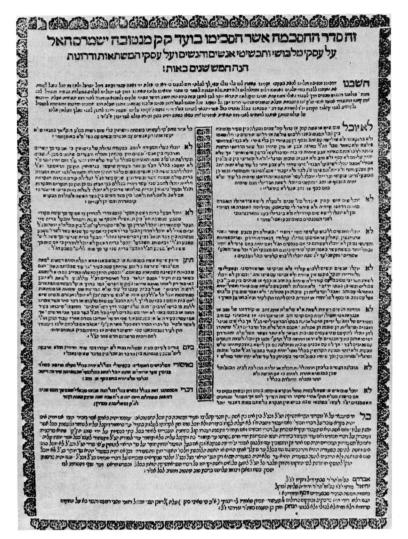

Pragmatica, Mantua, 1650 Sumptuary laws published periodically by the Jewish community to restrict the use and display of articles of luxury. The regulations became common in the Middle Ages when any ostentatious display of luxury would draw hostility from the surrounding Gentile communities.

authorities exerted themselves in suppressing, or at least limiting the vice—but to no avail. Mention has been made of Leone da Modena, who was a typical 'victim' of the gaming passion. Modena, who had attacked card-playing and dicing in his youthful treatise yet continued to do so all his life, challenged a prohibition of the Venetian Jewish community against it, and advanced talmudic arguments in support of his contention. He similarly opposed another prohibition, directed against tennis-playing on the Sabbath. This had been the subject of much learned controversy among Italian rabbis. Young Christians and Jews played the game with zest. In the learned responsum of R. Moses Provenzali there is a detailed description of the sport as practiced at the time. Naturally, there was betting involved, and the owner of the court was entitled to a percentage of the winnings.

Other not-so-Jewish pastimes practiced by Italian Jews included hunting. Some of the affluent bankers of Florence actively engaged in the sport. Bonaventura da Volterra sent his friend Lorenzo the Magnificent a buck and two fawns he had hunted. A band of Florentine Jews on vacation in the country whiled away

Playing cards, Venice, mid-eighteenth century. A deck of thirty-two playing cards in silver filigree box. The cards are painted in laquer colors on silver sheets. Amsterdam, Rijksmuseum, on permanent loan to Joods Historisch Museum.

their time by drawing up a Hebrew document parodying certain procedures of the law court in their native city. In it they mention some of their friends who were out setting traps 'for they spend all their time laying snares for kites and ravens'.

The education of Jewish youth in Italy included (as we have seen) several subjects not normally found in the curriculum of medieval Jewry. Italian Jews studied medicine and philosophy at university level, and on occasions—though rarely—were among the teachers of the 'studio'. Eventually the need was felt for a Jewish university. Even in Italy the universities received Jewish students only reluctantly. In the middle of the 15th century the Jewish communities of Sicily determined to found a Jewish university on the island. King John of Aragon and Sicily granted the communities authority to establish a 'studium generale', though unfortunately nothing is known of the functioning of the university. The same is true of another attempt a century later. R. David Provenzali of Mantua proposed the establishment of a Jewish 'studium' in Mantua and circulated a prospectus among the Jewish communities of Italy (1566). It is thought that the university did, in fact, function for a little while, though not for long.

This sometimes incongruous mixture of piety and licentiousness, learning and superstition, assimilation and loyalty to Judaism, is a characteristic of Italian Jewry in its heyday. It has been described with some justification as a unique phenomenon of a successful synthesis of culture and civilization rarely achieved elsewhere. Jewish scientists and philosophers, physicians and artists, translators and poets, were simultaneously Hebrew scholars or even officiating rabbis in their communities. At the same time the Jews of Italy made a profound and lasting impression on the learning and art of their environment.

EPILOGUE

A marked economic and cultural decline of Italian Jewry took place during the ghetto period. In due course there was a complete break with the spirit of the Renaissance, though the process took much longer than was warranted by circumstances. The new age of enlightenment and emancipation dawned during the second half of the 18th century. The ghetto age proper lasted for about two centuries, and came to an end—with a few exceptions—with the French Revolution.

Yet even in the physically and spiritually cramped quarters of the Italian ghetto, the muses were not completely silenced. A description of Jewish occupations in an Italian ghetto of the 18th century includes eight medical practitioners and fifteen musicians. The author of the publication containing the list was Benedetto Frizzi, a spirited defender of the Jewish viewpoint in the controversy over the granting of civil rights to Jews. The polemic engendered by the spread of revolutionary ideas and enlightenment produced modern anti-Semitic literature and its counterpart of Jewish apology. Frizzi's *Difesa* (Defense) was his reply to the political economist Giambattista Gherardo d'Arco, who had attacked the Jews in his *On the Influence of the Ghetto in*

Title page of Jewish communal tax ordinance, Mantua, 1722-3. Prepared by the ► Jewish authorities, the tax ordinance was circulated among the members of the community. A block sum was imposed by the town authorities on the communities who then apportioned it out individually. In Italy in the 17th to 18th centuries, communal dues were exacted by a tax on capital, known as *Capella,* the assessment being made by every individual under oath in the synagogues. All essential services for the community were paid for with this tax, as well as amounts due to the government as the price of toleration.

זה הספר לס'
נולקיס ינחוט

זה סדר
ההערכה
והתכהנה אשר שמו לשעבר מע' הנבחרים
מהק"ק במנטובה י'צו לפני כל חיים ולחים
למען על פיו ישקו ויתכהנו · ועתה
מחדש בני הועד הכללי יע"ו איר' ליום
כ'ר'ט חשון הת"פ פן אסרוהו ויקיימוהו
וקבלו עליהם פל פרט ופרט מפרטיו עם
איזה תיקון שנתחדם בו בעד ג' שנים
שתחילנ' בחדם כרצו תפ"נ ויתשלמנה לכל
חדם פיברארו תפ"ו הע"ל:

נדפס פה מנטובה
בבית השותפים כמ"ר יצחק נכמ"ר דוד
ירא וכמ"ר יעקב חבר טוב יצ"ו
ע"י העוסק נמלאכת בקדם נציר המדפיסים
יהושע נכ"ר מיכאל מסיצי יצ"ו
con licenza de Superiori

the State. The argument as such was not entirely new in Italy. As early as 1639, Simone Luzzatto of Venice, a friend and younger contemporary of Leone da Modena, published his *Discorso circa il stato de gl'Hebrei* (Discourse on the State of the Jews). In it the author examined the social and political conditions of the Jews in a non-Jewish environment, with special reference to Venice. Luzzatto has been described as an anticipator of the nineteenth-century learned publicist.

The Luzzattos became one of the most prominent Italian Jewish families in modern times. Moses Hayyim Luzzato is an important figure in Jewish literature. His Hebrew poetry is considered a major link between the medieval tradition and that of today. Luzzatto was born in 1707 at Padua, son of a rich silk merchant. Like many of his contemporaries he became a votary of the Kabbalah. In 1727 he created a secret circle for the study of mystical lore, and started writing esoteric compositions. These activities caused Luzzatto to be suspected of Sabbataianism (the secret remnants of the greatest Jewish messianic movement which had come into being in the 1660s). The adherents of the messianic sect were hunted down everywhere, and had to go underground. Now and then secret cells of Sabbataians were discovered, and were subjected to veritable witch hunts. Luzzatto's circle was rightly or wrongly suspected of Sabbataianism. The Venetian rabbinate compelled Luzzatto to hand over his mystical writings, and to foreswear similar activities in the future. From then on Luzzatto fought a losing battle with the Jewish communal authorities in Italy and elsewhere. In the end he died in Palestine, a young man, in 1746. Luzzatto was a sensitive poet who put new life into Hebrew-Italian poetry, which had become rather mechanical. Luzzatto was influenced by the general literary tendencies of his age and in his allegorical dramas, he modeled himself on Battista Guarini. He is regarded as a founder of the school of modern Hebrew poetry.

The third outstanding member of the family was Samuel David Luzzatto (1800-65). A native of Trieste, he became the outstanding exponent of modern Jewish-Italian culture. He was essentially self-taught, and became a scholar of considerable renown. He was heir to the tradition of Italian-Jewish scholarship, and at the same time became associated with the Jewish intellectual revival of Central Europe, the so-called 'Science of Judaism'. His range of interests has been described as dazzling. He rediscovered many important medieval texts, and published some of them in modern editions, such as the poetry of Judah Ha-Levi. Luzzatto prepared new Italian editions of the Bible and the Jewish prayer-book. He broke new ground in Hebrew philological research, Hebrew grammar and biblical exegesis. In addition he wrote on a large variety of Jewish subjects, historical, literary, liturgical, bibliographical, and so forth. Last but not least he was a prolific poet in his own right. Luzzatto was the commanding figure at the center of Jewish studies in nineteenth-century Italy, the Colleggio Rabbinico of Padua.

Notwithstanding the efforts of Luzzatto and of his friends, the impact of the Emancipation upon the internal life of Italian Jewry in many respects was destructive. Attempts at revival made at the turn of the 20th century produced only limited and short-lived results. Intermarriage and emigration took an increasing toll of the Italian-Jewish community, and the process of disintegration was tragically speeded up by the persecutions of World War II.

CHAPTER IV

Germany

by Dr. Hermann Goldschmidt

The first Jews to settle in Germany came in the time of the Romans, possibly before the beginning of the Christian era, and certainly centuries before Christianity reached the country. In 321 A.D., when Christianity was beginning to be the official religion of the state, Constantine the Great issued a decree canceling the privileges which the Jews in Cologne were at that time enjoying; until then they had been accepted and respected as fellow citizens. German Jewry really began to flourish at the time of Charlemagne. Toward the end of the 8th and at the beginning of the 9th century, Jews were enjoying full equality and taking an active part in public life; their number was growing rapidly, possibly because there were many conversions to Judaism. This close relationship between the Jews and Germans continued for three centuries of the Middle Ages and was of benefit to both communities, resulting in a Golden Age which ended in 1096 with the beginning of the First Crusade. This heralded the process of disintegration which gathered momentum throughout the Middle Ages and found its victims also among other peoples and other cultures; before long it led to the persecution of the Jews, which has continued ever since, relentlessly, century after century.

The Jews were never expelled from the whole of Germany, though for a quite extraneous reason: Germany was not yet united. There was always another '*Land*'—sometimes only a few

Interior of the synagogue at Worms (before its destruction in 1938). Completed in 1175, the synagogue was built in Romanesque style. Destroyed on *Kristallnacht*, 1938, it was rebuilt in 1959, incorporating the remains of the original synagogue. Attached to this synagogue stood the famous Rashi chapel, associated with the great medieval French scholar. Worms, Municipal Archives.

miles away—which was willing to offer them a home. Neverthe-less, many thousands died as martyrs, refusing to save themselves through baptism, even when this was offered to them under torture or on the stake. Tens of thousands were driven eastward, carrying their native civilization with them. Far fewer survived the persecution on German soil. Maintaining their ancient con-nection with the country, their character was determined by the relationship.

But even in those early days no profound fusion was pos-sible, if only because at that time intellectual communication took place not in German but in Latin. The Jews made the German language their own, but their thinking did not become part of German culture in spite of the fact that Albertus Magnus, Thomas Aquinas, and Meister Eckhart recognized the greatness of the Jewish philosopher Maimonides. 'Rabbi Moses' was of importance only to the Latin-speaking German intellectuals, who either did not know or did not care that there was also a Jewish minnesinger (minstrel), Süskind von Trimberg, who flourished in about 1215. According to one of his manuscript poems which has survived, he resigned from his court post when he found himself discriminated against because he was a Jew, and was not rewarded as he should have been.

In about the year 1000 there was in Mainz a seminary for talmudic studies led by R. Gershom ben Judah, who was called 'the Light of the Diaspora' (see chapter on France). For German Jewry, this seminary was of the utmost importance—it was the beginning of a vital chapter in its history, although scant mention is made of it in German annals. Until that time, Babylonian scholars had been the spiritual leaders of all Jewry; now European Jews took their place.

During the Middle Ages, the life of German-speaking Jewry reached its climax in 'German Hasidism'. Its two leaders were Samuel the Hasid (pietist) (c. 1115-80), who fled before the Cru-saders from Mainz and settled in Speyer, and his son Judah the Hasid (1150-1217), who was later active in Regensburg. This Hasidism stressed the intensity of religious feeling, as expressed in the Psalms, with a particular emphasis on moral behavior. The teachings of the movement are recorded in the *Sepher Hasidim* (the Book of the Pious). Judah the Hasid and St. Francis of Assisi were contemporaries though they did not know of each other; Meister Eckhart also lived at that time and wrote his *German Mysticism* without suspecting that a related Jewish mysticism had preceded him on his own German soil. The German Jews distinguished themselves by their great spiritual achievements, and they were also willing to suffer for them. This set them apart from both the French Jews of that time, who disappeared, and from the Spanish Jews, whose communities were driven into exile or, faced with the choice between death and baptism, chose apostasy in their hundreds of thousands.

In his *World History of the Jewish People*, Simon Dubnow describes the singularity of German Jewry in this way: 'When it was the fate of the Jews to become martyrs and outlaws, they defied all difficulties and knew how to withstand the heaviest pressure. They took over the national leadership from the French, sharing it with Spanish Jewry... They showed an unlimited power

Colophon, 1293. Colophon of a manuscript containing the Pentateuch, the Five Scrolls, and the sections of the Prophetical Books recited in the synagogue. The colophon consists of micrographic writing made up of biblical texts. A parchment script, it gives the name of the scribe as Solomon Hacohen and the date of its completion as 1298. Paris, Bibliothèque Nationale.

of passive resistance. Even the most terrible massacres did not result in any general apostasy from Judaism: the victims remained firm, the martyrs died bravely, without considering for one moment the possibility of saving themselves through sham baptism. In quieter times German Jews humbly accepted the state of being outlaws; they allowed themselves to be hurt but not broken...'

The Jews who left Germany during the late Middle Ages remained so passionately and so effectively faithful to their

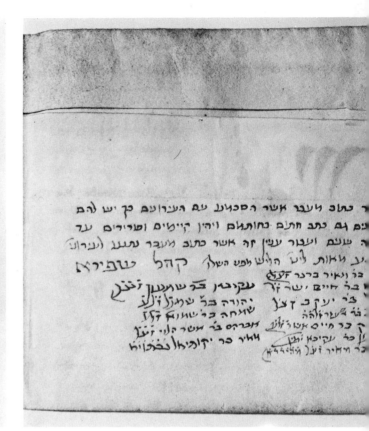

Left: *Charter of privileges*, Speyer, 1333. Document laying down the privileges of the Jewish Council of Speyer. It states that 'Judges, Council and citizens of Speyer make a contract with the Jews of Speyer', according to which the Jews' Council and the Jews' 'bishop' will be elected by the Jews without interference from the City Council. The Jewish Council will have twelve members and any of them who are members for ten years will have life tenure. The town puts its sexton at the disposal of the Jews to help them collect any fines above three pounds which they might impose, but the town receives a half of such money collected. It is dated 1333. Speyer, Municipal Archives, 1U 247.

Right: *Charter of privileges*, Speyer, 1333. Reverse of the same document as in the lefthand illustration, containing a confirmation in Hebrew with the signatures of the twelve Jewish Council members. Speyer, Municipal Archives, 1U 247.

language, that medieval German is alive to this day in Yiddish, with which the Jews excluded themselves from the language of their new surroundings. In the 18th century, most of the Jews spoke Yiddish. Those who, like Moses Mendelssohn, made the change to the new High German, were, however, able to join the mainstream of the culture; indeed, they were able to become an integral part of it at a time when Germany was making great intellectual progress. This explains the extraordinary position the Jews were to hold in the German-speaking regions, similar to that which they once maintained for several centuries in different countries in the Arab world. The lives of the Jews in Central Europe improved rapidly within a few decades; the Golden Age of German Jewry coincided with Germany's classical period; the two movements influenced, strengthened, and enhanced each other.

TOWARD EMANCIPATION

The Jews strove to free themselves from the limitations of the ghetto, that relic of the medieval feudal system which the rest of the population had already overcome, but which still kept the

Jews isolated from their surroundings. The term 'German Jew' is used here in the widest sense, including all the German-speaking Jews and ignoring the not inconsiderable differences between the groups of German, Austrian, and Czech nationals. German Jewry could at this time be broadly classified into three groups: the Court Jews and others enjoying patronage, Jewish peasants, and East European Jews.

As an instance of this class structure, the case of Moses Mendelssohn is very instructive. Mendelssohn went to Berlin at the age of fourteen in October 1743; exhausted and hungry, he had to go round half of Berlin in order to reach the single gate through which Jews were at that time permitted to enter, after being taxed like cattle. Yet at this time, there was in Berlin already a class of educated Jews whose lives were unrestricted and who were in contact with the leading intellectuals of the town.

Several hundred of the Jewish families who fled from Spain settled in Germany; they never sank to the level of the ghetto. For two or three centuries there were also in Germany and Austria a group of 'Court Jews' who flourished, especially during the eight decades between the end of the Thirty Years' War and the time of Mendelssohn's birth. They were appointed

וזאמרן נעש השבעת קידושין כידו וראה אותה אם הוא טוב טרוש
ויראה אותה עד אולעי עמשין ישאל אותה אם הוא טוב שלא שלום
שתהא קנין כסו ואחר חזירא להחתן והחתן נשכ לה
נאלבע השב הטוכ ואנקל ניר יתן ואמשרשבתי ועל
ועל עבים ישחרו אלאו שראו שהקרש אותה כראוי
והאמרך אחר אל החתן התנבת הלל והחתן שוב אחריו כל התינטא
אלה נאלה אלכ לי שאחר החתן מאליו ·

הֲרֵי אַתְּ מְקוּדֶשֶׁת · לִי · בְּטַבַּעְתָּזוּ
כְּדַת · מֹשֶׁה · וְיִשְׂרָאֵל ·

ואומרין לחזון אול טוב בקהל רב
והאמכך על הכתובה בידו וקורא אותה בקול רם בפני הקהל עם ב עבים
אחריש · ופתך והא ארכתוב יקח ספר הכתב ויקרא כאונ העב
שאו כב יראל כאותה שטו כתה אהומר
והשו עבים קבל קם מהחתן והלה על הכתוב ועל השחורת העגלים
בעגם
ואחר כל זאת · על האמכך מין שלב רחיים כאוחים שמחו לי ואמכך
שאו שמב בכרות הלל

כספר מצו
אימן ונכתה כה אן הארץ שנו ויכטו את רצפה · אימעי ארכתי ויכך
אותאם עלי · ונטביב ווש ב אוטם את הלות כך קורין אהל שגא כיעיתאו
נו סיך אמיך שאלאבן שעושה על לה סאון אהכתה שלן כונה הירכה
אם הלוב לשם וכמתה אודם ונחשה לי לחתונא עד שלמך שלחבני
אמעא אלה כלבה שהקלובן אורתה ·

Liturgical book, Germany, 1590. Parchment manuscript, containing prayers, and hymns for Sabbaths, *Hanukkah,* Purim, weddings and circumcisions. There are many illustrations in color depicting religious ceremonies, this one showing a marriage ceremony under the traditional canopy. Nuremberg, Germanisches Nationalmuseum, Hs. 7058.

Wedding rings: (a) Left. Gold, Germany, seventeenth century. A broad band with an engraved relief of flowers and leaves. On top is a tent built on fourteen pillars. On the top are engraved the words '*Maazal Tov*' (Good Luck). Inside the ring is the blessing recited by the mother of the house on lighting the candles at the commencement of the Sabbath. (b) Center. Silver with gilt, Germany, sixteenth century. On the band is a relief showing Adam and Eve in the Garden of Eden. Also under the tree is the serpent along with a deer, a lion, a unicorn, a goat, a horse, an ox and a camel. Inside the words '*Maazal Tov*' are engraved. (c) Right. Silver, Germany, sixteenth to seventeenth centuries. Band with silver plate shaped as an open book bearing the traditional formula 'The voice of the bridegroom, the voice of the bride' in Hebrew. Pforzheim, Schmuckmuseum 2009/420/421/419.

symbiosis, Adolf Leschnitzer charts the course of development. The first part covers roughly 1690 to 1812, the second 1812 to 1933, with turning points in 1754 and 1871. The first period of one hundred and twenty years saw the rise of several hundred families, who were the forerunners of Mendelssohn; during the second period all the German Jews—who numbered then about two hundred thousand—became citizens and were able to develop freely both intellectually and economically. The turning point of the first period came half-way, in 1754, and promised well: this was when the friendship between Lessing and Mendelssohn began. The turning point of the second period also came half-way, in 1871, and boded ill: this was when death began to threaten the Jews. Three times during this second one hundred and twenty years German nationalism reached a peak, and three times it turned into an anti-Semitic movement. After 1812, France lost her ascendency, and the new wave of nationalism which at arose at that moment discovered that it had in the Jews ready victims, completely at its mercy. Fanned by the recent victory over France, this exacerbated nationalism led in the first two decades after 1871 to the first outburst of real anti-Semitism. In the decade after 1933 it led to what Leschnitzer describes as 'the ghastly fifth act of a historic drama which, like a classical tragedy, ended in a catastrophe'.

to the royal courts, and encouraged to settle in Germany's main towns 'to promote general trade', as it says in a decree issued by the grand Elector of Brandenburg and Prussia in 1671. Like the Huguenots, Jews were welcomed—if they were well-to-do or capable—in the regions devastated by long and terrible wars, and the restrictions imposed upon the Jews languishing in the ghettos did not generally apply to them. They were to provide loans, supervise the currency and taxation, build factories, introduce industries, provision the armies, and encourage the economy.

Apart from these Jews living in the towns, there was a strongly rooted Jewish peasantry, which had been settled on the land for centuries, and there were also the so-called East European Jews, descendants of the German Jews of the Middle Ages. During Mendelssohn's lifetime, in fact, many of these 'East European' Jews became either Germans or Austrians when Poland was divided for the first time. Both Frederick the Great, king of Prussia, and Maria Theresa, empress of Austria, thoroughly disliked Jews, but a great many of them became their subjects when they and Catherine the Great carved up Poland among themselves in 1772. The one took Posen and the other Galicia, with their medieval Jewish settlements. There had been Jewish settlements on German soil without a break for many centuries; their enormous potentialities had again and again been suppressed. They were encouraged to contribute to Germany's development at the very moment when not only that country but the whole of Europe was being carried toward tremendous achievements. When Mendelssohn entered the modern era, he was not alone. He had forerunners, companions and a large following.

In his book *Saul and David* (1954), about the German-Jewish

Passover plate, Nuremberg, seventeenth century. Plate for the Passover *(Seder)* service. Silver. The insets depict biblical scenes and personalities (including Moses, Aaron, David and Solomon). The lower inset shows the rabbis (related in the Passover service) who stayed up all night in Bene Berak relating stories about the Exodus from Egypt. The words on the inside of the plate give the order of the Passover service. Amsterdam, Joods Historisch Museum, Inv. 222.

Two external events and a double achievement mark the late 18th century as the start of the modern age, for Jewry as for the world at large. The external events were, first, the independence gained by the United States of America through their victory over England. This translated into reality the declaration of their independence in 1776, which stated that all men are created equal, entitled to equal rights, including the right to live, the right to freedom, and the right to the pursuit of happiness. Secondly, in 1791, the French National Assembly in Paris, after much deliberation, accorded the right of citizenship to all French Jews, a right also accorded to the Jews of all the countries conquered by France during the following years.

The double achievement was the German translation of the Hebrew Bible, published in 1783 by Moses Mendelssohn as the climax of his endeavors, and his essay *Jerusalem; Concerning Judaism and Religion,* which was also a declaration of independence. In this essay he demanded not only the abolition of the restrictions imposed upon the Jews, but also that the freedom which he asked for them should be regarded as part of the general freedom of conscience. Humanism was the burning concern of the moment; it was not to bypass the Jews. It was repeatedly emphasized that the demand made by the Jews and made by others for them was of immediate concern and of general importance: as a criterion of the times and of progress, it stood in the forefront of the fight for freedom by everyone, for everyone.

Mendelssohn spoke as a representative of the Jews; he was the first 'conscious Jew' of modern times. He rejected the ghetto in favor of the general culture of his times, but also remained faithful to the medieval Jewish community. Having achieved recognition as a German writer and philosopher, he was entreated

Circumcision knife and case, Germany, 1677. Mother-of-pearl with semi-precious stones. The inscription gives the date and the name of the owner. The knife has a blade sharpened on both sides. The wooden box is decorated with incised flowers, the date and name of owner. Jerusalem, Israel Museum, No. 112/53.

◄ *Page from a miscellany,* Bingen, 1649. Manuscript containing rules for the calendar (illustrated by drawings of scenes related to the equinoxes and the solstices), a list of dates of fairs, and a kabbalistic work about the candelabrum and about Psalm 67. Berlin, Stiftung Preußischer Kulturbesitz, Staatsbibliothek, Inv. Ms. or. oct. 3150, fol. 78r.

Havdalah lamp, Germany, late seventeenth century. Light for *Havdalah* (end of Sabbath service) incorporating a box for spices (which are inhaled in the course of that service). Silver. At the foot stands a Jew with a *kiddush* cup and a spice box in his hands. At his head is a box with a drawer for the spices. Above, a gallery with ornamental dolphins and heads. At the side four movable parts into which the *Havdalah* candle was placed. The inscription on the sides gives the name of the owner. Tel-Aviv, Stieglitz Collection, No. 255.

Torah breastplate, Frankfurt, c. 1700. Silver, partly gilt. In the center, a holder in which was inserted the name of the relevant festival. On either side it is flanked by cherubs and other angels. Paris, Musée de Cluny, Strauss-Rothschild Collection, Inv. 12295.

by Johann Caspar Lavater to become a convert to Christianity. This startled him; suddenly he realized that if he did not want to become completely assimilated but wished to continue to live as a Jew in the Christian West, he would have to encourage all the other Jews to keep pace with him—and Mendelssohn chose to remain a Jew. In 1769, at the age of forty, he was a prize-winner of the Berlin Academy, a contributor to the *Library of Belles Lettres,* and to the *Letters on Contemporary Literature;* he

was a famous and celebrated author; from then on, he devoted himself exclusively to the Jewish cause, to what he called 'his nation'. Only after the Middle Ages had ended for all the Jews could Judaism itself enter the modern era; only then would the individual Jew be able to remain Jewish in the context of the new age.

And he succeeded! Certainly, it was only the beginning of a development which two centuries after Mendelssohn's 'return to Judaism' has still not reached its conclusion; but it was Mendelssohn, and he alone, who initiated this development among the Jews of the German-speaking regions. As a philosopher, he lacked Spinoza's powers of perception, and he was not as inspired in his religion as Baal Shem Tov; nevertheless, his philosophy was definitely an entirely new departure, so that all later Jewish opinions were in some way influenced by it: this applies not only to liberal but also to Orthodox Judaism, not only to the Jews who considered themselves citizens all over the world but also to the Zionists who advocated a Jewish state; it applied to Jewish scholarship and to the revival of the Hebrew language. After Mendelssohn, a retreat from progress was no longer possible.

With Mendelssohn, the Jews entered the modern era. He did not see the modern Jews as simply replacing the Jews of the Middle Ages, and when he demanded emancipation, he pleaded for them not as Jews but as human beings. He did not ask for the emancipation of their Judaism, which seemed to him to be their purely personal concern, to be preserved but not to be brought up to date. His enemies showed a clear discernment when they followed their excommunication of Spinoza and of the disciples of the Baal Shem with a proscription of Mendelssohn's writings. Every step toward Emancipation would help to outdistance the Middle Ages and thus change the image of Judaism. Mendelssohn made the distinction between the universal teachings of Judaism which were absolutely consistent with the new insights of the Age of Enlightenment, and between the divinely revealed legislation touching all aspects of the individual Jew's life. To make the distinction of accepting the Jew as an equal in public life but considering him as different at home could not be reconciled with a total view of life and was contradictory to the spirit of Judaism which concerns the whole of existence. When Judaism began to establish itself as a contemporary force, it was obliged to relinquish, sooner or later, its medieval principles, no matter how carefully and with what reservations it approached its own progress. Even those Jews who believed that they were remaining faithful to every essential aspect of medieval Judaism helped to hasten its decline by every small compromise with modern times.

Most sincerely, Mendelssohn maintained that he recognized the duties imposed by the Jewish view of life, which had always been valid and should remain so; yet when the official guardians of tradition proscribed his writings he was undeterred—as no medieval Jew would have been. Ignoring the ban, he completed his German translation of the Bible. The publication of *Jerusalem* in 1783 had brought him to the notice of the world; now he had also escaped from the ghetto of the mind.

141

The struggle for Emancipation continued, in spite of serious setbacks, in spite of periods of apparent stagnation, gradually drawing the Jewish communities into contemporary life; at the same time, endeavors were made to emancipate Judaism itself. Assimilation was rightly feared and was inevitable if the new era refused to accept Jews as equals and denied them the right to live openly and entirely as Jews. Anti-Semitism also played a role; the madness and the crimes of anti-Semitism again and again emphasized the uselessness of every attempt at assimilation, and made it more urgent that Jews should be accepted as equal though different.

'Traustein', Bingen, 1700. Red sandstone. The *'Traustein'* was the stone against which a glass was broken in the course of the wedding ceremony. It was formerly in the south wall of the Bingen synagogue. It is inscribed: 'The voice of mirth and the voice of gladness, the voice of the bridegroom and of the bride' (Jer. 7:34). On the bottom half of the stone is the biblical verse: 'This is the gate of the Lord: the righteous may enter into it.' Weddings were held in the open in front of this stone until 1832. Jerusalem, Israel Museum 199/22.

RELIGIOUS TRENDS

The first Jewish aspect to achieve some measure of equality was its religion, both in its Orthodox and in its liberal manifestations: Orthodox Judaism testifies to the constant values unaffected by the passage of time, while the liberal attitude bears testimony through being renewed by every new age. Orthodoxy derives from the core of Jewish teachings, which is untouched by history; in face of changes it demands constancy. Liberalism demands a constant keeping in step with the times.

The liberal form of the Jewish religion has been in existence since 1810 when Israel Jacobson built a new synagogue in Seesen

Mezuzah, Germany, seventeenth to eighteenth centuries. The *Mezuzah* is to be affixed to the doorpost. Of carved wood, it is in the shape of a tabernacle resting on four pillars. Through the window the parchment is visible showing the word *Shaddai* (Almighty); on the inside are selected verses from the Pentateuch. At the top is a small cupola crowned by birds' heads. Paris, Musée de Cluny, Inv. 12318.

Page from Darmstadt Haggadah, early fifteenth century. German *Haggadah*, so called because it belongs to a Darmstadt library. The illuminated *Haggadah* is one of the most characteristic forms of medieval Jewish art and this is one of the outstanding examples. It was written, and probably also illuminated, by Israel ben Meir of Heidelberg. Darmstadt, Hessische Landes- und Hochschulbibliothek, Inv. Cod. or. 8.

Portable Art of the Law, Vienna, early eighteenth century. The three crowns at the top represent the 'crown of the law', the 'crown of royalty' and the 'crown of priesthood' mentioned in the Mishnah (Avot 4:17). Paris, Musee de Cluny, Strauss-Rothschild Collection. Inv. 12239.

Facing page:

Torah Crown, Vienna, mid-eighteenth century. Silver and gilt. Biblical scenes are depicted, including the Binding of Isaac, Aaron and the High Priest, Jacob's Dream, David playing the Harp, Moses with the Tables of the Law, and others. Paris, Kugel Collection.

Torah covering, South Germany, eighteenth century. Right and left are depicted Jacob's Dream and in the center the Binding of Isaac. Basle, Judisches Museum der Schweiz, 72.

with an organ, held Confirmation services, and continued his earlier reforms. In 1818, a Reform Temple was established in Hamburg, modeled after a Berlin prototype and indicating the growth of a progressive Judaism; the Orthodox reacted by opposing all such developments. This conflict brought into the arena men who represented, together and in opposition to each other, every conceivable religious movement, from the extreme left to the extreme right. On the extreme right stood Samson Raphael Hirsch (1808-88). In order to keep the observances pure, he advocated an exclusive Orthodoxy, holding itself aloof from the rest of Jewry. Nearer the center stood R. Seligmann Baer Bamberger of Würzburg (1807-78), who advocated a comprehensive congregation, provided this did not interfere with his own strict Orthodoxy. On the extreme left stood Samuel Holdheim (1806-60), who believed in a break with tradition and an adaptation to the present, thus introducing Reform Judaism. The most important pioneer of liberal Judaism—which was initiated by several people—was Abraham Geiger (1810-74), who stood a little left of the center, and strove to combine the present with the past. He was one of the originators of modern Jewish scholarship, to whom the past was a source of energy to shape the present, and who saw this revival as a guarantee of the future. Compared with these men, the center looked rather dull but was nevertheless influential. Zacharias Frankel (1801-75), the father of conservative Judaism, rejected any unauthorized modification of traditional observances, but also believed that they were bound to be affected by the changing times.

Thus, religion gained a victory but paid too great a price in assimilation: the right, the left, and the center always treated it as 'a confession', that is, as 'a creed', referring only to a part of life. As a creed, it remained marginal and did not affect the much more comprehensive attention devoted to the countless other duties of everyday life in the countries where the Jews had made their homes. The creed was and remained the private and personal concern of each individual. The historical covenant which united Jewry was forgotten, or rather would have been forgotten, if the first step, the emancipation of religion, had not been followed by the second, the creation of Jewish scholarship. Finally, the third step followed, adding nationhood, in the light of the modern conception of history.

Jewish Scholarship

Judaism is a religion. Judaism is also scholarship—in Hegel's sense, a recognition of its contemporary meaning. This includes historical studies, concerned with a comprehensive representation of Jewish history which must lead to a total view of the history of mankind; it includes the history of philosophy, embracing all of man's spiritual development; the history of mysticism; the tremendously influential body of poetry and of art generally; it also includes philology, inasmuch as the cultures of other languages have been inherited and preserved by Judaism. It must

Curtain for the Ark of the Law, Rhineland, early eighteenth century. On either side, a Baroque column wound round with vines. On the capitals, amphorae with flowers. The lions at the top hold the miter of the High Priest. From the old synagogue in Cologne-Deutz. Cologne, Stadtmuseum.

also include a basic study of the development from antiquity to the Middle Ages and it must take in a consideration of the foundations of the modern era; it must look to the future, and consider history in the light of the biblical prophecies. To these and other aspects of scholarship, Jewish thought and learning has much to contribute.

Already in 1818, at the time of Hegel's arrival in Berlin, the conflict centered round the synagogue from which the liberal movement grew, with the ensuing Orthodox reaction. In that year, Leopold Zunz published his epoch-making lecture *Concerning Rabbinical Literature*. This work could well have broadened the influence of Jewish thought on the modern era, had external circumstances permitted the development of the latent Jewish forces. Together with Eduard Gans, Isaac Marcus Jost, Joel List, Moses Moser and others, Zunz helped found 'The Association for the Culture and Science of the Jews' in Berlin in 1818;

148

Hanukkah lamp, Frankfurt, early eighteenth century. The figure on the top is Judith holding the head of Holofernes. The arms of the candlestick reproduce the 'buttons and flowers' of the design of the original candelabrum in the tabernacle. On top of them are figures representing animals, hunters, and warriors. The base is held by four heraldic lions. Paris, Musée de Cluny, Strauss-Rothschild Collection, Inv. 12241.

Heinrich Heine became a member of it in 1822. This marked the beginning of the 'Science of Judaism'. But their *Journal for the Science of Judaism* appeared for less than two years (1822-3); the association was dissolved in 1824, and in 1825 its president, Eduard Gans, underwent baptism to be allowed to continue as Hegel's collaborator, that is, to become a professor. He was not the first member of the association to turn apostate; almost half a year previously, Heinrich Heine had taken the same step to collect an 'entrance ticket to European culture' as he called the certificate of baptism. Nevertheless, Jewish scholarship itself also

received its 'entrance ticket' during the 19th century; with each passing decade it became more and more apparent that Judaism had exerted an enormous influence upon the world of antiquity and the Middle Ages, and also made a considerable contribution to the supremacy of the Western world. The path which led to European culture and every important aspect of modern times did not bypass or lead away from Judaism, but led through Judaism to the future. Almost all the best of the 'emancipated' Jews of the 19th and early 20th centuries realized this too late, and only much later, there followed the logical step of establishing chairs for the study of Judaism at the universities—and Jewish scholarship remains neglected in the German-speaking regions to this day.

GABRIEL RIESSER

In 1783 Mendelssohn opened the way to Emancipation for German Jewry, after they had been settled in the region for nearly two thousand years. In 1943, the police closed the last offices of the *Reichsvereinigung* of the Jews in Germany, which marked the effective end of their settlement there. Gabriel Riesser died in Hamburg in 1863, at fifty-seven, eighty years after the first event and eighty years before the second. At the time of his death, Jewish Emancipation was such an accomplished fact that his contemporaries showed little interest in his life's work, though he had been a leading pioneer. Riesser was the first Jew to be made a judge in Germany; the appointment came in 1860, to the court in Hamburg, his birthplace, the town where at the beginning of his life he had been excluded from holding any office at all, and suffered much discrimination. Emancipation had come, certainly, and—thanks to Riesser, who remained a Jew—it was now being taken for granted.

Riesser did not think of his endeavors as a campaign on behalf of the Jews, nor did he intend that it should benefit Jews only, so that it was all too soon forgotten that it had in fact been a Jewish campaign. Riesser saw his struggle as a general one for the sake of right and freedom itself; it was a good Jewish attitude, with which he strove to benefit his country and humanity as a whole. In 1848 he became a member of the Frankfurt Council, and later a member of the German National Assembly, which held its meetings in the church of St. Paul; one of its best orators, he finally became its vice-president. He helped to shape the German constitution, which was completed seventy years later by another German Jew, Hugo Preuss. He was among the thirty-three delegates who invited the king of Prussia to become emperor of Germany on April 3 1849. He belongs not only

See illustration page 145.

Torah binders, Germany, 1737. Embroidered linen. These *Torahwimpel* or binders were presented to the synagogue when a boy made his first visit with his father. The scenes depicted express the wish that 'he should grow to happy manhood and enter under the marriage canopy'. The binders were 'donated by the child Jokel, son of the community president Aaron Katz'. Decorations include signs of the zodiac, the High Priest Aaron, and a wedding scene. Jerusalem, Israel Museum, Inv. 150/54.

Page from a Haggadah, Darmstadt, 1734. Parchment page from the manuscript of Passover service. The Hebrew text is accompanied by directions in Judeo-German. Amsterdam, Joods Historisch Museum, Inv. 22.

Torah covering, Germany, 1749. Velvet with gold embroidery. Made for the synagogue in Biebricht; the inscription relates that it was donated to the synagogue by the 'Eternal Light Association'. Jerusalem, Israel Museum, 151/16.

to the history of German Jewry but to German history; his great achievement assures him of a place also in modern Jewish history.

Every Jew today enjoys a privilege for which he has to thank Riesser's courage, without knowing it. The Jews of France are called not 'Jews' but 'Israélites'; Switzerland's communities are called 'Israelitic' congregations, 'Israelitic' associations; Riesser called his first publication, the daring manifesto of a young man of twenty-four, *The Position of the Adherents of the Mosaic Faith in Germany.* From the late Middle Ages, 'Jews' was a loaded

word. People generally regarded it almost exclusively as an insult, and it is frequently still used as such even today; the Jews were sensitive to it, and as modern citizens, they wished to be rid of the shame and dishonor which had been part of their Jewishness in the ghetto. In 1832 Riesser published the first issue of his newssheet concerned with religion and freedom of conscience and called it *The Jew*. Because Riesser had the courage to use this word, in spite of its undertones of hatred and contempt, the civic emancipation of the German Jews remained publicly related to their four-thousand-year-old heritage, placing the Judaism of modern times beside that of Antiquity and the Middle Ages. 'Our name is associated with an unjust hatred; ought we therefore to deny it, instead of doing our utmost to make it honorable? It is a historic name...'

The new era concerned not only the Jews who were at that moment alive but the history of the Jewish people; the burden of the past could not have been shed without sacrificing a profound heritage, which might at that moment have seemed expendable but which was essential for future survival. The positive aspects of history can only be fostered, as Riesser said, 'by tending the wounds caused by hatred'.

Eighty-four years later Martin Buber also called his publication *The Jew*, and rightly commented that Riesser had meant the individual Jew, for whose civic emancipation he was striving.

Circumcision bowl, Augsburg, eighteenth century. The bowl was used to collect the blood caused by the circumcision operation. Cologne, Stadtmuseum, 1928/385.

'Our paper is called by the same name, to designate not the individual but the representative of our people and its mission. We do not demand freedom of conscience for the adherents of a religious faith, but freedom to live and to work for a suppressed people. Today, the majority are treated as helpless victims of events; they must become masters of their own fate and have freedom of action, so that they may mature to fulfill their obligation toward humanity.' This expansion of the meaning of the term 'Jew', advocated in 1916 by the pioneer of the 'national emancipation' of the Jewish people, together with

Circumcision bowl, eighteenth century. Wood. The bowl is in the form of a milk ladle with a handle on which is incised the Hebrew for 'foreskin'. The holder was filled with sand, a candle put in and the foreskin burned (though this was an unusual custom). Basle, Jüdisches Museum der Schweiz, Inv. 35.

further interpretations added later, was not yet thought of by the champion of 'individual emancipation'; it would never have been possible to suggest them had it not been for Gabriel Riesser—and the twofold legacy of Theodor Herzl.

Theodor Herzl

Viewed superficially, Herzl's short life falls into one final decade, apart from the thirty-four years from his birth in 1860 until 1895 when, as the Paris correspondent of the Viennese *Neue Freie Presse,* he witnessed the degradation of Captain Dreyfus and the frenzy of a crowd seized with anti-Semitism, and felt a sudden call. When the public, watching the degradation of Captain Dreyfus, shouted: 'Down with the Jews!', Herzl finally realized that the Jewish problem was a political one, regardless of the religious and spiritual foundations of Judaism. 'Modern anti-Semitism is not a simple repetition of the persecution to which Jews have been exposed in the past. Only the ignorant could believe this.' In modern times, Judaism meant the Jewish people; therefore the problem was one of statesmanship and political power, it was 'a political problem concerning the whole world which the civilized nations will have to settle in council', for which the single solution, according to Herzl, was the Jewish State.

As a man speaking in the name of the Jewish people, he was taken seriously—more seriously than he could have hoped or expected. He negotiated with the sultan, spoke to the pope, greeted the German emperor at the gates of Jerusalem; traveling as a politician in Russia, he was received by the Russian statesman, Von Plehve. He went to England and won the support of the leading Jews and, what was more important, of the leading statesmen there. England could not at this time offer Palestine, which was still ruled by the Turks; Herzl was offered part of the Sinai peninsula, and a tract in Uganda (now in Kenya). At the time when Herzl was writing *The Jewish State,* he would have welcomed any South American country as an opportunity to establish Jewish sovereignty; later Palestine gained importance in his eyes; in the midst of his everyday political activities he enthusiastically described its future in the novel *Altneuland* (Old-New Land). He saw the offer of the tract in Uganda as a decisive step forward in the direction of the 'Promised Land'; this was considered a betrayal by the masses—especially in Eastern Europe—whom he had aroused and who passionately longed for the messianic 'Land of Israel'. Herzl had barely time to justify himself before he died. He introduced Jews to politics, that is, to the means of manipulating history, a test of maturity which every modern nation is obliged to pass. The struggle for civic emancipation during the 19th century had brought about a revival of Jewish religion and culture; now the

See illustration page 146.

demand by the Jews to be emancipated as a people called for practical changes. They demanded equality in the world community of peoples, as citizens of the Jewish state or any other state; Jews have been loyal citizens since their first exile, when Jeremiah commanded them to be loyal: 'Seek the peace of the city whither I have caused you to be carried away captives, and pray unto the Lord for it: for in the peace thereof shall ye have peace' (Jer. 29:7), while the rabbis crystallized this as 'the law of the state is the Law (of the Jews)'.

There was one revolutionary new factor, which would, for good or evil, in future be decisive in world politics: modern technology. What had been a dream for two thousand years had become practical politics, argued Herzl, 'because we have machines'. He noted in his diary that electricity had been invented 'so that the Jewish problem might be solved in its light'. 'Politics and technology, or rather, politics thanks to technology, the modern relationship between technology on the one hand and the political emancipation of the Jews on the other' is one of Herzl's legacies; in keeping with the most revolutionary beliefs of the 19th century, this intellectual people has been obliged to become practical.

His second legacy is the man himself. During the last decade of his life, Herzl sacrificed his fortune and that of his parents, the happiness of his family and his own life to his tremendous vocation. He was hated and despised and suffered ridicule. He bore a huge responsibility: by attracting the world's attention to the Jews he endangered their safety, yet it was in order to save them from far greater dangers, which he was the first to predict—once he had realized the relationship between modern politics and technology. He remained completely unselfish and was patient in leadership, asking nothing in return except a little confidence. It was a Jewish attitude, similar to that of the prophets of antiquity, of the teachers and martyrs during the Middle Ages. The man must be remembered not only by the Zionists and their descendants, the citizens of Israel, but by all Jews everywhere as one of themselves. Herzl deserves, too, to be remembered by the whole of mankind, because through working for his own people he worked for the peace, the freedom and the happiness of all. The following anecdote reads almost like a parable: during the preparations that were made for the First Zionist Congress in Basle, a newspaper was founded, which the majority wished to call *Homeward*; Herzl rejected this initially in favor of *Homeward to Humanity*, which carries biblical undertones of Zion and the profound meaning of the Jewish expectation of the Messiah. However the name he chose, and which was finally adopted, was *The World*.

THE JEWISH RENAISSANCE

The external achievement of modern Emancipation, the recognition of equality which the Jews gained as human beings, as citizens, as a people, was bound to be followed by a spiritual development. What has been called, since about 1900, 'the Jewish renaissance' by its pioneers and its teachers, was brought about largely by German-speaking Jewry; there were also drawbacks but no one can deny it this achievement.

In the spring of 1901 Leo Baeck published his comments on Harnack's *Lectures on the Essence of Christianity*, which he followed with *The Essence of Judaism* (1905), a statement on Judaism which

Left: *Spicebox*, Hamburg, mid-eighteenth-century. Silver. On two sides are clockfaces which can be adjusted to note the time of the end of the Sabbath. On the four corners, four synagogue officials are depicted; one is holding a *kiddush* cup, another the unleavened bread, the third a candle and the fourth a knocker used for arousing worshipers for early morning service. The tower is modeled after that of St. Nicholai's church in Hamburg (which was burned down in 1842). Hamburg, Museum für Hamburgische Geschichte, 1911/412.
Right: *Spicebox*, Austro-Hungary, eighteenth century. Silver filigree. The decorations include six musicians, a clock for setting the hour of the end of Sabbath and a weathervane in the shape of a lion. Amsterdam, Joods Historish Museum.

invited comparison with Harnack's *Essence of Christianity* (although without a mention of Harnack in the text). Harnack at the time was the leading scholar and theologian at Berlin University and the Prussian Academy. Leo Baeck was at that time twenty-eight years old and completely unknown. He was not content with defending himself, nor with refuting the arguments of the other, but visualized a future in which 'the essence of Christianity' might be included in 'the essence of Judaism'. He argued that when Christianity arose 'the pagans were ready to begin to accept the teachings of Judaism'. Chapters 49 and 56 of Isaiah indicate that Jews also were once active as missionaries;

Havdalah plate, Regensburg, mid-eighteenth century. Pewter. The Hebrew inscription, taken from that service, reads: 'I will lift the cup of salvation and call upon the name of the Lord'. (Ps. 116:13). In the center is the inscribed the beginning of the *Havdalah* service: 'Behold, God is my salvation'. Jerusalem, Sir Isaac and Lady Edith Wolfson Museum, Hechal Shlomo, Inv. 90/6.

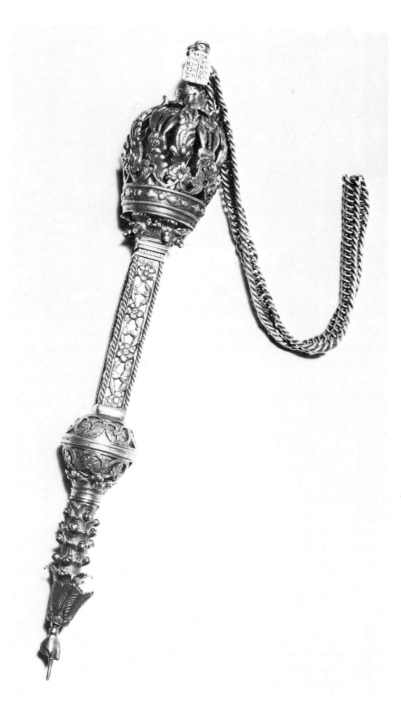

as exiles in Babylonia they were commanded to convert others and obeyed—until five hundred years after the beginning of the Christian era every twelfth 'Roman' was a Jew. With its belief in salvation, Christianity carried the idea much further; in consequence, the Jews suffered persecution and oppression. But a belief in the existence of the covenant from the revelation on Mount Sinai need not prevent a Jew from also believing in the revelations of Christianity. It was not this possibility, but the rejection of it that was a denial of faith. 'No mother hates her child, but the child often forgets and denies its mother.'

The two leading Jewish thinkers of the Middle Ages, Judah Ha-Levi and Moses Maimonides, both concluded that it was possible to accept all the revelations of related religions; following them, Baeck, with his image of a mother and her children, prepared the way for an acceptance of all the religions which derive from Judaism: Christianity, Islam, socialism. This affirmation was also a part of the essence of Judaism. A younger German Jew, Franz Rosenzweig, in his *Stern der Erlösung* (Star of Redemption) of 1921, maintained that only two of the revealed religions, Judaism and Christianity—and they alone—enhanced and supplemented each other; it might be said that they 'shared the work of salvation'. Rosenzweig went further than Baeck, granting the Christian 'daughter' equality with the Jewish 'mother', renaming them 'sisters' because—in the modern era—they were both children of the same past. This revolution began with *The Essence of Judaism,* in which Baeck maintained that

154

Book binding, Austria, eighteenth century. When a boy reached his religious majority *(Bar Mitzvah)* at the age of thirteen, it was customary to give him as a gift a special—and sometimes very elegant—prayer-book. Jerusalem, Sir Isaac and Lady Edith Wolfson Museum, Hechal Shlomo, Inv. No. 943-18-7.

Christianity and Judaism did not exclude each other but could and would have to exist the one with the other.

In 1915—ten years after Leo Baeck's *The Essence of Judaism*—Hermann Cohen published his *Concept of Religion in the System of Philosophy*. It came as a surprise to those who knew him. Cohen, already seventy-three years old, was the leader of the 'School of Marburg'; until then he had regarded religion as a primitive form of philosophy which he had attempted to make redundant in his *Philosophical System*. Although he still questioned its independence, he admitted that it had 'a special quality'; it should not demand that reason make concessions to it, but its special quality should make it acceptable to reason. The discussion taking place here was not unlike that between Baeck and Harnack, but this time it was held between a man's philosophy and his sense of religion. Until his death four years later in 1918, Cohen devoted himself to his *Religion of Reason Drawn from the Sources of Judaism,* and here the discussion ended in his conclusion that the future belonged to both. Cohen was first and foremost a philosopher, so that many of the 'School of Marburg' saw in his *Religion of Reason* a confirmation of their teacher's endeavor to achieve a 'pure consciousness'. Others, and especially Franz Rosenzweig,

saw in the *Religion of Reason* evidence of a fundamental change, in which the philosophy survives because of the religion. Just as Christianity is not harmed but strengthened through the vitality of Judaism from which it derives, just as a Jew is not a worse but a better citizen when he demands the emancipation also of his religion, so in the same way, a man is a better philosopher when he does not ignore the best part of himself while striving for a philosophy.

The new philosophy which took Judaism as its source was no longer merely a philosophy of religion, as it was practiced by Solomon Ludwig Steinheim, Solomon Formstecher, and Samuel Hirsch toward the middle of the 19th century, though their attempt to do justice both to philosophy and to Judaism was original and deserves respect. Steinheim wrote *Revelation According to the Doctrine of the Synagogue*; Formstecher published *The Religion of the Spirit* (based upon Schelling); and Hirsch followed Hegel in his *The Religious Philosophy of the Jews*. The same path was still being followed by Moritz Lazarus in 1900, and later by the extraordinary Oscar Goldberg, and later still by Hans-Joachim Schoeps, and by Julius Guttmann, whose *Philosophies of Judaism* was published in 1933. Again and again, religion is acknowledged

155

rather than understood; it could not be understood within the limitations of the 'philosophy of religion'. Although this did not ignore religion, it did not take it sufficiently into account.

There were others whose thinking was certainly influenced by their Jewish origins, but whose work was of interest to the world generally—from Moses Mendelssohn and Solomon Maimon or Moses Hess to Martin Buber, Jacob Klatzkin, Hugo Bergmann and Max Brod. Also doubtless conditioned by their Jewish heritage and frequently its spokesmen, whether they were aware of it or not, were others: Karl Marx and Ferdinand Lassalle, as well as Sigmund Freud, Edmund Husserl, Walther Rathenau, Gustav Landauer, Alfred Adler, Theodor Lessing,

Ernst Cassirer, Otto Weininger, Georg Lukasz, Ludwig Wittgenstein, Herbert Marcuse. There were some important mathematicians who were also philosophers: Carl Gustav Jacobi, for instance, as well as Georg Cantor, Hermann Minkowski and Albert Einstein.

THE ARTS

There was also a renaissance of modern Jewish art, both in the sense of a regeneration of the past as well as of independent achievements. Gustav Karpeles, for instance, in his *History of Jewish Literature* traces the relationship between modern Jewish

Scroll of Esther, Alsace, eighteenth century. Parchment. The scenes purporting to depict the Scroll of Esther in fact convey a vivid picture of Jewish merrymaking in eighteenth-century Germany. Jerusalem, Israel Museum, Inv. 2390-12-52.

Torah breastplate, Germany, 1763. Silver with gilt. The hands at the top are giving the priestly blessing. The inscription names the donors and gives the date the work was completed. Jerusalem, Israel Museum, Inv. 148/21.

wrote this about Kafka, whom he hardly knew, though they were roughly the same age and spiritually very close to each other: 'The men who wrote the Bible must have thought of God the way Kafka does. I have never read any book which reminded me so strongly of the Bible as his novel *The Castle*.'

Poetry is rare and significant, one of the supreme human achievements. Several women poets distinguished themselves. Beside Else Lasker-Schüler there were Margaret Susman, Gertrud Kolmar, and Nelly Sachs. They stand alongside the tragic figure of Paul Celan, perhaps the greatest of the post-Holocaust poets, whose *Fugue of Death* is a final requiem to the death camp victims. That German Jewry was overtaken by catastrophe must not obscure the fact that it proved itself extremely creative. Mombert and Kafka, whose subjects were least 'Jewish'—whose work does not 'show' that they were Jews—became increasingly aware of their Jewishness, as their posthumous papers have made

Circumcision hanging, Germany, 1772. Silk with silver thread. This cloth was hung on the wall during the circumcision ceremony, and reproduces the blessing said at the ceremony. It also gives the names of the donors. Jerusalem, Israel Museum, 152/98.

writings and the ancient tradition of the biblical and above all the talmudic Aggadah, the 'instructive stories' of antiquity and the Middle Ages. He draws a comparison between this and the relationship of Jewish scholarship to the Halahkah, the religious legislation. 'The Halahkah and the Aggadah are poetry and have their origins in the Bible. ...and once more the lovely Aggadah comes into its own.' Karpeles was right to rejoice. Heinrich Heine, Else Lasker-Schüler, Karl Wolfskehl, Alfred Mombert, and Franz Kafka—these are only some of the most important names in the vast literature produced by German-speaking Jewry. Their contribution to the spiritual development of Judaism has been enormous. In a letter dated May 25 1927, Franz Rosenzweig

Hanukkah lamp, Frankfurt, mid-eighteenth century. Silver. Rectangular box with eight oil lamps supported by four standing lions. At the right, a peasant with curved sickle. At the back, a *menorah* in a medallion and above, a crown held by lions. Nancy, Musée historique lorrain, Inv. 1140.

apparent: the influence of their origins increased as they grew in stature as writers.

There was a vast number of gifted Jewish men and women who wrote in German or distinguished themselves otherwise, as musicians for instance. Such were Gustav Mahler and Arnold Schönberg, who were preceded by Felix Mendelssohn-Bartholdy, Giacomo Meyerbeer, Jacques Offenbach, to mention only the most important ones. The *Philo-Lexikon* of 1937 lists the names of three hundred Jewish writers in the German language who were born in the 19th century; there is also a long list— including Moses Ephraim Kuh and Heine—of those belonging to an earlier period. The list continues into the 20th century and includes an increasing number of representatives of the other arts.

The artists struggled as artists. The Jewish artists struggled also as Jews. They were not granted the same opportunities as others and were expected again and again to prove their equality as human beings and their right to call themselves citizens of the country in which they were born—as if the country and its language had not belonged to them for many centuries through countless generations. There was another factor which decisively affected the German Jews, indeed all the Jews in the German-speaking regions: Jewish artists were never accepted without a certain reserve, if only because of the circumstances. Lessing's intimate friendship with Mendelssohn remained unique; none of the great men who came after him had the necessary spiritual

stature. Certainly, there was the memorable friendship between Karl Marx and Friedrich Engels, but both of them were German expatriates; it should not be forgotten, either, that Marx was a victim of Jewish self-hatred. There was also the friendship between Stefan George and Karl Wolfskehl, which was of benefit to their work and brought them a great deal of happiness; confronted with the need to make a choice, George chose to safeguard his writings and deserted his friend.

Rimmonim, Nuremberg, late eighteenth century. The design is of an eight-cornered, two storey tower. Cologne, Stadtmuseum, Inv. RM 1929/1224 a & b.

German Jewry became fully emancipated at a time when Germany was thriving culturally, but its creative powers were already waning or turning from the arts to other fields, so that Jewish creativity gave the impression of being a separate phe-nomenon, in spite of the fact that it was closely related to the genius of the German language and to German culture. And so, when Jews took over the leadership of German art during the later part of the 19th and the first decades of the 20th century,

Seder dish, Cologne, late eighteenth century The illustrations depict the four sons mentioned in the *Seder* service—the wise son, the wicked son, the simple son, and the son who does not know how to ask questions. Underneath is shown the paschal lamb. Cologne, Stadtmuseum, Inv. 1928/570.

Sabbath lamp, Nuremberg, late eighteenth century. The body of the lamp is in the form of a tower on which are two rows of panels depicting objects and scenes of a traditional nature. The scenes (on various sides of the lamp) include depictions of Mount Sinai, the Tabernacle, and possibly a gate of Jerusalem. Hanover, Historisches Museum am Hohen Ufer.

Hanukkah top, South Germany, early nineteenth century. Wood. The four-sided top had a Hebrew letter on each side corresponding to the initials of the Hebrew phrase 'For a great miracle occurred there'. The letters had numerical value and the person who turned to the highest number was the winner. Basle, Jüdisches Museum der Schweiz, Inv. 105.

it was seen not as sometimes to be welcomed, but to be deplored. There was to be no end to the conflict arising out of an equal love for Germany and for Judaism—a conflict no less pernicious for being unnecessary. To escape being rejected, some had themselves baptized, which did not make them more acceptable to their surroundings, who then considered them insincere; on the other hand, the Jewish community was neither willing nor able to support the artist and yet condemned him when, having to

Sukkah, South Germany, early nineteenth century. The *Sukkah* was the hut in which Jews dwelt during the Festival of Tabernacles as a memorial to the period spent by their ancestors in the desert. The decorations in this one copy a depiction of Jerusalem as well as showing scenes of the South German villages where it was made. It was first erected in 1825 in Fischach near Augsburg and put up by the village carpenter who may have painted it according to instructions (perhaps on the model of some manuscript). It was used by the family of the owner for many years but by 1910 was too unstable to be put up again. The planks were left in straw in a barn (which can be seen in one of the panels). In 1938, when the Nazis were in power, it was secretly loaded onto a truck in parts and sent to Jerusalem as part of the belongings of a new immigrant. The family donated it to the Bezalel Museum and it is now on permanent exhibition in the Israel Museum.

See illustration page 147.

Plate for Purim, Germany, c. 1800. The illustration in the center depicts the incident in which Haman had to lead Mordecai on the king's horse (Esther 6). It is embellished by the rabbinic story that Haman's wife, looking out of the window, assumed that Mordecai would be leading Haman, and emptied a pail of slops on Haman, under the impression that he was Mordecai. Around the rim is an inscription stating that the plate is a 'remembrance gift'. ... Jerusalem, Feuchtwanger Collection, Inv. 9247.

of four thousand years of 'world history' and the influences of the medieval ghetto, superimposed upon the previous close ties with Germany. Here, Emancipation occurred more suddenly, assimilation appeared more promising than in other countries. The Jews of Western Europe, demanding not privileges but equality, were more concerned with helping to bring about a new era of freedom, happiness, and peace for all mankind, than with the preservation of Judaism—which continued unchanged among the Jewish masses—especially in view of the fact that they found themselves discriminated against as much as before. Two years before the beginning of World War I—exactly one hundred years after the 'civic emancipation' in Prussia (March 11 1812)—Franz Rosenzweig found that as a Jew he could not become a university lecturer in spite of his excellent qualifications. He considered baptism, but at the last moment felt himself to be too much of a Jew to accept it. Others gave in. For decades, the German Jews, striving to keep step with German progress, were exposed to tremendous pressure. To withstand it often meant giving up all intellectual ambition, which went against the grain not only of the 19th century generally but of their own dynamism, of which the German Jews had suddenly become aware.

choose between two birthrights, he ceased to be a Jew for the sake of his art.

Attention has tended to be concentrated on Heine, Lasker-Schüler, Wolfskehl, Mombert, and Kafka; there were a great many others who deserve a biographical note and an evaluation of their work and who also showed that it was possible to remain loyal to Judaism and at the same time to be a native writer and artist. The two loyalties did not conflict, but supplemented and enhanced each other. But as far as Germany was concerned, this realization either came too late or was helpless in face of the worsening circumstances.

THE FINAL FLOWERING

German Jewry progressed in its spiritual development until it took its modernity for granted. On the tenth anniversary (1951) of the founding of the 'American Federation of Jews from Central Europe', Leo Baeck spoke of the contribution which German Jewry had made to the progress of Judaism, of Germany, of humanity as a whole, often indirectly and frequently with much anguish; he said that 'those who speak of it must do so reverently'. Its special qualities arose out of Judaism—which meant belonging both to a people and to a religion, the inheritance

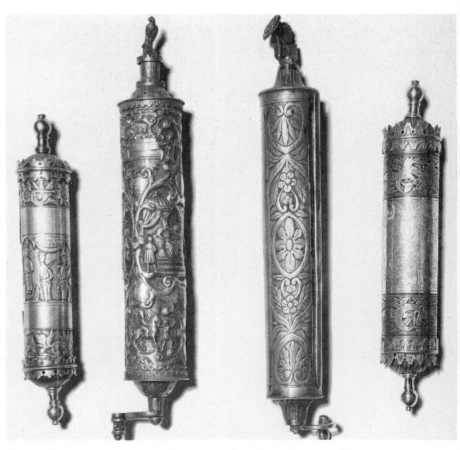

Four Scrolls of Esther in containers, Germany, early eighteenth century. Cologne, Stadtmuseum, Inv. RM 1928/384.

Finally, Judaism was denied for the sake of creativity. This applied to Friedrich Julius Stahl, the founder of conservative political science, to Eduard Gans, Hegel's leading collaborator, and the devout Johann August Neander, who also finally became an important professor of Christian theology. Creativity was the force behind Ludwig Börne, Heinrich Heine, Felix Mendelssohn-Bartholdy, and Ferdinand Lassalle—who also denied his origins, even though he rejected baptism. To this group also belonged Eduard von Simson, president of the German National Assembly (1848-9) and later the first president of the German Supreme Court. Others remained faithful to Judaism, among them Gabriel Riesser, more or less a contemporary of Stahl and Simson, and Leopold Zunz who laid the foundations of modern Jewish scholarship. His work was continued by others: Zacharias Frankel, Abraham Geiger, Heinrich Graetz, Moritz Steinschneider. They initiated younger men: Wilhelm Bacher (born 1850) and David Kaufmann (born 1852). Solomon Munk, born in Glogau, Silesia, was one of the world's greatest orientalists; he became Ernest Renan's successor at the Collège de France. Extreme poverty forced him to leave his birthplace, much against his inclinations, and—in the spring of 1828—his native country, after receiving a letter from Karl von Altenstein, Prussia's first minister of education, which contained the following passage: 'The Ministry wishes to inform you that it is not prepared to provide for your further education while you adhere to the Mosaic faith.'

'The world in which we live is heart-breaking,' Theodor Lessing wrote in 1930 in a small masterpiece entitled *Jewish Self-Hatred*; though not an exhaustive study of its theme, it was brave and original. Modern Judaism had progressed sufficiently to confront its own shadow. It did so firmly and with dignity, out of a profound sense of responsibility. This self-hatred, already taken into account by the Bible, causes not only pain but shame; it

Unleavened bread holder (for the Passover *Seder* table), nineteenth century. Silver with gilt. Below, two lions holding the Tables of the Law. Two doors open and inside are three gilt plates for the three pieces of unleavened bread (corresponding to the three divisions of the Jews: the priests, the Levites and the Israelites). On top, a *Seder* plate with six containers in different shapes: one like a wheelbarrow, another a vessel for making bread, another a wooden milk container, and another an eggcup. These held the various special features of the *Seder* service. The handles are eagle-shaped. Jerusalem, Feuchtwanger Collection, Inv. 369.

is a characteristic feature of the German version of modern Judaism. The German Jews made progress under great difficulties and with many an inner conflict; perhaps this is why they became the pioneers of modern psychology, from Joseph Breuer and Wilhelm Fliess to Sigmund Freud, who had a vast number of Jewish collaborators and disciples.

FRANZ ROSENZWEIG

'Education without end', sighed Franz Rosenzweig, echoing the Preacher's 'Of making many books there is no end' (Ecc. 12:12). The theory contained in so many books should at last be turned into practice. Jewish education and literature should affect Jewish lives, here and now. The great-grandfather of Franz Rosenzweig became (1807) headmaster of the Samson school in Wolfenbüttel in which, according to Leopold Zunz, its most famous pupil, hardly any subject but the Talmud was taught at that time. (Eventually, the Talmud was taught there less and less,

Wheelbarrow, Germany, nineteenth century. This was used as a holder of *haroset* (food eaten in the course of the Passover *Seder* service). The *haroset* symbolized the mortar forbidden to the Jewish slaves in Egypt. The Hebrew inscription recalls how the Egyptians embittered the lives of the Children of Israel in Egypt. Jerusalem, Sir Isaac and Lady Edith Wolfson Museum, Hechal Shlomo, Inv. 32/11.

Mahzor (festival prayer-book), Hammelburg, 1847-8. Parchment manuscript ▶ with leather cover and metal clasps. The illuminated page, with a decorated gate resting on two elephants, with turrets and figures, is taken from the Passover service and contains the beginning of the '*yotzer*' poems. Underneath the arch, Jews are shown baking the unleavened bread for Passover. Darmstadt, Hessische Landes- und Hochschulbibliothek, Inv. Or. Handschrift 13.

ישע מאשרים
יפזר זה מזבשרים
הזריעו פרידז בשרים
שיר השירים

Citron box, Germany (?), 1878 (?). The Hebrew inscription includes the biblical verse (Lev. 23:40): 'And ye shall take you on the first day the fruit of goodly trees, branches of palm-trees and boughs of thick trees and willows of the brook and ye shall rejoice before the Lord your God seven days.' Jerusalem, Israel Museum, Inv. 129/5.

until the 'Jewish Secondary School' was opened, in which it was not taught at all.) Not much more than a hundred years later, the great-grandson, after serving for four years in the trenches during World War I, completed his *Hegel and the State* and *Star of Redemption*, and decided to dedicate the rest of his life to Jewish scholarship. In January 1920 he sketched, 'dancing rather than writing', and within a few days, *Education without End* —a blueprint for a modern Jewish school.

The change which Rosenzweig advocated was being encouraged by external circumstances. For several decades everyone, including the Jews, had been affected by the drive for general education. Everywhere, evening classes were started, 'adult education' became all-important; there was a demand for fundamental changes in teaching methods. The Jews had a special problem, because Judaism has always been considered everywhere above all an 'education'; on this its very survival has depended. Through its teachings and through its observances, it has been passed on from generation to generation. A knowledge of Judaism alone is not enough, but a general education is also no substitute for it. Further education was a contemporary problem, and may have provided an additional impetus, but the Jews had to find their own solution, through founding their own educational institutions. This has from ancient times on been considered of such importance that the Talmud sanctions the turning of a synagogue into a school, where a school is lacking, but forbids the turning of a school (back) into a synagogue: 'learning' is more important than anything else.

At the opening of the Jewish Free School in Frankfurt-am-Main on October 17 1920, Franz Rosenzweig said that, though the obligation to learn was ancient and unalterable, a new approach was needed at the present time. The seclusion of the Middle Ages had been overcome, the world of study was no longer enough, and Jews as well must also live in the world and be at home in its wider civilization. 'Today, there is no one who has not been influenced, who has not absorbed something of another culture, if only a little Goethe,' Rosenzweig pointed out approvingly; in the Middle Ages it had been feared that outside influences would 'alienate' a Jew, whereas in fact they enriched him. At the same time, he talked of a return to Judaism as a means to progress. The 'new learning' must adopt a 'new approach': its starting point must be not the Torah but life; the way back to the Torah must be found through life. Nothing of modern life should be sacrificed or disowned, everything should be directed toward Judaism. Rosenzweig added that the best teacher would be the one who introduced most outside influences.

Until then, adaptation to the new age had meant certain compromises concerning religion, scholarship, and national feeling, and neglect or even rejection of the central aspects of Judaism —compromises which affected the whole of life. Rosenzweig believed that it was possible to be a modern Jew, to combine the 'alien' world with a spiritual return to Judaism: nothing was to be sacrificed, nothing disowned. As always throughout Jewish history, the heart remains Jewish. 'What I mean by Jewishness', Rosenzweig writes in *Education without End,* 'has nothing to do with literature. Neither with the writing nor with the reading of books. It is not even—may all modern spirits forgive me—something that is "experienced". At most, it is a part of life. Perhaps not even that. It *is* life.' This does not, of course,

Hanukkah oil-lamp, Germany, late nineteenth century. The eight lions served as candleholders. Above, the two lions holding the Tables of the Law. This is a nineteenth-century copy made in Germany of a type of *Hanukkah* lamp that was popular in Russia in the eighteenth century. Jerusalem, Sir Isaac and Lady Edith Wolfson Museum, Hechal Shlomo, Inv. 26/53.

Door of the Essen synagogue (before its destruction in 1938). It is decorated with ritual symbols designed by L.A. Riedinger.

apply to everyone, everywhere, always. Existence itself will confirm a Jew as a Jew, even when he does not practice or profess his Jewishness, only if he accepts the new teaching. 'All rules of behavior, whether Orthodox, liberal, or Zionist, produce caricatures of people, the more ridiculous the more strictly they are applied. There is only one rule which will ensure that a person will be a Jew and, through being a Jew, a worthwhile human being: the rule that there is no rule... Our ancestors had a word for it: confidence.'

About two years later, Rosenzweig fell seriously ill; he was unable to preserve the spiritual freedom proclaimed in *Education without End*. He had no worthy successor. German Jewry was to be denied the future which Rosenzweig had envisioned for it. But the way which he indicated to it was to be followed by Jewish communities elsewhere.

THE BIBLE TRANSLATIONS

To Jews for whom Hebrew was not their mother-tongue, a good translation of the Bible was essential if they were to feel close to their heritage. But in spite of this need, which continued to grow in urgency for the two and a half thousand years of the 'world history of the Jewish people', there have been few really successful translations of the so-called Old Testament. They include the Greek-language *Septuagint* of the Egyptian Jews, the *Targumim* (the translations into Aramaic), Saadyah's translation into Arabic, and the translations made by German Jews. The first decisive step was the simultaneous publication (1783)

of Moses Mendelssohn's translation of the Five Books of Moses and of the Psalms. The work of translating the Bible was undertaken in ensuing generations by various people, until the version by Martin Buber and Franz Rosenzweig, who began to collaborate in 1924 on the translation which the surviving Buber finished in 1961. Mendelssohn's predecessors date back to the 13th century, to the time of what Wolfskehl called 'the intimate influence of the medieval surroundings' which possessed great spiritual energy; the translations were first into Middle High German, and later into Yiddish. During the spiritual decline caused by the Crusades, an increasing number of men and certainly most of the women were no longer able to understand the Hebrew readings in the synagogues. The women, the common people, and finally the whole of German Jewry wanted to hear the biblical prophecies in the language of their daily life, and called for a translation which soon included the whole Bible.

In 1943, Karl Wolfskehl wrote, in a letter from New Zealand, that his greatest wish at the end of his life was 'to see the medieval verse translation of the Bible edited and published'; we do not know what manuscript he was referring to. Yiddish documents have always been shamefully neglected by scholars. To Isaiah Sonne, a professor at the Hebrew Union College in Cincinnati, Wolfskehl wrote: 'As you know, there are translations of Joshua, Judges, Samuel and Kings, all of them in stanzas like the *Nibelungen,* full of marvellous poetry. Everything has still to be done: the text has to be established, the question of authorship elucidated; even the date of composition is uncertain. I am convinced that these epics bear witness to the intimate influence of the medieval surroundings; they are a ray of light in a period of exile. Perhaps they are the only substantial epic poems of post-biblical times ever to have been written...'

In the 16th century, Yiddish translations were made of the Five Books of Moses, the Psalms and the Scrolls (The Song of Solomon, Ruth, Lamentations, Ecclesiastes, Esther); these have been preserved. Two complete translations of the Bible were made by Jekutiel ben Isaac Blitz from Wittmund and Josel Witzenhausen, and published between 1676 and 1679 in Amsterdam. Mendelssohn's translation, published a century later, was the first into standard German; in his introduction, written in Hebrew, he wrote: 'Since then, nobody has thought of undoing the harm by translating the Holy Scriptures into the language of our own day and age. Jewish boys capable of understanding the word of God have to learn it from the translations of Christian scholars.' That this translation was a landmark in Jewish history was obscured by the fact that Judaism continued to cherish its medieval attitudes, obstructing Mendelssohn's work, rejecting the renaissance even when it was not a threat but a promise; also, the incentive to intellectual progress disappeared when, as a consequence of the French Revolution, Jews were granted full citizenship. Mendelssohn's Bible was printed in Hebrew type, which certainly contributed to its immediate acceptance; more than thirty years were to pass before his German words were printed in German type. His work was interrupted by his untimely death; it took fifty years before the translation was to be completed.

Passover dish, Offenbach, c. 1920. Wood. The dish contains three tiers for the unleavened bread and seven holders for the ritual constituents of the meal. The inscription in German reads: 'Behold children; this is the bread of poverty that our ancestors ate in Egypt.' Offenbach, Klingspor Museum, Inv. 3108/20.

Embroidered hanging, Offenbach, 1924-6. Linen. Hung during Passover it contains selections of verses read at the Passover *Seder* service. Some verses are given in Hebrew, others in German. Offenbach, Klingspor Museum, Inv. 4258.

Synagogue in Düsseldorf (destroyed in 1938), 1904. Düsseldorf, Landesbibliothek.

The *Twenty-Four Books of the Holy Scriptures based on the Masoretic Text* was the work of Leopold Zunz and his collaborators, Heymann Arnheim, Julius Fürst, and Michael Sachs; it was published in 1837 and ran to several editions. (Shortly before, Gotthold Solomon published his *German Bible for Israelites for School and General Use,* which deserves a mention.) Zunz's achievement did not receive very much attention, partly because of the strong anti-religious tendencies of the time—which had nothing to do with anti-Semitism—and partly because of the conflicting tendencies among the Jews themselves. In 1859 Ludwig Philippson founded the Israelite Institute for Bible Study, because Jewish attendance at Protestant institutes frequently led to baptism. In opposition to him and to the translations by Christians, the Orthodox movement founded an institute in 1865, and Seligmann Bär Bamberger, Abraham Adler, and Marcus Lehmann began their translation. Philippson's *Israelite Bible* was published between 1839 and 1853; containing introductions, commentaries and summaries, it strove to be faithful, popular and readable. Solomon Herxheimer wished to counteract the tendencies of the times, 'the daily growing ignorance of Judaism and indifference to it on the one hand, and the fossilization of Jewish religious life on the other.' In 1842 he published his *Twenty-four Books of the Bible in Hebrew with a Faithful Translation, Continuous Commentary and Notes for Sermons.* The existence of 'faithful translations' made Jacob Auerbach think it necessary to produce an edited version for 'young ladies'. It was first published in 1858; he called it *A Pocket Bible for School and Home Use* and said in a preface that it ought not to be mistaken for the Bible itself. Samson Raphael Hirsch published

his translation of the Five Books of Moses in 1867, and of the Psalms in 1882; with its detailed and comprehensive commentary, it ranks with the works of Mendelssohn and Zunz. Hirsch left the Hebrew name of God or its synonyms untranslated, and had the German word *Gott* printed in spaced type. Mendelssohn had at least tried to find a translation and introduced the term 'the Eternal' *(Der Ewige)*, which was generally accepted and copied by Zunz, although it was inadequate; according to Mendelssohn's commentary to Exodus 3:14, he ought to have found a word expressing both the continuousness and the necessity of God's existence as well as providence.

Baden-Baden. Synagogue burning on November 10, 1938. On this night, ostensibly as a reprisal for the killing of a German diplomat in Paris, the Nazis organized the burning down of hundreds of synagogues throughout Germany, the destruction of Jewish shops, and the arrest of thousands of Jews. Windows of Jewish stores were shattered and this became known as 'the night of the broken glass' *(Kristallnacht).* Photo archives Yad Vashem, Jerusalem.

The 20th century saw two further complete translations: Simon Bernfeld's *The Holy Scriptures* (1903) and Lazarus Gold-schmidt's *The Holy Books of the Covenant* (1921). The translation by N. H. Tur-Sinai (Harry Torczyner) was revised and republished after the translator had emigrated to Jerusalem. In his introductions to the editions of his *Holy Scriptures* published in 1937 and 1954, Tur-Sinai wrote that his translation had been influenced by that of Zunz. It was originally intended for use in the liberal synagogues of the Berlin communities and leading liberal and conservative rabbis and scholars collaborated on it.

But the only translation which is really alive is that of Buber and Rosenzweig. The use which they made of German was determined by the structure of the Hebrew language; previously, both Jewish and Christian translators had ignored the undercurrents flowing through the original by means of related words. The translation was also distinguished by being printed in 'self-contained phrases to be read in one breath,' which was an attempt to return to the early oral tradition and make the Bible once more suitable for reading aloud. It also succeeded, as did some previous translations, in not obscuring the inspiration of the original. Rosenzweig wrote that the only justifiable translation of the divine name was one which concentrated not on the eternal aspect but on the presence, on immediacy. The only word which he found entirely suitable in every way was the personal pronoun, which expressed the three dimensions of the presence of God: He is spoken to, He speaks, He is spoken of... Only the personal pronoun in one of its three forms was equivalent to one of the three forms of God's presence. And Buber wrote: 'It was not possible for us to write "the existence" or "the presence", because this would have meant substituting a definite concept for a name with a dynamic meaning; it would have conveyed the "always"—Mendelssohn's "the Eternal"—rather than the continually new. It was a question of finding an equivalent which would arouse in the receptive reader the confidence emanating from the divine name; that is, the need was not for a concept of the presence of God but for a word which made this imme-

diate. The realization that the original name was a sort of pronoun indicated the solution. In our German version, therefore, we use I and MINE when God is speaking, YOU and YOURS when He is spoken to, and HE and HIS when He is spoken of.'

And so, it becomes once more possible to speak of Him, to hear Him and, above all, to speak to Him, to the God of the Jewish people and of all those who have inherited the Bible. This modern age questions the religious revelations, considering them almost idolatrous: but even now the voice is capable of moving the listener 'as always'. It was a decisive moment in Jewish history, a reawakening of Judaism, when Mendelssohn, by means of his Christology and the German language, revitalized the Jewish core of the Hebrew Bible. The climax came with the translation of Buber and Rosenzweig, which gave the Jews the self-awareness and the confidence to accept the Christian claim to a share in the inheritance not merely as a fact but as something to be welcomed. It is an encouraging sign that the Bible has commanded renewed attention in the context of modern life, it is a sign of encouragement to humanity: glad tidings not only for the Children of Israel, but for all people everywhere: 'It is a light thing that thou shouldest be my servant to raise up the tribes of Jacob, and to restore the preserved of Israel: I will also give thee for a light to the nations, that my salvation may be unto the end of the earth' (Isa. 49:6).

It is possible to contribute to the best of one's abilities and without reservation to the modern era, while remaining close to the biblical roots; German Jewry gave proof of this. The community remained faithful to the four thousand years of its people's history, while keeping faith with the present: having developed in the Jewish tradition, it was a contemporary community. The Jews who had their roots in the German-speaking regions made great progress, but it was limited by the fact that it took place in Central Europe, so that their greatest achievements—like those of Europe generally—are valid mainly as an inheritance for mankind in times to come. German Jewry was part of the Jewish people, just as the Jewish people is part of humanity as a whole.

CHAPTER V

The Netherlands

by Dr. Jozeph Michman-Melkman

The men we meet at the beginnings of the Jewish community in the Netherlands are remarkable, often impressive, personalities. There had been isolated Jewish families living here and there in the Middle Ages; but there was little to distinguish these Ashkenazi families from their brethren in Germany. They were exposed to persecution from the middle of the 14th century and it is virtually certain that when the republic of the Netherlands began its war of independence against Spain, there were no Ashkenazi Jews in the Seventeen Provinces. Spanish and Portuguese Jews had, on the other hand, already settled in the wealthy southern Netherlands in the 16th century and established their center in Antwerp. But they lived there as crypto-Jews or Marranos, for the Spanish rulers of the country, Charles V and later Philip II, enforced the same anti-Jewish laws as in metropolitan Spain, and enforced them with the same fanaticism. The successful revolt and proclamation of a republic by the seven Northern Provinces offered the persecuted Marranos opportunities of which they began to avail themselves by the end of the 16th and the beginning of the 17th century.

The contrast between the hesitant and slow settlement of Jews elsewhere and their settlement in the Netherlands is striking. Proud of their wealth and lineage, conscious of their economic importance for the young and still insecure commonwealth, they negotiated from a position of equality. Take, for instance, Don Samuel Palache from Fez, who arrived in the Netherlands as ambassador of the king of Morocco (1609), gained the confidence of Stadtholder Prince Maurice, and set out to fight Spain. Tradition has it that his home housed the first *minyan* (group of ten male adult Jews, the minimum required for communal prayer) of the Beth Yaacov community, and when he died in 1616, his funeral cortege included not only Jews, but also representatives of the authorities.

Even before this, Marranos had settled in Amsterdam and elsewhere, though without openly admitting they were Jews. The turning point in the life of the Marrano colony came in 1602. Apparently, they had invited an Ashkenazi rabbi, Uri Halevi or Philips Joosten, as the Netherlands texts call him, to serve as their minister, *shohet* (ritual slaughterer) and *mohel* (circumciser); so much, at least, appears from the minutes of his interrogation when he was arrested in 1603. Of the outcome of this interrogation nothing is known, but it is clear that Uri Halevi and his Sephardi friends now decided to admit their religion openly and establish a community, if not in Amsterdam, then in some other town in the Netherlands. This, at least, appears from a resolution taken by the Aldermen of Alkmaar on May 10 1604: 'At the request of Philips the Jew, in the name of several households of Jews and Jewish associates (i.e. Marranos), of the Portuguese and other nations... it is permitted that they may enter this town and stay and dwell there peacefully and secure even as any other good burghers... and confess their religion.' This was a first victory. It was to be followed soon by another, when the city council of Haarlem, after long negotiations, granted a similar charter to a group of well-to-do mer-

Emunot ve-Deot by Saadyah Gaon, Amsterdam, 1647. Latin title page of Saadyah Gaon's tenth-century philosophical work *Emunot ve-Deot* (Book of Beliefs and Opinions) printed at the press of Menasseh Ben Israel's son Joseph. The printing press set up by Menasseh Ben Israel in 1627 introduced Hebrew printing to Amsterdam, which remained the principal center of Jewish printing for the following century. Amsterdam, Bibl. Rosenthaliana.

chants from Amsterdam who also wanted to bring over their families from Portugal, Turkey, and Italy. The documents show that 'Belchior and Francisco Mendes and Michael Castro, *alias* Abraham and Isaac Franco and Michael Nehemie' were not only rich but also skilled negotiators. One may presume that in their negotiations they always kept an eye on Amsterdam, where the resistance of Church circles to Jewish settlement was much stronger than elsewhere. When finally Rotterdam also decided to invite Portuguese merchants to settle (1610), Amsterdam could not lag behind. Officially, Jews were not yet admitted, but *shehitah* (ritual slaughtering) took place, a prayer-book was published, a plot for a cemetery was bought, and a tender was issued for the building of a synagogue.

It was a strange situation, and even stranger in that not even all Christians enjoyed freedom of religion. In 1618, the Remonstrants (a sect which had seceded from the official Reformed [Calvinist] Church) wrote to Prince Maurice: 'Judge for yourself, high-born Prince, whether it be not a deplorable procedure that the Jews, overt enemies and detractors of our Savior, exercise their religion in the mightiest city of Holland, namely in Amsterdam, while we Christians, yea, even Protestants, are forbidden to do likewise.' It was indeed a problem, which became even more acute when the Jewish religion proved to be attractive to Christians. The rulers of the province Holland decided to solve it once and for all and requested two leading legal authorities, Hugo de Groot (Grotius) and Adriaan Pauw, to draft a Jewish statute. De Groot's report has been preserved; it is by no means as tolerant as one would have expected from so great a lawyer and fighter for intellectual liberty. The States of Holland refused to commit themselves to the detailed regulations which De Groot proposed, possibly as a result of the representations made by the Portuguese merchants in a counter-memorandum. At any rate, it was decided to leave a completely free hand to the different towns.

This amounted to a defeat for the Church circles who wanted to keep the Jews in bounds and found it hard to reconcile themselves to the charters which Rotterdam and Haarlem had granted. In fact, however, the legal situation of the Jews was not to change until the Emancipation. The other provinces followed the lead of Amsterdam, as they usually did, and left the towns to decide matters for themselves. This might well have led to arbitrary decisions; and indeed, there were towns where Jews were forbidden to stay overnight or where settlement was subject to restrictive rules, but they were the exception. In Amsterdam particularly, where, notwithstanding initial opposition, the large majority settled, the authorities took pains to assure that the *status quo* was not violated, and neither the aggressive sermons of the parsons nor the occasional complaints of the artisans had any effect. While the Jews did not become citizens (*'poorters'*), they were allowed to exercise any trade that had not been regulated by the guilds.

COMMERCIAL ACTIVITIES

That was all the Sephardim who settled in Amsterdam wanted; they were not after social or cultural integration in the Netherlands community. Their spiritual home was Spain, with its far higher cultural standards than those of the little republic. There existed a closed community of exiles, a Diaspora of Marranos, who maintained close relations with each other, primarily in the exercise of commerce. For that very reason they were able to make a unique contribution to the economic prosperity of the young republic. They did not—as has occasionally been claimed—lay the foundations for the economic power of the Netherlands empire in the 17th century, for their contribution was at first, certainly until the Twelve Years Armistice (1609-22), far too small for that. But there was a mutual influence: the Sephardi

Emunot ve-Deot by Saadya5 Gaon (in Hebrew). Amsterdam, 1647. The title page of *Emunot ve-Deot* by Saadyah Gaon (see previous illustration) in Hebrew. This work is one of the basic pillars of Jewish religious and philosophical thinking. The original Arabic version was translated in Spain by Judah Ibn Tibbon. Amsterdam, Bibl. Rosenthaliana.

merchants did certainly benefit from the fruits of the enterprise and daring of the Netherlands Golden Age. In turn, thanks to their worldwide connections and the use of their capital, they were able to offer the Netherlands republic opportunities which were readily accepted. Netherlands shippers carried the goods of the 'Portuguese' to all parts of the known world. They sailed for Angola in Africa, for Goa and Cochin in India, for Brazil, the West Indies and North America. Their agents were sent out to North and East Europe: they could be met as far abroad as Danzig, Posen and Zamosc. In those days of inadequate communications it was important that the Amsterdam merchants had relatives dispersed all over the world as a result of the Expulsion from Spain. Particularly close ties with Amsterdam were kept up by Hamburg and Venice, so that the former could become the basis for the Baltic trade and the latter for the Levant trade.

The increase in importance of the Jewish merchants in Amsterdam may be gauged from the growth of their numbers among holders of accounts with the Bank of Exchange. In 1609 only 24 of the 731 accounts were held by Portuguese merchants but by 1620 they numbered 106 out of 1,202. By 1674 there were 265 Jewish account holders out of a total of 2,031, or 13 per cent, while the Jews accounted for no more than 1½ per cent of the population. Though the size of the accounts shows that quite a few Christian merchants were better off than the richest Jews, there were, nevertheless, many small capitalists among the Portuguese Jews and their average wealth was considerably above that of the remainder of the Amsterdam population. The wealth and economic importance of the Portuguese Jews was not a matter of individuals, but of the group and of its contacts with other centers.

There were a few great merchants, like, for instance, Bento Osorio; later, there were Moses Machado, supplier to the Dutch and English armies under William III, and Francisco Lopes Suasso, who was able to lend the same William III two million guilders for his expedition to England. By the end of the 17th century the Portuguese Jews had begun to increase their capital considerably, and their initially minor share in industry grew at the same time. They were in sugar refining and in the tobacco industry—an important field in the beginning of the 18th century —and above all in the diamond industry, which in course of time was to become an almost exclusively Jewish occupation in Amsterdam.

Another trade in which the Jews could engage because it had not been preempted by the guilds was Hebrew book-printing. The first printing press was that of Menasseh Ben Israel (1626), who later was followed by others who achieved a wide reputation. The output of these presses was of such outstanding quality that the Jewish publishing houses of Amsterdam soon outgrew their modest beginnings and exported their books to all parts of the Jewish Diaspora.

Notwithstanding, then, the not inconsiderable restrictions hampering their economic growth, the Jews shared in the general prosperity of the Netherlands republic.

THE GOLDEN AGE OF NETHERLANDS CULTURE

The 17th century was the Golden Age of Netherlands culture, which shone particularly in the field of painting, but flourished in other domains as well, such as literature and science. The mutual influence of Netherlands culture and that of the Sephardi Jews is evident from the many mutual points of contact. One has only to look at Rembrandt's paintings to understand how he was fascinated by the Jewish types of his surroundings; and not by Jewish types alone: Jewish religious conceptions must also have been a source of interest to him, for he made four plates for Menasseh Ben Israel's book *Piedra Gloriosa,* an apocalyptic work interpreting the suffering of the Jews of Poland at that time, as a sign of the coming of the Messiah. There were Christians who converted to Judaism; on the other hand, there were Church authorities who wanted to convert the Jews, scholars who studied the Mishnah and the Talmud, and even a Christian poetess who composed Hebrew poems. But above all, the interest on both sides is evidenced by the disputations which took place in Amsterdam: the first dialogues between Christians and Jews in which the latter could express themselves freely and without having to defer to hostile authorities. The first dispute, as early as 1608, was between the Englishman Hugh Broughton and the physician David Farrar. Menasseh Ben Israel also defended Judaism in his *Vindiciae Judaeorum* and even, though cautiously, attacked Christian tenets in another book, *Conciliador.* So did another, less famous but far more learned author, the Amsterdam rabbi Saul Levi Morteira, whose *Providencia de Dios con Ysrael* specifically attacked the Calvinist doctrine of the official Netherlands Reformed Church; the book has never been printed, presumably because of its aggressive tone. The greatest of the Jewish apologists, though, was Dr. Isaac Orobio de Castro (1620-87), originally professor of medicine in Seville and later physician in Amsterdam, who had a learned disputation with an Amsterdam minister and even dared to publish a book against *La Vana Ydolatria de las Gentes.* So violent were the pronouncements of many of those who had only recently returned to the Jewish fold that the magistrates of Amsterdam finally decided to permit no more disputations between Jews and Christians; they were obviously afraid of a reaction in Church circles.

But it should not be thought that the polemics were directed only against Christians. There were also internal discussions, that were often no less fierce. The first we hear of them is in 1618, when the secular leaders of the Beth Jacob community, led by the physician Abraham Farrar, clashed with R. David Pardo. While Farrar and his adherents were rationalists who took a critical view of the Kabbalah and were even prepared to question rabbinical decisions, R. Pardo regarded this as backsliding into heresy. The conflict became so acute that the rabbi and some of his followers set up a new community: Beth Israel. Soon afterward, the city was to be the scene of an even more tragic dispute. At its center was Uriel da Costa. Uriel, who was born in Oporto in 1585, became treasurer of a church in 1608. He began to observe Marrano customs about 1610 and persuaded many of his relatives to do likewise. He fled to Italy with his mother and three brothers in 1614, and converted to Judaism, assuming the name of Uriel instead of Gabriel. A few years later he had set up in Hamburg; by 1627 he was in Utrecht, then by 1631 in Amsterdam. Riddles surround his life but his ideas, and particularly his argumentation against the immortality of the soul, aroused a wave of indignation in the Marrano Diaspora. Over the next twenty years, Sephardi religious scholars produced a flood of treatises, books, and even poems in defense of the immortality of the soul. Uriel was excommunicated. In 1640 he shot himself, leaving a work, *Exemplar Humanae Vitae,* which has reached us only in a version that has been mutilated by anti-Semitic hands.

Uriel da Costa's principal claim to fame, though, is as the

Portrait of Benedict Spinoza, c. 1670. Portrait of the famous Dutch philosopher (1632-77) by an anonymous Dutch painter. Though he had received a traditional education and his teachers had included Menasseh Ben Israel, Spinoza's unorthodox religious views led finally to his excommunication from the Sephardi community. The Hague, Gemeentemuseum.

precursor of the best known scion of the Jewish community of Amsterdam: Baruch Spinoza, like him a victim of excommunication. Unlike da Costa, Spinoza had been educated in the Jewish faith; perhaps even more important, he was born in Amsterdam and never left Holland. He refers to Holland as 'mea patria' (my fatherland) and is totally lacking in Jewish national feeling and respect for ancestral tradition. Spinoza was interrogated and excommunicated by the *parnassim* (synagogue wardens) and rabbis before his writings were published. One may assume that his heresies were not the sole reason for the measures taken against him: Spinoza's contacts with the Protestant sect of the Collegiants and with the atheists were regarded as a great danger, not only for the religious views of the Jews themselves but for their place in Dutch society, which might be undermined

by an 'unbeliever'. The surprising result of his expulsion from the Jewish community was that, notwithstanding the revolutionary nature of his ideas for the period, the authorities gave him less trouble than they did his Christian adherents. His philosophical system may be the most important contribution to Dutch culture any Dutch Jew has ever made, but at the same time it must be said that no Portuguese Jew of his time ever identified himself so closely with the Netherlands commonwealth or kept at such a distance from the Jewish community.

This may well account for why the reaction to his activities was so much less marked than it was in the case of Uriel da Costa. We know of one of his supporters who was also excommunicated: Dr. Juan de Prado, who soon afterward disappeared to Antwerp. He and Spinoza were the targets of an intelligent pamphlet from the fearsome pen of Orobio de Castro. But that is all we known of Spinoza in the Jewish community. This can perhaps be explained in part by the fact that at this time the mystical trend began to predominate in the Portuguese community. The spread of Isaac Luria's kabbalistic ideology in Italy dates from the years 1656-9, and in view of the close relations existing between Amsterdam and Italy, it is hardly surprising that in Amsterdam as well, rationalism had to make way for mysticism. The result was that by 1666, Amsterdam was ripe for the advent of the Messiah Shabbetai Tzevi (see chapter on Muslim Lands). Rabbis and congregants were thoroughly convinced that the Messiah was about to lead them to the Promised Land and refused to listen to the more sober voices of a few skeptics. As the community prepared itself to pay allegiance to the 'King of the Jews', their hopes were crushed by the report of his conversion to Islam. One result of this traumatic disillusionment was that from then on, the Portuguese Jews as a community resigned themselves to awaiting their fate in the Netherlands; returning to Spain was out of the question, and establishing a Jewish commonwealth in Palestine proved impossible. From then on, they regarded themselves as subjects of the Netherlands republic. The most exalted expression of this change of attitude may be found in the splendid synagogue which was built at the instigation of *Hakham* (chief rabbi) Isaac Aboab da Fonseca, a one-time follower of Shabbetai Tzevi. A Christian poet calls it

> *Chef d'œuvre de tous lieux sacrés,*
> *Du premier temple la mémoire,*

and indeed Bouman, its architect, drew his inspiration from the Solomonic Temple—or rather, from its reconstruction by Jacob Judah Leon, who became so famous for the model he had constructed that he was given the nickname Templo. This imposing, fortress-like structure was inaugurated in 1675 in a manner which a contemporary writer regards as fit for 'a festival celebrated in freedom and in the Temple rather than in exile and in a synagogue'.

The synagogue—called 'Esnoga'—was built with a view to the future. The community was flourishing, and its headmen expected membership to grow to larger numbers than was to be the case. The Sephardi immigrants had grown in stature and wealth with the Commonwealth. They were by now playing an important part on the Exchange, the operation of which has

Festive meal in the Sukkah, Amsterdam, 1722. From an engraving by Bernard Picart, depicting the Festive Meal in the *Sukkah* or the booth for the Festival of Tabernacles, which commemorates the forty-year wandering of the Israelites in the desert. The *Sukkah* seen here is that of a rich family while the one behind is that of a poor family. It has to be a temporary structure through which it is possible to see the stars. Amsterdam, Fodormuseum.

never been better described than by Joseph Penso in *Confusión de Confusiones*. We find many representatives of foreign powers among them, and their relations with the court of Stadtholder William III were close. Wealth also served to stimulate culture. In the stately mansions on the canals of Amsterdam and the luxurious villas on the road to Utrecht beside the river Vecht, the wives and children of the barons engaged in music, dancing, and poetry. The poetry, incidentally, was almost never in Dutch: some poetic societies used the Spanish language, but Hebrew also had its practitioners. Joseph Penso was seventeen when he wrote a Hebrew play, and other poets, like Moses Zacut, Solomon d'Oliveira and—in the 18th century—David Franco Mendes are also known to have produced Hebrew poems at an early age. That they were able to do so was due to the modern educational methods of the famous Talmud Torah school, which

stressed the study of Hebrew grammar and the actual speaking of the language—an approach which was far from general at the time. In their love of music, the citizens of Amsterdam took their cue from Italy. Works were written for religious purposes by such Amsterdam composers as Abraham de Caceres and the non-Jew C.G. Lidarti; from there, it was but a short step to operas and plays. In 1624, a play by Reuel Jessurun (*alias* Paulo de Pina), entitled *Diálogo des Montes* was even performed in the synagogue, but such frivolities were forbidden in 1639.

Not that the rabbis objected to poetry and music. On the contrary: in many of the dozens of pious societies which, in addition to their official activities, also offered an opportunity for the study of rabbinical literature, it was the custom to celebrate the conclusion of a Talmud tractate by the composition and reading of poems and dialogues, and in at least one instance by a play. In 1683, the poet-historian Daniel Levi de Barrios was familiar with at least twenty such societies, and there must have been many other similar associations. Another occasion for musical and theatrical performances was provided by the weddings of the leading families; if the family was particularly wealthy, a poet might be invited specially for the occasion. In this way, two eighteenth-century Hebrew poets have left plays and operas: Moshe Hayyim Luzzatto and David Franco Mendes. We know, however, of no Spanish or Dutch plays—proof that the environment was still felt as too foreign to invite participation in local cultural life. At most, there were rich Portuguese Jews who appeared as patrons of the arts.

THE ASHKENAZI COMMUNITY

The first Ashkenazi Jews must have reached Amsterdam about 1620. They held their first separate synagogue service in 1635, and in 1642 they bought a cemetery which is still in use. From 1648 on, many Jews from Eastern Europe went to the Netherlands. While the number of Sephardim in Amsterdam in 1610 was 400, and in 1674 their total number in the Netherlands—besides Amsterdam, the only place where Portuguese Jews lived was in the Hague—cannot have been much more than 2,500, Ashkenazi Jews in Amsterdam in that year already numbered 5,000. A century later, the Sephardi community had remained

Jewish burial ground, Amsterdam, 1670. Cemetery of the Sephardi community at Ouderkerk, near Amsterdam, from an engraving and etching by Abraham Blooteling, after Jacob Ruisdael. Jerusalem, Israel Museum.

Synagogue. By M. Pool Sculy. No. 1 is the rabbi; no. 2, the Ark coffer; no. 3 the Scrolls; no. 4 the *Hazzan* or cantor. Amsterdam, Rijksmuseum, engravings dept. Inv. no. 16:309.

almost static (3,000), while the number of Ashkenazi Jews in Amsterdam had grown to 19,000, with another 8,000 in the remainder of the country. Nevertheless the cultural impact of the Ashkenazim until the middle of the 18th century was disappointing. Admittedly, the Great Synagogue was inaugurated in 1671 —in other words, even before the Esnoga synagogue—and soon proved too small, so that it was followed by a few large and innumerable smaller ones, which surely indicates that there were at least a few Jews of sufficient wealth. The bulk of the Ashkenazi community, however, consisted of relatively poor Jews. In all

those years, the Amsterdam community produced no scholars. It is perfectly understandable that initially its rabbis had to be brought from abroad, but the practice was continued. By 1710, the Amsterdam community was large enough even to be able to invite one of the greatest scholars of the time, Tzevi Ashkenazi, known as *Hakham* Tzevi. It is, however, significant that when a conflict arose between him and the Portuguese chief rabbi, Salomon Ayllon, the aldermen of Amsterdam finally intervened in R. Ayllon's favor and *Hakham* Tzevi was forced to leave the city in 1714. The Ashkenazi community acknowledged its debt to *Hakham* Tzevi to the extent that his descendants held the office of chief rabbi of Amsterdam for more than a century. The family also produced many chief rabbis and rabbis for other places in the Netherlands.

Whether these can be regarded as Dutch rabbis, however, is another question. In the 18th century, at any rate, they cannot, for even Jacob Moses had been educated in Poland and was unfamiliar with the Dutch language and with conditions in Amsterdam. The same goes for his predecessors and for other

◄ *Ketubbah,* Rotterdam, 1648. Marriage contract on parchment etched by Shalom Italia, 1648. Italia was born in Mantua and settled in Amsterdam. Coming of a family of printers, he made his name as an engraver and miniaturist, doing many copperplate borders for the *Ketubbah* and *Megilah.* Here he depicts wedding scenes from the Bible, those of Eve, Sarah and Rachel on one side, traditional wedding scenes on the other. The name of the groom in this wedding: Isaac Pereira; that of the bride: Rachel, daughter of Abraham da Pinto. Jerusalem, Israel Museum.

Halitzah ceremony, Amsterdam, 1683. This copper etching shows the so-called *Halitzah* ceremony in which the brother of a man who died childless is relieved from his obligation to marry the widow. This ceremony involves the widow removing the brother-in-law's shoe and reciting the biblical formula: 'So shall be done to the man who shall not build his brother's house.' Dutch artist unknown. Jerusalem, Israel Museum, 2725-10-51.

scholars who reached the Netherlands more or less by chance. They often published their works in Amsterdam, because the Amsterdam printers produced good work; but they had acquired their learning elsewhere. Their daily language was Yiddish, and was to remain so until the second half of the 18th century.

The Portuguese Jews also applied themselves by preference to Spanish and Hebrew, but the difference was that they were prosperous and had had a share in the rich Spanish civilization. The bulk of the poor Ashkenazim were unable to reach a cultural level equal to that of the Sephardim. Notwithstanding

וככה תאכלו אתו מתניכם חגרים נעליכם ברגליכם ומקלכם בידכם פסח הוא לה

Seder meal on Passover, Amsterdam, 1695. The engravings are by Abraham ben Jacob in imitation of the engravings in Matheus Merian's *Icones Bibliae*, Basle, 1625. The quotation at the bottom is taken from the *Haggadah* service and reads: 'And thus shall you eat it, with your loins girded, your feet shod, and a staff in your hand'. It was a custom among many Jewish communities to enact this scene at the Passover table to recall the Jews in Egypt on the eve of the Exodus. Amsterdam, Bibl. Rosenthaliana.

the steady growth of the Amsterdam community, it continued for years to look up on the one hand to the greater scholarship of the East European centers and on the other to the social position of its Portuguese coreligionists. There were a few rich families who monopolized the office of *parnassim* (synagogue wardens) and who exercised unlimited authority over their communities. Tobias Boas, the Hague banker, was one of the advisers and moneylenders of the stadtholder's court and the government. He even represented the Jewish communities of Amsterdam and Rotterdam in audiences at the court, and presumably had a hand in the *démarche* of the Dutch Ambassador Burmania when he protested to Maria Theresa against the expulsion of the Jews from Bohemia and Moravia. This certainly was the case with another great banker, Benedict Levie Gomperts of Nijmegen, who had followed his family from nearby Cleves in Germany.

Gomperts, member of a widespread family, had interests not only in the Netherlands (particularly in Amsterdam and Amersfoort), but also in Germany and England. The most famous Ashkenazi, though, in the second half of the 18th century, was Benjamin Cohen of Amersfoort, first a tobacco merchant but later also a banker, whose relations with the court were so close that Stadtholder William V and his wife Wilhelmina even stayed at his house.

However, it should not be forgotten that most of the Dutch towns did not admit Jews, or admitted them only subject to restrictions. The great wealth and cultural achievements of a few individuals cannot conceal the fact that few Jews could make more than a bare living. This is particularly the case in Amsterdam, which had a very large Jewish proletariat. As a result, the Ashkenazi Jews found their contacts with their surroundings

Circumcision, Amsterdam, 1722. Circumcision as depicted in Picart's *Cérémonies et Coutumes Religieuses,* with, in attendance, the father of the child, the godfather, the *Mohel* (circumciser) and the rabbi. The Chair of Elijah, on which the child is placed before being circumcised, can also be seen. The woman with a cross is a Christian servant. Amsterdam, Fodormuseum, Inv. no. A. 10258.

mainly among the less prosperous classes. If one is to believe stories from the 18th century, there were a fair number of pickpockets and prostitutes among them—hardly surprising in an international port. Significantly, a considerable number of Yiddish words found their way into the slang of the Dutch underworld. On the other hand, Yiddish, which the Jews continued to use until well into the 19th century, soon absorbed Dutch words and expressions.

Relations between the Portuguese and Ashkenazi Jews were to change radically in the second half of the 18th century. By 1762, hints of the incipient changes are to be found in the writings of Isaac de Pinto, a rich and learned Portuguese Jew. As a *parnas* of the Portuguese community, he had to deal with increasing poverty among many of its members, who had lost their money through unlucky speculations and the ill-fortune of the Netherlands republic. Nevertheless, de Pinto felt far superior to his Ashkenazi brethren, as appears clearly in his con-

troversy with Voltaire. But soon afterward, another Portuguese Jew of Amsterdam, Mordechai van Aron de... (the surname is not mentioned) in a Dutch periodical took a very different line: the Portuguese-Jewish nation, he states, has had its summer; the High German Jews (as the Ashkenazim are formally called in Dutch) on the other hand, most of whom arrived destitute, '(are) being regarded by us Portuguese with a good deal of contempt, but (are) in fact more industrious and economical than we are; they have survived their winter and see better times approaching. They are rising, we are sinking.'

EMANCIPATION

But the times that were in store for the Ashkenazim were hardly better ones. The war with England, the subsequent domestic strife, and finally the French conquest in 1795 brought

Preparations for the Passover Festival, Holland, 1725. Etchings from Bernard Picart's *Cérémonies et Coutumes Religieuses* showing the preparations for the Passover Festival a) the search for leavened bread; b) The *Seder* (Passover) meal. The scenes depict a ceremony in a Sephardi community. (a) The night before Passover a search is made for any (leaven) bread inadvertently overlooked which is then burned and a special blessing recited. In fact some leavened bread is deliberately left in a corner so that the ceremony can be carried out. (b) 1) The plate with hard-boiled egg and roast shankbone of lamb, commemorating the Temple offerings. 2) Plate with bitter herbs which symbolize the bitterness caused by the Egyptians to the Israelites in Egypt. 3) Contains a mixture symbolizing the mortar the Jews were forbidden to have in Egypt. 4) Salt water in which the bitter herbs are dipped. 5) The father is breaking the unleavened bread in his hand. All the Jewish household servants are participating. 6) Serviette under which one piece of unleavened bread is hidden. 7) On the floor the basket where unleavened bread is kept. Amsterdam, Rijksmuseum, engravings dept.

L'EXAMEN du LEVAIN &c.

A. La Maitresse de la maison, qui met du PAIN LEVE en divers endroits, afin que son Mari qui en fait la recherche en trouve.

Le REPAS de PAQUES.
chez les
JUIFS PORTUGAIS.

1. Le Plat ou est un Os d'Epaule d'Agneau, avec un Oeuf dur.
2. Plat ou sont les Herbes Ameres.
3. Plat de Figues Pommes Amandes Canelle &c. hachees et toutes ensemble, representant la matiere dont ils faisoient les Briques en Egypte.
4. Plat avec la Sauce pour tremper les Herbes Ameres.
5. Moitié du Gateau les Levites, dont le Pere de Famille rompt des morceaux, qu'il distribue a tous ceux qui sont a table. N.B. tous les Domestiques Juifs sont a la même Table avec lui.
6. Serviette sous laquelle le Gateau a été caché.
7. Panier ou sont les Matsot, ou Pain de Paques.

hardship to the Dutch, and to the Jews even more. At the same time, almost overnight, an entirely new generation arose that sought to realize the ideals of the French Revolution: liberty, equality, and fraternity. The supporters of the emancipation of the Jews were exclusively members of the upper middle class, and, while their writings and speeches castigated the social evils prevailing in the Jewish communities, for which they held the *parnassim* responsible, it soon became clear that their real aim was civic equality. Strangely enough, they had to fight their battle on two fronts: notwithstanding the victory of the French Revolution and the establishment of the Batavian republic, the revolutionaries in many parts of the country, and notably in Amsterdam, objected vehemently to the admission of the Jews as full-fledged citizens. But the majority of the Jews was equally opposed to change. Both the *parnassim* and the masses remained faithful to the House of Orange and rejected the revolution. Moreover, they feared that equal rights would also mean equal

duties; specifically, they were concerned about compulsory service, abolition of the autonomy of the communities, and the introduction of the Dutch language. Both parties tried to influence the political representatives of the nation. The innovators, such as the lawyer Moses Solomon Asser and his son Carolus, the physician Hartog de H. Lemon or the mathematician Littwak, were closer in their views to the leading figures of the republic. In imitation of the French revolutionaries, they established themselves as a club, Felix Libertate, which engaged in propaganda among the Dutch revolutionaries. On the other hand, the *parnassim* succeeded in gaining understanding for the opposite viewpoint among conservative and religious delegates.

The result was the unique debate which began on August 22 1795, and was wound up on September 2 with the adoption of the Decree on the Civic Emancipation of the Jews. In this debate, two parties confronted each other: those who regarded the Jews as a nation and therefore wanted to deny them citizenship, and

Yom Kippur or Day of Atonement, Holland, 1725. The Day of Atonement as celebrated by the Ashkenazi Jews in Holland. The Day of Atonement is the most solemn day in the Jewish calendar when Jews beg for forgiveness for sins committed. On this day a white garment *(Kittel)* is worn during the service. Amsterdam, Rijksmuseum, engraving dept.

184

Esther Scroll with case, Holland, mid-eighteenth century. Esther Scroll printed on parchment with copper engravings illustrating scenes from the Bible story printed in Holland in the mid-eighteenth century. The silver case of the same period is from Germany. On the scroll, the beginning of the Esther story is visible, with the blessings (on the right) said before the reading. Tel Aviv, Stieglitz Collection.

those for whom the Jews were individuals. The debate is remarkable for the almost complete absence of any note of anti-Semitism or pseudo-anti-Semitism, and on reading the reports today, one is more than once tempted to side with the opponents, who spoke appreciatively of the Jews' belief in the Messiah who was to lead them back to their ancient homeland. Eventually, the decree was passed by a large majority, presumably due to backstage pressure by the French ambassador. But even though the decree was adopted at a time when the country was virtually a French province, the Restoration of 1815 brought no attempt to tamper with Jewish Emancipation; and until the rise of National Socialism, no political party ever proposed to deprive the Jews even in part of their civic rights.

In the Jewish community of Amsterdam, the debate was conducted on a less lofty level. While the municipal authorities were on the side of Felix Libertate, the *parnassim* could count on

Rabbi medal, Amsterdam, 1735. Silver medal commemorating the appointment of Rabbi Eleazar ben Samuel from Brody (Galicia) as rabbi of the Ashkenazi community in Amsterdam. This medal caused a great controversy as it portrayed the graven image of the rabbi. Jerusalem, Israel Museum.

Omer calendar, Holland, eighteenth century. The painted wooden *Omer* calendar was used for the counting of the *Omer* — the forty-nine-day period of semi-mourning between Passover and Pentecost. The holes are for a peg which was moved forward from day to day. The Hebrew in the center is the blessing recited before the counting of the *Omer* at the evening service. Jerusalem, Israel Museum.

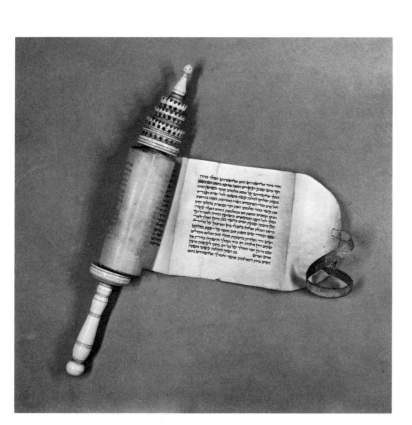

Ivory megillah, Holland, eighteenth century. Handwritten Esther Scroll, rolled on an ivory holder with carved top. Here, the beginning of the book of Esther. Cologne, Stadtmuseum, Inv. No. 1928/418

Etrog box, Holland, mid-eighteenth century. The *etrog* box served to keep the citron fresh during the week-long Festival of Tabernacles. Inscribed below: 'Fruit of Citrus Tree'. Jerusalem, Sir Isaac and Lady Edith Wolfson Museum, Hechal Shlomo, Inv. No. 25/7.

Bookbinding, Holland, 1770. With the inscription *Five Books of the Torah.* Silver, 1770. Tel Aviv, Stieglitz Collection.

the support of the masses, who even threatened the innovators with violence in the synagogue. In 1796, the men of Felix Libertate took an unprecedented step: they left the community and established a new one, Adath Jeshurun, with its own chief rabbi (Rabbi Isaac Ger, son of a Swedish convert to Judaism), its own synagogue and its own cemetery. Adath Jeshurun has sometimes been called the first Reform synagogue; unjustly so, for the changes in the synagogue service were minor and the rabbi was strictly Orthodox. The differences with the old community lay in the field of national and communal politics, though the spokesmen of Adath Jeshurun also used social arguments to incite the masses against the *parnassim.* It is characteristic of the times that the battle was fought mainly with pamphlets written in Yiddish, proof that Dutch had by no means become the daily language among the Jews. At one moment it seemed as if Adath Jeshurun would prevail over the old community. After a coup d'état instating the Jacobin trend in the Batavian republic (January 1798), the new magistrates of Amsterdam deposed the *parnassim* and replaced them by Jews who shared their ideas (*manhigim*). This, however, only increased the unrest, and by June 1798, they had to be replaced by more moderate personalities. The authorities did try to make peace between the quarreling Jews, and in 1802 the government even ordered the two communities to reunite. But in vain: the reunion did not take place until 1808, on the order of Louis Napoleon, Napoleon's brother, who had by then been made king.

To judge by the letter, the reestablishment of unity would seem a victory for the old community, though in actual fact the innovators had won the day. Most characteristic for the

Decanter for Kiddush wine, Holland, nineteenth century. Cut glass decanter for *Kiddush* wine used for the sanctification blessing on Sabbaths and festivals with inscription of the months of the year followed by the names of holidays. Amsterdam, Joods Historisch Museum, Inv. no. 300.

187

course of development is perhaps the man who became the head of the new organization created by Louis Napoleon: the High Consistory. Its appointed chairman was Jonas Daniel Meyer (1780-1834), a brilliant lawyer who was to play a leading part in Dutch Jewry. As a grandson of Benjamin Cohen, the enormously wealthy banker who had been a *parnas* in Amsterdam, Meyer had connections with the old community. He had a considerable influence on the king, who, unlike his famous brother, wanted sincerely to help the Jews. Meyer had represented the old community at the Assembly of Notables which met in Paris in 1806, but neither the High German nor the Sephardi community sent a delegation to the Paris Sanhedrin, though Adath Jeshurun did. One may assume that Meyer had been able to prevent the king from forcing the old communities to take part in the Sanhedrin.

The 'High Consistory of the High German Communities in the Kingdom of Holland' soon developed activities which were in agreement with the new ideas. External decorum in the synagogue service was encouraged, the use of the Dutch language was promoted by means of a Bible translation, and great efforts were made to reduce the large number of private *minyanim* (Jewries). All these measures had the support of the king, who, on Meyer's advice, sought to remove all obstacles to complete equality for the Jews, such as the refusal of towns to appoint Jews to municipal office. The king even went as far as to decree that wherever the weekly market was held on Saturday, it was to be shifted to another day of the week. Another measure, however, taken by the king at the insistence of his brother, provoked serious resistance: the formation of a special Jewish army corps that was to take part in Napoleon's war against Russia. In spite of the propaganda and pressure of the High Consistory, the volunteers included a number of officers but hardly any other ranks, so that the project had to be dropped.

Our only reason for mentioning this abortive plan is the

Louis Bonaparte's entry into Amsterdam, 1808. The Jewish citizens of Amsterdam, standing on the terraces of their synagogues (Portuguese synagogue, left, and Ashkenazi, right) greet the entrance parade of Louis Bonaparte. An etching by Langendijk. Amsterdam, Rijksmuseum, Rijksprentenkabinett.

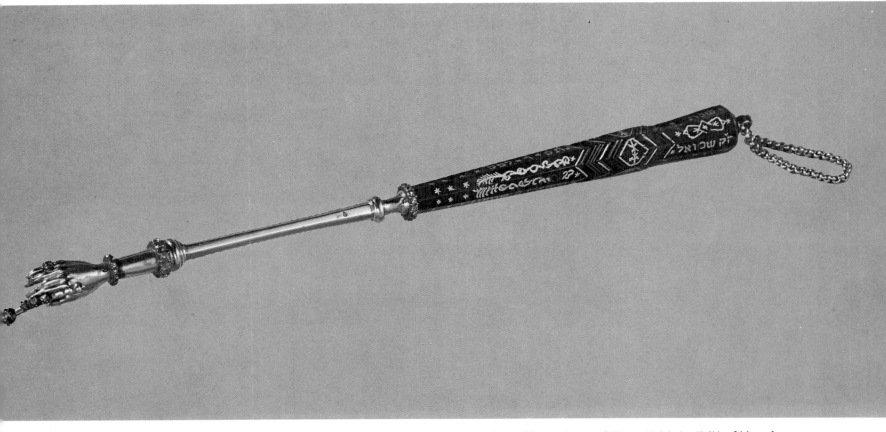

Torah pointer, Amsterdam, 1754. This gold and jasper Torah pointer bears the inscription: 'Samuel Zanwel, son of Simon Polak (or Falk) of blessed memory and his wife Mirele, daughter of Tobias Boaz (famous banker at the Hague) Amsterdam, 514 (=1754)'. Paris, Musée de Cluny, Strauss-Rothschild Collection, 12334.

light it casts on the mentality of the leading figures in the Jewish circle grouped around Jonas Daniel Meyer. They wanted to raise the Jews from their inferior station and bring them up to the level of the best of the other nations. Because of the outcome of their efforts, they are now often judged unfairly and regarded as assimilants who had no higher purpose than to curry favor with non-Jews. This takes no account of the fact that many of the innovators strove for a better future for the Jewish people and were often inspired by Jewish national feelings. Running side by side with the struggle for Emancipation, the second half of the 18th century marked the revival of Hebrew literature among the Ashkenazim, just as it came to its end among the Sephardim. In the Netherlands, it reached its peak in the beginning of the 19th century, when an association of Hebraists, 'To'elet', was founded under the inspiring leadership of Dr. S.I. Mulder. An undoubted influence of Mendelssohn, and perhaps even more of his collaborators Naphtali Herz Weisel (Wessely) and Solomon Dubno, can be felt: the latter two lived in Amsterdam and had great influence on the younger generation. Nevertheless, the Hebrew revival movement shows a specifically Dutch trend, if only in its choice of subjects. Moses Lemans, for instance, an outstanding Hebraist and mathematician, wrote a great epic work on the war between the Netherlands and Belgium, while Gabriel Polak, the most industrious if not the most gifted of the circle, translated many works from Dutch and Latin literature. Even greater is the group's impor-

tance in the field of education. Not only were nearly all of them teachers, but they turned out valuable Hebrew study books and dictionaries, and above all translations of the Bible and liturgical works.

These translations also had an additional function: they helped to make the Jewish masses, who continued to use Yiddish, familiar with the Dutch language. It was one of the means used to turn the Dutch Jews, who in the 18th century had always been referred to as 'the Jewish nation', into a religious community and to organize them into what, following the Christian pattern, called itself a 'Church Association'. In this respect, King William I, crowned in 1815, continued the work of Louis Napoleon. He, too, was strongly influenced by Jonas D. Meyer, whom he appointed as secretary of the National Commission on the New Constitution (1815), where the Jew Meyer had to keep the balance between twelve Protestants and twelve Catholics. The degree of activity which King William I deployed in Jewish affairs is astounding. Even by 1814, he had signed two decrees regulating the structure of the High German Israelite and Portuguese Israelite Church Associations and prescribed where the six chief rabbis were to reside. The celebration of marriages and funerals, the appointment of *parnassim*, budgets—everything was regulated by royal decree. In 1817, a decree was issued on the education of poor Jewish children, and in the same year, provision was made for the examination of teachers and rabbis, teaching by unqualified and foreign personnel was prohibited, and a com-

Jonas D. Meyer, 1780-1834. Famous jurist, president of the board of Jewish synagogues and secretary of the National Commission on the New Constitution of the Netherlands, shown in a lithograph by J.A. Daiwaille after a painting by Louis Moritz. Amsterdam, Rijksmuseum, Rijksprentenkabinett.

sions that the Jews felt them as a threat to their life or existence. Admittedly, certain offices, particularly representative ones such as that of mayor, were never open to Jews. On the other hand, there were certain professions in which Jews could easily make a career for themselves from the beginning of the 19th century.

One profession in particular owes its development in the Netherlands to a very large extent to the Jews: the law. We have already mentioned some lawyers, Jonas D. Meyer and the Assers. The latter family produced a host of jurists, the most

Miniature Sabbath stove, Holland, beginning of nineteenth century. Possibly a model. As the lighting of a fire was forbidden on the Sabbath, these stoves kept the food warm for twenty-four hours. Of brass and iron. Amsterdam, Joods Historisch Museum, Inv. No. 23 b.

pulsory national syllabus was introduced. In 1818, local authorities were ordered to provide grants for Jewish communities in accordance with their numerical strength. The king also encouraged the building of new synagogues, and in 1827 even awarded a 'medal of honor' for the publication of Jewish educational works. While most of these measures can be attributed to Jewish advisers, it is clear that the king was serious about applying the principles of emancipation: complete equality for the Jews, to be achieved by, among other things, the elimination of all differences between Jews and non-Jews which, in the king's view, were not of a religious nature.

The king's efforts were in the first place successful among the well-to-do Jewish circles. As in Germany, there were those among them who went so far as to abandon Judaism. Conversion never, however, assumed epidemic dimensions in the Netherlands, on the one hand because the Jewish community was a long-standing, closed circle which it was not easy to abandon, and on the other hand because the anti-Jewish feelings rife among a large part of the population never assumed such dimen-

famous of whom was the Nobel peace prizewinner, Tobias M.C. Asser. The first Jewish professor of law was J.E. Goudsmit of Leiden, who was to be followed by dozens of others, including E.M. Meyers, whose dismissal from his chair in Leiden by the German occupation authorities in 1940 caused such a degree of unrest that Leiden University had to be closed. The Supreme Council, Holland's highest law court, has probably never been without a Jewish member. As chance would have it, its president at the time of the German occupation was a Jew, L. Visser. On that occasion, Visser proved himself a man of principle and a conscious Jew. Of the five Jews who were Cabinet members during the last century (not a large number as such), four were Minister of Justice.

Another profession in which the Jews had excelled was medicine. Even in the 17th century there were famous Jewish doctors, and in the 18th century, Jews were the first protagonists of vaccination. However, it was only much later that the universities opened their doors to Jewish members of the medical profession.

In considering the part played by the Jews in the life of the Netherlands, we cannot overlook the figure of Samuel Sarphati, a physician whose manifold activities doubtless sprang from a strong social motivation. He founded a company for the manufacture of flour and bread, but when he realized that in doing so he had not succeeded in abolishing poverty, he attempted to provide employment by restoring Amsterdam's position as an international center by such means as the organization of exhibitions. Since there was no suitable space for his purpose, he built an enormous complex to fill this need; and for this building to be put up in suitable surroundings, he exerted pressure on the municipal authorities until they started to follow the example of Paris by establishing new suburbs with wide avenues. This, of course, stimulated the need to provide accommodation for visitors, and it was Sarphati who took the initiative for the construction of the first—and to this day the most representative—modern hotel in Amsterdam.

Sarphati would of course not have succeeded in all this without the help of the bankers. Karl Marx spoke contemptuously of the many Jewish bankers of Amsterdam, though on investigation they are somewhat less ubiquitous than Marx's anti-Semitic cast of mind made them out to be. Most of them, like the Bischoffheims, were branches of foreign enterprises. But there were two financiers who played a highly important role in the Netherlands. The first was Lodewyk Pincoff, whose energy was the driving force behind the development of Rotterdam. The career of Pincoff, who was even elected to the First Chamber (the Netherlands Senate), came to a sad end when the African Trading Company, which he had founded, went bankrupt. He escaped to America and was sentenced *in absentia*. His fall resulted in an anti-Semitic campaign which not only made its mark in the press, but also resulted in a cooler attitude toward the Jews in ruling circles. The man feeling this most immediately was the banker A.C. Wertheim, who in a sense may be regarded as Sarphati's successor. In addition to being a banker, Wertheim was also a Liberal politican, with considerable influence in his

Dr. Samuel Sarphati, (1813-66). The enterprising Dutch physician, whose multiple activities usually had a social motivation behind them, in a lithograph by S. Áltmann. Amsterdam, Rijksmuseum, Rijksprentenkabinett.

party. But the most interesting aspect of his personality is his attitude to Judaism. Wertheim was completely detached from Orthodoxy. In Germany he would no doubt have found his place in a Reform synagogue; in the Netherlands, this Jew who desecrated the Sabbath and violated the dietary laws in public was for years president of a 'Church' Association which was committed to a position of rigorous Orthodoxy—a position which Wertheim defended with great spirit. His statement 'Not a stone of the fort' became the slogan of the synagogue, whose Orthodox rabbis and unorthodox lay leaders joined forces to prevent the rise of any Reform movement in the Netherlands, and this attitude prevailed until far into the 20th century.

THE MODERN PERIOD

By the end of the nineteenth century, Dutch Jewry was in the throes of far-reaching economic, sociological, political and cultural changes. In Amsterdam, the Jews had played a major part in the diamond industry ever since the 17th century. When the South African diamond fields were discovered, demand for cut stones rose enormously, causing an unprecedented prosperity in this industry, which attracted more and more Jewish dealers and workers (the 'Cape Period', 1872-6). The boom passed and was

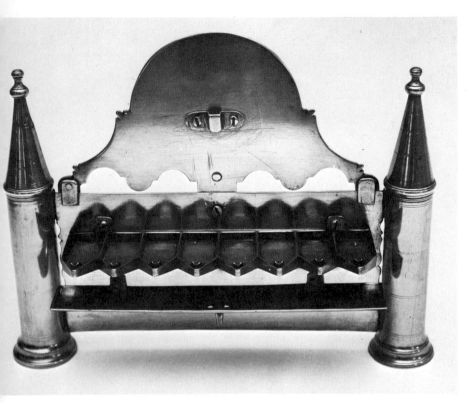

Hannukah lamp, Holland, early nineteenth century. Strasbourg, Musée Alsacien, Société pour l'Histoire des Israélites d'Alsace et de Lorraine.

Brass Hanukkah lamp, Holland, end of nineteenth century. Tree, animal and flower ornamentation, with eight oil lamps. Cologne, Stadtmuseum, Inv. No. 1927/710.

followed by a severe slump. But unlike what had happened in former days, the workers would no longer rest content with the steps their employers proposed to meet the crisis in the old-fashioned manner; Socialism had taken a hold on them, and their demands and arguments in the trade union movement were radical. In these hard times, there developed 'a sharp, almost hostile division between Jews and Christians' among the diamond-cutters. This was brought to an end principally by the great Dutch trade union leader Henri Polak (1860-1943), who founded the General Netherlands Union of Diamond Workers (Algemeene Nederlandsche Diamantbewerkers Bond) in 1894. Owing to Polak's organizational talents, the ANDB was soon to become the strongest trade union in the country and was capable of resisting the anarchistic trends which threatened to overwhelm the Socialist movement. To counter the danger of anarchism, Polak and eleven others founded in 1894 the Social-Democratic Workers Party, in which he played a leading role for many years and which he was to represent in Parliament.

The trade union movement, too, owes much to Henri Polak, who, after a bad disaster for the Netherlands workers, played a major role in establishing the Netherlands Federation of Trade Unions in 1906; in its beginnings, the new Federation was greatly influenced by the ANDB with its excellent organization and ample financial means. The growth of trade unionism and Socialism led at first to serious conflicts within the Jewish community. Henri Polak, of course, played his part in this conflict, though later events were to prove that he held strong Jewish convictions and even supported the rebuilding of the Land of Israel.

In his writings he never denied his Jewish origins and interest. Most of his Jewish fellow-Socialists, however, thought differently. The Jewish proletariat, which turned Socialist in the beginning of the 20th century, regarded the Jewish religion as 'opium' and, unlike the East European Jews, never developed an independent road to Jewish Socialism. Even more hostile was the attitude of the Jewish intellectuals of the Marxist Left, who eventually found themselves in the Communist party and whose leader, David Wynkoop, son of a well-known rabbi and Hebrew grammarian, completely cut his ties with all things Jewish. Still, for all their internationalism and atheism, the Jewish quarters of Amsterdam retained a markedly Jewish feel, reflected in their characteristic dialect and perhaps also in strong intellectual aspirations. Not many years later the sons of diamond-workers, hawkers and small shopkeepers were to be found among the intellectual élite of the Netherlands.

In the hundreds of Jewish communities outside Amsterdam, things were different. Here, there was no coherent Jewish proletariat, and the Jews were strongly aware of being a small minority that was different from the general population. With a few exceptions, they had a hard time making a living. Hawker, market dealer, cattle dealer, butcher—those were their main trades. Here again, things changed at the end of the 19th and the beginning of the 20th century: the hawkers began to benefit from the development of industry, the market dealers from better communications and commercial expansion. Thus they became manufacturers and wholesalers, mainly in the textile trade. In the eastern Netherlands, a number of Jewish families

192

(Menco, Spanjaard, Hedeman) succeeded in establishing large factories and developed the district of Twente into the center of the Dutch textile industry. Another industry, first established by a Jewish trader in a small village, was the margarine factory of Van den Berg, which was to grow into the worldwide Unilever concern.

This increase in prosperity was paralleled by another development: the Jews began to leave the small villages for the cities. Amsterdam attracted the greatest numbers, but the other cities, Rotterdam, the Hague, Utrecht, and Groningen in the north also saw their Jewish population grow at the expense of the country. Obviously, this process toward urbanization also had the effect of making many Jews, who in their former small communities had kept faith with their religion, lapse into religious indifference or even leave the Jewish community entirely.

The beginning of the 20th century was therefore a time of crisis for the Dutch Jews. Their progress was faster than that of the general population, and at the same time their birthrate, which had been very high, trailed off rapidly. The number of mixed marriages increased; in Amsterdam, even, it was the highest of all the great cities in Europe. The demographic decline was further reinforced by the considerable numbers of those who opted out of the Jewish community on the grounds of atheism.

Not that the role of the Jews diminished. We have already seen how important they were in the Socialist movement: the

Silver circumcision medal, Utrecht, 1845. Circumcision medal given by Judah ben Eliezer, a *Mohel* (circumciser) from Utrecht, to all the children he circumcised. The chair seen here is the Chair of Elijah or circumcision chair; on the other side the name of the child and date of the ceremony were engraved. Jerusalem, Israel Museum.

number of Jewish Labor leaders who were elected to Parliament or municipal office was considerable. The Liberal party, too, had numbered Jews among its leading members ever since Wertheim. No less important was their part in cultural affairs. The first of the Dutch Jewish painters was also the greatest: Jozef Israels (1824-1911). He had not yet detached himself from the Jewish community, and his Jewish identification inspired some of his best works, such as the *Son of the Old People and the Scribe*. His son Isaac Israels, also a talented painter, belonged to a different

period already, in which the rich Jews were embarrassed by their poorer brethren, but still felt most at home in their own circle, the *haute juiverie*. Later painters never came up to the standards of Jozef Israels.

Glass goblet with silver base, Holland, 1860. Glass with Hebrew inscription giving the name of the donor and the person to whom it was destined. Silver base with Dutch silver mark. Hamburg, Museum für Kunst und Gewerbe.

Sculptors were rare among Dutch Jews; one of them, Jozef Mendes da Costa (1863-1939) was not only known for monumental works, but also for figurines and groups in *grès cérame*, which reflect his social consciousness as much as his Jewish ties. He was obviously influenced by the new social movement. The same is true to an even greater extent for the writers, the most famous of whom, Herman Heyermans, was the Netherlands' greatest playwright and whose plays concerned themselves mainly with the sufferings of the working class. When Heyermans wrote about Jews, however, he was usually so critical as to be nearly hostile. In his novel *Diamond Town* and his play *The Ghetto* he depicts figures that are less than sympathetic. To his credit it must be said that he later admitted this bias frankly, at least as far the play is concerned.

The rise of Socialism inspired many other Jewish writers; not a few of them directed their attention to the Amsterdam ghetto or the small Jewish country community, and enjoyed great fame in their time, although they have no message for later generations. An exception must be made in the case of the gifted children of a rural rabbi named De Haan: Jacob Israel and Carry. Jacob Israel, a talented lawyer, regarded himself as a great poet, though in actual fact his gift for prose may have been greater. Swaying from one extreme to the other, he began his career as an atheist-socialist teacher in Haarlem and ended it as a fanatically Orthodox Jew who sought the friendship of Arabs in order to fight Zionism and thus became the victim of the first political murder committed by Jews in the modern Land of Israel. His sister was more consistent in her atheism and her rejection of Judaism, but she never denied her origins, as is shown by her touching description of her youth and her religious experiences in the paternal home.

This love of the Jewish milieu, though often enough combined with a measure of self-hate, is characteristic of the Dutch and particularly the Amsterdam Jews. It is hardly surprising to find it in a city where the Jews had for three centuries accounted for one tenth of the population and thus had created and developed a sphere that was particularly their own. It was a sphere which did not fail to attract non-Jews, many of whom sought to identify themselves with it, a tendency most marked in the world of the theater and cabaret. There have been many great Jewish actors—the greatest of them was Esther de Boer van Ryk, who owes much of her fame to her appearances in Heyermans' plays—while the greatest of Dutch cabaret entertainers, Louis Davids, was also a Jew. In fact eventually even the lines between Jew and non-Jew became completely blurred. Jewish speech and Jewish patterns of living left such clear traces in the world of the arts, that the absence of this milieu was painfully noticeable after World War II.

ZIONISM

In this prevailing atmosphere, it is scarcely surprising that the Jewish national movement was confronted with specific problems. Most Dutch Jews were so deeply convinced of the effec-

tiveness of the Jewish-Gentile symbiosis in Holland that they could not believe in any danger to the Jews and felt sure that the few existing traces of discrimination would disappear in course of time. Not that Dutch Jewry lacked those who felt strong ties with Jews in other parts. The closeness of the link with the Land of Israel is evident from the establishment of a fund-raising organization for the benefit of the Jews in the Holy Land: Pekidim and Amarcalim of the Holy Land (1810), in Amsterdam. This organization, headed by the bankers Lehren, became a factor of importance in the support of the Jews of Jerusalem and also helped strengthen the Jewish community. The Lehren brothers were pietitst who came into conflict with the prevailing rationalist-assimilationist trend. Their group still had its followers in the 20th century, but its influence was negligible.

Zionism on the other hand, basing itself, as it did, on the principle of emancipation, was able to gather a following from the very beginning. One of the first Zionists was the banker Jacobus H. Kann, who was among Herzl's early collaborators. In the Netherlands, the Zionist movement soon had to fight on two fronts: it was violently opposed by the Orthodoxy and condemned by all the Dutch chief rabbis with the exception of Dr. J.H. Duenner. On the other hand, the Socialist Jews regarded Zionism as a reactionary movement, which was therefore a danger to the worker and must be fought. As a result, there were only two Zionist nuclei until the time of the end of World War I: those Orthodox circles which followed Duenner's lead, and members of the free professions. This situation was changed by that war. Neutral Holland absorbed a number of refugees, particularly from Belgium, and they soon started to deploy an intensive Jewish national activity. Under their influence, the Jewish national movement in the Netherlands began to be more active in propaganda, education, and cultural affairs. Young religious leaders became enthusiastic Zionists and Socialist opposition weakened. A strong Jewish youth movement, which militantly promoted Hebrew and a pioneering movement came into existence. During the 1920s, growth remained comparatively slow, but the great change came with the rise of Hitler in Germany, particularly after 1933. The seven years until the Netherlands themselves were occupied by the Germans were a restless time. The thirty thousand or more German Jews who escaped to Holland brought the Dutch Jews face to face with questions which could not be answered without a complete change of orientation. Who was responsible for their maintenance? Should one insist on keeping the borders open, or would this undermine the position of the Netherlands Jews? Was the stream of refugees a portent of what Holland must expect, or would the country be able to preserve its neutrality again, as it had done in World War I? To look after and help absorb the German Jews, a mighty apparatus was set up under the leadership of the diamond merchant A. Ascher and the historian D. Cohen. This committee to all practical intents took over responsibility from the Government, which was extremely reluctant to admit the refugees. In the discussion over their admission, the vast majority of the Jews spoke in favor of a policy of open borders,

The Jewish Bride by Joseph Israels, 1903. Israels (1824-1911) depicted the general everyday life in Holland as well as specifically Jewish scenes, particularly from 1883 onward. This Dutch-Jewish painter has often been called the most significant figure in Dutch art since the 17th century. Amsterdam, Rijksmuseum.

German round-up of Jews, February 1941. Jews kneeling on the Jonas Daniel Meyerplein after a round-up by the German police during the occupation of the Netherlands. Of the 140,000 Jews in Holland at the outbreak of the war, some 80 per cent perished. There are today 22,000 Jews in the country.

notwithstanding the possible consequences for the Netherlands. Most Dutch Jews, however, fostered illusions as to the inviolability of the country which now appear incomprehensible. Only few had premonitions of the terrible disaster which was to befall Dutch Jewry.

WORLD WAR II

If we are to understand what happened in the Netherlands between the years 1940 and 1945, we must remember that the Netherlands had not known war for more than a hundred years.

The Jewish bride. Famous work by Rembrandt. Rembrandt lived in the Jewish quarter of Amsterdam and was attracted by Jewish types whom he depicted in portraits and biblical themes; thirty-seven out of his two hundred male portraits are of Jewish personalities or types. Among his sitters were Dr. Ephraim Bueno and Menasseh Ben Israel. Amsterdam, Rijksmuseum.

Interior of Portuguese synagogue, Amsterdam, 1675. A rare example of a synagogue interior painted by a major artist, Emanuel de Witte, in 1675. The building and interior have remained unchanged until the present day. Jerusalem, Israel Museum.

Peace and contentment had become national characteristics. The law was obeyed to the letter as were all official orders, for no one considered the possibility that a criminal government might take advantage of this obedience to lead peaceful citizens astray. There was one small group which sided with the Germans, but even one section of the Dutch National-Socialists rejected anti-Semitism. All this, however, did not prevent the Dutch officials from following the German decrees meekly, even if they were contrary to the Netherlands constitution and international law. The eyes of the population were not opened until the

Germans began to use brute force and arrested a few hundred Jews in Amsterdam, herded them together and deported them to the concentration camp of Mauthausen. Amsterdam reacted with a total worker's strike (February 1941), which spread to other places in the neighborhood as well. It was a unique and courageous act of solidarity with the Jews; for the Jews, however, the effect of the strike was only moral. The Germans, taught by experience, continued their actions by means of quasi-legal decrees and thus brought the majority of the civil service and the police over to their side. Concentration camps were established;

Interior of Maastricht synagogue, 1839-40. A fine Dutch synagogue interior. The women's gallery can be seen upstairs; the reader's desk is in the center, the Ark at the end, and, above it, the Ten Commandments.

the one in Westerbork served as a transit camp to the death camps of Auschwitz and Sobibor. Of the 140,000 Dutch Jews, more than a 100,000 were deported, and only a few thousand of these returned. Many of the others perished as well. Among the non-Jewish population, a considerable number were prepared to give shelter to the Jews, in spite of the danger to life which it involved. It is assumed that some twenty thousand Jews went underground; about half eventually were found by the Germans.

Even during the war, there had been isolated complaints in the underground press about the failure of the Dutch population to reject German anti-Jewish discrimination unanimously. The complete extent of the disaster, however, did not come out until after the war. The numbers of the victims spoke a language that could not be misunderstood. The terrors of Auschwitz and Sobibor became known. Reports, accounts, diaries appeared, the most famous being that of Anne Frank. The feeling of inadequacy became a trauma of the Dutch people after World War II. Theologians became aware of the relation between Jew and Christian and pleaded for a total revision of the Christian view of Judaism. Artists identified with Jewish suffering and wrote of it, spoke of it, illustrated it. It seemed that the Jews had never occupied the Dutch people's attention so much as when they had become numerically a completely unimportant minority.

And what of the Jews themselves? The shock of the apocalyptic events left unmistakable traces. The Jewish community shook off its self-satisfied attitude and regained an awareness of its links with Jews elsewhere. This appeared first and foremost in the massive emigration to Palestine and later to Israel, which proportionally exceeded that of all other Western countries. Many Dutch Jews, though, also emigrated to other countries, Canada, Australia, and particularly the United States. But there are yet other aspects that reflect the catastrophe. The prose and poetry of the Dutch-Jewish writers is pervaded by the memories of what happened to them or to the Jews in general. More than ever the Jews in the Netherlands are aware of their Jewish identity.

One may ask whether this is not a passing phenomenon. The Catastrophe operated selectively and the intellectual and financial upper strata of the Jewish community were comparatively the least affected. Hence, though only one-sixth of the Jews have survived and remained in the Netherlands, the share of the Jews in Dutch cultural and economic life seems no less than before the war. At an estimate, there are some fifty Jewish professors, and dozens of writers, poets, composers and other artists. Unfortunately, however, this seems to be an Indian summer which presages no new growth. Not only is the community numerically so small that it depends on other countries, mainly on Israel, particularly for its spiritual needs, but the demographic conditions are particularly unpromising. The birth rate is lower than that of the general population. The favorable climate, the absence of discrimination, and the general prosperity encourage further blending with the non-Jewish environment. Jewish consciousness and the sympathy and often admiration for Judaism among the non-Jews are not sufficient to counteract this trend.

The three hundred and fifty years of Jewish existence in the Netherlands thus form a complete self-contained entirety, framed by two great disasters for the Jewish people: the Expulsion from Spain and the Nazi Holocaust. During that period, the Netherlands Jewish achievement, economically and culturally, has been considerable. But while the first part of the period, until the Emancipation, is characterized by a Jewish community which was closed off from its environment and in close contact with Jews elsewhere, the second half presents the opposite picture: separation from the Jewish world and ever greater participation in the Dutch society. The Jewish national revival was on the point of reversing the trend, when the great Holocaust put an end to all thought of independent development, and all that remained was the memory of a great past.

CHAPTER VI

England

by Dr. Vivian D. Lipman

In England, various factors hastened the change from medieval Western society based on feudalism and the Church to the modern concept of a national state with a centralized government: its geographical situation as an island; the loss of most of its Continental possessions at a relatively early date; the Black Death, after which a new and free form of agricultural society gradually replaced the feudal system. Because England had a head start on her Continental neighbors, she experienced her anti-monarchical revolution a century and a half earlier than France and almost three centuries before Russia. And though after a brief interlude the monarchy was restored, never again was the power of the Crown able to stifle freedom of thought or conscience.

Faces of medieval English Jews, thirteenth century. These six faces come from caricatures drawn on thirteenth-century English official documents and show individuals as they appeared to their contemporaries. Reading downward these are: a) the great financier Jurnet, son of Isaac, of Norwich, shown crowned, with three faces; b) Mosse (Moses) Mokke, son of Abraham, also of Norwich, wearing the Jewish spiked hat (?); c) Mosse's wife, Avegaye (Abigail); d) Aaron, 'son of the devil', of Colchester, wearing a cowl and with the Jewish badge in its English form of the two tables of the law; e) an unnamed English Jew of 1234, with a pair of scales; f) Hake (Isaac), another Norwich Jew, of 1289. Jewish Historical Society of England.

As a result, England subsequently enjoyed practically three hundred years of growth, during which she was for a period indisputably the richest and most powerful nation in the world. Even the struggle for political emancipation of the mass of the population was conducted within constitutional limits despite the fact that at times the atmosphere was dangerous. By the end of the 19th century, therefore, England was the envy of the less privileged nations of the world.

The image which has impressed itself on outsiders—and one that persisted until the mid-20th century, when it has been replaced by that of a permissive society—was a land where it was 'always afternoon', where the country house weekend was the epitome of pleasant and gracious living; where freedom of the individual and the press were supreme; where no secret police knocked on the door at night.

England in modern times has on the whole adhered to this image in respect of the Jews. When the *Jewish Chronicle* wrote on the outbreak of the 1914 war, 'England has been all to the Jews, the Jews will be all they can to England', it was expressing the sentiments of an Anglo-Jewry composed mainly of immigrants and the sons of immigrants, which had been absorbed into the established community and many of whom had no other aim than to live as 'Englishmen of the Jewish persuasion'. Even in the half century which has followed, loyalty to Britain has not, on the whole, conflicted, except perhaps temporarily, with Zionism and pride and affection for the State of Israel. For the appeal of life in England since the Resettlement has been the tolerance and freedom which has facilitated the absorption of people from different backgrounds and with different ideals and has molded them into a national entity while allowing them to preserve their separateness in matters of religion in its widest sense.

It was not, however, always so. Anglo-Jewish history falls into three clearly defined periods: the Middle Ages when Jews were a restricted, more or less tolerated, minority until they were expelled in 1290; from then until 1656 when Jews were not supposed to be in the country openly at all; and from 1656—the Resettlement—since when they have enjoyed virtually complete social and, from 1858, political equality.

THE MEDIEVAL PERIOD

Jewish society is, to some extent, a reflection of its environment, and thus in the Middle Ages the Jews in all countries were particularly conditioned by the surrounding society, a state of affairs that applied to medieval England as well as to Continental communities. Since the Anglo-Jewish community was an extension of northern French and Rhineland Jewry, the same conditions could, to a large extent be found. The Jews were the king's chattels, driven to moneylending because all other means of livelihood were denied them. (In England, they could not hold rural land in a feudal society, and were debarred therefore from agriculture. Even in the towns they could not practice a craft because they were denied membership of the craft guilds which operated on a religious basis.) While they were useful in providing money they were generally protected; but exploitation eventually reduced their profitability both as moneylenders and as royal 'milch cows' to be taxed on every conceivable pretext and sometimes none at all. This was the pattern of the Anglo-Jewish medieval settlement, which began under the Norman kings and was summarily ended by Edward I in 1290 when he realized, after a trial run in Gascony, that the impoverished community brought him in less than he could obtain by confiscation of their effects on expulsion. His action, the first general expulsion of Jews—as distinct from local expulsions—set a precedent which was followed by Philip the Fair of France, who banished the French Jews in 1306, and by Ferdinand and Isabella of Spain in 1492.

Yet during the two centuries of Jewish settlement in England there had been periods of reasonable security. The Jews had first come to England either in the reign of William the Conqueror or in that of his successor William Rufus, who hardly rates as an orthodox Christian and who is reported to have offered to turn Jew if the Jews could defeat the bishops in theological disputation. Some crossed the Channel after disturbances in Rouen at the time of the preaching of the First Crusade (1096). Certainly in times of strong government in the 12th century the Jews were favored by the Crown. The Charter granted them under John in 1201 confirmed the privileges they had enjoyed under Henry I and these were substantial. They were free to travel, a right to which medieval rabbis attached great importance as indicating a free status; they enjoyed a large measure of communal autonomy; they were exempt from the courts of the local lords and of the Church and subject only to royal justice. In twelfth-century England they were thus a favored class, but their position was eroded as the 13th century advanced and the power of the Church with its growing intolerance and anti-Semitic legislation permeated all sectors of English life.

Earlier the Church as a whole, as distinct from particular dioceses, had been prepared to tolerate the Jews. They were the descendants of biblical characters with whom the populace, through the stories told them by their priests, were familiar. True, they were infidels but they were regarded as witnesses to the origins of Christianity and it was hoped that they would eventually accept conversion. Bernard of Clairvaux, for example, had condemned attacks on Jewish communities by Crusaders and the papacy never at this time supported accusations of ritual murder and indeed often tried to combat them. But with the Third Lateran Council in 1179 the attitude changed. Social intercourse between Jews and Christians was discouraged; Jews were even forbidden to employ Christian servants. The measures were largely ineffective in England at that time though no doubt they contributed to the anti-Jewish feeling which found expression in the attacks on Jews in 1189-90. The 1179 decrees, however, were only a prelude to the harsh impositions of the Fourth Lateran Council in 1215, which not only repeated earlier decrees but also insisted that Jews should wear distinctive dress. In England, this was generally avoidable on payment until in 1253 the wearing of a badge was made compulsory, as were restrictions on building new synagogues, employing Christian servants and settling outside established communities, for which a licence was hence-

forth required. And under Edward I the screw was turned still tighter with the expulsion of Jews from certain towns which were the dower of the queen mother, who was fanatically anti-Jewish.

The influence of medieval Anglo-Jewry on its environment was small. The social and neighborly intercourse which evidently existed in the earlier period when Jews and Christians often rode together on journeys or visited one another's homes and drank together, was later forbidden by both the Church and secular authorities, though this did not prevent a number of Christian guests attending, despite ecclesiastical warnings against doing so, a particularly lavish Jewish wedding held in Hereford in 1286, for which they were placed under the ban of the Church.

It is of interest, however, that the Jews of medieval England did not live in ghettos. True they congregated in certain streets—one of which was generally called 'the Jewry'—close to a place of royal protection, to the market, and to their synagogue, but their houses were not separated by any physical barrier from those of their Christian neighbors.

Nor were all urban houses which have survived inhabited by Jews. Often a house has been wrongly attributed to Jewish ownership because it was thought that only a Jew could afford such dwellings. In fact, most Jews could not afford them either and it is only a minority, such as the so-called Music House of the Jurnet family in Norwich and the Jew's House at Lincoln identified with Belaset, which can definitely be stated to have been built and lived in by Jews.

It is thus obvious that it would be a mistake to assume that all Jews were rich magnates. The Anglo-Jewish medieval community, consisting at its peak of between four and five thousand souls, produced a number of rich financiers during the two hundred years of its existence. But there was a much larger number of individuals who existed by negotiating small loans among villagers or petty burghers, probably by a bit of pawnbroking or by working for richer coreligionists either directly, or by producing the consumer goods they needed. There also seems to have been a criminal element among the Jews and there are records of crimes of violence as well as offenses against the Forest Laws.

Medieval Prejudices

England has the doubtful distinction of being the first European country in which was heard the accusation of ritual murder in the Middle Ages. The story of the murder of William of Norwich in 1144 is an unpleasant example of the use made by calculating interests of an incident which, in fact, probably need never have been connected with Jews at all. But once the suspicion had been aroused that the boy found buried in a wood outside Norwich at Easter had been the victim of Jews celebrating the festival of Passover, there were unscrupulous persons prepared to make a martyr of the boy for the material benefits accruing to the Church from pilgrims who would come in the hope of miraculous cures or to do penance for their sins. However, it is only fair to record that the accusations were not accepted unanimously and that there were local churchmen who opposed the assertion that William was a martyr murdered by the Jews. Since the 19th century attempts have been made to discover from the evidence the true cause of William's death. The present author, having regard to the state of undress of the corpse, the ill-treatment of the body and the fact that he was gagged, has come to the conclusion that the boy was the victim of a sexual crime.

The surprising part of the matter would seem to be the small amount of anti-Jewish feeling aroused. The sheriff as the king's representative extended protection to the Jews of Norwich and accompanied them to the ecclesiastical court to which they were summoned, reminding the clerics there assembled that the Jews were accountable only to the king. The matter soon died down and the subsequent murder of a leading local Jew was not really due to it.

How different, though, the hostility aroused and the massacres perpetrated when the preaching of the Third Crusade—the first to make any impact on England—inflamed Christians against the 'infidels' in their midst. Debtors seized the occasion of the current anti-Jewish feeling to cause riots and to burn the records of transactions in which they were involved. The massacre of the York community in 1190—during the festival of Passover—has taken its place in medieval martyrology with the destruction of the Rhineland communities at the end of the 11th century. The situation in Norwich in 1144 must be compared, too, with the story of St. Hugh of Lincoln, another tale of a boy martyr but one which occurred in 1255 when the climate of opinion had hardened against the Jews. Though the boy, it is now accepted, probably died accidentally while playing, a forced confession was extracted from the Jew living nearest to the spot where he was found and a large number of Jews was arrested, many of whom perished.

Deteriorating relations between Jew and non-Jew were aggravated in the long reign of the weak, pious and anti-Semitic Henry III (1215-72), who was ably abetted by his violently anti-Jewish wife. The Jews suffered from the increasing exactions of the Crown, from the worsening climate of opinion and from the disorders following the baronial rebellion against the king.

LEARNING AND POETRY

Within their own community, however, Anglo-Jews often led a rich intellectual life. In an age when only a small percentage of the population could read and write, the Jews were generally literate in Hebrew and often in Latin and Norman-French as well. Indeed many business documents which have survived were obviously written by the signatories themselves. Anglo-Jewry kept in close touch with the communities of Northern France, particularly before 1204 when Normandy was lost to the English king. They received eminent scholars from abroad. Abraham Ibn Ezra is reputed to have visited England in 1158, and it was while Yomtov of Joigny was living in York in 1190 that he was among the Jews who committed suicide in Clifford's Tower.

The community also produced scholars of its own. Probably the greatest Jew in England in the Middle Ages was Elijah Menahem of London who was scholar, financier and physician and who lived from about 1220 to 1284. Various commentaries, including one on the Passover *Haggadah,* survive as well as a series of halakhic decisions. The *Etz Hayyim* of Jacob ben Judah Hazan of London was written as late as 1287, only three years before the expulsion. A code of law with liturgy and poems, the codification takes the same general form as other contemporary works of a similar type, such as the *Mishneh Torah* of Maimonides. It is in two parts, sixty chapters in the *Sepher ha-Torah* which is largely concerned with liturgical, ritual and matrimonial law, and forty-nine chapters in *Sepher ha-Mishpat,* mainly on civil law. It also contains the complete prayer-book of medieval Anglo-Jewry and their Passover *Haggadah.* Incidentally, the text of the medieval Grace after Meals would seem to confirm that scholars enjoyed high status, for unlike the modern version, there is a prayer for their increase.

It might appear that medieval Jewish scholarship was unequal, concentrating on Talmud, responsa, and grammar, the last particularly favored not only in Jewish learned circles but among the Christians. In actual fact, a famous medieval Hebrew poet, Meir of Norwich, who survived the expulsion and whose works were preserved for centuries in the Vatican Library, provides evidence that the standard of Anglo-Jewish literature was in no way inferior to that of Continental Jewry. The story of the discovery of his existence is a remarkable one. He might have remained completely unknown but for the fact that a fourteenth- or fifteenth-century scholar, probably German, copied out the poems and that they reached the Vatican. Still the poet's name might not have been known but for the fact that his signature is there in acrostic form—'Meir' in some of the short poems; 'Meir son of Elijah the *Hozeh* (seer)' on another occasion; and in a long poem on the Exodus, 'I am Meir, son of Rabbi Elijah from the city of Norwich which is in the land of the Isle called Angleterre...' If his work survived so fortuitously, is it not likely that there were other authors of caliber whose works have disappeared?

There were, too, patrons of scholarship and scholars among the medieval magnates of Anglo-Jewry. For until modern times scholarship was not generally a separate occupation. To devote time to study and to esteem scholars was the pride and pleasure of many businessmen (aided, no doubt, in the Middle Ages by the fact that moneylending left time for other pursuits). Many had libraries or at least collections of books, and in a number of cases the rich financier was also steeped in religious learning and capable of sitting on a *Bet Din* (rabbinical law-court). Some, like Elijah Menahem of London, were physicians. And, in a period when herbs were important in the treatment of illness, it was a Jewish doctor in Norwich who owned the first private herbarium in England.

The 'Synagogue' statue outside Rochester Cathedral, mid-thirteenth-century. Mid-thirteenth-century figure, one of a pair of the conventional Church and Synagogue contrasted figures, with a broken banner and tablets of the law reversed. Dean and Chapter of Rochester Cathedral. Photo R.H. Langden.

Menasseh Ben Israel, 1636. Menasseh Ben Israel (1604-57), rabbi, author, and printer, of Marrano origin, came to London to appeal to Cromwell to allow the Jews to resettle in England. Although his name is indissolubly associated with the Resettlement, he probably died a disappointed man, believing his mission to have been unsuccessful. He was drawn by Rembrandt in the Jewish quarter of Amsterdam, where he spent most of his life. Amsterdam, Rijksmuseum.

CHRISTIAN HEBRAISTS

Jewish doctors certainly treated well-to-do Christians and there were other social relationships between Jews and Christians. But at a time when there was quite an important school of Christian Hebraists in England, it would be interesting to know where these obtained their knowledge of Hebrew. Not necessarily, the evidence would seem to show, from Anglo-Jews. Just as the Jews of England and Northern France were closely linked, so too were English Christian scholars with their colleagues in Paris, and in Paris there was a lively school of Hebrew studies. There, Jewish commentaries, particularly Rashi, were extremely popular among Christian students of the Hebrew Bible. But in view of the fact that the aim of Christian Hebraists—such as the thirteenth-century Dominicans and Franciscans who studied the Old Testament to draw its heirs closer to Christianity—were not always the pursuit of learning alone, Jewish scholars would have been chary of

teaching them and thus putting a weapon into their hands voluntarily. On the other hand, converts would have had no such scruples. Nevertheless, there is some reason to believe that Roger Bacon, the Franciscan friar and philosopher, Herbert of Bosham, and Maurice, Prior of the Augustinians at Kirkham, may have studied with Jewish teachers. Maurice mentions that in his youth he spent three years learning Hebrew and transcribed forty Hebrew Psalms, the Jews themselves admiring his calligraphy. Roger Bacon, a friend and admirer of the famous thirteenth-century Bishop of Lincoln, Robert Grosseteste, who sponsored a literal version of the Psalms, wrote that there was no difficulty in finding Hebrew teachers for 'there are Jews to be found everywhere'.

Two cases are known in Anglo-Jewish medieval history of Christians whose study of the Hebrew language had unexpected results in an age which took its religion seriously. The Dominican friar Robert of Reading became a proselyte and died as a martyr in 1275 under the Hebrew name Haggai. A more romantic story is that of the unnamed deacon who came from Coventry to Oxford University and whose study of Hebrew and of the charms of a local Jewess with whom he fell in love led to his conversion and marriage. Charged with desecration of the host, he was found guilty and burned alive, though his wife seems to have escaped punishment.

We cannot attribute to Anglo-Jewry any *Haggadot* or other manuscripts of artistic workmanship, like those of Continental Jewries, although it is conceivable that English examples of this type of work may have been produced but may not have survived. On the other hand, there remain in England stained glass windows and medieval statuary and it is tempting to speculate on how far the Christian artists used models from the Jewry for their Old Testament characters. Was Terah, for example, still looking out from the window of Canterbury Cathedral, drawn from life? Was he based on a Jew seen by the artist walking in the street, even down to the detail of his medieval Jewish spiked hat? Indeed were characters in morality plays later in the Middle Ages based—apart from biblical stories in the Vulgate—on earlier representations when the Jews were there to be observed or on some folk memory handed down from generation to generation?

For after the Expulsion what remained was a memory—a few streets bearing ever afterward the name 'The Jewry' or 'Old Jewry', a few stone houses, a few converts to Christianity in the Domus Conversorum, a few visitors, Jewish physicians, for example, called in by monarchs and important personages and allowed to practice their religion during their stay. In Norwich, the tradition of Abraham's Hall (the property of Abraham, son of Deulecresse, a wealthy Jew, burnt on what was probably a trumped-up charge of blasphemy in 1279) survived until the 18th century, for an inn on the site had as its sign Abraham offering Isaac for a sacrifice. The cult of boy-martyrs persisted

See illustration page 215.

until the Reformation particularly in literature. A century after the Expulsion, for instance, the Prioress's Tale in Chaucer's *Canterbury Tales* describes such a killing. It purports to take place in a town in Asia, where:

'...all these Jews conspired
To chase this innocent child from earth's face
Down a dark alley-way they found and hired
A murderer who owned that secret place;
And as the boy passed at his happy pace
This cursed Jew grabbed him and held him, slit
His little throat and cast him in a pit.'

But as the last verse showed, the inspiration was:

'O Hugh of Lincoln, likewise murdered so
By cursed Jews, as is notorious...'
(transl. Nevill Coghill)

Finally, there remained in some English cathedrals a symbolic reminder in the form of two statues contrasting the Church Triumphant and the Synagogue Dejected, a motif found elsewhere on the Continent, notably at Strasbourg Cathedral.

THE SECRET SETTLERS

The Expulsion of the Jews from Spain in 1492 and their forcible conversion in Portugal in 1497 added a new element, which heralded the eventual Resettlement. It also coincided with one of the turning points of world history, the discovery of the New World, and the subsequent movement of trade and civilization from their Mediterranean past to the Atlantic. Antwerp and later Amsterdam and London superseded Venice and Genoa as the richest entrepots; they became key centers in Jewish life, and in the return of the Jews to England.

The Marranos, the new Christians from Portugal, played an important role in this process. Jews at heart, they masqueraded as loyal Catholics and attended Church services but found also the opportunity to attend secret Jewish services among themselves. The courage of these people; the risks they ran day after day, year after year; the fear of exposure—with its awful consequences—which they faced as they went about their everyday pursuits; the natural decline in their religious knowledge generation by generation through lack of Jewish education and practice until all that remained were vague memories of an ancestral cult—all these factors might have influenced a less determined race to forget the past and accept the advantages that conformity offered. Yet such was not to be. Obviously many were lost to Judaism but there remained a vital element to play a significant part in Jewish history and to convert the term of contempt 'Marrano' (meaning 'pig') into an honored name in the course of the centuries to come.

One portent for later times was that the Marranos' safety depended on their being indistinguishable in dress and behavior from their neighbors. This normally meant living as Catholics, and after the Reformation in England (although some in the Low Countries and England eventually did live as Protestants), as Catholic foreigners. Since in England they were obviously 'Portuguese', it would be expected that they should be Catholics. Dissimulation was essential for survival. The Inquisition kept close watch on all suspected of Judaizing—indeed our knowledge of the Marranos in England is basically derived from denunciations and spies' reports in the Inquisitorial archives. Discovery, once a Marrano fell into the Inquisition's hands, meant prison, with examination under torture; if he refused to recant, the stake.

Marranos were in England from the end of the 15th century, but while there were probably individuals present throughout the 16th and early 17th centuries, life in organized communities was not continuous. Established groups there were secretly holding religious services and following Jewish practices, both in London and, for one period at least, in Bristol. A woman such as Beatrice Fernandez of Bristol was able to observe the dietary laws even when traveling and staying at inns on the journey. And the great house of Mendes of Antwerp employed a Marrano agent who boarded ships at Southampton to tell Portuguese travelers whether it was safe for them to continue their journey to Antwerp in search of greater religious freedom or whether it would be wiser, if at the time the Inquisition was particularly active in the Low Countries, to disembark in England and wait awhile. Probably by the end of Elizabeth's reign the Marranos were often known to be Jews and 'Portuguese merchant' was synonymous with Marrano. But their usefulness as doctors or providers of intelligence to the ministers of the Crown made it expedient not to seem to notice their real character.

Jews did arouse, however, hostility among the foremost writers of the age, especially in the period when Rodrigo Lopes, Queen Elizabeth's Marrano physician, who dabbled in Portuguese politics, was executed in 1594 for allegedly plotting to poison the sovereign. It is now generally accepted that, while he may have been involved in some intrigue, he was not engaged in treason against his royal patient. Christopher Marlowe's *Jew of Malta*, first performed in 1592, is supposed to have been based partly on the career of Joseph Nasi, who became the sultan's minister and duke of Naxos; reports about him, combining truth with lurid imagination, had long been circulating in England. Shakespeare's Shylock was surely an amalgam of all the anti-Semitic accounts that he had ever heard in a country where no professing Jews were to be found and where Lopes, though a foreigner, would not have had outward characteristics which in other circumstances would have been regarded as Jewish. Yet Shakespeare was too great a playwright to make Shylock unmitigatedly villainous. There is a pathos, which though it may have owed nothing to any insight into Jewish teaching or suffering, does, nevertheless, bear witness to the playwright's comprehension of a fellow human being's capacity for feeling, even though he was a despised Jew. It also shows that Shakespeare had no illusions that Christianity automatically engendered goodness:

'Hath not a Jew eyes? hath not a Jew hands, organs, dimensions, senses, affections, passions? fed with the same food, hurt with the same weapons, subject to the same diseases, healed by the same means, warmed and cooled by the same winter and summer, as a Christian is? If you prick us, do we not bleed? If you tickle us, do we not laugh? If you poison us, do we not die? and if you wrong us, shall we not revenge? If we are like you in the rest, we will resemble you in that. If a Jew wrong a Christian, what is his humility? Revenge. If a Christian wrong a Jew, what should his sufferance be by Christian example? Why, revenge. The villainy you teach me, I will execute, and it shall go hard but I will better the instruction.'

By the mid-17th century the climate had changed again. When the Resettlement of the Jews in England was achieved in 1656, it was due to a combination of factors in the English environment—political, religious, economic, and social.

Politically, the Civil War and the republican government which followed occupied a period of less than twenty years, but their effects for English history were lasting. Gone for ever was absolute monarchy as conceived by the early Stuarts. Gone was the power of the Church of England to impose conformity, as was found when attempts were made after the Restoration. Even though those outside the established Church did not obtain full political rights until the 19th century, they were not, except for brief periods, such as the time of the so-called 'Popish plot', in any physical danger. And the fear that a Catholic monarch with Catholic descendants might endanger the *status quo* (religiously and politically) which had been built up, led to the Revolution of 1688 and the replacement of James II by William of Orange.

THE INFLUENCE OF THE OLD TESTAMENT

The religious factors were perhaps even more important. The Puritans, divided into sects though they were, read and loved the Bible, and particularly the Old Testament, for its own sake and not merely as a prelude to Christianity. Their interest had been aided by the availability of printed books in the century since the discovery of the printing process. In 1611, the publication of the Authorized Version gave Englishmen the opportunity to read the Bible in magnificent and poetic English, translated from the original Hebrew and not from garbled versions of other translations. And until the 20th century, when the Bible is no longer required reading, generations of Englishmen responded to its inspiration. Both as creative writers or as regular readers they knew and were influenced by its contents and noble style. Even now, often without realizing it, English people (and perhaps Scots and Welsh even more) use biblical expressions or phrases as part of everyday speech: for example, 'there is nothing new under the sun', 'nation shall speak peace unto nation', 'how are the mighty fallen', 'the voice of the turtle', 'the little foxes', (the last two were titles of plays also). Shakespeare was reared on an earlier translation of the Bible and was familiar with its contents, as were his audiences. It was said of Milton that he thought in Hebrew though he wrote in English. Everywhere in the early part of the 17th century—and indeed in the non-conformist religious revivals at the end of the 18th century and in the 19th century—preachers, outside the court circles, modeled

their discourses on the language of the Bible, and used long quotations from its pages. They and the reading of the Bible itself helped to form not only the moral outlook but also the literary style of future generations. The imagery and the Bible-based simplicity of Bunyan's prose, for instance, had a distinct effect on eighteenth-century prose writers.

The Hebrew Bible's influence on the English-speaking world was not limited to speech or sermon. Biblical ideas on individual liberty as analyzed by seventeenth-century Puritans influenced the framing of the Bill of Rights in 1689 (which in turn was the basis for the American Constitution). In this connection, it is interesting to consider how the pride of place given to various books of the Bible has changed with the centuries. Thus the subjects which had influenced earlier generations, such as those concerned with Law, history and political theory, were superseded in the 19th century by the Prophets. Their ideas on social justice accorded well with the growing social conscience of the economic and social reformers who were campaigning for legislation to prevent the exploitation of the poor.

Of course, until the religious indifference of the 20th century, the Jews themselves, despite a minority of defectors, had been conditioned by their biblical heritage, reading it both in the original Hebrew and in the vernacular; taking pride in its records as their own history; studying its laws and relating its contents to contemporary conditions. They gloried in being the People of the Book, irrespective of their own religious Orthodoxy—a state of affairs which exists in modern Israel where Bible study and Bible reading are not exclusively the preserve of the religiously observant as it is, to some extent, in modern Britain.

It is not surprising, then, that in the Bible-conscious society of seventeenth-century England, many of the Puritans should have felt a sympathy for the descendants of the biblical characters they revered, and should have been prepared to have them living openly in England. Some advocates of readmission had, of course, an ulterior motive, hoping that freedom and toleration would lead to eventual conversion of the Jews; others believed that a great ill had been done to the Jews by England in the Middle Ages and that the time had come for redress; while still others thought that they were really members of the Ten Lost Tribes of Israel and should honor their brethren. Puritan terminology often spoke in Hebraic terms, even referring to their enemies as the 'uncircumcised'.

THE RESETTLEMENT

Crucial, of course, for the Resettlement was the personality of the absolute ruler, Oliver Cromwell. Tolerant in religion, prepared to let those of other faiths live freely so long as the security of the state was not endangered, he saw the economic advantages which could accrue to England from the readmission of the Jews, who, he hoped, would enrich London at the expense of Amsterdam.

This economic factor was brought to the fore by the small group of Marranos who settled in England from the 1630s. Led by Antonio Fernandez Carvajal, a wealthy merchant and shipowner who had lived in the Canary Islands, several of them had connections with the Islands and their trade. Others came from Brazil (where Marranos had flourished in a brief period of Dutch rule) and from the Marrano settlements in Amsterdam and Hamburg. In addition to their economic importance as importers of bullion, precious stones, dyestuffs and sugar, some at least acted, like their Elizabethan predecessors, as suppliers to the Government of military intelligence, which their overseas commercial relations made it easy for them to collect. Although living outwardly as Catholics, they met privately for Jewish worship in Carvajal's London house. An incident in 1656, however, induced them to declare themselves openly as Jews.

England was at war with Spain and the ships and cargoes of Spanish nationals were therefore liable to seizure. Information was laid against one of the Marrano merchants, Antonio Rodrigues Robles, and the seizure of his goods followed as 'enemy property'. Robles appealed to the Lord Protector for restitution, claiming that he was not an enemy alien but a Jew. He was supported by the evidence of a number of his fellow Marranos, who likewise declared their real identity.

MENASSEH BEN ISRAEL

This incident occurred during the one-man campaign for open Resettlement of the Jews in England conducted by Menasseh Ben

The Bodleian bowl, c. 1280(?). Bronze bowl with Hebrew inscription, found in Norfolk about 1696. Apparently 13th century and possibly originating in the medieval Jewish community of Norwich in Norfolk. Oxford, Ashmolean Museum.

Israel, Amsterdam rabbi, scholar, and publicist, himself of Marrano origin. Menasseh Ben Israel's own life bears out the contention that in certain parts of the world, at least, the lot of the Jew was easing. He had lived most of his life in Amsterdam, where the worst he had to fear was periodic bitter quarrels with his own congregants and with his professional colleagues. By the outside world he was regarded as an authority on Jewish affairs, the representative Jew of his era. Diplomats sought him out, savants consulted him. Theologian, writer, acquaintance of Rembrandt, who has immortalized his features, he was a celebrated and respected figure in the non-Jewish world, a noted preacher whose large audiences included many Gentiles as well as Jews. His advocacy of Jewish Resettlement in England, because the exclusion of the Jews from that one country prevented the messianic redemption, set the seal of respectability on the movement. His book, the *Hope of Israel,* published in 1650 in Latin, was soon translated into English and was a 'runaway best seller'. When, therefore, he added the weight of his prestige to the pleas for readmission already made, the strength of the case both on practical economic grounds and on the grounds of religion was well-nigh unassailable.

Menasseh Ben Israel had arrived in London in September 1655 and in October waited on the Council of State, presenting to Oliver Cromwell his *Humble Address to the Lord Protector* and a petition for the repeal of laws against the Jews and for their readmission on specified, and somewhat restrictive, terms. This petition was eventually referred on December 4 1655 to a distinguished assembly of lawyers, politicians and merchants. Almost at once the two senior judges answered that there was no legal bar to the readmission of the Jews but the four succeeding sessions produced opposition on points ranging from theological prejudice to mercantile jealousy; and even those who favored official readmission would have imposed severe social, as well as political, disabilities on the Jews. At the end of the fifth session on December 18 1655, Cromwell dissolved the Conference. The Robles incident, already described, followed in March 1656 and on March 24 another petition was presented to Cromwell. This was signed not only by Menasseh but by the leading Marrano residents, who had admitted their true faith in the Robles case. This petition had no political implications, no messianic overtones. It asked simply for tolerance for the right to meet privately for prayer and to bury the dead according to Jewish rites.

Until recently it was thought that this petition was never answered and that, since Robles' property was ordered to be restored on May 16 1656 by the Council of State, this was as far as the Council went; that because there was no record of a specific permit to resettle, none was given, and that Cromwell, unable to extract a positive decision, merely connived at the Resettlement of the Jews. That theory has been called into question by Cecil Roth who discovered that in the minute book recording the proceedings of the Council on precisely the day (June 25 1656) it was due to discuss the matter, the relevant pages had been torn out deliberately. The discussion therefore is likely to have taken place and the conclusion to have been favorable, a result which was conveyed to the waiting Jews, including Menasseh Ben

Israel, either by word of mouth or by a written communication (perhaps both) which has since been lost. Who suppressed the pages of the minute book is unknown but it is likely that the responsibility lies with one of the opponents of Jewish resettlement, wanting the next government to regard the return of the Jews as a personal whim of Cromwell's which did not have to be honored by his successors.

Menasseh Ben Israel, however, was disappointed that the terms on which he desired a settlement to be based—including communal autonomy, control over immigration and a special oath of allegiance—were not conceded. In fact, his ideas belonged to the past, to a different age and one to which Anglo-Jewry to its advantage never had to subscribe. Even though there were some attempts in the next half century to make terms and conditions, neither Charles II nor his successors would agree and Anglo-Jewry developed, as have all the best British institutions, without any written constitution at all. It was this quiet, unobtrusive beginning of the modern community which has molded it and influenced its history ever since.

It must be admitted, however, that England from the Resettlement until modern times has always been a backwater so far as Jewish intellectual life is concerned. It has had neither the numbers nor the Jewish learning of Continental communities; neither the traditional scholarship of Eastern Europe nor, when it came, the scientific and philosophical approach of the German *Wissenschaft*. Even when the reservoir of scholarship moved from its traditional environments, the new centers were the United States and later Israel, and Great Britain was bypassed. Anglo-Jewry has, nevertheless, played an important part in modern Jewish history though this has often been conditioned by the attitudes of the host society and, in some cases, by accident rather than by conscious design. The leading role of Britain in world affairs in the 19th century gave British Jews an opportunity to seek to intervene to improve the conditions of Jews in other lands; and the relationship of Britain to Palestine and the Jewish national home in the 20th century also meant that British Jews had a special position in world Jewry. But the prominence of Anglo-Jewry after 1945 was due largely to the fact that, after the European Holocaust, it was the largest Jewish community in Europe, apart from that in Russia which was sealed off from the mainstream of Jewish life for half a century. Numerically it has been overtaken in the 1960s by France which has received a large influx from North Africa. Anglo-Jewry's importance has thus been, in its different ways, out of all proportion to its size or capacities.

THE EARLY SEPHARDIM

The Jews from the Resettlement enjoyed a social equality with all other dissenting groups in England. There were one or two attempts to levy special taxes on them, but these did not persist; and while they suffered from certain political disabilities, these were shared until the 19th century by others who were Christian Englishmen, not members of the Established Church. Perhaps the most important special disability, since so many of the Jews were

Jacob Sasportas (1610-98). Sasportas was *Haham* of the Spanish and Portuguese Congregation in London from 1664 to 1666, when he left for Amsterdam on account of the great plague. Engraving by P. van Gunst. London, Spanish and Portuguese Jews' Congregation. Photo Freeman, London.

immigrants, was their inability to be naturalized, even by private Act of Parliament, because of the need for a Christological oath. But endenization was a workable substitute; and the Jews of England had less of a special status than any other Jews in Europe until the end of the 18th century (probably even less than the favored Jews of Holland).

It was, of course, easy for the Sephardim to pass unremarked among the general populace. After all, they were Westerners. And though they were after 1656 free to meet for prayer in their synagogue, outside they demonstrated no special mannerisms which marked them off as Jews, though they were obviously recognized as a distinct group by Addison, writing in the first issue of *The Spectator* in 1711: 'I have been taken for a Merchant upon the *Exchange* for above these ten years, and sometimes pass for a *Jew* in the Assembly of Stock-Jobbers at Jonathan's.' They quietly went ahead in the years that followed the Resettlement, consolidating their position, welcoming other Sephardi merchants into their ranks, and, in the reign of William III, having their numbers reinforced by the wealthy Amsterdam Jews whom the

tions); and Princess Anne (the future queen) who was reported to have visited the synagogue in 1681, later, according to tradition, presented a piece of timber from a man-of-war to serve as one of the beams in the roof of the Bevis Marks building (since her husband, Prince George of Denmark, was Lord High Admiral, there is some plausibility in this story).

The Sephardi community continued to grow. A recrudescence of the Inquisition between 1720 and 1735 caused perhaps 1,500 refugees, whose families had remained secretly loyal to Judaism for over two and a quarter centuries, to emigrate to England. Increasing numbers arrived from Italy, especially from Venice and Leghorn—families like the D'Israelis and the Montefiores; others came from Morocco and Gibraltar (especially in 1781 when the civilian population was evacuated at the beginning of the siege).

In the early years of the Resettlement, the Sephardim had been the sole, and later the dominant, Anglo-Jewish religious group. But soon their numerical predominance was challenged (although their social and financial leadership remained throughout the 18th century).

THE COMING OF THE ASHKENAZIM

When the medieval communities of France and Germany had been faced with expulsion in the 14th and 15th centuries, the trend had been to move east, particularly to Poland, which, under enlightened rulers, had welcomed a Jewish middle class and the economic benefits they had brought. By the middle of the 17th century, however, the era of tolerance was over and the ruling class was intent on persecuting the Jews and restricting their activities. In 1648, the Chmielnicki massacres unleashed migration westward, a movement which continued for the next three centuries (see chapter on Russia and Poland). Though the first Ashkenazi immigrants in England worshiped in the London Sephardi synagogue, the only one in existence, they were soon sufficiently numerous to organize their own synagogue about 1690 and buy their own burial ground, and they had sufficiently wealthy members to facilitate their endeavors. The Great Synagogue was opened in 1726 (it was to be tragically destroyed by enemy action in 1940). Unlike the situation of the Sephardim, Ashkenazi sources of recruitment never dried up and by the end of the 18th century they had become numerically the stronger element in Anglo-Jewry, though the prestige of the Sephardim, with a community of only about 2,000, still remained paramount.

The first Ashkenazi immigrants—and the wealthiest—came from Hamburg. This is true of both Benjamin Levy and Moses Hart as well as Hart's rival Mordecai Hamburger (the son-in-law of the woman diarist Glückel of Hameln), the founder of the Hambro synagogue—which, in fact, may owe its name as much to its patronage by immigrants from Hamburg as to its connection with Hamburger. Of the leading characters of Anglo-Jewry in the earlier part of the 18th century, both lay and religious, many others also had some connection with Hamburg or with its sister community Altona. But by the end of the century the notable

Haham David Nieto, 1654-1728. The most scholarly and versatile of Anglo-Jewish rabbis, writing in Italian, Spanish and Hebrew on many subjects. Painting by David Estevens, engraving by J. McArdell. London, Spanish and Portuguese Jews' Congregation. Photo Freeman.

monarch encouraged to settle in England. Their synagogue flourished, and they were fortunate to appoint as a *Haham* (chief rabbi) David Nieto, a man of outstanding scholarship and personality who guided their affairs from 1701 to 1728, and who headed a modest flowering of literary activity in his own congregation.

By the end of the century the first synagogue was too small and was replaced by the magnificent Bevis Marks synagogue, which was opened in 1701.

The impression made on non-Jewish visitors to Sephardi services varied with the occasion. Pepys, attending on *Simhat Torah,* found the synagogue 'a bear garden'; John Greenhalgh, another observer, being present on a Saturday, was impressed (as much by the wealth of the community as by its religious devo-

212

personalities, such as Levi Barent Cohen, Aron Goldsmid and Eliezer Isaac Keyser had come from Holland, or from some other great city such as Vienna (as Baron Lyon de Symons) or Frankfurt-am-Main, the home of the Rothschilds. By this time, some of the scholars and religious functionaries were being drawn from the great reservoirs of learning in Poland.

Among the poorer immigrants, there was a different trend, and one which has not yet been fully investigated. It would seem that many of them came from small German communities, particularly from towns in the south of that country. The pressure to move, until 1768 at least, was not caused so much by active persecution as by economic needs. Rules in the German states about the activities of Jews were often stringent. Prussia under Frederick the Great, while almost encouraging rich Jews, would hardly tolerate poor ones. In many cases, while a man was permitted to earn a living sufficient to bring up a family, this right would not be extended to his sons, who, when they were ready to found families in their turn, would have to move on. England, in which they were free to operate, proved attractive, and in the earlier part of the century, the agents on the Royal Mail packet boats would grant free passes to the poor and passage across the English Channel for a nominal sum. Alternatively, the gradual immigration of this type of Jew may well have been accelerated by the *Haidamak* disturbances, which reached their climax in 1768, causing refugees from Poland to crowd into Germany and to displace German Jews who then moved west. This influx of Polish Jews into small towns with limited economic opportunities may have caused some of the more enterprising among the native population to seek a livelihood elsewhere. Such a situation was seen in England in the 1840s when the poor Irish immigrants drove the Jews out of much of the market trade.

In any case, the 18th century saw additions to the Jewish population in England, causing its increase from about 1,000 in 1700, to 6,000 by 1740, 8,000 by 1750 and 20,000 by 1800. Since the Napoleonic Wars caused a considerable decline, though not a complete halt, to further arrivals, it may be assumed that this figure remained substantially the same in 1815, though natural increase has to be taken into account in a period when the general population was rising too and when some estimates put the Jewish population in 1815 at between 25,000 and 27,000.

THE ENLIGHTENMENT

In the 18th century, both Sephardim and Ashkenazim were conscious of the importance of education, though in the early part of the century the Sephardi schools were superior in the teaching they provided. There, boys were taught Hebrew, English and Spanish or Portuguese (the conservative Sephardi community,

while using English freely in their everyday lives did not see fit to replace Portuguese by English in synagogal minutes until as late as 1819).

The onset of the eighteenth-century Enlightenment had its effects even among the English Jews. There were some early attempts at freethinking. For example, the German-born physician, Meir Loew Schomberg, who built up a large fashionable practice but quarreled with both his Jewish coreligionists and the Royal College of Physicians, wrote a Hebrew treatise in which he not only worked off a good deal of personal spite but also suggested that one could be a good Jew by belief in God without observance of the practical and ritual commandments (it is perhaps significant that five of his six sons became Christians).

Another eighteenth-century Jewish preoccupation with intellectual problems is that of an anonymous writer who dealt with the problem of Jewish education in an open society and the purpose to which it should be devoted in a work written in Judeo-German: *Sepher Giddul Bannim* (The Education of Children), published in London in 1771. The anonymous author may have been the physician George or Gompertz Levison (a pupil of the pioneer of surgery, John Hunter). His book advised on methods of teaching Judaism to children from their earliest years so that they might learn to love and appreciate their heritage, but its author accepted the view that religion existed in a secular context.

Eventually, the modernizing trends which on the Continent produced the Enlightenment, were not without their more modest parallels in the Anglo-Jewish establishment. About 1770, there began, after a period of intellectual stagnation, a revival of Hebrew printing in London and the production of prayer-books and Bibles with English translation—notably by David Levi, the humble but indefatigable scholar who, while eking out a living as a tradesman, was a one-man Jewish publication society.

A revolution in the wider field of education was brought about by Hyman Hurwitz and Joshua van Oven. Hurwitz, an immigrant from western Poland, an area within reach of the influence of the Mendelssohnian Enlightenment, opened a private school in Highgate, where he became a friend of Coleridge. In his school he introduced modern methods of tuition, hitherto unknown in the *heder* of Anglo-Jewry and brought a scientific attitude to the mapping out of a program of Jewish education. This school, subsequently transferred to Kew, became under Hurwitz's successor, Neumegen, the school to which most of the leading families of the communal Establishment sent their sons in the second and third quarters of the 19th century. Hurwitz subsequently became the first Anglo-Jewish professor as Professor of Hebrew at the newly founded University College, London.

Perhaps even more widespread was the influence of Joshua van Oven. The physician of the Great Synagogue and an amateur Hebraist of note, he was a pioneer of communal reorganization. Van Oven made a lasting contribution by converting in 1817 the small charity school of the Great Synagogue (which dated from 1732) into a voluntary school on the lines of those being founded by the National and British Societies for the Church of England and Nonconformists. It was this school which, as the Jew's Free School, became the largest primary school and gave

◀ *Portrait of Dr. Fernando Mendes,* by Catherine da Costa, 1722. Dr. Mendes, a Marrano court physician (d. 1724), who accompanied Catherine of Braganza when she went to England to marry Charles II, was painted by his daughter, the first Anglo-Jewish woman artist. London, Jewish Museum.

Sir Moses Montefiore, 1840. Painting by Solomon Hart, R.A., 1840. Sir Moses Montefiore (1784-1885), the famous philanthropist, is shown in Lieutenancy uniform and holding the Ottoman sultan's *firman* condemning the Damascus ritual murder libel. He was the first English Jew in modern times to be knighted. London, Spanish and Portuguese Jews' Congregation.

Rabbi Solomon Hirschell (1762-1842). Painting by F.B. Barlin. Born in London where his father was rabbi, he was brought up in Germany. He embodied the forces of tradition and was also the first rabbi of the Great Synagogue to act as chief rabbi for the Ashkenazim of Britain and the British colonies. London, National Portrait Gallery.

successive generations of the Jewish proletariat a grounding in secular education, an indoctrination in English standards and an injuction to fidelity to Jewish religious tradition.

Even the traditional chief rabbi, Solomon Hirschell, who at the end of his life resisted the coming of religious reform, showed some adjustment to modern ideas—he was, after all, brought up in Berlin, where his father, Hart Lyon (former rabbi of London) was rabbi and acquainted with the circle of Moses Mendelssohn. Hirschell, incidentally, was the first prominent English rabbi to be of English birth (although of European upbringing); and he was the first who could be called a chief rabbi, whose authority was generally recognized by Ashkenazi congregations beyond London and indeed in the British colonies overseas.

SOCIAL LIFE IN THE 18TH CENTURY

As the 18th century advanced, some Jews began to fulfill the hopes that had been entertained by those English Christians who had considered that in the congenial atmosphere of England they would convert. Some of the proudest Sephardi families who had retained their loyalty to Judaism during two centuries of threatened persecution were assimilated and married into the English upper class. Moses Mendes, a minor poet, was baptized, and others, even if they did not convert themselves, encouraged their children to enter the English aristocracy. Samson Gideon, the great financier of the mid-19th century, secretly retained membership of the Sephardi community, but he married a Christian and had his children baptized. He did this to support

Preceding page:

Portrait of a medieval Jew, Canterbury, c. 1178. Stained glass window of c. 1178 in Canterbury Cathedral, showing Terah, father of Abraham, wearing the characteristic medieval Jewish red pointed hat and the long robe. Dean and Chapter of Canterbury Cathedral.

Bevis Marks synagogue, London, 1701. The oldest surviving synagogue in Britain was opened in 1701 in Bevis Marks in the City of London, for the Spanish and Portuguese Jewish community. It is similar to, but smaller than, the Spanish and Portuguese Synagogue of 1675 in Amsterdam. The scene, a color engraving from a watercolor, was painted in 1817 by a member of the community, Isaac Mendes Belisario, an artist who exhibited at the Royal Academy. London, Collection of Spanish and Portuguese Jews' Congregation. Photo Freeman, London.

his unsuccessful claim to a baronetcy or peerage; and it is clear from a letter to his son, when the latter was created a baronet while still a schoolboy at Eton, that Samson Gideon's overriding ambition was to found an English landed family.

Many among those Jews who remained within the fold were accused of worldliness, of ostentation in dress and behavior, of levity. Rabbi Hirsch Levin (or Harz Lyon), rabbi of London's Ashkenazi Great Synagogue from 1757-64, castigates his flock for dressing like Gentiles, while their womenfolk in decollete dresses and fashionable wigs endeavor not to appear daughters of Israel. They associate with English people even on Christian feasts when they dress better than on their own. They eat Christmas pudding, visit theaters and operas, coffee houses and gaming houses. And they are lax about Jewish observances.

Yet the interest in theater and opera which he condemned was a manifestation of the interest which Jews had (and have) in music and which made them patrons of the great musical figures of the time, such as the young Mozart when brought to London by his father, and Handel, whose *Judas Maccabeus* they, together with the composer's royal patron, turned from a failure into a success when Handel was boycotted by the English nobility. It was the same spirit of interest in the arts which George Bernard Shaw a century and a half later praised when he commented on the influence on the theater of the absence of rich nonconformist families and the presence of rich Jewish families.

Jews of the upper class certainly mixed socially with non-Jews; they were among the guests of Horace Walpole and, in an age of laxity, when the clergy were often younger sons of the aristocracy or landed gentry, holding livings donated by their

'Moses and Aaron', by Aaron de Chavez. This painting, showing Moses and Aaron with the Ten Commandments in Spanish and Hebrew, was over the Ark in the Creechurch Lane Synagogue. The artist, Aaron de Chavez (d. 1705) was the first recorded Jewish painter to work in England. London, Spanish and Portuguese Jews' Congregation. Photo Freeman, London.

families, and not celebrated for their spiritual qualities, Jewish owners of country houses were even to be found playing cards with the local parson.

Members of the community did not fail to do the fashionable thing and have their portraits painted by the famous painters of the period, Reynolds, Gainsborough or Romney. Judging by what remains in England's historic synagogues and in the Jewish Museum, communal dignitaries and rabbis also patronized lesser artists, so that the interest aroused in the modern viewer is rather that of the historian than the art connoisseur.

EARLY ANGLO-JEWISH ARTISTS

The community was also producing artistic talent of its own. Aaron de Chavez painted a famous picture of Moses and Aaron for the first Bevis Marks synagogue in 1674. Martha Isaacs was chosen to paint the portrait of Rabbi David Tevele Schiff in 1765, though her career in England ended soon after, when she left to settle in India. Abraham de Lopes Oliveira was a silversmith whose ritual objects—particularly ornaments for Scrolls of the Law and Sabbath lamps—were of the highest standard, so that the needs of the community, which, in the early days of the Resettlement had either been supplied from Amsterdam or by non-Jewish craftsmen such as John Ruslen, were at a later date catered for by native-born Jewish masters. By the end of the century, Naphtali Hart, a Jewish silversmith, was in partnership with a Scotsman, Duncan Urquhart, and while their firm specialized in the elegant tea services fashionable at the beginning of the 19th century, they also followed a profitable side-line by making *kiddush* cups for ceremonial occasions. However, the plate presented annually to the Lord Mayor of London from the end of the 17th century by the Jewish community as a gesture of their goodwill, though it depicted a theme of Jewish significance, seems to have been executed by non-Jewish craftsmen.

There were also immigrant artists, Solomon Polack from Holland, and Solomon Bennet from Poland, a portrait painter and engraver. The latter's portrait of the chief rabbi, Solomon Hirschell, which appeared in a pamphlet of 1808 by Levi Alexander, entitled *'The Axe to the Root'; or Ignorance and Superstition evident in the Character of the Rev. S. Hirschell,* did not improve the bad relations already existing between the two men. Bennet, in fact, although considered highly as a painter in Germany where he lived for many years, is better known as a controversialist than an artist among Anglo-Jewry.

Sabbath lamp, London, 1734. English eighteenth-century silver lamps for the Sabbath are rare. This one, dated 1734, is by the Anglo-Jewish silversmith, Abraham de Oliveira, who was responsible for many Jewish ritual objects. This lamp is similar to contemporary Dutch models and contains six parts (hook, crown, ball, lamp with seven burners, drip-pan and pendant finial). London, Jewish Museum.

Lord Mayor's plate, London, 1737. Beautiful silver plate with English inscription recording presentation to 'Sir John Barnard, Knight, Lord Mayor of the City of London by the Body of Jews residing in the said city, anno 1737.' In the center of the plate there is an imaginary coat of arms of the Tribe of Judah. Jerusalem, Israel Museum.

FROM PEDDLER TO PUGILIST

In the 18th century, many of the needs of the rural housewife, who visited a market town infrequently and the metropolis perhaps once in a lifetime, if at all, were supplied by various kinds of itinerant salesmen. Among these was the bearded Ashkenazi peddler, generally a recent immigrant, depicted in caricature by Rowlandson and others or in the porcelain statuettes of the period. He made his way with his pack on his back, visiting the remote and outlying countryside districts and providing the inhabitants of isolated areas with the haberdashery and the baubles they would otherwise have had to go and get from afar. Many of these itinerant tradesmen formed the nuclei of provincial communities, for when they saw the opportunity, they would settle down and turn jeweler, silversmith, tradesman, or, in the ports, navy agent.

At the end of the social scale were the old clothes men, eking out a meager living from buying secondhand clothes and selling them to the lower-class Englishmen who, until the mid-19th century, could not afford to buy new clothes and wore the

cast-offs of the more affluent. Poverty and unemployment increased among the unskilled Ashkenazi immigrants, many of whom found that the hopes they had had of making a living in England bore no resemblance to reality. Some took to crime and it was after a robbery with violence committed by Jews on the inhabitants of an isolated farm at Chelsea, that the Government imposed its prohibition on the issuing of free passes which had enabled Jews to come to England from the Continent. Another notable crime, though committed in France in 1791,

A Jewish pedaler, c. 1760. Derby ware statuette of a Jewish peddler who is wearing an East European fur-edged hat and long coat. National Art Collection Fund, Lady Ludlow Collection.

The Jewish boxer Daniel Mendoza (1763-1836). Daniel Mendoza whose skill made him the most famous pugilist of his time is shown in his second and successful fight with the previous champion, Richard Humphreys, on May 6 1789. Engraving by J. Grozer after Thomas Rowlandson. Alfred Rubens Collection.

had repercussions in England, for the Jewish thieves who stole the du Barry diamonds brought them to their criminal contacts in London. However, in this affair, a Jew was also on the side of the angels, for when the jewels were shown to Lyon de Symons, he not only recognized them but was instrumental in apprehending the criminals. It may be that the character of Fagin, familiar to readers of Dickens' *Oliver Twist,* and considered an anti-Semitic portrait, would have found its place in late eighteenth-century London, though it was out of date when the book was written in the 1830s. For by that time Anglo-Jewry was more typically represented by its sober and respectable middle class.

Previously, however, Daniel Mendoza taught the poor self-defense and by his own success as a pugilist won the respect of the general population for his people. The conscience of the established community had been aroused by the plight of the poor in the 1770s and 1780s. Societies were set up to teach the poor trades and crafts, to give them the means of subsistence, and to apprentice youths so that they might earn a living in tailoring or in one of the other occupations then followed by Jews.

In the mid-18th century, an effort was made to facilitate the naturalization of Jews but the storm caused by the 1753 Jew Bill, though a limited measure, led to its almost immediate repeal. Henceforward the Jews passed out of legislative history until the emancipation of the Roman Catholics and Nonconformists in the early 19th century engendered action to obtain equal political rights for the Jewish community, by then almost all native born.

However, another facet of governmental activity in the 18th century was a happier augury for the future. When Empress Maria Theresa expelled the Jews of Prague in 1774, George II and the British Government, with no ulterior motive, made representations to have the decree rescinded, thus providing the first instance of a European government acting in the interests of an alien minority. In the 19th century, such cooperation between the Anglo-Jewish community and the British Government to help persecuted Jewries abroad was to be a feature of foreign policy.

This later cooperation of Jewry and the British Government was aided by what was originally merely a matter of protocol—the protest of the Ashkenazim at their exclusion from the loyal greetings extended by the Sephardim to the new king, George III, on his accession to the throne in 1760. The compromise solution between the two communities, that the Sephardim and Ashkenazim would join together on matters of mutual interest, though at first resulting in intermittent consultations only, was the nucleus of the Board of Deputies, the representative Anglo-Jewish organization of the 19th and 20th centuries. Its activities and recommendations on behalf of Jewish communities both at home and abroad have been listened to by the British Government and its agencies, though its influence has depended on Britain's relationship with the Jews at the time. Thus, in the 19th century, when Britain's policies coincided with Jewish aspirations, the Board was a powerful organization whose specialized knowledge was respected. On the other hand, the exact opposite is true of the 1940s, when the Zionist-orientated Board was in conflict with the Labor Government which was rigid in its opposition not only to a Jewish state but to the admission of all those survivors of the concentration camps who wished to settle in Palestine.

Silver Kiddush cup, London, 1810. Plain goblet with rounded foot. Hebrew inscription recording presentation to the Jewish community in the Kent port of Sheerness by Moses bar Michael in 1811. By the London silversmith Thomas Daniel, 1810. Jewish Historical Society of England, University College, London. – *Silver citron box,* London, 1817. Engraved with Hebrew and English inscription recording presentation by the chief rabbi, Solomon Hirschell, to Aaron Joseph, warden of the Great Synagogue, London, on his marriage, 1817. The box unscrews to hold a citron *(etrog)* used on the Feast of Tabernacles. By the London silversmith Samuel Hennell. London, Jewish Historical Society of England, University College. – *Silver goblet,* 1812. Presented to Dr. Coltman by the Jews of Liverpool for his services to their poor, 1812. By Duncan Urquhart and Naphtali Hart. London, Jewish Historical Society of England.

On Thursday the 9th of May ~ were married, at Horder's Rooms, Minories, by the Revd Solomon Hirschell, Samuel Hilbert Israel of St Maria Axe, Shoe Maker Row & Bridge St Blackfriars Esqr & the beuty amiable, & highly accomplished Miss Fanny DeSymons. Vide. Times Chronicle, Post, &c &c.

The Israel-de Symons wedding, 1822. The chief rabbi, Solomon Hirschell, marries under the traditional canopy Samuel Hilbert Israel of Clapham to Fanny, youngest daughter of Baron Lyon de Symons (the couple became the parents of Sir Barrow Helbert Ellis, Indian civil servant). London, Jewish Museum.

NEW ARRIVALS

By the end of the 18th century, therefore, there existed a community of about 20,000, of whom 2,000 were Sephardim and the rest Ashkenazim. While the majority, numbering some 15,000, lived in London, there were provincial communities of varying size in a score of other town-ports like Plymouth and Portsmouth, country towns like Exeter, fashionable resorts like Bath and Brighton, and one or two of the rising manufacturing centers like Manchester.

Not only the numbers but also the composition of the community had undergone changes in the preceding hundred years and it was particularly noticeable among its leadership that very few of the families who had originated among the Marranos remained within the fold. Consequently leadership in the 19th century fell to those families which had arrived from countries

such as Italy during the middle of the 18th century. The Mocattas and the Montefiores, fairly modest on their arrival, became the magnates of nineteenth-century Anglo-Jewry.

Among the Ashkenazim, where wealth and social status were not so great, the assimilatory process was slower. Although individual members of famous families and their descendants did convert or marry out of the faith, the likelihood was that the family itself, or at least a branch of it, would remain Jewish so that the name would survive. An example is the Goldsmid family. While Abraham and Benjamin's children were lost to Judaism, Sir Isaac Lyon Goldsmid was a great figure in nineteenth-century Anglo-Jewish history. The Cohen family, founded by Levi Barent Cohen, who came from Amersfoort in Holland in the third quarter of the 18th century, is another instance of a family whose descendants married into every well-known Anglo-Jewish family; while the nineteenth-century Rothschilds made it a definite policy to allow daughters to marry into the general population—where the prize was sufficiently high—but discouraged such practices among the sons, a formula which proved successful until the 20th century.

THE PERIOD OF EMANCIPATION

The 19th century is rich in famous Anglo-Jewish individuals—Moses Montefiore, David Salomons, various Rothschilds, the first Lord Swaythling—men of action and achievement. Anglo-Jewish talent found its outlet in organization, in building up a series of institutions, which, firmly based, have survived continuously for more than a century. The tendency is in keeping with the English environment. The importance of character in Victorian England is stressed over mere book learning; the social legislation of the period bears witness to the growing awareness of the rich and influential that they have a duty toward their social inferiors; the principles of *laissez-faire* are gradually made to retreat before government control; the supremacy of the family and of a puritanical code of morality succeed the permissiveness of the pre-Victorian era.

Nathan Meyer Rothschild and his family, c. 1821. Painting by W.A. Hobday. The founder of the English branch of the Rothschilds (1776-1836) has his fourth son, Mayer Amschel (1818-84) on his knee. His wife holds the youngest child, Louise (1820-94); next are Charlotte (1802-59), Lionel Nathan (1808-79), Anthony (1810-76) and Nathaniel (1812-70). On the floor, Hannah Mayer (1815-64). London, Jewish Museum.

223

The Jews of England found themselves in sympathy with this code generally. The interaction of Jewish teachings and of Victorian Bible-based morality led to harmony in ideas and practice. The respectable, hardworking Jewish community of the mid-19th century was content to parallel Christian church-going by regular synagogue attendance; to strive for better material conditions for themselves and their families; and to support their communal leaders in the struggle for political equality, which entered its long final phase when the granting of Catholic emancipation in 1829 made it seem unreasonable that only the Jews should be excluded from political power.

It is probably true that, like the suffragettes more than half a century later, the emancipationists were a minority movement, the mass of the Jews being prepared to accept the *status quo*. In the period after the 1832 Reform Bill which gave a limited extension of the franchise, the momentum gradually grew, especially since in local government and in such privileges as the freedom of the City of London—without which retail trade within the City was forbidden—the barriers were falling fast. By 1855 there was a Jewish Lord Mayor of London, Sir David

Baron Lionel Nathan de Rothschild, 1835. Painting by Moritz Daniel Oppenheimer. A protagonist in the struggle for Jewish emancipation and the first Jew to sit as a member of the House of Commons (1858). He financed the purchase of the Suez Canal shares in 1875. London, National Portrait Gallery.

Sir Isaac Lyon Goldsmid's house at 20 Spital Square. The house of a Jewish patrician in East London, before the wealthy merchants and financiers moved their homes westward. Goldsmid (1778-1859), wealthy banker and the first Jewish baronet in England (1841), built himself a villa at Regent's Park in the 1820s. Historical Buildings Section, London County Council.

Salomons, and neither he nor Sir Moses Montefiore, who had been Sheriff of London from 1837 to 1838, had to compromise their Judaism in any way to execute their civic duties. The non-Jewish support was also impressive. Lord Macaulay was a powerful advocate and the approbation of individuals was backed by the voice of the City of London which was prepared, to all intents and purposes, to be disfranchised for eleven years rather than abandon the Member of Parliament it wanted, Baron Lionel Nathan de Rothschild, and elect a more 'acceptable' candidate. The stumbling block through these final years was not the House of Commons but the die-hard members of the House of Lords, many of whom genuinely believed that by admitting Jews to the ranks of politicians, and thereby allowing them to

The first Lord Rothschild taking the oath in the House of Lords, 1885. Painting by B.S. Marks. Nathaniel Mayer, first Lord Rothschild (1840-1915) is shown taking the oath in the Jewish manner, with head covered. Politically a Conservative (unlike his Liberal father), he was the acknowledged lay head of the Anglo-Jewish community. First Jewish peer, he was one of the outstanding Jews of his time. National Portrait Gallery.

become potentially members of the British Government, they would be jeopardizing the survival of Britain as a Christian country. The solution to the problem in 1858 allowed each House to determine the form of oath to be taken by its members—the unacceptable part of the existent oath being the phrase 'on the true faith of a Christian'. By the time Nathaniel Rothschild was raised to the peerage in 1885 such controversies were completely out of date and he was able to take his seat without opposition.

JEWS IN BRITISH POLITICS

But the thirty years' struggle had had the effect of aligning the Jews with the Liberals and Radicals who had supported their claims against Tory extremism, though Conservatives like Disraeli and Bentinck had spoken and voted in favor of Emancipation. By the 1870s, however, Jews were joining the Conservative party and were being elected to Parliament as Conservatives. In 1874, Saul Isaac became the first Jewish Conservative M.P. and he was followed shortly afterward by the more talented Lionel Louis Cohen and Henry de Worms (later Lord Pirbright). Nor did the Rothschilds maintain their former Liberalism. The

second Lord Rothschild was a leading figure on the Conservative benches in the House of Lords in the early 20th century.

The move away from the Liberals in the 1870s was due partly to the growth of anti-Semitism in the Liberal Party due to its opposition to what it considered Disraeli's cynical eastern policies. While the Liberals were hostile to Turkey because of her cruelty to her Christian subjects, Disraeli was prepared to overlook these misdemeanors in the pursuit of his conception of British interests—the protection of the route to India, 'the brightest jewel in the English crown', from Russian infiltration. Nevertheless, the Liberal Party still attracted Jews of the caliber of Sir George Jessel, Solicitor General in 1871, and in the early 20th century, Herbert Samuel (the first Viscount Samuel), the first professing Jew to be a member of a British Cabinet, and Rufus Isaacs (the first Marquess of Reading).

The decline of the Liberal Party in the 1920s and 1930s caused many of its adherents to transfer their allegiance to the growing Labor Party, though numbers of Jews have remained Liberals by conviction. For many years, Jews were out of sympathy with Conservatism, though in local government in the 1960s they featured prominently on Conservative-dominated councils. On the other hand, socialist doctrine proved attractive

The old clothes market in Petticoat Lane, c. 1860. Old clothes dealing was a typical Jewish occupation until the mid-nineteenth century and the old clothes markets were in the heart of London's Jewish quarter. Alfred Rubens Collection.

to Jews, whether the descendants of proletarian Russian immigrants of the 1881-1914 period or intellectuals. Since 1945 their numbers in the House of Commons have been proportionately high, with a considerable number supporting the left wing of the Party. Indeed, until persecution of the Jews as Jews by the Russians, and even as late as the Hungarian rising of 1956, many Jews were members of the Communist Party. For what has happened is that, with the loosening of religious ties, Jews have gone searching after 'other gods' and have sought their redemption in Marxism, socialism or one of the fashionable creeds which have an ephemeral appeal.

THE RUSSO-JEWISH IMMIGRANTS

The most important social change within the life of Anglo-Jewry came with the period of mass immigration from Eastern Europe in the years between 1881 and 1914. Anglo-Jewry increased in these years from 65,000 to 300,000, London Jewry from 46,000 to 180,000. This was only a part of a much wider movement which, as a result of tsarist persecution, brought a million Jews from Eastern Europe to the Western World. There had been a few immigrants, of course, from Eastern Europe into Britain before the 1860s, and a small but steady flow in the later 1860s and 1870s. In 1881, however, the assassination of Alexander II was followed by pogroms spreading a wave of terror through many provinces in south-west Russia. Similar persecutions over the next decades added to the flow of emigrants.

It was not only from the Russian empire that the immigrants came. There was also a steady flow from the Austro-Hungarian territory of Galicia, where the cause was poverty not persecution, and from Rumania, where governmental anti-Semitism became a tradition.

So much alien immigration provoked mounting opposition and a Royal Commission was set up to produce a report in 1903. Although it recommended no general bar against immigration but only attempts to prevent the concentration of immigrants in particular areas, an Aliens Act was passed in 1905 which sought to limit immigration generally. However, in the British tradition, it allowed entry to genuine refugees from religious or racial persecution; and within a few years the number of such refugees obtaining entry to Britain rose again. It was the war of 1914, not the Aliens Act, which really ended the mass migration from Eastern Europe.

The newcomers provided a complete contrast to the assimilated Anglo-Jewish community, in which they were at first not altogether welcome. Their habits and their dress were different, and they knew no English. They were a distinct element over-crowding the East End of London and forming ghettos in the large provincial cities, appearing conspicuous wherever they went. The opposition which alien immigration provoked aroused fears of anti-Semitism; and the Jewish Board of Guardians, feeling that its resources were unequal to coping with the far greater number of applicants for its help, offered them inducements to return to their countries of origin. It was not until

Israel Zangwill (1864-1926). Painting by W.R. Sickert. An author and dramatist of versatile talents, Zangwill will probably be best remembered for his description of life in the London Jewish immigrant quarter, where he was brought up and taught as a young man. Especially popular are *Children of the Ghetto, Ghetto Tragedies* and others in the same vein. London, Jewish Museum.

the Kishinev pogroms that the Anglo-Jewish community accepted the fact that the flow of immigrants would not cease and that the new arrivals had come to stay. Thereafter, a united community fought attempts to restrict immigration. It was largely due to their efforts that the Aliens Act did not, as events proved, turn out to be the complete barrier to immigration which had been feared.

The immigrants formed, in the years before 1914, a world of their own. This world was sympathetically depicted by Israel Zangwill, born in 1864 and himself the son of an immigrant, though like his own 'grandchildren of the ghetto' removed from it by education, by profession, by associates and, in his own case, by out-marriage. He was an early and enthusiastic supporter of Herzl, though he severed his connection with the Zionist movement when the Seventh Congress refused Britain's offer of Uganda as an alternative home for the Jews.

In his famous *Children of the Ghetto,* Zangwill brought to life the East End community, its hopes, its achievements, its poverty, its religion, and its conflict between the Orthodox older generation and the modern younger people. Here is found what no sociological or statistical report could give—an understanding of the effects of their experiences on the people themselves. And because Zangwill was a Jew from the East End, albeit of a generation earlier, before the mass immigrations, the incidents he describes are often based on actual occurrences or on Jewish laws and practices which would be unknown to Gentile writers. Many of the characters in the book are thinly disguised portraits of personalities well known in the East End of London in the last twenty years of the 19th century. The saintly Reb Shmuel, for example, is based on the much loved rabbi Jacob Reinowitz (a *dayyan* or judge of the chief rabbi's court), who combined strict religious practice and great learning with tolerance toward those who brought their problems to him; the ultra-pious mystic N.L.D. Zimmer was the original of Karlkammer in the book; Harry S. Lewis, the editor of the *Jewish Standard* (on which Zangwill worked) was the model for Raphael Leon, who has a leading role in *Grandchildren of the Ghetto*; Melchizedek Pinchas has been identified with Naphtali H. Imber, the composer of *Ha-Tikvah*; and, as the model for Moses Angel, Zangwill used his own father. Like Moses Angel, the elder Zangwill's heart was set on Jerusalem; and, as soon as he could afford it, the son enabled the father to settle there.

Zangwill in his short stories also portrayed Jewish suburbia —Dalston and Highbury—as well as Jewish life in the provinces, in Eastern Europe and in the United States. It is significant that his writings on Jewish themes have proved the most lasting of his many works.

A novel of the Jewish provincial ghetto had to wait a further generation until in 1922 Louis Golding's best-seller *Magnolia Street* did for Manchester what Israel Zangwill had done for London. The book, although popular in its day, does not have the same charm and warmth as Zangwill's work, although it is now of interest as recording a social milieu which has disappeared.

THE ELITE

Communal authority remained with the Anglo-Jewish elite well into the 20th century. In the Jewish, and indeed the Victorian English spirit, the Establishment was very much a family affair, with the Rothschilds at the top and a group of other closely knit families ruling Anglo-Jewish institutions. These families intermarried with one another; they lived near one another in town; even in the country they clustered their country houses in close proximity, as in the Rothschild territory on the Buckinghamshire-Bedfordshire border, or in Kent.

Some of the magnates derived a special prestige from their association with royalty—particularly 'the Marlborough House set,' the entourage of the Prince of Wales for some thirty years before his accession to the throne as Edward VII in 1901. There had, of course, been contacts between the royal family and Anglo-Jewry before. William IV's brother, the duke of Sussex,

'*Brighton Front*', 1861. Abraham Solomon (1823-62) depicts Brighton Front in 1861, when it was past its fashionable zenith under the Regency but still a favorite resort for many, not least London's wealthier Jews. Tunbridge Wells Art Gallery.

The North London synagogue, 1868. This synagogue, by the Jewish architect Hyman Henry Collins, was the first public synagogue built in the popular middle-class residential areas of North London of the time (Barnsbury, Canonbury, Highbury, and others). Jewish Historical Society of England.

for instance, was a keen orientalist and a patron of Jewish charities and institutions; but the friendship of the Prince of Wales with members of the Rothschild family was a new departure in that it brought prominent Jews into close regular association with the heir to the throne and thus, *ipso facto,* into the highest rank of English society. The Prince of Wales, excluded by Queen Victoria from any active role in the work of government, took over the leadership of London society which his mother had abandoned in her widowed seclusion. The Marlborough House set, over which the Prince presided, showed by its very position the reaction against the austere thought of Buckingham Palace. Membership of the English landed aristocracy was not a necessary qualification—indeed almost the reverse. Wealth, intellect, charm were the qualifications; above all, the

ability not to be boring. The first Lord Rothschild and his two brothers, the brothers Reuben, Arthur and Albert Sassoon, Sir Ernest Cassel, Baron de Hirsch, Sir Felix Semon, the physician, and Sir George Lewis, the most fashionable solicitor of the day, were all within the circle—although not all were active members of the Jewish community. The prince would stay at the homes of some of his Jewish friends and, where the matter arose, would accommodate himself to their religious duties. The prince's fondness for the company of his Jewish friends and his tastes for Jewish humor naturally aroused considerable comment. It is reasonable to infer that Edward was attracted by the combination of luxury and taste, the sense of something interesting and different, which these Jewish magnates with their Continental or Oriental backgrounds could contribute.

LEADERSHIP AND SOCIAL SERVICE

The Jewish upper class as a whole, however, while less glamorous than the members of the royal entourage, were men with a social conscience. Their prosperity did not make them indifferent to the needs of their poorer coreligionists. They felt it their duty to take communal office, to man the committees of the voluntary organizations, and they spared neither their time nor their energy in the causes they upheld. Not everyone was a Moses Montefiore who retired from business at the age of forty to devote himself to good works. Lionel Louis Cohen, for instance, did his day's work on the Stock Exchange and in Parliament before turning to his Board of Guardians activities.

Much of the work done epitomized the Jewish ideals of charity. It is not enough according to Jewish teaching to make a donation and then to turn one's back; consideration must be given to the use to which the money is put, and to the dignity of the recipient who must not be allowed to feel himself a beggar, of no account to anyone. From this evolved the Board of Guardians' practice, side by side with emergency relief, of helping the poor to help themselves. Loans were granted to start businesses, to tide a man over a period of bad luck, and systematic efforts were made to teach trades. In certain aspects the Board was well ahead of current non-Jewish practice. The employment of a sanitary inspector, although intermittent, was instrumental at least in limiting epidemics in 1855 and 1866; and similar regular work in the housing field in the following decades pioneered environmental health work by voluntary bodies and local authorities.

At the end of the 19th century, the Board of Guardians, though opposed to providing general medical services, was among the first to combat and treat tuberculosis. Moreover, when its methods, advanced in the early days of its existence, fell behind current ideas based on replacing philanthropic action with trained professional staff, the Board was flexible enough to adapt itself to the new techniques. In the mid-20th century, the Board had to fit in to the framework of the Welfare State, dealing increasingly with the needs of old people and of other social groups whose problems do not stem primarily from poverty; and after a century of work as a Board of Guardians of the Jewish poor, it reflected these changes by renaming itself the Jewish Welfare Board.

In education, too, the Jewish community were pioneers. The Jews' Free School has already been mentioned and it was followed by similar schools providing elementary education for large numbers of poor Jewish children in the East End of London. Under the patronage of the Rothschilds and other communal magnates (who patronized their own particular school) these schools flourished. Their standards were high, due to the intelligence and devotion of Jewish schoolteachers and the keenness of the pupils themselves. Many an immigrant child of the 1881-1914 period owed his later success to the anglicization he received in these schools. The Jews' Free School (JFS), for instance, was one of the first to organize vocational training. In the 1930s, when many of its pupils were still living in unsatis-factory conditions, it equipped the senior girls to teach home economics in a Jewish context. It is perhaps significant that, though this East End school was destroyed by enemy action in World War II, its successor, the JFS Comprehensive School is again a leading institution in the field of Jewish and secular education, and one of the more successful examples of the new and not yet fully proven comprehensive education in Britain.

THE RELIGION OF THE VICTORIAN JEW

The location of the postwar JFS outside the former Jewish quarter of East London is only one indication of the movement of the Jewish population away from its traditional home in the East End. In the 1930s, the wealthier children of the immigrants followed the practice of their predecessors and abandoned the East End in search of gardens, bathrooms and the status of suburban living. The attraction of suburbs for Jews had, of course, started in the mid-19th century when there was a similar movement out of the center of London by the growing middle classes. For the Jewish middle class of the 19th century the results of prosperity were new communities followed by new synagogues to serve the growing populations of the West End, North and North-West London. Previous self-imposed limitations on the building of new synagogues had to give way to the realities of a situation in which most synagogue-goers were people still walking to synagogue on Sabbaths and festivals, yet living miles from the synagogues existing at the beginning of the 19th century.

It was as a result of these movements of population and the increase of synagogues in residential areas that in 1870 the London Ashkenazim formed a United Synagogue. Although the United Synagogue was founded and run by laymen as an umbrella organization for the offshoots of the original Great Synagogue, its earlier years were closely associated with the chief rabbinate of the Adlers. Nathan Marcus Adler (1803-90), who succeeded Solomon Hirschell as chief rabbi, had a university doctorate and a German training; he was, while strictly Orthodox, a modern pastor and an organizer. He was succeeded in 1890 by his son, Hermann, who had previously acted as his father's deputy. Hermann Adler, like his father, was a traditionalist, but more willing to consider some innovation. These processes of modernization and adjustment within the Anglo-Jewish religious establishment provide another outstanding example of the Anglo-Jewish genius for organization rather than spirituality. Anglo-Judaism under the Adlers aimed to keep within it the majority of the Anglo-Jewish community, whether doctrinally Orthodox or more permissive in practice. Once again the Anglican compromise set the example for Anglo-Jewish imitation. Perhaps this helps to explain why the Reform Synagogue—whose origins in 1840 had only a limited relation to theological issues and whose early members included individuals like Sir Francis Goldsmid, meticulous in their religious observance—and the later Liberal Jewish movement never attracted a mass membership either in London

Lionel Louis Cohen (1832-82). A *Vanity Fair* cartoon of 1886. As founder of the United Synagogue and the Jewish Board of Guardians, Conservative Member of Parliament and stockbroker, Cohen represented the lay leadership of the Anglo-Jewish religious establishment. (Photo George Miles).

Lib

Hyman Hurwitz, 1846. Born in Poland, Hurwitz (1770-1844) became a pioneer of the 'Enlightenment' in England. An educational reformer and founder of a famous school, he was first Professor of Hebrew at University College, London. Litho by J.M. Johnson from a picture by Kirkafer. London, Jewish Historical Society of England.

or in the provinces. At present, the Progressive community numbers 40,000 out of a total Jewish community estimated at some 420,000.

A contributory factor was, perhaps, that the mid-19th century immigrants from Germany who so powerfully developed the Reform Movement in the United States did not make so marked an impression on the Anglo-Jewish community as a whole;

they were probably relatively fewer and many of them, as persons of broad European culture, speedily assimilated into the wider community.

The Russo-Jewish immigrants of the 1881-1914 period, who in other countries created a new and separate community, did not remain long isolated from the previous Anglo-Jewish community; nor did they, on the other hand, completely alter its character and institutions. Instead, they gradually assimilated into the established Anglo-Jewish community while also slowly influencing its ways. The reasons for this phenomenon must be set out in some detail, becuse they provide the key to the understanding not only of the relations between Jews and non-Jews but also of how the Anglo-Jewish community developed as it did in the late 19th and first half of the 20th century.

THE JEWISH ATTITUDE TO ENGLAND

Throughout the 19th century, England had acquired a special reputation in the eyes of Jews the world over. The tolerance of her own attitude toward the Jews compared favorably with the anti-Semitism, overt or implicit, of Continental Europe. In England, Jews could acquire wealth, property, positions of influence, the friendship and sympathy of their Government and also of their fellow citizens. For this was an age when Englishmen could still be aroused to moral indignation by reports of persecutions abroad; and they crowded meetings held, under distinguished auspices, to protest against ill-treatment of Jews in Russia and elsewhere. The completion of Emancipation in 1858 removed any reservations about Jewish political equality. Finally, the unequaled prestige of Britain throughout the world naturally had its effect on the standing of Britain in Jewish eyes.

All these factors come together in the journeys of Sir Moses Montefiore to aid his hapless brethren. He made them with the support of the British Government, traveling at times in a British warship, bearing an English title; he was granted a distinction by the queen to mark his success. His efforts were regarded by some as a demonstration of British influence in the Near East. It was natural therefore that Jews all over the world should see some equation between British and Jewish interests and regard Britain differently from other nations.

The philanthropic and political activities of Montefiore were designed to hasten the day when Jews abroad would obtain similar privileges to those enjoyed by their coreligionists in England. With the belief in the compulsive power of continuous progress current among the Victorians, it was inconceivable that there should ever be retrogression. True, the day of liberation was long in coming but that it would eventually arrive was never doubted. Thus is significant that Montefiore, with all his love for the Holy Land, never advocated mass immigration as a solution to Jewish ills. That was left to a more realistic and cynical age which had learned by bitter experience that general enlightenment was a mirage, though in England there was a group of non-Jewish writers in the mid-19th century who, before the days of political Zionism, advocated a Zionist program.

The Nineteenth-Century Novelists

Novelists, poets, and dramatists in the 18th century had been generally anti-Semitic, or at best neutral, in their treatment of Jewish characters. The 19th century, however, saw a desire among great English writers to do the Jew honor. Trollope, it is true, was anti-Semitic, but Dickens, after Fagin in *Oliver Twist* redressed the balance by creating the too-good-to-be-true Riah in *Our Mutual Friend*. In Scott's romantic medieval novel *Ivanhoe*, Rebecca was noble as well as beautiful and, unlike Shakespeare's Jessica, staunch in her religious loyalty. Disreali made Sidonia a combination of an idealized Rothschild and an equally idealized Disreali, an impossibly heroic and superior figure. Even the writings of lesser known Jewish authors, such as the poet and novelist Grace Aguilar, helped to give a more sympathetic, and indeed a truer, picture of Jewish life and ideals. As a result the public were given a different picture of the Jew from the old clothes men of caricature or even the characters of missionary novelists who, depicted in the course of exchanging their Jewish darkness for the light of Christianity, were represented with varying degrees of accuracy.

In the later 19th century, however, an unfavorable view of Anglo-Jewry came from certain Jewish writers who castigated the materialism, the ostentation, the lack of religious sincerity of the wealthy middle class whom they classified as card-playing philistines. Two novels particularly set the tone and thereby

The Montefiore family, 1797. Painting by R. Jelgerhuis. Sir Moses' father, Joseph Elias Montefiore (1759-1804), and mother Rachel (1762-1841) with the young Moses, then thirteen, holding a book; his brother Abraham (1788-1824) and two of their sisters. A typical Anglo-Jewish middle-class scene of the period. London, Jewish Museum.

Grace Aguilar

Grace Aguilar (1816-42). A writer of novels on Jewish subjects, Grace Aguilar brought Jewish ideals to the knowledge of the Victorian reading public. Her most popular work, *Vale of Cedars,* describes the trials and tribulations of Spanish Marranos. Alfred Rubens Collection.

give a picture of the social life and attitudes of a section of the population, not necessarily representative of the whole.

In 1888 Amy Levy's *Reuben Sachs* depicted the milieu of Bayswater and Maida Vale, suburbs of fairly recent Jewish settlement: 'Books were a luxury in the Leuniger household. We all have our economies, even the richest of us; and the Leunigers, who begrudged no money for food, clothes or furniture, who went constantly into the stalls of the theater, without considering the expense, regarded every shilling spent on books as pure extravagance.' Another example of her criticism is that: 'Born and bred in the very heart of nineteenth-century London, belonging to an age and a city which has seen the throwing down of so many barriers, the leveling of so many distinctions of class, of caste, of race, of opinion, they had managed to retain the tribal characteristics, to live within the tribal pale to an extent which spoke worlds for the national conservatism.

'They had been educated at Jewish schools, fed on Jewish food, brought up on Jewish traditions and Jewish prejudice.'

But even more contemptuous of Maida Vale society was Frank Danby (alias Julia Frankau, the mother of the novelist Gilbert Frankau) in *Dr Phillips—A Maida Vale Idyll* published in 1887. 'All the burning questions of the hour are to them a dead letter; art, literature, and politics exist not for them. They have but one aim, the acquisition of wealth. Playing cards at each other's houses is their sole experience of the charms of social intercourse; their interests are bounded by their homes and those of their neighboring brethren.'

Yet a little reflection shows how partial were these charges. The cultured cosmopolitan Jew, especially the Central European, was responsible for much patronage of music, the theater, and the arts, not only in London but in provincial cities like Manchester and Bradford.

The great sympathetic Jewish novel of the 19th century was written by a non-Jewish writer. George Eliot's *Daniel Deronda* was published in 1876. It is the story of a young man brought up as a Christian who discovers his origins, reverts to Judaism and, finally, with his Jewish bride, leaves England to settle in Palestine. The inspiration behind the writing of the book is said to have come from Emanuel Deutsch and the character of Daniel was reputedly based on Colonel A.E.W. Goldsmid, himself half-Jewish by birth, but who returned to Judaism and later led the English branch of the early Zionist society *Hovevei Zion* (Lovers of Zion). Through the mouth of one of the characters, Mordechai Cohen, George Eliot voices Jewish aspirations which cannot be faulted in a world where the State of Israel is an accomplished fact but which must have been startling, indeed ludicrous, to many mid-nineteenth-century Jewish men of property: this was made clear by Amy Levy in *Reuben Sachs* where the book is mockingly described by one of the characters as 'George Eliot's elaborate misconception'.

Mordechai's words therefore are more sympathetically received by a later generation than that for which they were written, though there was obviously gratitude for the understanding of Jewish tribulations displayed by a world-famous non-Jewish writer. '...There is a store of wisdom among us to found a new

Professor Samuel Alexander O.M. Bronze sculpture by Sir Jacob Epstein. The Australian-born Jewish philosopher (1859-1938) was awarded the prized distinction of the Order of Merit (in 1930). London, Ben Uri Art Gallery.

Jewish polity, grand, simple, just like the old—a republic where there is equality of protection, an equality which shone like a star on the forehead of our ancient community, and gave it more than the brightness of Western freedom amid the despotisms of the East. Then our race shall have an organic center, a heart and brain to watch and guide and execute; the outraged Jew shall have a deference in the court of nations as the outraged Englishman or American.'

And the last word on the matter came from Daniel himself: 'I am going to the East to become better acquainted with the condition of my race in various countries there... The idea that I am possessed with is that of restoring a political existence to my people, making them a nation again, giving them a national center, such as the English have, though they too are scattered over the face of the globe.'

In an age when Englishmen were traveling to the Middle East, the Jew fulfilled the romantic, exotic role which in the 20th century has passed to the Arab. Lord Shaftesbury, after his period of conversionist activity, was an advocate of Jewish statehood; Laurence Oliphant was another of the pre-Zionists; while Disraeli, though he had been baptized as a boy of thirteen, was profoundly influenced by his Jewish origins, even inventing ancestors from the Spanish Sephardi aristocracy to fulfill his cravings for romance. His visit to Palestine, his Jewish friendships, his novels were the vital background to the Eastern policies he pursued when at last in the 1870s political power was indubitably achieved, even though his pro-Turkish and anti-Russian line did not directly affect Jewish development in Palestine.

However, despite the few who looked to Palestine, the vast majority of Jews in the 1870s were content with their lot in England and, when the immigrants came after 1881, they had no other promised land in mind than England or America, to which some to them were unable to continue their projected journey because of lack of the passage money. Although these Russo-Polish immigrants flocked to Herzl's meetings and thrilled to his words—in contrast to the 'West End' Jews who cold-shouldered him and the chief rabbi, Hermann Adler who called Zionism an 'egregious blunder'—paying their small contributions to Zionist funds, they had no desire themselves to move on again. England, despite the initial hardships they were enduring, offered opportunities to their children and to themselves to better themelves. The scholarship won by the immigrant boy, Selig Brodetsky, to Cambridge University was a cause for pride to the whole East End community and a presage of what might be for their own children in the future.

The Beginnings of Anglo-Jewish Letters

It is a customary generalization on Anglo-Jewish history that periods of religious observance have alternated with laxity and suicidal assimilation. Observance has coincided with immigrations of Orthodox refugees who have either led to their own lives completely separate from the native-born community or have injected their own fervor into it, until such time as they—or their children—have integrated, and the process has has to begin all over again. The Napoleonic Wars, which slowed down—though they did not stop—immigration for a generation, left by 1815 a largely native-born community. It was the educated members of this community which cooperated, under the leadership of Isaac Lyon Goldsmid, in setting up the first secular university in Great Britain, University College, London, at which Jews could take degrees and in which (as already mentioned) for the first time at a British university, a professorship, that of Hebrew was held by a Jew, Hyman Hurwitz. During the next four decades scholars came from abroad either as political refugees or attracted by the greater freedom possible in England: Emmanuel Deutsch, the Silesian-born talmudist who worked at the British Museum; Louis Loewe, who came from Berlin to be oriental secretary to the duke of Sussex, accompanied Sir Moses Montefiore on many of his missions, and was the first principal of the Jews' College and later of the Ramsgate College; Adolph Neubauer of Hungary,

who joined the Bodleian Library in 1868 and was Reader in Rabbinic Hebrew at Oxford from 1884 to 1900 Solomon Schiller-Szinessy, also of Hungary, who fought in the Hungarian rising of 1848, was Minister of the Manchester congregation and subsequently Reader in Rabbinics at Cambridge.

Yet their impact on general Anglo-Jewish life was limited. In spite of the scholars, in spite of men and women who combined Jewish with secular culture, in spite of the various literary societies and the attempts to promote an interest in and knowledge of the Hebrew language and literature, the sole lasting achievement of this period was the foundation of the *Jewish Chronicle,* which outlived all its rivals and remains the only flourishing publication in Anglo-Jewry to this day. It was fortunate in its editors, and particularly in that Abraham Benisch, himself of Bohemian origin, established the paper on a sound commercial basis while not neglecting learned contributions, a reflection of his own scholarly interests. He it was, too, who advocated settlement in Palestine and laid down a practical program for the enterprise; and it is noteworthy that in later years, despite the hostility of the Anglo-Jewish establishment, the Zionist platform always found support from editors of the *Jewish Chronicle.*

While the majority of the Jewish scholars were from abroad, Britain and its colonies were not without native-born Jewish scholars in the 19th century. This was particularly true of the 1880s and 1890s when there was a surge of Jewish literary activity, albeit inspired largely by the Rumanian-born Solomon Schechter. This interest in the Jewish past was symbolized by the great Anglo-Jewish Historical Exhibition at the Albert Hall in 1887, which made a tremendous impact both in the Anglo-Jewish community and outside; it was an achievement, because of its scope and the pioneering work involved, even greater than that of the exhibition held at the Victoria and Albert Museum in 1956 to celebrate the tercentenary of Jewish Resettlement. One by-product of the 1887 exhibition was the foundation in 1893 of the Jewish Historical Society of England, which, because of the European Holocaust, is probably the last surviving Jewish learned body of its age in Europe.

The circle around Schechter included Israel Zangwill; the philosopher and theologian Claude Montefiore; Lucien Wolf, journalist and authority on foreign affairs; Israel Abrahams, later Reader in Rabbinics at Cambridge; and Joseph Jacobs, folklorist and social scientist, who subsequently left for America and was an editor of the *Jewish Encyclopaedia.* It will be noted that, in the slightly amateurish tradition of English scholarship, most of the group of British-born scholars were men with other occupations.

If one seeks to estimate the contribution of nineteenth- and early twentieth-century Anglo-Jewry to English scholarship it must be admitted that they do not play the same role as Jews in Germany, Italy, or France. Even so, there were many brilliant individual contributions: Samuel Alexander (1859-1938), the philosopher, who was born in Australia but educated at Oxford, where in 1882 he became the first professing Jew to be elected to a fellowship, was an outstanding figure by any standards. A systematic philosopher whose *Space, Time and Deity* has been regarded as the most thorough treatise on philosophy to appear in

England since Hobbes, he was not only a metaphysician but a philosopher deeply interested in ethics and esthetics. But, apart from Alexander, one should mention the Shakespearian scholars, Sir Sidney Lee, editor of the *Dictionary of National Biography* and Sir Israel Gollancz, a founder of the British Academy and its first Secretary.

JEWS IN THE ARTS

In art, the scene is varied. The beginnings were conventional enough: Solomon Alexander Hart (1806-81), Royal Academician, Professor of Painting and Librarian of the Royal Academy, painted large historical scenes in the grand manner as well as

Day of Atonement, 1919. This oil painting of 1919 by Jacob Kramer represents the simple, fervent piety of the Jewish immigrants from Eastern Europe. The artist himself was born in the Ukraine in 1892. Leeds, City Art Gallery.

238

pictures on Jewish themes, including some contemporary pieces. Abraham Solomon (1824-62) was a genre painter of scenes of social respectability but executed with careful and effective craftsmanship. Far different was his more gifted younger brother Simeon Solomon (1835-1905). Beginning as a Pre-Raphaelite—Burne-Jones said he was the greatest artist among them—his earlier paintings have, as Swinburne said, a strange beauty in the drawing of the faces. He was, however, an unstable character and succumbed to excesses of sex, drink and drugs. After a spell in prison, he died in an East London workhouse.

Camille Pissarro was in London as a refugee during the Franco-Prussian War and his son, Lucien (1863-1944) married in England, and did most of his work there. His post-Impressionism influenced the work of English painters of his time. Solomon J. Solomon (1860-1921) was a fashionable portrait-painter of Edwardian society and also had important public commissions: he was a committed Jew. In this he differed from Sir William Rothenstein (1872-1945), although the latter, in his early career, painted a number of Jewish scenes in the strictly Orthodox Machzike Hadath synagogue in East London. Rothenstein was, by origin, one of an assimilated German Jewish family of Bradford. But the Russo-Jewish immigration soon produced in England (as in Paris) its own artists. Alfred Wolmark (1876-1961), David Bomberg (1890-1967), Mark Gertler (1892-1939) and Jacob Kramer (1892-1962) were among this group, Bomberg and Gertler being born in England of recent immigrant parents. Wolmark startled Edwardian galleries by his use of color. Bomberg, Gertler and Kramer, however, while seeking for a time to develop in England a Jewish style that would represent the Yiddish culture of their origins, were more restrained, less addicted to fantasy, more sober in their colors than the analogous Russo-Jewish painters elsewhere, such as Chagall—perhaps because of the sobering influence of the English environment. An outstanding sculptor was Sir Jacob Epstein who, coming from New York, settled in London in 1907. His works varied from bronze portrait busts to monumental sculptures (such as the one adorning the rebuilt Coventry Cathedral).

English Jews also played a minor but respected role in other branches of the arts. Thus that most 'typically British' of songs *A Life On The Ocean Waves* was one of eight hundred songs composed by Henry Russell (1813-1900), whose son Sir Landon Ronald (1873-1938) was a noted composer, conductor, and principal of the Guildhall School of Music. But it was essentially as performers that Jewish musicians were best known—among them the pianists Moiseiwitsch, Solomon, and Dame Myra Hess who founded and ran a series of lunchtime concerts at the National Gallery during World War II; the violinists Yehudi Menuhin and Ida Haendel who both made England their home; and Lionel Tertis who was responsible for the renewed recognition of the viola as a solo instrument.

In literature, a number of Jews have made their mark including the poets Siegfried Sassoon, Isaac Rosenberg and Humbert Wolfe who all made their reputation in the World War I period (when Rosenberg was killed), and the historian Philip Guedella. In the 1950s the impressive record of English drama was spearheaded by a number of Jewish dramatists including Harold Pinter, Arnold Wesker and Peter Shaffer with Lionel Barth scoring successes in musical plays. Well-known younger poets included Dannie Abse and Jon Silkin.

THE IMMIGRANTS AND THE ESTABLISHMENT

By the time of the 1881-1914 immigrations, the established community, although generally traditional in religious observance, was culturally assimilated. The immigrants from countries where they had lived self-contained lives were an element distinct from the native-born community. Just as in the cultural field they published Yiddish newspapers, which tried to resist the official community's policy of anglicization, there was some degree of conflict between their religious institutions, grouped around the small *chevrot* or conventicles and the official religious establishment.

Yet this conflict should not be exaggerated. Some groups among the immigrants, regarding the official community as insufficiently Orthodox, maintained their separatism. But the majority realized that they had in common with the United Synagogue establishment the use of the German or Polish ritual of prayer. Thus, although the immigrant may have found services at a United Synagogue somewhat cold and unemotional—and the membership charges prohibitive, at least initially—he would not have been at a loss in following the liturgy nor could he have condemned its Orthodoxy out of hand. This meant that as the immigrants became more anglicized and began to ascend the social scale, they were attracted from their own *chevrot,* which had been formed into the Federation of Synagogues at the instigation of the first Lord Swaythling in 1887, and often joined the United Synagogue, membership of which became a status symbol to them and their children in the same way as membership of a Reform Congregation was a status symbol in the United States. The results can be seen almost a hundred years later. Whereas the United Synagogue, despite much non-adherence, maintains its dominant position in the Anglo-Jewish community, the Federation of Synagogues has lost regular worshipers in its synagogues, many of which, in areas abandoned by Jewish inhabitants, have had to be closed or amalgamated.

ACHIEVEMENT IN INDUSTRY AND COMMERCE

In the economic field, the great increase in the numbers and influence of the British middle class, one of the most significant factors in nineteenth-century English social history, had repercussions on the Jewish community. It created a demand for consumer goods, which the Jews were particularly adept at satisfying,

◄ *Portrait of the artist's mother*, 1911. Born in the Jewish quarter of East London of Polish-Jewish parents, Mark Gertler (1892-1939) depicted the immigrant types of his childhood. London, Tate Gallery.

Seder plate, England, 1925. An English modern silver copy of the early 17th century majolica plates used for the ritual constituents of the Passover Eve ceremony and with the headings of the service in the center. Silver versions of the same type are found in Holland in the 18th century and elsewhere. Jerusalem, Israel Museum.

thereby themselves acquiring considerable wealth and moving into the ranks of the middle class. Among them were such men as Marcus Samuel who imported and sold shells from the Far East, later manufacturing the elaborate shell ornaments, without which no Victorian household would have been complete. To this economic enterprise of the father, the world was to owe 'Shell' oil, for when the son (later the first Viscount Bearsted) sought a name for his new oil company, he honored the commodity on which the family's first fortune had been founded.

Primarily, however, Jewish initiative caused innovations in the clothing trade and thereby a social revolution whose magnitude cannot be overestimated. For the first time, a working man in the middle of the 19th century could be as good as his master. He was able to buy new, cheap clothing cut in the same fashion as that worn by the wealthy. It is true that the material was not so fine nor the workmanship of bespoke standard—'one man, one garment' tailoring remained in the 19th century largely the prerogative of the non-Jewish craftsman. But the gap between the classes was narrowed by the fact that all had the opportunity, in the cities at any rate, to wear clothes which superficially looked alike. Tailoring for this new market, itself growing as the prosperity of the country increased, proved a profitable venture.

This contribution of E. Moses and Son (and suchlike firms) in the mid-19th century was taken further by Montague Burton in the early 20th century, with his chain of stores marketing the ready-made clothing manufactured in his modern factory. Yet

probably the greatest contribution to 20th century merchandising was made through the firm of Marks and Spencer, who, under Simon Marks and Israel Sieff, changed fundamentally the whole pattern of shopping and the attitude toward buying clothes. By dealing direct with the manufacturer and eliminating the middleman, they were able to reduce prices drastically, while, at the same time, because of the size of their orders, being able to insist on a high quality and design.

RELIGION AND EDUCATION

The Jewish immigration of the 1930s from Central Europe, unlike the proletarian influx from Eastern Europe, was a middle class movement, the refugees being wealthy or comparatively wealthy, educated, with technical know-how, and so were able quickly to acquire economic independence. German and other refugee Jewish scholars, scientists, artists and businessmen made a great contribution to Britain in peace and war. Special mention should perhaps be made of the artists, who have influenced their English surroundings in a way even greater than that of their predecessors of previous immigrations. Joseph Herman, born in Warsaw, who came to England in 1940, made his home among the Welsh miners and portrayed their daily life at work; Hans Feibusch, born in Frankfurt-am-Main, became famous as a painter of murals for English churches; Benno Elkan, whose candelabrum is one of the artistic treasures of the Knesset, also executed similar works for England's national shrine, Westminster Abbey.

It is perhaps remarkable that synagogues in Britain have not as a rule commissioned similar works from Jewish artists, or indeed buildings from Jewish architects of the first rank. In the 20th century, particularly since 1945, there have been a large number of Jewish architects but synagogues have generally been designed either by non-Jewish architects or by less prominent Jewish architects, a welcome exception being the small synagogue at Belfast by Eugene Rosenberg. Perhaps this failure to appreciate the contribution that outstanding artists could make to the synagogue is due to the continued 'provincialism' of Anglo-Jewish religious life. Continental Jewry did appreciate this potentiality but the German and other Central European immigrants did not make the overall impact on Anglo-Jewish religious life that might have been expected. If they were Orthodox Jews, they either formed their own communities—where learning was of supreme importance—or joined the United Synagogue. Their influence on that organization was in one sense strong and persistent. Better educated in Judaism than their Anglo-Jewish counterparts, they gave the latter a feeling of inferiority so that the old easy-going

The Jewish family, 1913. Russo-Jewish immigrants depicted by Mark Gertler ▶ (1892-1939). The mass immigration of refugees from Russian oppression (1881-1914) produced densely packed ghettos in London and other large cities. The distinctive garb and features of the immigrants attracted the attention of contemporary artists from outside and later from inside the immigrant community. London, Tate Gallery.

241

tolerance fought a losing battle against the more rigorous logic of the newcomers.

Yet there must be proper appreciation of the reason for the awareness and for the closing of the ranks of the 'faithful'. In the past, when assimilation became strong, there were prospects of new immigrations and new infusions of enthusiasm. Religion was still a force in the land unrivaled by the counter-attractions of materialism. But the position has changed. Those who guard the Jewish heritage in Britain are conscious of the flight away from traditional Judaism, of the indifference to Jewish education and of the growing number of out-marriages. The old aristocratic families have merged or are gradually merging with the surrounding society. And the children and grandchildren of the East European immigrants, often the victims of wartime evacuation and divorce from a Jewish background, have been unable to transmit any Jewish teaching, of which they themselves are often ignorant, to their children. Now the Jewish school—especially the primary school under the auspices of the Zionist Federation, which enjoyed increasing success in the 1960s—stands, in many cases, as the only bulwark against complete assimilation. As in so many aspects of life in the non-Jewish as well as the Jewish world the school has superseded the home, the teacher has succeeded to the rights and duties abdicated by the parents.

In England there is the danger that, for many, the Jewish past will become passé. Already Jewish moral attitudes and behavior, which were cited by non-Jewish observers as being admirable examples for the general community, have been decried and abandoned. While alcoholism and violent crime remain alien to Jews, the strong family life characteristic of Jewish communities is disappearing. The divorce rate matches that of the general community, illegitimate births have risen sharply, and drug-taking is on the increase. The Jewish young, like their non-Jewish counterparts, have succumbed to the persuasive influences of the permissive society.

THE INFLUENCE OF ISRAEL

One hope for Anglo-Jewry lies in its commitment to Israel which has grown with the years and which may be the supreme factor in the retention of Jewish identity. The process has been a slow one and, interestingly, the Zionist connection with England was, in the early days, greater than its ties with Anglo-Jewry. Theodor Herzl, it is true, found support from Israel Zangwill, from Leopold Greenberg, the editor of the *Jewish Chronicle* and from a minority of other English Jews. He was able, by the force of his personality, to win over Lord Rothschild who had previously been hostile. He received the adulation of the poor immigrants in the East End of London. But his great achievement was that, in pursuit of his aim of obtaining legal recognition for his claim to Eretz Israel, he won over such members of the British Government as Joseph Chamberlain, then Colonial Secretary. He was so attracted by the possible English connection that at the Fourth Zionist Congress held in London, he declared: 'England the great, England the free, England with her eyes fixed on the seven

seas will understand us. From this place the Zionist movement will take a higher and higher flight, of this we may be sure.' Although the offer of Uganda by the British Government was rejected by the majority of Zionists whose object was the traditional homeland or nothing, the interest in Jewish nationalism evinced by the British Government at this early date was only the forerunner of things to come.

The fortuitous development, unperceived at the time, was the immigration of Chaim Weizmann, the young Russian scientist who chose to make his home in Manchester instead of in Switzerland or Germany, and thereby changed the course of history. In his spare time, Weizmann indoctrinated a group of young Manchester intellectuals—Harry Sacher, Leon Simon, Simon Marks and Israel and Rebecca Sieff. They became his disciples in Zionism. He won over the influential editor of the *Manchester Guardian*, C.P. Scott, whose newspaper henceforward promoted the Zionist case. Thus when the 1914-18 war prevented communication between Zionist leaders whose national states were not on the same side, the English group, reinforced by Nahum Sokolow, who had been sent by the Zionist Movement to London, was ready to take over the direction of the campaign.

Much has been written in Leonard Stein's definitive book *The Balfour Declaration* about the various motives which led to the granting of the Balfour Declaration by the British Government in 1917. The misconceptions regarding the power of Russian Jews to influence events in Russia in that year of revolution; the effect such a promise would have on American Jewry's attitude to the war; the underestimating of Arab reactions; the benefits which would accrue to Britain strategically from having a Jewish national homeland in Palestine. All these, as well as the desire to do justice to the Jews and the influence of Weizmann and Herbert Samuel—whose importance has been underestimated—affected the issue and made it expedient as well as desirable that some gesture should be made to encourage Jewish aspirations. Lloyd George, Balfour and Sir Mark Sykes were genuinely uplifted by the idea of Jewish independence but even so the original concept of Palestine *as a national home* for the Jews was watered down in the final version of the Balfour Declaration:

'His Majesty's Government view with favor the establishment in Palestine of a National Home for the Jewish people, and will use their endeavors to facilitate the achievement of this object, it being clearly understood that nothing shall be done which may prejudice the civil and religious rights of the existing non-Jewish communities in Palestine or the rights and political status enjoyed by Jews in any other country.'

At the time the difficulties caused by the change of formula and the later interpretations placed on it were not envisaged by anyone. The enthusiasm of the Jews was unrestrained; the fact that the Mandatory Power which was to administer the country would be Britain was felt to ensure a smooth and happy future for those Jews who wished to settle in Palestine. And the first High Commissioner appointed was a Jew, the same Herbert Samuel, whose memorandum to the Prime Minister in 1914 suggesting a national home in Palestine had brought forth the comment from the prosaic Asquith:

'I have just received from Herbert Samuel a memorandum headed "The future of Palestine". He goes on to argue, at considerable length and with some vehemence, in favor of the British annexation of Palestine, a country the size of Wales, much of it barren mountain and part of it waterless. He thinks we might plant in this not very promising territory about three or four million European Jews, and that this would have a good effect upon those who are left behind. It reads almost like a new edition of *Tancred* brought up to date. I confess I am not attracted by this proposed addition to our responsibilities, but it is a curious illustration of Dizzy's favorite maxim that "race is everything" to find this almost lyrical outburst proceeding from the well-ordered and methodical brain of H.S.'

The disillusionment was swift. Difficulties in colonization, Arab riots and a policy of appeasement toward their intransigence, the various Royal Commissions sent out from England to solve the Palestine problem—all led to unsettled conditions and mounting hatred. The German immigration of the 1930s brought a new element into the *Yishuv* (Jewish community) which became a refuge for some of those who could escape from the Nazi terror.

Exterior of Belfast synagogue, Northern Ireland. This is perhaps the only modern communal synagogue in the British Isles by a leading contemporary Jewish architect (Eugene Rosenberg, C.B.E., architect of St Thomas' Hospital, London; of Warwick University and many other university and hospital buildings; and of Gatwick Airport). The main building is circular, with a covered entrance corridor. Yorke, Rosenberg and Mardall.

243

דע לפני מי אתה עומד

But the notorious 1939 White Paper, limiting Jewish immigration to a maximum of 75,000, after which the gates would be permanently closed, was followed by World War II, when thousands of Palestinians enlisted in the British forces.

When peace came, the tragic losses to Jewry were fully revealed: 6,000,000 dead. The survivors, broken in mind and body, wanting only to go to Palestine, were obstructed by the restrictive policy administered by the new British Labor Government, which in pique passed the whole problem on to the United Nations. Then followed commissions, a period of suspense and in November 1947, international opinion expressed in the UN General Assembly agreed to the partition of Palestine and the establishment of a Jewish state.

In the twenty years since the birth of the State in 1948, though a massive *aliyah* (immigration) from Britain has not materialized, the moral effects of the existence of the State have been profound, giving Anglo-Jewry a new pride and self-respect. The Jew no longer feels that he should be quiet in the hope of passing unnoticed by his enemies. As the Six-Day War showed, Jewry, whatever views had been held previously and however loose the ties had been, found a unity of purpose in a one-hundred-per-cent commitment to the Israel cause. As a result, there has been an increase in migration to Israel since 1967, particularly of young families from England.

Nor is the interest confined to Jews. Adventurous youth has found in Israel one of the few countries of the world where idealism and endeavor are still considered important. They have spent vacations on *kibbutzim* or following their profession in development areas. When volunteers were required to work on the Masada 'dig' the response from applicants in all walks of life was overwhelming, despite the fact that by joining the enterprise they would be out of pocket.

While there has been no pressure on British Jews to emigrate, there have been those who have responded to the challenge offered by Israel; those who have acted on their belief that only in Israel is it possible for a Jew to live a full and uninhibited Jewish life.

THE FUTURE

Anglo-Jewry's contribution to British life has been undoubted—in commerce, the arts, science, letters, philosophy and in public life generally. To Jewish life, on the other hand, its contribution has been more limited—no giants of piety, no major contributions to scholarship. And yet British standards of conduct, of public life, and even British habits have become readily assimilated by Jews, even immigrants of the first generation, and have thus been passed into the general corpus of Jewish experience.

The future of Anglo-Jewry as a community is at best uncertain. The demographic trends—in so far as they can be discerned—are not favorable: declining rates of births, lower marriage rates within the community than in the general population, and so on. Demographically, the outlook is for a declining community, presumably no longer to be reinforced periodically by transfusions of foreign immigration. The process of assimilation to the general community is what can only be expected in an open society.

The answer to this in Jewish history has been the inner resources of the Jewish community, its spiritual leadership, its tenacity of religious observance, its devotion to its traditional learning. Yet it is precisely these which are lacking in the Anglo-Jewish community today. The struggles of Israel during the last twenty-odd years, culminating in the experience of the Six-Day War in 1967, produced a general feeling of sympathy, of fraternity, of pride. But it is questionable whether sentiment and fund-raising can in themselves ensure the survival of a religious community. Insofar as the feeling of identification is deepened in particular individuals, this logically leads to emigration to Israel and the loss to Anglo-Jewry of some of its younger, more vital elements. If the feeling of identification with Israel led to a widespread study of, and proficiency in, the Hebrew language, things might be different: but of this there is little evidence as yet.

The Anglo-Jewish community has been traditionally based on religious affiliation. Can it remain as an entity in a society in which the cementing force of religion is limited to a minority, however devoted? This is a question which only the future can answer. Yet one thing is clear: the story of Anglo-Jewry is not yet over, nor the unique relationship between Jewish culture and English civilization.

◄ *Interior of Belfast synagogue,* Northern Ireland. The picture shows the eastern side of the synagogue with the Ark in which the Scrolls of the Law are kept, and to the right, a candelabrum used on the festival of *Hanukkah* (dedication). The covering of the Ark and the candelabrum are bronze, the work of Nehemia Azaz, an Israeli sculptor living in England. Yorke, Rosenberg and Mardall.

CHAPTER VII

United States of America

by Rabbi Abraham Karp

THE JEWS COMES TO AMERICA

In early September 1654, twenty-three Jews arrived in the town of New Amsterdam to found the first Jewish community in what is now the United States. The twenty-three came from Recife in Brazil, having been forced to leave that city when it was recaptured by the Portuguese from the Dutch.

The immigration of Jews to America in the 17th and 18th centuries was part of the general movement of the center of the Western world from the Mediterranean to the Atlantic. The discoveries of the 16th century turned the attention of nations and men to the promise of the Americas.

Tales and evidence of the great wealth of the new continents in commodities and in land filled the dreams of the daring and raised the hopes of the hungry: for hungry they were in increasing numbers, with the population of Europe growing at an unprecedented rate and rapidly becoming urbanized. New frontiers were needed to support the poor, that could be exploited by the enterprising. America became the goal and destination, and the Atlantic, a route to new hope and new life.

It is estimated that the Jewish population of the United States at the time of the first Federal Census in 1790 was between 1,300 and 1,500. Small as it was in number, the Jewish community felt itself an important and integral part of the new nation. The western world, nurtured on the Bible, knew and lived with the Hebrews and 'seed of Abraham' without ever having met a Jew. In Colonial America, the works of Josephus were second only to the Bible itself. Though numerically few, the Jews of Colonial America nevertheless constituted distinct figures on the landscape.

In the first three decades of the republic, the Jewish population increased from fewer than two thousand to fewer than three thousand, while the general population trebled. In the next three decades, 1820-50, the general population doubled, but the Jewish population soared to some fifty thousand—a seventeenfold increase! The difference is attributable to one factor: immigration.

America was open for immigration, and the condition of the Jew in Europe was such as to make the enterprise most attractive.

The Congress of Vienna, convened in 1815 to restore Europe to its pre-Napoleonic ways, set off a wave of reaction in which the Jews suffered greatly. Newly granted rights were revoked and new oppressive measures enacted and enforced. The unsuc-

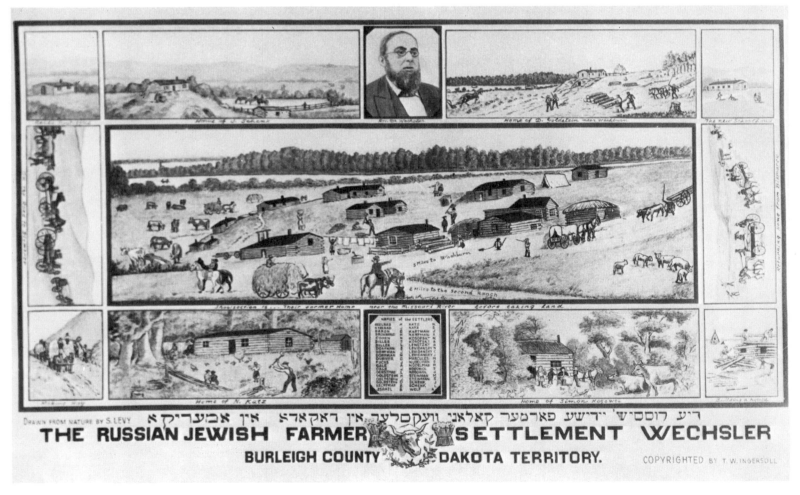

The Russian Jewish Farmer, Settlement Wechsler, 1865. The paper was founded in 1865 by Dr. Judah Wechsler in Burleigh County, Dakota Territory, and the illustrations drawn from nature by S. Levy. Jewish agricultural colonies were founded in the mid-west and far-west in the second half of the 19th century; all were short-lived. American Jewish Archives.

247

THE OCCIDENT,

AND

AMERICAN JEWISH ADVOCATE.

VOL. I.]   NISSAN 5603, APRIL 1843.   [No. 1.

INTRODUCTORY REMARKS.

It is a time-honoured custom, that when an Editor appears for the first time before the public, he is to state something of the course he means to pursue, and of the subjects he intends laying before his readers. In our case, this is hardly necessary, since the name of "Jewish Advocate" amply shadows forth that we mean to devote our pages to the spread of whatever can advance the cause of our religion, and of promoting the true interest of that people which has made this religion its profession ever since the days of the great lawgiver, through whom it was handed down to the nation descended from the stock of Abraham. But this general view may, perhaps, not be sufficiently detailed for many whom we would gladly number among our readers; and we will therefore briefly state our object in assuming the editorship of this new periodical, and of the course it is our firm determination to pursue.

With regard to our object, we state candidly, that the plan of a religious periodical did not originate with ourself, nor did we approve of it when it was first suggested to us. We thought then, and still think, that newspaper knowledge is at best but superficial; for, to make a paper or magazine really interesting to the general public, (and for such a one it is our duty to labour in our present vocation,) much matter must be admitted which is more pleasing in its nature than instructive, and the variety, which is to be constantly furnished, will naturally prevent long and continuous articles being given, although they might be extremely rich in information, even such as the people stand most in need of. We dreaded, moreover, that despite of the greatest care which we could bestow, articles might at times gain admission which

VOL. I.   1

The Occident, April 1843. Page 1, volume 1 of *The Occident,* edited by Isaac Leeser. For a quarter of a century, the remarkable Isaac Leeser (1806-68), minister, editor, translator of the Bible and prayer-book, textbook editor and communal architect, ran the high-quality magazine *The Occident* (from 1843-68). He was the first to introduce English sermons in the American synagogue. American Jewish Historical Society.

cessful revolutions of 1830 and 1848 and the reaction which followed gave further cause for Jewish uneasiness. Add the despair which ensues when hopes become shattered, and all the conditions were ripe for migration.

In the 1830s and particularly in the 1840s Jews arrived in significant numbers, mainly from Bavaria. They founded congregations in the existing communities and established communities in such cities as Boston, Hartford, New Haven, Albany, Syracuse, Rochester, Buffalo, in the northeast; Baltimore, Columbia, Augusta, Columbus, Mobile, New Orleans, and Galveston in

the south; and Cincinnati, Cleveland, Chicago, Louisville, Milwaukee, Pittsburgh, Columbus and Indianapolis in the midwest. The De Sola-Lyons Calendar of 1854 listed ten congregations in the new state, California.

In 1820, the American Jewish community was largely native-born, English-speaking, small in number and rapidly assimilating. By 1850, it was largely a German-speaking, immigrant community beginning to establish those institutions and organizations which would give it structure and identity.

Jewish immigration from Germany to the United States showed a dramatic increase during the period of political and civic reaction in the central European countries affected by the Revolution of 1848. The Jewish population of the United States increased in the decade 1850 to 1860 from some fifty thousand to one hundred and fifty thousand.

Among the new immigrants were a growing number of Jews from Eastern Europe. American Jewry, in the three decades which followed the mid-century, was made up chiefly of immigrants from the 'German' countries of Central Europe, with a significant admixture of East European Jews from Russia, Poland and Rumania.

As the Jews of Europe joined their neighbors in flight to the New World, so the American Jew joined fellow Americans in moving westward. Individual Jews could be found in many pioneer settlements, and Jewish communities dotted the entire map of expanding America.

In the decades of the Civil War and Reconstruction, Jewish immigration greatly decreased. The first attempt at a Jewish population survey, undertaken by the Board of Delegates of

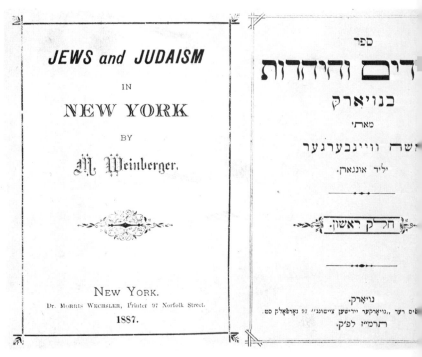

Jews and Judaism in New York, 1887. This work in Hebrew describes Jewish religious and cultural life in the New York immigrant community by the Hungarian-born rabbi Moses Weinberger, 1887. American Jewish Historical Society.

Weighing and Delivering Matzot, New York, 1870. Leslie's *Popular Monthly* carried a series of pictures depicting the method of baking *matzot* (unleavened bread for Passover) and its weighing and distribution in New York in 1870. American Jewish Historical Society.

American Israelites in 1877, placed the number of Jews in the United States at 230,257.

Few events had greater influence on the course of American Jewish history than the assassination of Alexander II, 'Tsar of all the Russians', in March 1881. This assassination touched off pogroms in more than a hundred Jewish communities (see chapter on Eastern Europe). Physical persecution, political oppression, and economic disabilities set in motion a wave of immigration which brought two and a half million Jews from Eastern Europe to American shores in the half-century from 1880 to 1930. The mass migration began in the 1880s and was brought to an end for the Russian Jew by the Revolution of 1917 and for the Polish Jew by the restrictive American immigration law of 1924.

In the decade 1880-90, some two hundred thousand Jews emigrated from Eastern Europe; in the following decade the number doubled. The very great majority came from Russia-Poland, but an appreciable number also arrived from Galicia, Hungary and Rumania.

Economically, America was ready to receive them. The depression of the early seventies had come to an end, and the country was again expanding, geographically and economically. The industries needed new labor, and the new laboring class needed purveyors of food and clothing. The Jewish immigrant became the small merchant and clothing worker to supply this need. In small towns across the country he opened stores; in the large cities he entered the shops.

Well into the 20th century immigration continued to be the single most important factor in the American Jewish historic experience. Some six hundred thousand Jews came to the United States in the last two decades of the 19th century. Three times that number arrived in the first two decades of the 20th.

Some 95 per cent of the immigrants originated in Eastern Europe. Most came directly to America; some had remained for shorter or longer periods in West European countries. The rise of Hitler in 1933 precipitated a migration of German Jews to America in significant numbers, and some one hundred and fifty thousand arrived in the years which followed World War II.

The fifty thousand Jews of America in 1850 constituted 1 per cent of world Jewry. The million Jews in 1900 were 10 per cent of the world's Jews. Today America's six million Jews constitute almost half of world Jewry.

An Old Faith in the New World

The Jews of New Amsterdam, while yet petitioning for rights of domicile and trade, established a congregation, 'Shearith Israel', in 1655. A century later, the Newport, Rhode Island, Jewish community of some fifteen persons, turned to the established New York congregation for help in erecting its own synagogue. The beautiful building, now a national shrine, still stands in that seaport city. By the end of the Colonial period congregations had been established in New York; Newport; Philadelphia and Lancaster, Pennsylvania; Richmond, Virginia; Charleston, South Carolina; and Savannah, Georgia. Religious functionaries were imported, trained and maintained. Kosher meat was provided, burial grounds were consecrated, marriages solemnized. All things considered, there was a flourishing religious life in Colonial America, including the publication of the prayer-book in an English translation by Isaac Pinto in 1766 in New York.

Jewish religious development was fostered in the general atmosphere of Colonial America, where religion pervaded all of life. Many of the colonies were founded by religious groups, some for religious purposes.

A busy street on the old East Side. The pushcart was the open-air store of the Lower East Side of New York. This district was the first area of residence for most East European Jewish immigrants, who were poor and skilled in no craft. Because many of them had been petty traders at home, they carried on the same type of business in New York. American Jewish Archives.

There were, then, observant Jews and those who had thrown off the 'yoke of Commandments'. In formal public manner the faith was maintained. Congregations were organized, synagogues built, boys circumcised. The early minute books of New York's Congregation 'Shearith Israel' give evidence of serious and far-reaching congregational activities At the same time we derive a picture of waning personal religious observance. Public religious institutions were founded and maintained but personal piety fell victim to the atmosphere of the free frontier which was Colonial America.

Immigrants. A New York East Side street scene. The order of economic ascent for many Jewish merchants was from peddler to pushcart to store to department store. American Jewish Archives.

Although Jews most often married other Jews, intermarriage was common, if officially condemned. The necessities of life made it acceptable in deed if not formally approved by the community. There was considerable social integration in the frontier communities and Jews became, through marriage, members of some of America's socially elite families. Most often it was a choice between religious loyalty and bachelorhood as against the married bliss that an intermarriage promised. Many remained Jews, some practicing, participating Jews in their lifetime, but their children entered the majority society.

IN THE EARLY REPUBLIC

The *Savannah Republican* of April 21 1820 reports:

'On Wednesday the Grand Lodge of Georgia, and the subordinate Lodges of this city, assembled in Solomon's room, for the purpose of making the necessary arrangements for the laying of the cornerstone of a Hebrew Synagogue, about to be erected in this city.'

The assembly then proceeded to consecrate the ground and lay the stone. After an 'Anthem from a band of music', Thomas P. Charlton, Grand Master of Georgia spoke:

'This ceremony is a beautiful illustration of our happy, tolerant and free government. Everyone here is permitted to adore the eternal after the dictates of his conscience...'

The erection of a synagogue became an event of public celebration. The synagogue, as it were, gave to the Jewish community a place of worth and equality in the general community. The Constitution guaranteed freedom of religion for all. The Jew, whose history taught him to cherish rights more than most, accepted this right as a mandate. The American Jew established and maintained a synagogue in answer to his spiritual needs as a Jew. He also did so as an American, for a synagogue was also part of the American religious landscape.

In Colonial America religion held sway. Toward the latter part of the 18th century deism and atheism gained acceptance and respectability. The decades which followed the American Revolution saw a vast decline in the prestige of the religious establishment and in the place of religion in the life of the people. But in the early 19th century there was a great religious revival throughout the country. De Tocqueville was struck by the vast power religion had over the lives of the American people. Churches were built and filled. Religious concerns like salvation, the state of one's soul, the power of grace, the need of baptism were topics of conversation and controversy. The clergy was esteemed, and newspapers, magazines and countless books and pamphlets recorded their words and views. Laws were enacted to preserve the sanctity of the Sabbath. Religion was a chief American concern.

The Jews could not help being influenced by this atmosphere. Believers founded congregations and erected synagogues for their own spiritual needs; nonbelievers helped maintain them because it was the American thing to do. In city after city, a small group of Jews would establish the Jewish community by

Immigrants and immigration. The view of the Statue of Liberty in New York harbor brought a surge of hope for a new life to some two million Jewish immigrants, arriving mostly from Eastern Europe following pogroms and anti-Semitic persecutions in their countries of origin. American Jewish Archives.

organizing a congregation. Mrs. L. Maria Child writes in her *Letters From New York* (New York and Boston, 1843):

'Last week (September 1841) a new synagogue was consecrated in Attorney Street, making, I believe, five Jewish synagogues in this city, comprising in all about ten thousand of this ancient people. The congregation of the new synagogue are German emigrants, driven from Bavaria, the duchy of Baden, and other lands by oppressive laws. One of these laws forbade Jews to marry; and among the emigrants were many betrothed couples, who married as soon as they landed on our shores... If not as "rich as Jews", they are now most of them doing well in the world, and one of the first proofs they gave of prosperity, was the erection of a place of worship.'

The Touro Synagogue, Newport, 1763. An architectural masterpiece, the Touro synagogue of Newport, Rhode Island, has been designated a national shrine. The building was consecrated in 1763, and its architect was Peter Harrison. American Jewish Historical Society.

An event of prime significance to Jewish religious life was the founding of the Reformed Society of Israelites in Charleston, South Carolina, in 1825 'for promoting true principles of Judaism according to its purity and spirit'. Five years later it published its own prayer-book. Isaac Harby, the moving spirit of the Society, describes its purposes in the *North American Review*, 1826:

'The principal points aimed at by the reformers, are order and decency in worship, harmony and beauty in chanting, the inculcation of morality and charitable sentiments upon individuals, and the promotion of piety toward the Deity. In these things, the Society believes, consist religion, virtue, and happiness; in these, the salvation of every rational and immortal being.'

The Society did not long survive Harby's departure from Charleston. Thus ended a native American attempt to establish Reform Judaism. In retrospect, the Society did triumph when Beth Elohim, the mother congregation from which its adherents had seceded and which they later rejoined, itself became a Reform congregation.

Viable Reform Judaism was an importation from Germany. The American atmosphere was hospitable to it and it flourished on American soil as nowhere else in the world. Reform had its

American beginnings in the religious societies Emanuel in New York and Har Sinai in Baltimore, organized by German immigrants in the early 1840s. The Baltimore congregation brought to its pulpit the eminent rabbi, David Einhorn, whose ideology dominated American Reform Judaism throughout the 19th century. In 1846 a young Hebrew teacher from Bohemia, Isaac Mayer Wise, arrived in America and began a rabbinical career which in time bestowed upon him the deserved tribute of 'architect and builder of Reform Judaism in America'.

The traditional forces were not idle. In 1826, the first prayer-book with English translation was published in America. The Hebrew text was 'Carefully Revised and Corrected by E.S. Lazarus and Translated into English from the Hebrew by Solomon Henry Jackson.' Both were American Jews. A decade later Isaac Leeser translated and published the Daily, Sabbath and Holy Days and Festivals Prayer-book in six volumes; the Pentateuch with translation in 1845, and a *Book of Daily Prayers... according to the custom of the German and Polish Jews* in 1848.

It should also be recorded that in 1840 the first ordained rabbi to serve in America, Abraham Rice, arrived in Baltimore where for many years he was a spokesman for Orthodox Judaism.

Traditionalists and Reformers

The growing self-awareness of mid-nineteenth century America had its Jewish expression in the desire to establish an American Judaism. Its chief exponents were Isaac Leeser and Isaac Mayer Wise. The former, a German immigrant who became *hazzan*-minister of Sephardi congregations in America, was a traditionalist and expressed his 'Americanism' by introducing the English sermon and inspiring the first Sunday school. He had faith that America would be hospitable to a traditionally religious and highly cultured Jewish community if only the Jews willed it and matched will with enterprise and accomplishment. He set out to establish the institutions which would fashion such a community.

Isaac Mayer Wise, an enormously energetic and optimistic newcomer from Bohemia, believed that Judaism would in time become the religion of enlightened modern man. But first it had to be modernized and democratized, or better still, 'Americanized'. He thus became the exponent of a moderate pragmatic Reform Judaism, based on the pressures and practicalities of modern, democratic living. Thus for example, the prayer-book which he prepared and vigorously promoted was a modified traditional order of services with Hebrew text and facing German or English translations. Modernity ordered the elimination of hopes for the restoration of sacrifices. References to a Messiah

The Touro synagogue, Newport, 18th century. The interior of the same synagogue as above, built in 1763, as it looks today. The design of this interior is reminiscent of the Sephardi synagogue in Amsterdam. American Jewish Historical Society. ▶

and return to a homeland were eliminated, for America was Zion, 'Washington our Jerusalem'. Appropriately, he titled this prayer-book, *Minhag America* (The American Rite).

Overriding any individual differences and preferences was the conviction that American Jewry needed unity, and American Judaism, some kind of central authority. Reform and Traditionalist elements were brought together at a conference convened in Cleveland in 1855. Unity demanded compromise. Leeser's compromise consisted in attending a conference planned and dominated by Reform Jews; Wise's in accepting the Talmud as the authoritative interpretation of the Bible.

The conference did not lead to unity. It strengthened division and led to subdivision. Leeser and Wise dissolved their 'partner-

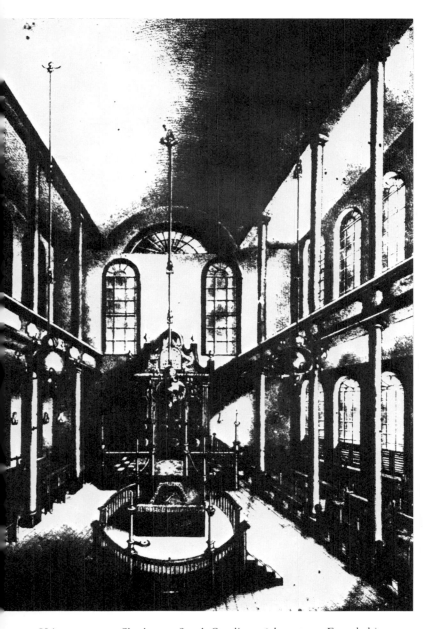

Hebrew synagogue, Charleston, South Carolina, 18th century. Founded in 1795, the Hebrew synagogue was designed by Solomon Carvalho. Owing to the town's liberal constitution, Charleston in South Carolina became a leading Jewish community in the US through the first quarter of the 19th century. The synagogue was destroyed by fire in 1838. American Jewish Historical Society.

ship' with recriminations which grew progressively more acrimonious as the years went on. The Reform group of the East, led by Rabbi David Einhorn of Baltimore, attacked the conference and dissociated itself from the Reform movement of Wise, rejecting it as puerile and retrograde, and accusing its chief proponent of opportunism. The rift between the moderate, practical Reform of the West and the radical, ideological Reform of the East divided the movement for three decades. Whatever chance Leeser had of giving leadership to, or exerting influence on, the East European Orthodox immigrant, he lost by consorting with the enemy, Reform.

In Philadelphia in the late 1860s, Reform and Traditionalist elements each marshaled their forces and undertook enterprises which would foster their interests. Isaac Leeser, supported by the Board of Delegates of American Israelites and the Hebrew Education Society of Philadelphia, organized and served as provost of Maimonides College, the first Jewish seminary in America. It opened its doors to four students in 1867 and died for lack of support four years later. In an attempt to heal the rift between the Reform parties of East and West, a conference was called in November 1869. It was convened and dominated by the triumvirate of the East: Rabbis David Einhorn and Samuel Hirsch of Philadelphia and Samuel Adler of New York. Wise and Max Lilienthal came from Cincinnati. A set of principles prepared by Einhorn was accepted. The conference concluded, the rabbis went their separate ways, having failed to bring their points of view any closer.

Religious practice and ideology were being fashioned not in conferences or seminaries, but in the individual congregations. The congregations of Colonial America were all Sephardi and continued their distinctive ritual even after a majority of their membership was Ashkenazi. The new immigrants from Western and Eastern Europe alike were pleased and proud to become associated with the existing Spanish-Portuguese synagogues, which in their eyes had the twin virtue of being 'native American' and aristocratic to boot. Not until the beginning of the 19th century was the first Ashkenazi synagogue founded, Rodeph Shalom of Philadelphia; and it was only in 1825 that a group of English Jews left Shearith Israel to organize B'nai Jeshurun in New York. With increased immigration, congregations proliferated. By 1860 there were perhaps two hundred congregations, permanent and temporary (meeting for the High Holy Days only), in more than one hundred cities and towns. There were the old Sephardi synagogues, traditional synagogues of the Western European type, and Reform congregations. The first East European synagogue, the Beth Hamidrash, was founded in New York in 1852. A contemporary report in *The Occident* states:

'Its founders were few, and they established it in poverty... in affliction, deprivation and straightness they watched over its early rise... Now (1857) it is supported by about eighty men in Israel...'

As a typical East European synagogue:

'It is open all the day... There is daily a portion of the law expounded publicly... every evening, when the people rest from their daily task... there are persons who study the law

Rebecca Gratz (1781-1869), by Thomas Sully. Rebecca Gratz was a noted and beloved member of the Philadelphia Jewish community through the first half of the 19th century, and is said to have been the prototype for Scott's characterization of Rebecca in *Ivanhoe*. She is credited with having founded the first Jewish Sunday school. American Jewish Historical Society.

for themselves, either in pairs or singly... it is filled with all sorts of holy books... on Sabbaths and festivals, in the evening and morning... the house is full to overflowing...'

Even on the remotest frontier, Jews gathered for prayer. In *The Occident* of December 22 1859 is the report:

'...In this town and county of San Diego, there number some twelve or fourteen Israelites. These scattered few of God's chosen people agreed to unite in the observance of the sacred festival of the New Year, as well as in the solemnities of the Day of Atonement... On the eve of that memorable day, a worthy citizen, named M. Manasse, journeyed fifty miles to be with us, and complete the number designated and requisite to form a congregation.'

A small number of the congregations were served by rabbis, many of them former teachers or minor religious functionaries, who, in the freedom of America, took the liberty of conferring ordination upon themselves; and some added the degree and title 'Dr.' as well. Wise, whom we have already met, Lilienthal and Rice came to America to seek opportunity to serve. Others, like David Einhorn, Samuel Adler, and Benjamin Szold, were brought by their congregations. The desirability of American-

born and American-trained rabbis was felt by thoughtful and concerned leaders of the community. Simon Tuska, a graduate of the university of Rochester, went to Breslau in 1858 to study in its seminary. Temple Emanuel sent some young men to Germany for rabbinic training. Of these, Bernard Drachman returned to serve as an Orthodox rabbi, and Felix Adler to found the Ethical Culture movement. The first viable seminary was established by that master builder, Isaac M. Wise. He first fashioned a lay organization, the Union of American Hebrew Congregations, as a base for support, in 1873.

The 'Call for Convention' which called the Union into being stated its purpose:

'To establish a Jewish Theological Institute... in order that some of our youth, conversant with the language of the land, should be educated for the Jewish ministry...'

'On the third of October 1875, the college was formally and solemnly opened in the city of Cincinnati...,' the college's president, Isaac M. Wise, reported. 'The class consists of seventeen students...,' he continued, one being a college freshman, thirteen high school students, three due to enter high school. 'Twelve of these students are American-born and five European.'

The American Jewish community was beginning to stabilize its institutions and to establish its own forms of religious education.

ORTHODOX, CONSERVATIVE, REFORM

'Perhaps one third of the Jews in the United States are still Orthodox, another third neglect religion except on the greatest days of the religious year... another third are in various stages of Reform...,' wrote James Parton in 1870. The East European immigration which followed added to the first two groups, and introduced a new phenomenon in Jewish religious life in America: the active anti-religionists. The latter, consisting of Socialists, anarchists and a variety of freethinkers, launched all manner of anti-religious projects. Periodicals in Yiddish and Hebrew (such as *HoEmes,* edited by Chaim Enowitz) launched regular and sustained attacks, and books and pamphlets were published to argue the falsity of religious doctrine and to portray organized religion as a retrograde, reactionary force. Religious laws and customs were scoffed at and religious leaders attacked in spoken and written word. Perhaps the most dramatic anti-religious projects were the *Yom Kippur* balls, held on *Kol Nidre* night, 'to eat, drink and make merry,' while other Jews were observing the day in prayer and fasting.

Within organized religious life there was heightened strife and contention which led to the current divisions into Orthodox, Conservative and Reform. To be sure, there were those who pleaded for one uniform American Judaism. Jacob Goldman, who had traveled widely in the United States, argued in his *The Voice of Truth* (Philadelphia, 1870):

'The *Jehudim* of the different parts of Europe, etc. have brought into this country their different *minhagim*... Our Rabbis, D.D.'s, Reverends, Preachers... are holding on to

The Hebrew Purim Ball at the Academy of Music, New York, 1865. The Purim Ball illustrated was held in New York on March 14 1865. Charity balls were popular in mid-nineteenth-century America. The Hebrew Purim Ball was a highlight of the New York Jewish social season. One of the guests has come disguised as a *Hanukkah* top or *dreidel.* American Jewish Historical Society.

their various *minhagim*... In the name of God, in the name of all Israelites whose hearts are still accessible... in the name of all Jewish American citizens, prepare... a code of *minhagim* common to all, and to be adopted by all of us survivors of the year 1870! Look upon our posterity! They are no longer Polander, German, Russian, English, Portuguese; they are Americans, and will and can have nothing more useful than "a *minhag* of America"...'

The Union of American Hebrew Congregations established in 1873 and its Hebrew Union College, founded two years later, were intended to serve all of American Israel. Indeed, the traditionalist Sabato Morais, minister of the Mikveh Israel Congregation of Philadelphia, served as a college examiner. But the issues which divided American Jewry were stronger than the wish to establish an American Judaism. Which prayer-book was to be used for an 'American Judaism': the traditional, the moderate reform *Minhag America* of Isaac Mayer Wise, or the radical *Olat Tamid* of David Einhorn? An increasing number of leading congregations were holding their main religious service of the week on Sunday morning. Others denounced this as the rankest apostasy. There were those who were most meticulous in their observance of the laws of *Kashrut,* while others termed it a remnant of an ancient barbaric cult and poked fun at 'kitchen Judaism'. Some congregations left the Union (now becoming more pronouncedly Reform) on this issue. The conflict came to a dramatic head at the banquet celebrating the First Commencement of the Hebrew Union College in 1884. The first course served caused the observant Jews present to leave the dinner and the movement. Visible insult had been added to the long-standing verbal attack on Jewish traditional usage. Such disparity of views on religion, law and custom inevitably led to division.

The break was long in the making. For three decades there had been division between Reform Jews and Traditionalists.

Within the group there was further division, between moderate and radical reform, and between West European and East European traditionalists. The ever-increasing immigration of Jews from Eastern Europe caused a restructuring: the Reform groups drew closer to one another in their desire for separation from the new immigrants. It has been suggested that radical reform gained the victory over moderate reform, because the 'native' Jew was convinced that its form of religious life and worship would keep the new immigrant out of the Temple.

All the elements of Reform Judaism joined in a conference held in Pittsburgh in November 1885 'for the purpose of discussing the present state of American Judaism... and of uniting upon... plans and practical measures...' Nineteen rabbis deliberated for three days. Isaac Mayer Wise presided, but the leading spirit was Kaufmann Kohler, a son-in-law of David Einhorn. The radical Reform of Einhorn dominated the proceedings. The eight-point platform was a forthright and succinct statement of an extreme Reform viewpoint on God, the Bible, *Kashrut,* priesthood, nationalism, Jewish mission, immortality, and social justice. It remained the most authoritative statement of Reform Judaism for half a century.

The East European immigration had its effect on the Traditionalist camp as well. The West Europeans were not at ease with the East European Orthodox Jew, and he in turn would

The Temple at Atlanta (exterior). Colonial, Byzantine, Romanesque, Gothic, neo-classical — American synagogical architecture often reflected the architect's and building committee's views of the nature of Judaism. Note here the Ionic portico. American Jewish Archives.

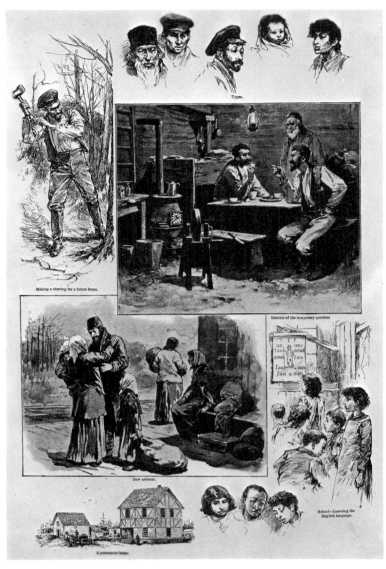

The Jewish colony at Woodbine, New Jersey. This colony was founded by the Baron Hirsch Colony Society. The New Jersey agricultural colonies established by the Baron Hirsch Fund were the most successful Jewish agricultural settlements in America. American Jewish Historical Society.

not look for religious leadership to a Sephardi *hazzan,* such as Sabato Morais, or a moderate reformer like Alexander Kohut. The West European traditionalists and the moderate reformers of the 'historical school' (spiritual disciples of Zacharias Frankel, principal of the Jewish Theological Seminary of Breslau), repelled by the ever-increasing radicalism of American Reform, now joined together in common endeavor to found a Jewish Theological Seminary. Its purpose would be to assure 'the preservation in America of the knowledge and practice of historical Judaism as ordained in the Law of Moses and expounded by the prophets and sages of Israel in biblical and talmudical writings...' It began instruction in 1886.

The East European Orthodox Jewish community was growing in size and self-awareness. For a quarter of a century, since 1860, its leading rabbinical figure had been R. Joseph Asch. With his death in 1887, an Association of the American Orthodox Hebrew Congregations was organized 'in order to create an intelligent Orthodoxy'. This task was to be entrusted to a chief rabbi, who would 'be the leader in the battle which must be waged to keep the next generation faithful to Judaism in spite of the educational, social and business influences, which in America are so powerful as to make our sons and daughters forget their duty to... (their) religion...' Rabbi Jacob Joseph of Vilna came as chief rabbi to a community fired with great hopes and high enthusiasm. It proved to be an ill-fated undertaking in all ways. Ill-conceived and utterly mismanaged, it aroused antagonisms and rivalries in the community and brought personal tragedy to the rabbi. But it also marked Orthodoxy in America as an independent, self-conscious force.

In the three years 1885, 1886 and 1887, three events took place which concretized the division of American religious Jewry into Orthodox, Reform and Conservative movements. Each group had made its decision to strike out on its own, and undertook an endeavor from which there was no turning back. Each enterprise was also in accordance with the nature and particular brand of the movement.

Reform Judaism, which had rejected the binding authority of a received tradition, had to meet in conference and adopt a platform which would state its ideological position and commitment. Orthodoxy, accepting the authority of the received legal tradition, needed a rabbinic figure of such stature as to become accepted as the symbol, transmitter and executor of that authority. The Historical School (called Conservative Judaism), committed to the relevance of the entire Jewish historical experience and the evolutionary character of Jewish Law, established a school for the scientific study of Judaism by its rabbinical students.

The tripartite division of the American Jewish religious community into Orthodox, Reform and Conservative Judaism continued and became formally institutionalized in the 20th century. Each group had its rabbinical seminary, lay and rabbinical organizations. Each movement also underwent change. Reform continued its drift away from tradition for the first two decades of the 20th century. A return to traditionalism then began, at first hardly perceptible, then slowly developing, and finally bursting into great activity in the years which followed World War II. An increasing number of rabbis who were ordained by the Reform seminary, the Hebrew Union College, came from an East European Traditionalist background. A significant number came under the influence of Zionism, which turned their attention and interest to Jewish peoplehood and Jewish culture. This interest became a commitment that they brought to their movement and their individual congregations. A comparison between the Pittsburgh Platform of 1886 and the Columbus Platform of 1936 shows up the new trends in Judaism which transferred the emphasis from the credal formulation to the ongoing historic spiritual experience of the Jewish people. The mass influx of sons and daughters of East European immigrants into the Reform congregations permitted and stimulated a return to traditional forms in the temple and a reintroduction of ritual into the home. The Sabbath eve service on Friday night replaced the Sunday service as the main service of worship. The use of Hebrew in the liturgy increased. *Bar* and *Bat Mitzvah, Kiddush,* and even *Havdalah* became part of Reform practice. The formerly proscribed head-covering for men was made optional in many congregations, and some reintroduced a form of the *tallit* for pulpit wear. The return to tradition continued, with committees and commissions now charged with the responsibilities of revitalizing the Sabbath, and preparing new prayer-books and a new *Haggadah,* with all indications that they will be far more traditional in form and content than those currently in use.

Conservative Judaism in the era of Solomon Schechter, 1902-15, was an ideological reaction to Reform. It was a reaffirmation of the autority of Halakhah, as a living, albeit changing, system of laws, usage, customs and traditions. It placed emphasis on the total historic religious experience of the Jewish people, and held precious all Jewish cultural and spiritual creations. In later decades, it came into competitive confrontation with Orthodoxy. Many Orthodox congregations turned Conservative in the hope of retaining the interest and loyalty of the rising generation. Graduates of the Jewish Theological Seminary founded Conservative congregations which drew their membership from the Orthodox camp.

The Conservative emphasis on Zionism and Jewish culture won for it the adherence of elements of the Jewish community which so far had been content to be accounted part of Orthodoxy. The chief influence on the movement in the years between the wars when it stood in ideological and practical contention with Orthodoxy was Mordecai M. Kaplan, who espoused a liberal

The Temple Ohalei Sholom, Brookline (Mass.). American synagogue architecture followed no single design or pattern. All modes and all styles were reflected in its architecture. American Jewish Archives.

260

theology, urged a reinterpretation of traditional belief and a reconstruction of traditional forms. His definition of Judaism as a total civilization—'the evolving religious civilization of the Jewish people'—became the basic position of his Reconstructionist movement. In consequence, Jewish culture in its totality, language, literature, art, music were stressed. The synagogue was turned from a House of Worship into a spiritual, cultural, educational, social center for congregation and community.

The earliest experiences of East European Orthodoxy in America were a complete disaster. The immigrant transplanted Old World synagogal forms to the New World. They answered his own spiritual needs, but could not win the interest or allegiance of his children. The reaction was a withdrawal from the American scene, into self-contained communities and spiritual and cultural isolation. Forward-looking leaders, taking example from the neo-Orthodoxy of Samson Raphael Hirsch of Frankfurt-am-Main, launched an attempt at making the traditional faith at home in the modern world. It took the form of a *yeshivah*-university, where young men would receive modern high school and college training while studying the sacred texts in the traditional manner in an Orthodox religious atmosphere.

The Yeshiva University and Rabbi Isaac Elchanan Theological Seminary has now put forth a generation of rabbis, teachers and lay leaders who have given great vitality to Orthodoxy. Orthodox Jews were to be found on college faculties, in the laboratories and in communal and cultural life. The Orthodox congregations took on new life, though the price has sometimes been the adoption of new forms borrowed from coreligionists on the left: mixed seating, English prayers and readings at services, the *Bat Mitzvah* ceremony and others. In the years since World War II there has been a growth of a re-emphasis on traditionalism in certain sectors of Orthodoxy, occasioned by the immigration of Hasidim from Central Europe, and a new militancy on the part of native-born Orthodox leaders as they stand in con-

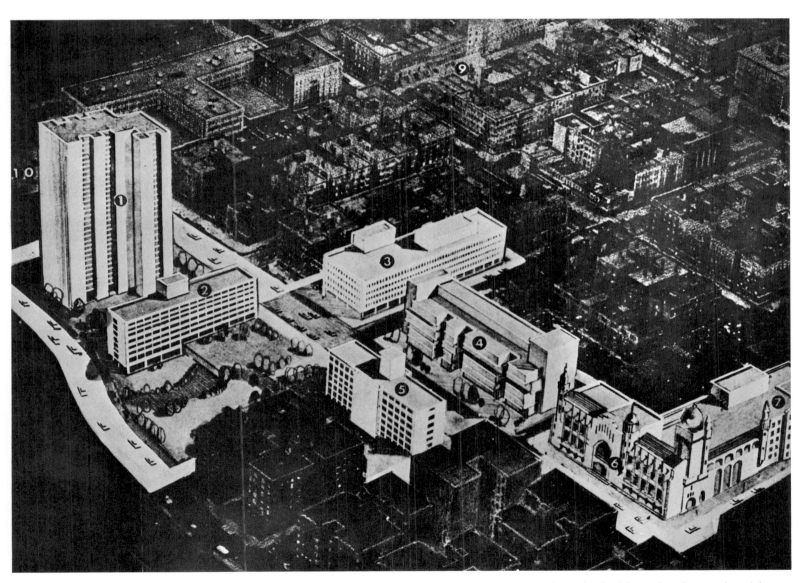

Plan of the main center of Yeshiva University. Yeshiva University, New York City, was the first American University under Jewish auspices. It traces its origins to 1886, before merging and being elevated to a university in 1945. It combines rabbinical and secular studies and among its many branches particularly notable is perhaps the Albert Einstein College of Medicine.

Modern Jewish-American tapestries. Stone, metal, wood, glass, cloth are all used in synagogue art. Samuel Wiener Jr.'s woven tapestries adorn the vestibule of Temple Beth El, South Orange, New Jersey. Hebrew letters and symbols are used: tablets, Torah, *shophar*, star and lyre. *Contemporary Synagogue Art*.

frontation to what they term the 'deviationist' movements of Conservative and Reform Judaism.

In recent decades Reform has been characterized by an attempt to rediscover tradition and to tackle the challenge it presents. The majority of rabbis and laymen are committed to the ever-widening influence of Traditionalism, but a few have sounded the alarm that this is a reactionary and retrogressive tendency. Orthodoxy has discovered the world outside, and most leaders and committed laymen are grappling with its implications and demands—with a small but significant number advocating great caution or actual withdrawal. Conservative Judaism continues to stress the total Jewish civilization, placing its em-

phasis on Jewish cultural creativity, educational enterprise, and communal activity.

The American Jew, having viewed America as a 'melting pot', then as a land of 'cultural pluralism', is now beginning to react to a new image of America: America as a land of 'ethnic assimilation and religious differentiation'. America as a nation demands political unity and civic concern, but it also fosters religious diversity. The Jew, sensing this, has made synagogue affiliation his expression of Jewish association. Salo Baron points out: 'In Western Europe and America, the religious factor has retained its preeminent position in the scale of communal values... the religious congregation has continued to attract the relatively

Ark. Wood carving in synagogue art, Temple Israel, Charleston, West Virginia. Milton Horn's door for the Ark of Temple Israel, Charleston, West Virginia. Left: Moses receiving the Torah. Right: Bezalel carving the Cherubim (Exodus 35). Photo Estelle Horn, *Contemporary Synagogue Art.*

CULTURE AND EDUCATION

In the religious revival which swept through early nineteenth-century America, missionary activity played a central role. There were missionaries to the Indians and missions to the peoples of Asia, Africa, and the Islands. Nor were the Jews forsaken. The 'American Society for Ameliorating the Condition of the Jews' by converting them to Christianity was founded in 1819, when there were hardly three thousand Jews in the country. The next year *Israel Vindicated; Being a Refutation of the Calumnies Propagated Respecting the Jewish Nation: In which the Objects and Views of the American Society for Ameliorating etc... are investigated. By an Israelite* was published in New York.

most constant and active participation of a large membership... total congregational membership in the United States vastly exceeds, numerically, Jewish membership in purely philanthropic undertakings.'

America considers the Jews to be members of a religious community, a view shared equally by the Jews themselves.

Congregation Israel, North Shore, Glencoe (Ill.). The graceful, stately, ethereal synagogue that the architect Minoru Yamasaki fashioned of concrete and glass for Congregation Israel, standing on the shores of Lake Michigan in the Chicago suburb of Glencoe. *Contemporary Synagogue Art.*

Menorah. The use of metal in synagogue art. A stylized *menorah* of nickel, silver and steel by Seymour Lipton for Temple Beth El, Gary, Indiana. Photo Oliver Baker, *Contemporary Synagogue Art.*

In 1823 *Israel's Advocate or The Restoration of the Jew Contemplated and Urged,* a missionary journal, began publication. Within a year Samuel H. Jackson began the publication of *The Jew, Being A Defense of Judaism Against All Adversaries and Particularly Against the Insidious Attacks of ISRAEL'S ADVOCATE.*

For two years, this first Jewish periodical in America was published monthly, engaging in vigorous polemic and argument.

The generation of the 1820s through the 1840s had grown up in freedom and seized the opportunities it provided. Jews entered the arts, professions and public service, a few with modest success. Daniel L. M. Peixotto became president of the Medical Society of the City and County of New York, while Dr. Jacob De La Motta served as secretary of the Medical Society of South Carolina. Samuel B. H. Judah and Jonas Phillips were playwrights and literary figures of some distinction. Isaac Harby was a newspaper writer and editor. Naphtali Phillips published *The National Advocate,* edited by Mordecai M. Noah.

Mordecai Manuel Noah was the most fascinating American Jew of the first half of the 19th century. A famed playwright and a founder of native American drama, he edited a number of newspapers, and attained considerable political influence as a leader of the Tammany Society. He was a man of pronounced opinion and forceful character; he apparently delighted in controversy. His public service included the offices of Surveyor of the port of New York, high sheriff, and consul to Tunis. He was the first to advocate the establishment of a Jewish agricultural settlement and a Jewish college in America and his dedication of Grand Island as a refuge for persecuted Jews is well known. He was indeed a man of many parts.

Rosa Mordecai reminisced about the first Hebrew Sunday School organized by her great aunt, Rebecca Gratz, in 1837:

'On the table was a much worn Bible containing both the Old and New Testaments... Watt's Hymns, and a penny contribution box "for the poor of Jerusalem..." The "Scripture Lessons" were taught from a little illustrated work published by the Christian Sunday School Union. Many a long summer's day have I spent pasting pieces of paper over answers unsuitable for Jewish children...'

The Sunday School idea, like its textbooks, was borrowed from the Protestant neighbors and adapted for Jewish use.

In the 1840s and 1850s congregations and individuals opened schools for Jewish children where a full curriculum of general and Jewish subjects was taught. A typical curriculum would include in Hebrew studies: Hebrew reading, translation of the prayers and the Pentateuch, some Hebrew grammar, Jewish religion taught through a Catechism, and biblical history. The secular studies might include: reading, writing, arithmetic, grammar, geography, spelling, composition, rhetoric, music, and language instruction in German or French. The outstanding private all-day schools (which boarded students as well, at a fee of about $200 for board and tuition) were the Misses Palache's school for girls, and Dr. Max Lilienthal's school for boys. Hyman B. Grinstein, in his *The Rise of the Jewish Community in New York,* states:

'Lilienthal's students wore a special uniform; they used German and French in everyday conversations... It became the outstanding Jewish school in New York City.'

There was sharp division in the Jewish community on the question of all-day schools. Some maintained that they alone provided an adequate education for the Jewish child. Others opposed them as being separatist and divisive of the community. With the secularization of the free public schools beginning in the late fifties, and the removal of specifically Christian readings and practices from many of them, the enrollment in the all-day schools declined. By the 1860s economics and a desire for full integration had their effect. The Jewish child now received his education in

See illustration page 281.

Mural. The mosaic mural 'The Call of the Shophar' by Ben Shahn (1898-1969), one of America's leading artists, in the vestibule of the Temple Oheb Sholom, Nashville, Tess. The call of the shophar turns everybody's attention to the *menorah* which is kindled by God's spirit. Ben Shahn was born in Russia and settled in the United States in 1906. Photo Bill Preston.

the public school. Attempts at congregational afternoon and evening schools were, with some notable exceptions, sporadic and haphazard. Some private schools carried on, but Jewish education was and remained at a low level, until the communal institutions and agencies took on the job decades later.

The creation and promotion of Jewish literature in mid-century and in the decades which followed was largely the enter-prise of two men, Isaac Leeser and Isaac Mayer Wise. In 1843 Leeser established—and for twenty-five years edited—the first Jewish periodical in America, *The Occident.* (Jackson's *The Jew* had been devoted almost wholly to anti-missionary polemics.) He also prepared and published children's textbooks; translated and published the Sephardi and Ashkenazi prayer-books; translated the Bible into English: organized the first Jewish Publication Society in 1845, which published fourteen little volumes of popular literature as *The Jewish Miscellany* series; and published ten volumes of his own sermons and addresses. Wise founded the weekly, *The Israelite,* in 1854, edited and wrote most of it for many years; a year later he began the publication of *Die Deborah* in German; he wrote historical and polemical works as well as popular novels; he helped establish the first publishing house devoted to Jewish literature, Bloch and Company; and began the practice of publishing the *Annual Proceedings of the Union of American Hebrew Congregations.*

In addition to *The Occident* and *The Israelite,* other papers, the *Asmonean* and *The Jewish Messenger* in New York, *Sinai* in Baltimore, and *The Gleaner* in San Francisco, had readers and influence. The Hebrew and Yiddish press in America began their activity in this period as well. Joshua Falk's *Avnei Yehoshua,* homiletical commentary on the Ethics of the Fathers, the first Hebrew book written and printed in America, was published in 1860. *Shir Zahav Likhvod Yisrael ha-Zaken* (1877) contains three poems in Yiddish, and is therefore acclaimed as the first Yiddish book printed in America.

YIDDISH IN AMERICA

Among the earliest Jews to come to America were Yiddish-speaking Ashkenazim. It is even suggested that the very first Jew to reach the new continent, Jacob Barsimson, was an Ashkenazi Jew. Since Yiddish remained the language of German Jews until the middle of the 19th century, the language was heard already with the arrival of the first Jews.

There are extant a considerable number of Yiddish letters written by and to Jews in Colonial America. The famous Gratz brothers, Bernard and Michael, who lived in Philadelphia in the latter half of the 18th century, wrote in Yiddish, as did their townsman, Jonas Phillips. Yiddish words and phrases dot the correspondence of the New York merchant Uriah Hendricks and the well-known patriot and financier, Haym Salomon.

The first large Jewish immigration wave, in the middle of the 19th century, consisted of residents of towns and villages of the German states, mainly Bavaria. They sought consciously to use the German language and suppress Yiddish, first to establish their credentials as devotees and practitioners of German culture, then in high esteem in America, and later to distinguish themselves and be distinguished by others from the Jewish immigrants from Eastern Europe.

Yiddish cultural activity and creativity in America begins with the first 'wave' of East European immigrants who came in the wake of the Polish uprising of 1863.

THE YIDDISH PRESS

Interest in the Franco-Prussian War of 1870 and the Russo-Turkish War in 1877 became the impetus for the establishment of the Yiddish press in America. The lithographed *Yiddische Zeitung* began to appear in 1870, and *Die Post* a year later. A half-dozen years later the *Israelitische Presse* of Chicago began its brief career. The language of the early press was a Germanized Yiddish; their social view, conservative, and favorable to religion. Their existence was precarious, their appearance, weekly, monthly or 'on occasion'.

Ezekiel Sarasohn, who with his father Kasriel Zvi Sarasohn established the Yiddish press on a firm foundation, described their early struggles:

Park synagogue, Cleveland (Ohio). The Park Synagogue of Cleveland, Ohio, by the German architect, Eric Mendelsohn (1887-1953), opened a new and exciting chapter in American synagogue architecture. It welded building with landscape and placed a house of worship in a park setting. Mendelsohn was a noted architect in Germany before having to leave when the Nazis came to power. After a spell in England and Palestine, he settled in the United States. Photo Hastings and Willinger, *Contemporary Synagogue Art.*

Periodicals began to proliferate in the early years of the century. In time the leading journals were the *Zukunft,* and Chaim Zhitlowski's literary journal *Dos Naie Leben* (1908). The editorial goal of Liessin for his *Zukunft* reflected the mood of much of the periodical press of the time. The goal of Yiddish literature would be not only 'to combine the pleasant with the useful' but to place before the reader 'the entire radiant world of science and progress, as well as the intellectual world of art and esthetic enjoyment.'

The Yiddish press, dailies and periodicals, attained the widest circulation and greatest influence in the 1920s and 1930s. The 1924 restrictive immigration laws, which brought Jewish immigration to a virtual end, dealt a heavy blow to the Yiddish press. The young American Jew today is no longer ashamed of 'Hebrew characters', but very few are able to read Yiddish.

Today, the *Forverts* appears daily in New York, as does the *Freiheit*. Canada's Jews can read the *Kanader Adler* of Montreal and the Toronto weeklies, *Daily Hebrew Journal* and the *Vochenblatt*. Some two dozen Yiddish periodicals representing a variety of Jewish ideological positions and cultural interests are now published in the United States and Canada.

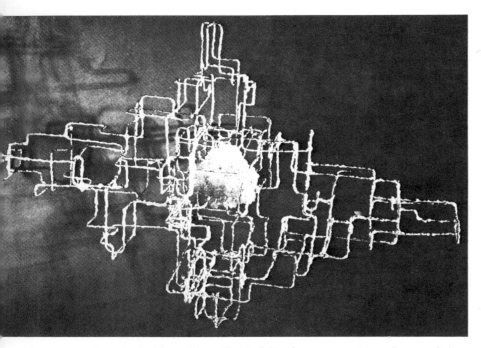

Eternal light. The architect, Percival Goodman, was a pioneer in commissioning works by contemporary artists for his synagogue buildings. Ibram Lassaw's Eternal Light of bronze and calcite crystal (hung before the Ark of the Law) is in the Beth El Synagogue, Springfield, Mass. *Contemporary Synagogue Art.*

THE YIDDISH THEATER

Hutchins Hapgood wrote at the turn of the century:

> 'In the three Yiddish theaters on the Bowery is expressed the world of the Ghetto—that New York City of Russian Jews, large, complex, with a full life and civilization. In the midst of the frivolous Bowery, devoted to tinsel variety shows, 'dive' music halls, fake museums... the theaters of the chosen people alone present the serious as well as the trivial interests of an entire community.'

The Yiddish theater in America had its beginnings in the early 1880s when members of Abraham Goldfaden's troupe arrived as immigrants and presented some of the plays of 'The Father of Yiddish Theater'. In 1891 a gifted playwright, Jacob Gordin, and the leading actor of the Yiddish stage, Jacob P. Adler, joined forces to present the first play 'worthy of serious consideration', *Siberia*. The early theater was dominated by the folk operettas of Goldfaden and by Gordin's serious plays.

The theater began to attract literary figures of high talent who made the Yiddish state a cultural force in the Jewish community. Among them were Leon Kobrin who wrote realistic plays on American themes; and David Pinsky whose plays expressed his Labor Zionist orientation, a passion for social justice and a love for the Jewish people. The works of Sholem Aleichem and Isaac L. Peretz attracted large audiences. Outstandingly popular were

'Most Polish and Lithuanian Jews came from small towns. The older ones among them did not have the slightest need for a newspaper... The younger ones, those who had some education, read German newspapers and gradually English newspapers... The very young were ashamed of a newspaper with Hebrew characters.'

The East European immigration, which was but a trickle in the 1870s, turned into a stream in the 1880s as a result of the restrictive May Laws. It enabled the Sarasohns to establish the daily *Yiddisches Tageblatt* in 1885, which attained wide readership and influence and was published till 1928 when it merged with the *Morgen-Journal*. The newspapers of the day were also journals of opinion. The *Tageblatt* represented the Orthodox viewpoint; its competitors, *Der Volksadvocat* and *Die Volkzeitung* were critical of the religious 'establishment'. The *New Yorker Yiddische Folkzeitung* attempted to speak for both Socialism and the nascent Jewish nationalism represented by the *Hibbat Zion* movement. Morris Rosenfeld, the 'poet of the ghetto', began his literary career in this paper in 1886. Indeed, the newspapers were also literary journals and represent the first blossoming of Yiddish literary activity in America. The 1890s saw the beginning of the famed Jewish daily, *Forward (Forverts)* which in time, under the editorship of Abe Cahan, became the largest Yiddish newspaper in the world, and still appears daily. The outstanding Yiddish journal of literature and thought, *Die Zukunft* (still appearing monthly) began its life in 1892. Its most distinguished editor was the poet, Abraham Liessin. The Socialist *Zukunft* was preceded by two years by the anarchist *Freie Arbeter Shtimme,* which also continues to appear.

The Asmonean, 1849. Volume I, No. 1, page 1 of *The Asmonean,* appeared on ▶ October 2 1849. The periodical press of nineteenth century America was greatly enriched by *The Asmonean* of New York which was its first weekly and was founded by Robert Lyon. American Jewish Historical Society.

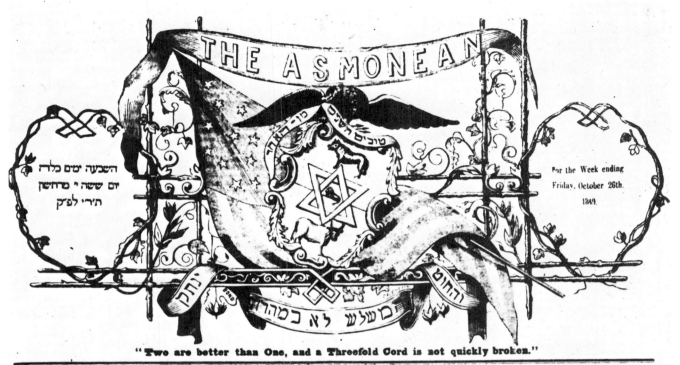

THE ASMONEAN

השבעה ימים מלא
יום ששה ‏ מרחשן
תירי לפק

טובים
מ‏ד‏‏‏

For the Week ending
Friday, October 26th.
1849.

נחם

יהוה

מעשׂ לא כמהר

"**Two are better than One, and a Threefold Cord is not quickly broken.**"

VOL. I.—No. 1.   "KNOWLEDGE IS POWER."   { ROBERT LYON, PUBLISHER, 140 Nassau St., New York.

The Asmonean

HAS THE PATRONAGE AND SUPPORT OF THE MINISTERS AND PRESIDING OFFICERS OF THE FOLLOWING CONGREGATIONS IN THE CITY OF NEW YORK:

שארית ישראל   Crosby St.   בני ישרן   Elm Street,
שער תפלה   Wooster St.   אנשי חסד   Henry St.
שער השמם   Attorney St.   רודף שלום   Attorney St.
שערי צדק   White St.   עמו אל   Chrystie Street.
     בני ישראל   Pearl Street.

Subscribers Names received by the following gentlemen :

NEW YORK.

THE REV. DR. LILLIENTHALL.
THE REV. S. M. ISAACS.
BACH, J. L., 146 William Street.
DITTENHOEFER, I., 44 Beaver Street,
GOLDSMITH, H., 4 West Broadway Place,
HART, H. E., 137 William Street,
HABER, ISAAC, 134 William Street,
ISAACS & SOLOMON. 53 Nassau Street,
LEVY MARK, 49 Maiden Lane.
LEVETT, Dr. M., 628 Broadway,
MAWSON, BROTHERS, 161 Water Street,
MORRISON & LEVY, 134 William Street,
SIMONS, E. & H., 33 Maiden Lane,
SOLOMON & HART, 243 Broadway.
WOOLF, M. 61 Maiden Lane.
WALTER, I. D., 40 Beaver Street.

SYRACUSE.

LEVY SYLVESTER.

PHILADELPHIA.

LYON, SAMUEL, Bookseller, Chestnut Street.
MAWSON, E. S., North Third Street.

ST. LOUIS.

LEVY, LEWIS M.

NEW ORLEANS.

BARNET, MICHAEL, Camp Street,
GOLDSMITH, HABER & CO.
HART, ISAAC.

MOBILE, ALA.

MORRISON, JOS.

☞ Agents are wanted in every City of the Union.

NOTICE.

THE ASMONEAN is sent to various persons not at present on the Subscription List, with a view to canvass for their patronage.

Trustees of Synagogues, Congregational and Society Officers are solicited to lend their co-operation.

Booksellers and Agents will be allowed twenty per cent. on all Subscriptions canvassed for and remitted.

Agents are wanted in all sections.

TO OUR SUBSCRIBERS.

In the circular announcing our intention to publish this Journal, we set forth that the Asmonean would be devoted to the advocacy of a congregational Union of the Israelites of the United States, and the general dissemination of information relating to the people. That its columns would be open to all and every communication appertaining to our Societies, our Congregations, our Literature, and our Religion. That all Foreign and Domestic News would be collected up to the latest moment prior to going to press, and that all matters of public interest, would be temperately commented on. At the commencement of our labors, we deem it necessary to repeat this statement, in order that there may be no misconception of the purpose and intention of the proprietors of this Journal. Emanating from a zealous desire to incite the cultivation of a *Unity of action* between the learned and the philanthropic of Israel, and of diffusing amongst our brethren, a better knowledge of the principles of the Jewish Faith, the paper comes into existence perfectly unfettered and unpledged. Free from the trammels of the schools of casuistry, we are disposed to act according to the maxims of our sages דרוש וקבל שכר " Investigate and acquire merit," this we hope to do soberly and humbly, craving at the hands of our co-religionists, who are better qualified, every aid and assistance which it is in the power of eminent talent to grant to those less gifted than themselves, for it is the duty of all Israelites to further every undertaking having a tendency to dissipate existing prejudices, and induce a better understanding of the true interests of Israel as a religious brotherhood. What is the value of ambition which seeks distinctions in the pursuits of commerce, the labors of the bar, or the senate, compared with that which seeks the elevation not merely of the individual, but of the Jewish people ! " No man can hope to attain eminence as a Jew, or glory in remaining one, until he has done his share in removing the prejudices of darker times." It is with these sentiments, and not in a spirit of arrogance, that we have assumed the grave responsibility of directors of a public Journal. As journalists, we may lack experience, but we are not deficient of zeal in our desire of preserving our national integrity, and averting the curse of infidelity from our people.

Our arrangements for obtaining intelligence respecting country congregations are at present incomplete. We shall at the earliest moment appoint correspondents in every section of the States, and by the exercise of unremitting enterprise, make our paper the means of concentrating the energies and resources of the believers in Israel.

Whenever the subscription list of the Journal warrants it, or the demands of our Advertisers encroach on our Columns, we will increase the size of our paper. Correspondence from all parts of America and Europe relating to our people, may be transmitted at the Editors charge. Communications appertaining to private interests must necessarily be post-paid.

SPEEDY JUSTICE.

Our State Legislature with a host of legal empyrics, have been for many sessions, the former actively, the latter for themselves, profitably employed in pruning and training, extirpating and replanting the prolific vine called the CODE, exhibiting at various times certain portions as plants of extraordinary vigour, capable of resisting the insidious action of the many caterpillars crawling about the Courts, and of affording shelter and protection when necessary, yet, were a stranger to enter several of the Courts, and observe the mode in which the business is conducted, he would conclude that *speedy justice* was a term without meaning, and that there were many places to dispel *ennui* in the city, besides those enumerated in the published lists of amusements of the day. The San Francisco method, with its rough and ready call on the posse commitatus, its instanter election of judges, and impanneling of juries, with all the passions strong upon them, is far better worthy of adoption than New York's retinue of enquiring justices, investigating and petty juries, and sentencing judges; if the proceedings upon all the late trials of importance are to be considered fair specimens of the administration of justice. Witness the late reports of the mode of obtaining a juror in the cause of the people against Judson and others. Now, was it possible to find a citizen with a gleam of intelligence beyond a beast of burthen, who had not heard of the Astor Place disturbance, of the slaughter of many persons on the eventful night in May, yet the admission of such knowledge, made by calling things by their proper term, and a public tumult is a riot, if riot have any meaning, was held to be a ground of incompetency in a juryman, and in the case of the people against John Price, for the murder of G. W. Campbell, at Baltimore, where the Court decided that no man who had read the accounts of the murder as published in the newspapers, could be competent to sit as a juror, as his reading must have created an impression of the guilt of the prisoner, and therefore, after calling 900 talesmen, and spending three days at an enormous expense to the county, they were obliged to remand the prisoner, and change the venue.

We will suppose, (which was the fact) a man to be found dead, under such circumstances as leave no doubt that his death proceeded from the violence of others, would a man be morally incompetent to sit as a juror, because a grand jury had returned a true bill, or the proposed juryman had read an account of the murder, and believed that it had been perpetrated. What has his reading to do with the evidence to be offered in the case, for on that, and that only, is the verdict to be founded. We refrain from offering all that occurs to us upon the ruling of the trier in these cases, but we cannot resist calling the judges attention to the fact, that many of the decisions tend to lower public estimation of common law as men of the legal authorities we instance one point which strikes us as particularly rich. In re Judson. — The court suggested to the triers

the dramas of Sholem Asch. The best products of European dramatists were also adapted for the Yiddish stage.

The stars of the Yiddish stage were the cultural heroes of the ghetto and each had his adherents and advocates who formed loyal, spirited, partisan claques.

In 1918 there were twenty-four Yiddish theaters in America, no less than eleven in New York City. Maurice Schwartz, through his Yiddish Art Theater, brought the Jewish stage to its triumphant heights. He gathered about him a gifted group, but it was his vision, enterprise and will that welded the Yiddish Art Theater into one of the greatest of repertory companies. From this group Muni Weisenfreind went on to become an outstanding movie star under the name of Paul Muni, and Joseph Bulow to be a prominent actor of the American stage.

Of the beloved stars of the Yiddish theater perhaps none had more devoted 'fans' than Boris Tomashefsky, the idol of the working girl, and Molly Picon, the *gamine* musical comedy star.

The theater reached its heights in the 1920s and early thirties. Its decline since has been rapid, although there has been a limited revived interest in the Yiddish stage in recent years.

YIDDISH POETS AND NOVELISTS

American Yiddish poetry had its origins in complaint and protest. The immigrant's golden dreams turned to bitter dross when he reached the shores of the Promised Land. Freedom and wealth were the promise America held out; reality offered a dingy tenement, back-breaking sweatshop labor, a grinding poverty which enslaved body and soul. Morris Rosenfeld expressed the plight and plaint of the immigrant in a series of simple, sentimental, bitter poems like the descriptive *I Am a Millionaire of Tears,* and *My Little Boy* which became the anthem of the sweatshop worker. 'I have a little boy... who is my whole life... but seldom, seldom do I see him... I leave for work when he's still asleep... and return from my labor after he's gone to bed...' His songs of immigrant life became the folksong of the immigrant. A contemporary, David Edelstadt, was the poet of angry protests and cry of rebellion. He died at at tender age of the immigrant affliction, tuberculosis. Morris Winchefsky's poetic cry is classic: 'You can kill only our body, our flesh, but not our holy spirit.'

The most gifted of American Jewish poets was Yehoash (Solomon Bloomgarden). His poetry, universal in theme, draws upon Jewish sources and uses Jewish images. A man of spiritual tendency, his poems breathe deep national feelings and some rise to psalm-like feeling and expression. His major life's work was the translation of the Bible into Yiddish 'in a style that purified and enriched the Yiddish language itself.'

Die Yunge was a name given to a group of writers whose work began to appear before World War I. One of the group, Joseph

Title page of Yiddish translation of Bible by Yehoash, 1941. One of the great works of literary scholarship in America was the translation of the Bible by the American Jewish poet Yehoash (Solomon Bloomgarten) into a poetic and contemporary Yiddish. Yiddish was the major language among the Jews of America up to World War I, but its use has been declining since. American Jewish Historical Society.

Opatoshu, described its creed: 'Yiddish literature ceased to be an educational tool and became an end in itself. It assumed artistic standards...' It was a kind of 'art for art's sake' movement, and the poets and writers turned from themes of tears and struggle, of social protest and upheaval, in toward impressionism, mysticism, individualism.

The famed and beloved Sholem Aleichem spent his last years in America and incorporated his views and experiences in his works. Sholem Asch lived for many years in America and wrote of American Jewish life. Israel Singer was a novelist and playwright of rare power. His brother, Isaac Bashevis Singer, writes in Yiddish, though he has attained his fame through English translations. Hayyim Grade is considered the outstanding Yiddish novelist today.

Yiddish scholarship is fostered by YIVO, the Yiddish Scientific Institute, which boasts an outstanding library and archives. It has

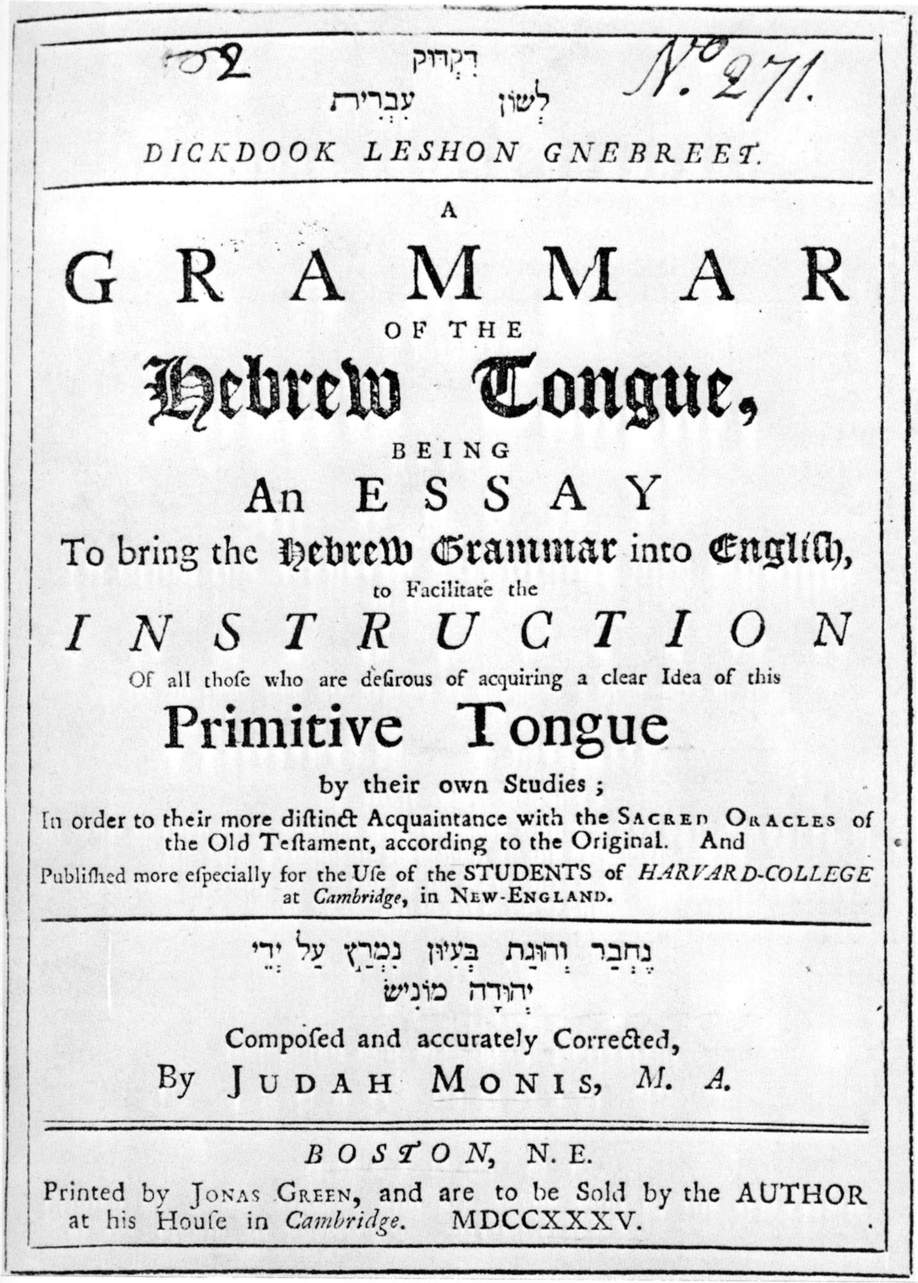
דקדוק
לשון עברית
DICKDOOK LESHON GNEBREET.

A
GRAMMAR
OF THE
Hebrew Tongue,
BEING
An ESSAY
To bring the Hebrew Grammar into English,
to Facilitate the
INSTRUCTION
Of all thoſe who are deſirous of acquiring a clear Idea of this
Primitive Tongue
by their own Studies;
In order to their more diſtinct Acquaintance with the SACRED ORACLES of the Old Teſtament, according to the Original. And
Publiſhed more eſpecially for the Uſe of the STUDENTS of *HARVARD-COLLEGE* at *Cambridge*, in NEW-ENGLAND.

נחבר והוגה בעיון נמרץ על ידי
יהודה מוניש

Compoſed and accurately Corrected,
By JUDAH MONIS, *M. A.*

BOSTON, N. E.
Printed by JONAS GREEN, and are to be Sold by the AUTHOR at his Houſe in *Cambridge*. MDCCXXXV.

The first Hebrew grammar in America, 1735. There was great interest in early Jewish history and in the Hebrew language in Colonial America during the first decades of the 19th century and many editions of Josephus and Hebrew grammars were published: Judah Monis' was the first to appear in America. Judah Monis was probably born in Algiers and left for New York in 1716 and Boston in 1720. He was instructor in Hebrew at Harvard until 1760. American Jewish Historical Society.

a staff of distinguished scholars and has an enviable list of scholarly publications in the field of Jewish history and language study. It carries on the great scholarly tradition begun by YIVO in Vilna. In a sense it is a symbol of the transplanting of Yiddish culture from the Old World to the New.

Hebrew Literary Creativity

The typesetter of the above-mentioned little Hebrew volume *Avnei Yehoshua,* which was published in New York in 1860, recorded the historic importance of this publication:

> 'I give thanks that it is my good fortune to be the typesetter for this scholarly book, the first of its kind in America...'

To be sure, books in Hebrew had appeared in America since 1735 when Judah Monis published his *A Grammar of the Hebrew Tongue... for the Use of the STUDENTS of HARVARD-COLLEGE at Cambridge, in NEW-ENGLAND.* Those which followed were grammars, lexicons, prayer-books, and editions of classic texts. Many were meant for Christian divines and their more scholarly congregants.

The first printing of the prayer-book in Hebrew occurred in 1826, 'The Hebrew Text carefully Revised and Corrected by E. S. Lazarus'. A decade later Isaac Leeser began the publication of his six-volume edition of *The Form of Prayer According to the Custom of the Spanish and Portuguese Jews* (Philadelphia 1837-8), with his own translation into English. He did the same for the Ashkenazi prayer-book in 1848. A number of editions of the traditional *Siddur* and the holiday *Mahzorim* were put out by the publisher and printer W. L. Frank of New York.

Various Reform prayer-books appeared in the mid-19th century, containing more or less Hebrew. *Minhag America* (1857) of Isaac M. Wise; *The Order of Prayer* (1855) by L. Merzbacher; *Olat Tamid* (1858) of David Einhorn, and a series of prayer-books by Benjamin Szold (beginning in 1861) were the best known and most widely used.

The first Hebrew Bible in America was published in Philadelphia in 1814. With a Latin introduction and notes and with vowel points it was intended for the Christian Bible student and reader. The subsequent edition in 1848 already took the Jewish reader into account for it boasted the editorial supervision of Isaac Leeser. Three years earlier Leeser put out a Pentateuch for Jewish congregational use with Hebrew text and his own English translation.

Beginning with the 1860s, contributions by American Jews began to appear in European Hebrew periodicals. The *Ha-Maggid* (published in Lyck) of 1864, for example, contains reports and articles from San Francisco, St Louis, Detroit, Chicago and New York.

The second and third Hebrew books published in America were of greater interest and significance than the first, for they dealt with the American-Jewish scene. *Emek Rephaim* (1865) by M. E. Holzman is a vigorous and at times vitriolic attack against American Reform rabbis, notably Max Lilienthal and Isaac M. Wise. 'A sect has arisen in Israel who attempt to form a code of worship... men who call themselves Doctors, and who are in fact destroyers of all that is sacred.' *Tuv Taani* (1875) by Aaron Zevi Friedman was a 'vindication of the Jewish mode of slaughtering animals for food called *Shechitah*.' It was in response to an accusation by the Society for the Prevention of Cruelty to Animals that the Jewish method of slaughtering was 'cruelty, needlessly inflicted'.

In the wake of the abortive Polish uprising of 1863 an immigration from Eastern Europe began. Though small in number, it brought to America readers of Hebrew and some Hebrew writers. Among these was Zvi Hirsch Bernstein, a pioneer of both the Yiddish and Hebrew press in America. In 1871 and for some five years he published the first Hebrew newspaper, *Ha-Zofeh ba-Arez ha-Chadashah*. The periodical served the new immigrants as a tie to the Old World, and helped introduce them to the New. Thus, for example, the reader became acquainted with Henry Wadsworth Longfellow, whose poem *Excelsior* was translated by Henry Gersoni.

The second East European immigration, that of the 1880s, produced a Hebrew reading public of such size as to encourage the establishment of three Hebrew weeklies in New York. Michael L. Rodkinson, who later translated the Talmud into English, published *Ha-Kol*; Ephraim Deinard, bibliographer and polemicist, whose bibliographical acumen and enterprise helped establish the major Jewish libraries in America, put out thirty-two issues of *Ha-Leumi*; and Wolf Schur began the publication of *Ha-Pisgah*. The last-named continued his publication efforts in Chicago, Boston and Baltimore, undaunted by financial difficulties and undiscouraged by indifference and rebuff. He was active in promoting early Zionism and combating assimilatory tendencies in American Jewish life.

The Society for the Advancement of Hebrew Literature in America published the Hebrew literary monthly, *Ner Ma-aravi* (1895-7). The Society's president was K. Z. Sarasohn, who established the first successful Yiddish daily in America; its treasurer was J. D. Eisenstein, author, anthologist, and encyclopedist, whose ten volume *Ozar Yisrael* encyclopedia in Hebrew is a landmark of Jewish scholarship in America.

The new century witnessed a rebirth of Hebrew literary creativity in America. The annual East European Jewish immigration, which had numbered in the thousands, now was counted in the hundred thousands. Among them were men of literary achievement and enterprise. The new Hebrew literary society bore the name of *Mefizei Sfat Ever* (Disseminators of the Hebrew Language). The mood was more optimistic, the goal more elevated, not merely to preserve a bit of Hebrew, but to establish Hebrew creativity. In 1909 and again in 1913 a Hebrew daily, appropriately titled *Ha-Yom* ("The Day"), was launched. Though short-lived, it is evidence of the mood of optimism.

The young Hebrew writers were in and of America. They received their general cultural education in America. In turn, many took American themes for their poetry. The first among them was Benjamin N. Silkiner, who in 1910 published an epic poem of Indian life, *Mul Ohel Timorah* (Facing Timorah's Tent). Ephraim E. Lisitsky's *Medurot Doakhot* (Dying Campfires) deals with the same theme. The American Negro as well as the Indian provided Lisitsky with material. Negro folklore and the suffering of the American Negro is found in his *Be'Ohalei Kush* (In Negro Tents). The poet and philosopher Israel Efros writes of the tragedy of the Red Indian and treated another American theme, the California gold rush, in an epic poem *Zahav* (Gold). In the writings of Simon Ginsburg, Hillel Bavli, Simon Halkin we find

American themes; the last-named translated Walt Whitman's *Leaves of Grass*. As an indication of how much at home they felt in America and how much they appreciated the English language and its literature, Silkiner, Lisitsky, Efros, Bavli, and Halkin each undertook to translate plays of Shakespeare.

Why the preoccupation with the experience of the American Indian and Negro? The poets express a sense of identification of the American Jew fighting for spiritual survival on American soil with the plight of the Indian who struggled to preserve life on his soil and the Negro struggling to preserve a sense of proud identity. The fine student of Hebrew literary creativity in America, Jacob Kabaloff, states:

'They felt at home in the natural beauties of America and in its literature. And they wished to transmit their appreciation of the American spirit as their contribution to modern Hebrew letters. In so doing, they helped free American

Hatzofeh B'Eretz Hachadashah, 1871. The first page of *Hatzofeh B'eretz Hachadashah*, appearing on June 11 1871. It was the first Hebrew periodical founded in America, and edited by Tzevi Hirsch Bernstein. The Hebrew periodical press reached its height in the 1920s, and the number of periodicals and readers has been declining since. American Jewish Historical Society.

Hebrew writing from the dominance of the Russian Jewish center and to give it character of its own.'

The leading Hebrew periodical in America today is the weekly, *Hadoar*. For many years it was edited by Menahem Ribalow who made it the central organ of American Jewish literature. He added supplements for the younger readers, edited the annual *Sepher Hashanah Li-Yhudei Amerika,* and founded the *Ogen* publishing house. The central body promoting Hebrew culture and literature is the *Histadrut Ivrit* (Organization for Hebrew Culture). The *Massad* Hebrew summer camps inspired the Hebraically-oriented Ramah camps of the Conservative Movement and Camps Yavneh and Sharon.

The cultural dependency of American Jewry on Europe came to an end with the Holocaust. The establishment of the State of Israel has revived interest in the Hebrew language. Israelis who have settled in the United States brought the Hebrew language with them and many serve as its most zealous advocates. The growth of the day school movement is producing a goodly number of Hebrew-reading and Hebrew-speaking American Jews. The increasing number of American Jewish youth who visit Israel, and students who spend a year or more there, are all sources of encouragement to those who espouse Hebrew cultural creativity in America.

The American Jewish community must look to its own resources for its spiritual life even though it can receive inspiration and strength from the cultural forces and institutions in the State of Israel. In the end, however, it is a question of will and enterprise in the American community. In the field of Hebrew cultural and literary creativity, American Jewry can look to a past of achievement but a future of uncertainty.

SCHOLARS AND SCHOLARSHIP

In 1901 a work which boasted of itself that 'for the first time the claims to recognition of a whole race and its ancient religion are put forth in a form approaching completeness,' was published in New York City. The boast was not an overstatement, for the twelve-volume *Jewish Encyclopedia* remains a landmark of Jewish scholarship. It speaks well of the state of Jewish scholarship in America at the turn of the century that it felt secure enough to undertake as monumental a project as the first Jewish encyclopedia. It speaks well, too, of the cultural interest of the Jewish community that the publishing firm Funk & Wagnalls had sufficient confidence in it to sponsor the venture.

The preparation and publication of the Encyclopedia stimulated scholarly activity in America and turned the attention of world Jewish scholarship to America. Though leading Jewish scholars of the world were joined in the enterprise, the great bulk of the work fell on American Jewish scholars. To be sure, almost all of these were European-born and European-trained, but it is important to note that scholarship accompanied Jewish immigration to the New World.

On the editorial board one finds such names as Cyrus Adler, American-born, first recipient of a doctorate in Semitics in America, an important scholar, who in a distinguished career in service of American Jewry, served as president of both Dropsie College and The Jewish Theological Seminary of America; Richard Gottheil, Professor of Semitic Languages, Columbia University, and President of the Federation of American Zionists; Marcus Jastrow, distinguished rabbi and author of the ever-useful and scholarly *A Dictionary of the Targumim, the Talmud Babli and Yerushalmi, and the Midrashic Literature* (1886-1903); and Kaufmann Kohler, later to serve as president of the Hebrew Union College, whose works on various aspects of Jewish thought and theology are lasting contributions to the field.

The youngest member on the editorial board was Louis Ginzberg who in the next half-century became the acknowledged leader of American Jewish scholarship. Trained in the *yeshivot* of Eastern Europe and in German universities, he became a master in virtually every area of Jewish learning. His *The Legends of the Jews* brings the reader a multi-volume collection of the *aggadic* material on biblical personalities and incidents. He brought to his studies of law, liturgy, ritual and custom, not only full knowledge of Jewish sources but a mastery of cognate material and disciplines. The three-volume *Perushim ve-Hiddushim bi-Yerushalmi* (A Commentary on the Jerusalem Talmud) deals only with the first four chapters of the tractate *Berakhot,* but in so broad a manner as to constitute a work on Jewish law, theology, history and culture.

A year after the publication of the *Encyclopedia,* Solomon Schechter was brought from Cambridge University to head the Jewish Theological Seminary. A scholar in theology, *aggadah* and liturgy, and a scholarly popularizer, he became a masterly statesman of scholarship. He brought to the faculty of the Seminary a body of scholars unsurpassed by any institution of Jewish learning. Chief among them was the aforementioned Louis Ginzberg. His colleagues were Alexander Marx, historian and bibliographer, who made the Seminary library the greatest repository of books and manuscripts ever assembled; Israel Friedlaender, scholar of the Bible and Judeo-Arabic, whose untimely martyr's death while on a mission to Eastern Europe brought to an end a career of infinite promise; Israel Davidson whose *Otzar ha-Shirah va-ha-Piyyut* (Thesaurus of Medieval Hebrew Poetry, four volumes, 1924-33) is the basic work of medieval Hebrew poetry and liturgy; and Mordecai M. Kaplan, American-trained rabbi, educator, theologian, and religious leader, who has been the single most important influence on American Jewish religious life and thought. His emphasis on the total Jewish cultural experience as the necessary spiritual expression of Judaism, his radical theology and his espousal of Zionism and Jewish cultural activity and creativity have had wide influence beyond the Reconstructionist Movement which he founded and heads.

The faculty of the Seminary has continued in this distinguished tradition. Louis Finkelstein has made distinguished contributions to the field of Rabbinics; Professor H. L. Ginsberg and Robert Gordis are biblical scholars of note; Shalom Spiegel has continued the faculty's contributions to medieval Hebrew literature; Abraham Joshua Heschel, scion of Hasidic aristocracy, by birth and spirit, is the most widely read and highly regarded Jewish theologian in America. The faculty is headed by Professor Saul

Lieberman. His works on the Palestinian Talmud, the *Tosefta,* and the influence of the Hellenistic civilization on Jewish life and thought in talmudic times, mark him as the preeminent scholar of Rabbinics in the world today.

In 1917, the Jewish Publication Society issued a new translation of the Bible done by a group of American Jewish scholars. Although the preface states that the board of editors contained 'an equal representation of the Jewish Theological Seminary... the Hebrew Union College... and Dropsie College...,' most of the translations were done by men associated with the Hebrew Union College.

The College's faculty has made a signal contribution to Jewish scholarship. Jacob Z. Lauterbach wrote with authority on the talmudic age; David Neumark's has been a distinguished contribution to the history of Jewish philosophy; Max L. Margolis, Julian Morgenstern and Harry M. Orlinsky have enriched biblical study; Jacob R. Marcus has done pioneering work in American Jewish history and founded and heads the American Jewish Archives; the president of the College, Nelson Glueck, was a distinguished archaeologist.

Talmudical study and scholarship in the East European tradition is carried on in the third great institution of higher Jewish learning, Yeshiva University. Its most influential faculty member is Dr. Joseph B. Soloveitchik, scion of a distinguished family of talmudic scholars, who is a world-renowned authority on Jewish Law and philosophy. Dr. Bernard Revel, its first president, succeeded in fashioning a school which blended sacred and secular studies. Under the imaginative and energetic leadership of his successor, Dr. Samuel Belkin, it has branched out into a multi-school institution, ranging from high school through medical school.

Scholars of originality and accomplishment have abounded. Brilliant linguistic insight and daring conjecture mark the work of the biblical scholar, Arnold B. Ehrlich, author of *Mikra ki-Peshuto* (The Bible in its Plain Meaning). Originality and daring is also the hallmark of the historian, Solomon Zeitlin, of Dropsie University, the Philadelphia institution for graduate studies in Hebrew and cognate subjects. One must also mention Alexander Kohut's monumental *Aruch Hashhalem*, completed in America, as well as Meyer Waxman's five-volume *History of Jewish Literature*, and Menahem M. Kasher's twenty-volume compendium of *midrashim* on the Bible, *Torah Shelemah*.

Two universities, Harvard and Columbia, have made great contributions to Jewish scholarship through their eminent faculty members: Harry A. Wolfson and Salo W. Baron. Wolfson undertook a rewriting of Western philosophy. He presents Philo as the seminal thinker whose philosophic concerns and concepts dominated European philosophy until Spinoza. Salo W. Baron is a preeminent historian, who has mastered the entire Jewish historical experience. He sees Jewish history against the background and in the setting of world history. His three-volume *The Jewish Community* is the first study of the Jewish community as an institution considered chronologically and topically. He attributes its viability to its ability to accommodate itself to new political conditions and social challenges, while remaining steadfast in its values and preserving its inner patterns. *A Social and Religious History* (now fourteen volumes up to 1650) is a complete reassessment of Jewish history stressing its uniqueness in its emphasis on social patterns and relationships, and spiritual goals. Baron's influence is exerted not only through the written word but also through the works of many young historians who trained under him.

It should be noted that American Jewry and its institutions of higher learning are now producing its own scholars. Professors of various aspects of Jewish studies, born and trained in America, now grace the faculties of such leading universities as Harvard, Yale, Chicago, California, Pennsylvania, Brown, Brandeis, and Columbia as well as the Jewish institutions of higher learning. There is a justifiable mood of optimism about the future of Jewish scholarship in America.

EDUCATION IN THE AMERICAN SETTING

The history of American Jewish education is one of the accommodation of traditional Jewish forms to the needs of the American scene. In broad terms, this means that the strong influence of individual congregations in the United States has had some effect on weakening the community structure of traditional Jewish education.

Democracy itself can be responsible both for strengthening and weakening an educational program. To the extent that democratization means lack of centralization, educational programs in the United States tend to be directed by the local community, or in the case of religious education, by the local parish or congregation. In certain cases this allows for freedom, creativity, and strong educational programs. But just as frequently this lack of centralization can be the cause of low standards and indeed a complete breakdown in educational programming.

Programs of Jewish education can come under various forms of sponsorship. In certain countries the organized Jewish community has taken on this responsibility. In others there is an arrangement or accommodation with the public school system whereby funds are chaneled into Jewish-sponsored and Jewish-oriented schools. In America Jewish education is largely congregation-oriented.

The American environment encouraged the growth of congregations. Indeed, early American public education was largely parochial, that is, church or parish sponsored. Jews followed suit and the early congregations were quick to organize such services as cemeteries and schools that had till then been communal. These were all-day schools where the student was exposed to the whole gamut of curricular interests, secular as well as religious. In the mid-19th century, Jewish boys and girls also received their total education in private all-day schools conducted by rabbis and Jewish 'educators'.

With the expansion of the American community in the second half of the 19th century, public education gained a foothold and was rapidly dissociated from the churches. The early synagogue-sponsored Jewish schools and the private schools began to dissolve as Jews sent their children to the nascent public school system. As the free and universal public school grew to dominate the American scene, Jews began to conduct their programs of Jewish education in supplementary fashion with children attending either congregational or community-sponsored religious schools on Sunday morning and/or on weekday afternoons after public school. A small minority of Jewish parents rejected this arrangement and sent their children to all-day Jewish schools, the first of which was the Yeshivat Etz Haim, established in 1886.

It was the supplementary type school, most notably the afternoon religious school, which gained the strongest foothold in the United States during the late 19th and early 20th centuries. Initially, these schools, the Talmud Torahs, were sponsored by communities. However as the national religious movements grew, Reform, Conservative and Orthodox synagogues established their own schools. During the fifty years from World War I to the present, the sponsorship of Jewish education changed radically from approximately 90 per cent of schools under communal organization to the same percentage today being under congregational sponsorship.

One of the effects of this has been to create a large number of small and unviable school units. While there may be as many as two thousand different Jewish schools in the United States today, the great majority of them are quite small with enrollments ranging from thirty to a hundred. There are, however, a significant number of large congregational schools, with adequate funds and enrollments of above five hundred.

Following the end of World War II there has been a significant rise in enrollments in Jewish all-day schools. Previously they had tended to be concentrated in the greater New York area and attracted children only from Orthodox homes. Currently enrollment in day schools is well in excess of fifty thousand pupils. Almost one in every ten Jewish students enrolled in any sort of Jewish school is enrolled in a day school. The figure is even higher in the large metropolitan areas where the motivation for day-school enrollment is not only religious or cultural, but results from the difficulties facing the urban public school systems.

Almost half of the Jewish school population at any one time is enrolled in Sunday school programs. These are deemed inadequate by all three religious movements. The Conservative movement has all but eliminated the Sunday school for the middle grades. The greatest strength of the Sunday school lies in the Reform movement. Reform congregations however are more and more turning to the afternoon supplementary school which is strongest in the Conservative movement. Orthodox weekday afternoon education has been weakened to some extent by the loss of a considerable number of pupils to the day-school movement. Day schools tend to be community-sponsored or inter-congregational while afternoon and Sunday schools are almost exclusively congregationally oriented.

The curricula of the afternoon schools sponsored by the three movements tend to be remarkably alike and the areas of difference are more structural than ideological. That is, Conservative and Orthodox schools usually require more hours and more years of attendance than Reform congregational schools. The emphasis on Hebrew in each of the schools is considerable, though achievement does not always match emphasis. The greatest level of achievement takes place in the day-school setting both because of the amount of time devoted to Jewish studies during the course of the week and also because pupils tend to react with more seriousness and greater motivation toward a school which is not supplemental to their general schooling.

There are eleven accredited Jewish teacher-training institutions in the United States, which do not, however, graduate sufficient teachers to meet the needs of the schools. Many graduates gravitate to other fields. Some use teacher-training as the first step toward the rabbinate. As often as not, the student of a teacher-training college in the United States is studying simply for the sake of the knowledge gained and has no professional aspirations in the field of Jewish education.

Significant strides have been made in supplementing programs of Jewish education through the use of summer camps. Hebrew is the spoken language of some of these camps and the educational personnel has full control over the atmosphere they establish. Significant numbers of Jewish teenagers and college students visit Israel for short periods and an increasing number study in the various universities in Israel.

Despite many false starts and often blind gropings, significant advance has been made in the field of Jewish education. These have benefited as yet only a small number of Jewish children. Valiant efforts are now being made to make available to significant numbers of American Jewish children the successful educational experiences pioneered and advanced by the progressive day schools and the imaginative supplementary educational endeavors.

IN AMERICAN LITERATURE

'If the statistics are right,' wrote Mark Twain in 1896, 'the Jews constitute but 1 per cent of the human race... Properly the Jew ought hardly to be heard of; but his contributions to the world's list of great names in literature, science, art, music, finance, medicine and abstruse learning are way out of proportion to the weakness of his numbers.'

Nowhere in the Diaspora has the Jewish contribution to general culture been more remarked upon than in twentieth-century America. In the late 1950s and the sixties, Jewish writers were widely considered to form the dominant 'school' in literature and criticism. Any best-seller list throughout this period contained one or more books written by Jews and usually concerning Jews.

This eminence was achieved after the great mass of East European immigrants, or their children, had learned the language and found themselves at home in the new land; and after writers, publishers and the reading public, horrified by the Holocaust and enchanted by the establishment of Israel, found a new interest in Jews as a subject.

In the 19th century the poetry of Emma Lazarus (1849-87) gained depth when she turned from classical themes to her own people's heritage and promise. She spoke of past glories and a restored Zion, urging 'Let but an Ezra rise anew, To lift the banner of the Jew'. It is her verses that are inscribed in the base of the Statue of Liberty, inviting:

> 'Send these, the homeless, tempest-tost to me.
> I lift my lamp beside the golden door.'

'It is from the Russian Jews, who are the mass of poor Jews in America, that the real contribution to American life is likely to come, because their aspirations are spiritual, their imagination alive,' wrote the editor of *Harper's Weekly* in 1916. In 1917 appeared *The Rise of David Levinsky,* the best novel of Abraham Cahan, founder and editor of the influential Jewish Daily *Forward, (Forverts).* This classic describes the coming of the penniless *yeshiva bachur* from the Russian *stetl* to New York in the 1880s, as Abe Cahan himself had come. The book tells of the 'rise' of its hero to multi-millionaire clothing manufacturer, sacrificing along the way the piety, the love of learning, the ideals of social justice, and even the hope for simple family joys that might have been his heritage as a Jew.

The Promised Land was the name given by Mary Antin to the new country, and the title she chose for her paean of praise in 1912 to the freedom of America in contrast to the repressions of the Old World. She decided to discard Jewish ties and assimilate into the beckoning new society.

The lot of the immigrant was treated by others with less starry-eyed optimism. Anzia Yezierska found poverty and near-desperation, as told in *Hungry Hearts* in 1920; yet she was sustained, as she reiterated thirty years later in her autobiographical *Red Ribbon on a White Horse,* by loyalty to Jewish ideals and the hope that America might yet become the golden land of justice the immigrants had envisioned.

Problems and disillusionments of the newcomers, and the defections of the second generation to the ephemeral lures of American society, were treated sympathetically by Myron Brinig in *Singermann* (which takes place in Montana); by Sholem Asch in *East River;* by David Pinski in *The House of Noah Eden,* Charles Reznikoff in *By the Waters of Manhattan,* Louis Zara in *Blessed is the Man.*

Negative aspects of ghetto life, its poverty, narrowness and ugliness, and the purported desperate greed of its offspring, were made much of by writers such as Ben Hecht, Samuel Ornitz, Budd Schulberg, Jerome Weidmann; and by leftist writers of 'proletarian' literature like Michael Gold in the thirties.

The bewilderment of a Jewish immigrant child whose parents were having their own struggle to find their place in the new world is feelingly evoked by Henry Roth in *Call It Sleep.* Terrified by his sordid surroundings and by his paranoiac father, the boy clings to his mother. He almost meets death while striving to find the glory that he has somehow glimpsed as hiding in the heart of the rote Judaism he is being forced to learn at *heder.*

A masterly, panoramic novel of second-generation Jews growing to young adulthood in the Chicago of the thirties is *The Old Bunch,* written by Meyer Levin in 1937. The relationship of child to foreign-born parents, the conflict of traditional ideals with youthful drives for success or freedom, the love of learning and the desire to serve humanity that characterize several of the 'bunch'—all ring true in this superb picture of American life.

That the Jews were not accepted in the American intellectual world until the 1940s was made most clear by the experience and report of Ludwig Lewisohn. This erudite young man found in graduate school in the early part of the century that a Jew had no place on an English department faculty.

'We boast of equality and freedom,' he said bitterly; but the disappointment opened his mind to new self-awareness as a Jew. His novel *The Island Within* and autobiographical works such as *Upstream* tell of the hopelessness of trying to find fulfilment through intermarriage and assimilation. 'To rise from my lack and confusion into a truly human life,' he concluded, 'it was necessary for me to affirm the reintegration of my entire consciousness with the historic and ethnic tradition of which I was a part.' It was as a loyal member of his own group that a Jew could make his greatest contribution to the pluralistic American society.

Most brilliant of the analysts of the place of the Jew in history and in the modern world was Maurice Samuel, who upheld the peculiar virtues of his people with a pride born of deep knowledge. This graduate of Manchester University never ceased educating himself. He taught himself Yiddish so that he could better understand his people's tradition, and became the great popularizer of Peretz *(Prince of the Ghetto)* and Sholem Aleichem *(The World of Sholem Aleichem).* In later years, he taught himself Russian to be able to write profoundly on the Mendel Beilis case in *Blood Accusation.*

With keen insight and mastery of polemic, Maurice Samuel put forth challenging hypotheses. He found, in *The Great Hatred,* the basis for anti-Semitism in amoral man's rage against the group which imposed moral restraints on his pagan passions. Reading *The Gentleman and the Jew* convinces one that the world suffers through its idealization of the Gentleman's role, who fights, kills, and admires power and honor; while the Jewish ideal, that of the peace-loving, moral, cooperative human being, is the one that might yet save the world.

Following World War II, one novel after another dealt with the Jew as pitiable victim of anti-Semitism. Arthur Miller's *Focus* and Laura Hobson's *Gentleman's Agreement* treated the question through gimmicks, in each case having as hero one who is really a Christian mistakenly regarded as a Jew, and who thereby has his eyes opened to the wrongs being perpetrated. Two of the three young men in Irwin Shaw's *The Young Lions* are Jews; Noah, who is a victim of barracks anti-Semitism, has no Jewish background at all, since he has been raised in foster homes. Norman Mailer's powerful novel of the war in the Pacific and the many American types who fought it, *The Naked and the Dead,* contains two Jewish characters, Goldstein and Roth, who are marked only by their 'authentic' and 'unauthentic' acceptances of the predicament of being a Jew.

Portraying the shallowness of upper-middle-class Jews of New York, Herman Wouk in his best-selling *Marjorie Morningstar* shows a college girl pursuing the American dream of stardom and success, but eventually becoming a Westchester matron who sends her children to Hebrew day school. Unlike the more negative writers whose knowledge of Judaism is sketchy, Wouk is a learned and committed Jew, whose *This Is My God* well expresses that commitment.

Charles Angoff's multi-volume saga beginning with *Journey to the Dawn,* of the life of a literate, sensitive American Jew, David Polonsky, is probably the most comprehensive fictional study of American Jewry since the turn of the century. As he describes it, it is 'multi-generation in structure and takes in every aspect of Jewish life in the United States: Americanization, assimilation, Zionism, secularism, the various religious denominations, Jews in industry and the professions, anti-Semitism and intermarriage.'

The Holocaust and the founding of the State of Israel were of course reflected in many of the postwar books. Leon Uris's *Exodus* became a popular source of knowledge about the events leading up to and following the establishment of the state. Meyer Levin wrote *Eva,* about a survivor of Nazi persecution, and *The Stronghold,* about a distinguished group of Europeans and the moral questions that plague them at the time of the Nazi surrender.

The greater literature on the Nazi experience has been written in Yiddish or Hebrew, or one of the European languages. Elie Wiesel, survivor of Auschwitz, whose works are in the main translated from French into English, can be counted among American writers. *Night* is his greatest single statement; while *Dawn, The Accident, The Town Beyond the Wall,* and *The Gates of the Forest* all speak to the conscience of the survivors of Nazism—not only those who were actually in the camps, but all men.

DRAMA AND POETRY

In drama and in poetry, Jews continued in the 20th century to make their contribution. Socially conscious Jewish playwrights of the thirties and forties like Clifford Odets and Elmer Rice showed the shortcomings of American life sometimes through the medium of Jewish characters. Lillian Hellman in a serious vein and such well-known lighter playwrights as Samuel N. Behrman, George S. Kaufman, and Neil Simon were mainstays of Broadway. In musicals, up to the point where Sholem Aleichem's *Tevya* stories became the basis for the smash hit *Fiddler on the Roof* in the sixties, and in the movie and television industries from their very beginnings, Jews have been singularly prominent.

Arthur Miller in the sixties was considered by many the foremost American playwright. His works, such as *Death of a Salesman, All My Sons, The Crucible,* deal not with overtly Jewish characters but with what might be called Judeo-Christian ethical questions of man's duty to family, self and society.

Poets of earlier stock, such as Louis Untermeyer and Babette Deutsch, both known also as critics and anthologizers, contributed much to American poetry in the first half of the century. After World War II, others rose into prominence. Karl Shapiro, champion of a more humane and emotional style against the leading

Saul Bellow (1915-). Saul Bellow is an outstanding representative of a group of Jewish novelists which dominated the American literary scene in the 1960s. His novels are rich in Jewish themes and expression. American Jewish Archives.

school of 'cerebral' (and often anti-Semitic) poets led by Pound and Eliot, gathered his best works into *Poems of a Jew.* In it he speaks of the Jew as 'man essentially himself, the primitive ego of the human race... absolutely committed to the world.' On the liberation of Israel, he writes, echoing Judah Halevi:

> '*When I think of the battle for Zion I hear*
> *The drop of chains, the starting forth of feet,*
> *And I remain chained in a Western chair.*'

Others whose Jewishness added depth and furnished subject matter for their poetry include Howard Nemerov, Hyam Plutzik, Delmore Schwartz and Muriel Rukeyser, who writes:

> '*To be a Jew in the twentieth century*
> *Is to be offered a gift. If you refuse,*
> *Wishing to be invisible, you choose*
> *Death of the spirit, the stone insanity.*'

Charles Reznikoff wrote lovingly of Judaism in such poetic lines as these in praise of Hebrew:

'Like Solomon,
I have married and married the speech of strangers;
None are like you, Shulamite.'

The most brilliant expression of love and understanding of Jewish tradition is that of Abraham M. Klein, a Canadian, whose masterpiece of prose-poetry, *The Second Scroll,* sums up the entire range of Jewish history, wandering, suffering, longing and glory. A brief love poem reads:

'How shall I cherish thee?
How shall I praise
Thee, make thee lovelier than is the case?
One does not don phylacteries
On Sabbath days.'

The leader of a cult of outspoken, free-living 'beat' poets of the fifties and sixties, many of them young Jews, is Allen Ginsberg. His howls against society's infringement on the individual soul include *Kaddish,* an unmodulated lament for the warping of his youth by the presence of his psychotic mother.

With the coming into dominance of the 'Jewish school' in American literature in the 1950s, the number of writers' names becomes overwhelming. Jewish critics also multiplied in numbers and in influence. Norman Podhoretz (editor of *Commentary,* the monthly sponsored by the American Jewish Committee), Leslie Fiedler, Irving Howe, Alfred Kazin and Theodore Solotaroff were among the leading arbiters of literary taste.

Isaac Bashevis Singer, like Sholem Asch before him, is a Yiddish writer living in New York, who, in translation, has been adopted as a favorite by the American reading public. Singer's *The Slave,* telling of a survivor of the Chmielnicki massacres (see chapter on Poland and Russia) and his forbidden love for a Polish woman, is, like his many other works, a haunting tale, emphasizing the mystical and offbeat elements in Jewish folk tradition.

The most revered writer for some years, especially among the young, was John D. Salinger, whose characters in *The Catcher in the Rye* and in the Glass family saga exemplify alienation, sensitivity, and the search for meaning. These characteristics, considered by many to be at least 'half-Jewish' (as are the Glass family), in the nuclear age seem typical of young people.

In his incisive stories collected in *Goodbye, Columbus* and in his novel of academic intermarriage, *Letting Go,* Philip Roth astutely comments on the bourgeois failings, spiritual insufficiency, and loss of identity of the American Jew. Charles Angoff once characterized one type of Jewish novel as being 'racked with self-degradation and obsessed with various aberrations, sexual and otherwise.' Exactly fulfilling this earlier description was Roth's best-selling novel *Portnoy's Complaint.* In its self-pitying ridicule of monstrous Jewish mother and sex-obsessed son, it has been said to 'cap—or put a yarmulke on—the American-Jewish genre.' In the literature of Jewish self-hatred, this can be said to be true.

Often named as the two top Jewish writers in America are Bernard Malamud and Saul Bellow. Both portray modern man seeking fulfilment or salvation. A difference pointed out by Joseph C. Landis is that in Malamud's parables, 'reluctant, less-than-ordinary men, seeking only to survive, unlikely candidates for moral greatness, grow into heroes that illustrate his theme of the ability of any man to redeem himself by acquiring moral identity,' while 'Bellow's heroes are more often conscious seekers of fulfilment, in essence intellectuals, driven like Henderson by a persistent "I want, I want, I want".'

In Malamud's *The Assistant,* Frank Alpine, amoral drifter, through his association with the good Jewish grocer, rises to the discipline of moral law and becomes a Jew. In *A New Life,* and in many of his short stories, the battered, well-meaning *schlemihl* gains a kind of nobility in failure. *The Fixer* again reveals the pattern: a little man, attacked by fate (the blood accusation against

Norman Mailer (1923-). Novelist, social critic, literary fashion-setter, creator of a new genre in literary expression, Norman Mailer is a major force in the contemporary American literary scene. American Jewish Archives.

Ernest Bloch (1880-1959). Ernest Bloch brought Jewish themes and nuances to his musical compositions in such works as the *Israel* symphony, *America* symphony and the *Shelomoh* rhapsody. His example inspired and encouraged a host of young Jewish composers to do the same. Born in Switzerland, he studied at the Geneva Conservatory in 1911-5. In 1917, he settled in the United States. American Jewish Archives.

Mendel Beilis is the prototype for the plot), gains greatness as he seeks only to survive.

Saul Bellow, better versed in Jewish as well as in general culture than most men, brings vitality and intellectual power to his works. Augie March seeks fulfilment by following adventure wherever it leads him, longing to become a better person than he is; Henderson, the rich and powerful, is driven to darkest Africa to seek purpose.

'The pay-off Jewish novel', as it was called upon its appearance in 1965, is *Herzog,* which details a neurotic, twice-divorced intellectual's musings and searchings as he seeks to improve the world and recapture his identity—finally concluding

that, when there is nothing left to say, the best first step is to set one's own house in order, as well as one can. A later novel of Bellow's, *Mr. Sammler's Planet,* received much critical acclaim and seems to be a more positive statement in Bellow's quest for meaning.

The popular fiction of today has even embraced the rabbi as a protagonist. The writing of Herbert Tarr, Harry Kemelman and Chaim Potok, among others, are entertaining and have given insights into the inner workings of Jewish life in the US. The Jewish contribution to and coloration of the current American literary scene is stated in a lead article in the *New York Times* book review (May 30, 1965), titled 'Some of Our Best Writers':

'There seems to be a dominant school at any given time in American fiction: in the 1920s it was realist-naturalist; in the 1930s it was proletarian; in the 1940s and early 1950s it was southern. We live now in the time of Bellow, Malamud, Mailer, Salinger, Roth.'

MUSIC

Music is an integral ingredient of the Jew's life. It accompanies him as he prays, studies, celebrates and mourns. It is therefore not surprising that Jewish music in America is as old as the Jewish community. The chief function of the Sephardi *hazzan* was to chant the service, and services were held as early as 1655.

In the early decades of the 19th century more varied and complex musical activity was begun. In 1818 Shearith Israel of New York, the oldest congregation in America, organized a synagogue choir. The practice quickly spread to New York's other leading congregations, Anshe Chesed and Temple Emmanu-El. By 1849 the choir of Temple Anshe Chesed, under the direction of Cantor Leon Sternberger, was regularly performing the very popular choral synagogue music of Sulzer and Lewandowsky. At a concert given by Temple Emmanu-El in 1853 to raise funds for a new organ a program of sacred music was performed by its choir accompanied by a concert orchestra.

Among the first volumes of Jewish music to be published in America is a work entitled *Principal Melodies of the Synagogue from Ancient Times to the Present.* It was issued by the Jewish Women's Section of the 'Parliament of Religions' held in Chicago in 1893 in conjunction with the Columbian Exposition. Alois Kaiser of Temple Ohev Shalom in Baltimore and William Sparger, of Temple Emmanu-El in New York, two leading cantors of the day, acted as editors for this first attempt to document the development of Jewish music. In addition to the historical material, the volume contains an anthology of the traditional modes, a collection of melodies used on the Sabbaths and festivals, and compositions by a number of European and American composers of the day.

Mordecai Manuel Noah (1785-1851), by John Wesley Jarvis. Newspaper editor, ▶ playwright, politician, communal leader, Mordecai Manuel Noah was the leading American Jew during the first half of the nineteenth century. He was United States Consul to Tunis 1813-15, sheriff of New York County, and even planned to settle a Jewish city of refuge on the Grand Island in the Niagara River.

Rimmonim by Myer Myers, 18th century. Myer Myers was a leading silversmith of Colonial America. The Shearit Israel synagogue of New York and Mikveh Israel of Philadelphia contain examples of his artistry. American Jewish Archives, Courtesy of Mikveh Israel Congregation, Philadelphia.

Torah crown. Ilya Schor recreated the world of East European Jewry in his own stylized fashion. His artistic creations abound with men, women and children of the Hasidic *stetl* (small town). The crown is at the Oheb Sholom Synagogue, Nashville. Photo J.J. Breit, *Contemporary Synagogue Art.*

With the arrival of great numbers of immigrants from Eastern Europe in the late 19th and early 20th centuries, East European *hazzanut,* which had by then reached its pinnacle in Europe, was introduced to America. Many of the cantors who had created the Golden Age of *hazzanut* in Eastern Europe began to find their way to America, and soon after a procession of talented choir directors followed. The cantors and choir directors brought with them the music of the 'old country'. With the exception of the number of hymnals produced for use mainly in Reform congregations, no Jewish music of any consequence was published in America until after World War I.

In the late 1920s a small group of talented composers began to create a new musical literature which reflected the cultural, social and artistic realities of the time. By 1930 the names of Abraham W. Binder, Jacob Beimel, Jacob Weinberg, Herbert Fromm and others were already well known as composers of music for the American synagogues.

The most significant new work to be created for the American synagogue was *Avodat Kodesh* by Ernest Bloch. It was a work for cantor, chorus and orchestra. Ernest Bloch arrived in America in 1916 already established as a composer of first rank. Among his works are the beautiful violin suite, *The Baal Shem Suite,* and the moving *Schelomo,* a Rhapsody for cello and orchestra.

Bloch's contributions were many. He was a particularly gifted composer who was able to combine the nuances of the musical impressionism of the day with the romanticism of an earlier period in an especially appealing amalgam. He was an inspiration to a whole generation of young composers, allowing and even encouraging his Jewishness to permeate all of his creative works. He showed the world that Jewish music could be accepted within the sacred temples of classical music on an equal footing with the music of other peoples.

In the years immediately following World War II such great names in European music as Darius Milhaud and Mario Castelnuovo-Tedesco turned to writing serious Jewish art and synagogue music.

More recently, a crop of young composers has emerged who are as closely related to American cultural life as to the synagogue. One example would be Samuel Adler who occupies the influential chair of composition at the Eastern School of Music and has more than a hundred published compositions to his credit.

While the list of composers who devoted themselves to Jewish creativity is a respectable one, a much larger list of Jewish composers turned their attention to the creation of classical music. Among their works are many on specifically Jewish themes. The multi-talented Leonard Bernstein, for example, created first the *Jeremiah Symphony* followed later on by his massive work, *Kaddish,* and still later by a new setting to a number of psalms entitled the *Chichester Psalms.*

In the performance of music, Jews far outnumber, proportionately, the instrumentalists of any other people. The roster of the leading instrumentalists of the first half of the 20th century is filled with names like Heifetz, Menuhin, Elman, Milstein, Rubinstein, Feuermann, and Stern. A number of great Jewish singers achieved world prominence. Among these are the tenors Jan Peerce and Richard Tucker; the soprano, Roberta Peters, and the baritone, Robert Merrill.

Jews have made a signal contribution to the American musical theater. Jewish names abound among composers of music for the American theater: Leonard Bernstein, Richard Rogers, Irving Berlin, Jerry Herman, Sheldon Harnick are but a few of the most successful. The breakthrough of jazz as a serious musical form was due almost entirely to the genius of George Gershwin who began as an apprentice composer in the Yiddish theater and turned to Broadway's Tin Pan Alley to realize his great musical ambitions. His was the first jazz composition to receive a performance in Carnegie Hall.

One must also add the names of Mark Blitzstein, who achieved fame in the thirties as a composer of music dramas on the social issues of the day; Aaron Copland, whose music for the ballet, opera and symphony hall are among the finest of its kind; Jerome Kern who became one of the masters of the early Broad-

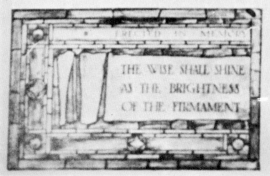

Memorial window, 1909. This memorial window was designed by American-born sculptor, Moses Jacob Ezekiel, a leading artist of the 19th century, for the Temple Keneseth Israel, Philadelphia. He studied and had studios in Berlin and Rome. The window was erected in memory of Isaac M. Wise, father of Reform Judaism in the United States. American Jewish Archives.

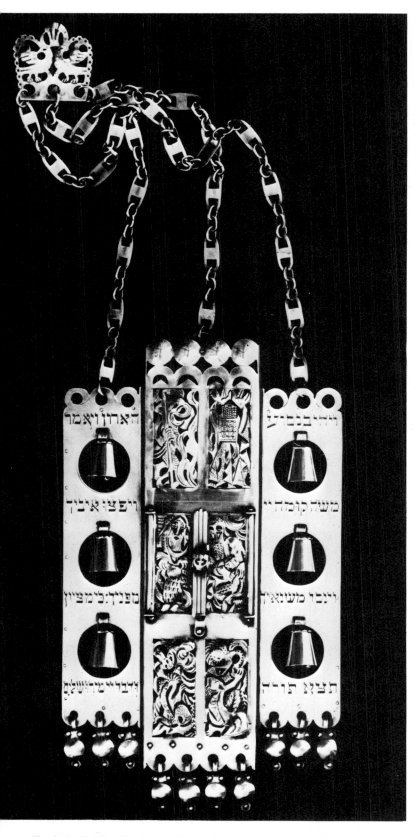

Torah shield. The Torah shield contains the traditional bells. The Hebrew inscription is the words chanted by the congregation as the Torah is taken from the Ark. 'When the ark journeyed ... For out of Zion shall go forth the Law, and the word of the Lord from Jerusalem'. The shield was made by Ilya Schor, the Polish-born artist who settled in the US in 1941 and gained a great reputation for his outstanding work on religious objects made in silver. The shield is in the Temple Beth El, Great Neck, New York. *Contemporary Synagogue Art.*

way musical period; Arnold Schoenberg who revitalized the whole field of musical composition with his twelve-tone scale; and Kurt Weill who came from Nazi Germany to continue a distinguished musical career.

IN ART

Philanthropic patrons of the arts such as the Guggenheim and Lewisohn families have long been well-known in America. In the second half of the century, other Jews have emerged in disproportionately large numbers as benefactors, patrons and fosterers of art in every sizable community throughout the country. The fact that they are particularly known as collectors of modern art may in part be due to the fact that the art of previous centuries has largely been bought up by 'older' families and museums. Openness to new forms, however, seems typical not only of the patrons but also of the many American Jewish artists themselves, whose number increases each year.

Jewish artists born in Eastern Europe and coming to America around the turn of the century, many of them studying for some time in Paris, brought modern European influences with them. Max Weber, whose work included nostalgic and gently humorous evocations of East European life, went from Cubism to what has been called the style of 'New York Expressionism'.

In a more realistic style, tending toward the romantic, the brothers Moses and Raphael Soyer portrayed sympathetic human figures, often scenes of Jewish or immigrant life.

During the Depression and Roosevelt years, Jewish artists, among others, often subsidized by WPA commissions, expressed strong social consciousness through their work. William Gropper, a Marxist from the Lower East Side, used the medium of violent caricature to great effect. Others whose work tends toward caricature and moral comment are Joseph Hirsch and Jack Levine, whose detailed, agitated paintings evoke the effect of hallucination.

The work of many of the artists, while not forming any 'Jewish school', expresses elements of Jewish background, such as the biblical themes of Ben Zion, and the Byzantine or Persian effects of the primitive, Morris Hirschfeld. David Bekker and Hyman Bloom often painted or drew scenes of the *stetl,* or ghetto, as does the younger Leonard Baskin, whose sculptures also continue to explore Jewish themes.

Todros Geller's strong feeling for Jewish culture came into full evidence when he was asked to create synagogue windows and other Jewish functional art. Ben Shahn, basically a lithographer and lover of letters, used his dramatic artistic gifts to further social causes in which he believed, and to add to Jewish ritual art as well.

The Jewish Museum in New York, under the auspices of the Jewish Theological Seminary, with Stephen Kayser as its first director, presents Jewish ritual and historical art, as well as shows of current and often controversial artists.

Jewish sculptors, beginning with Antokolski of Russia, have emerged to prominence in the past century. In America, Moses Jacob Ezekiel, born in Richmond in 1844, was well known in his

287

lifetime as a good portrait sculptor. A large group of American Jewish sculptors were born in Eastern Europe, many of them spending parts of their lives in Rome, Paris or London as well as New York. Enrico Glicenstein's many-sided realistic and expressive talent is seen in wood and terra-cotta moldings and in marble forms, including busts of Rabbi David Einhorn and Lincoln, done in the United States.

William Zorach, master worker in structural forms in stone and wood, living most of his life in Cleveland, taught and influenced a large school, including the outstanding Chaim Gross, Maurice Glickman, Nat Werner, Berta Margoulies, and Minna Harkavy. The 'classic antique' style in American sculpture has been represented by Saul Baizerman and Maurice Stern.

See illustration page 283.

A leading sculptor, Jacques Lipchitz, whose themes of struggle and emotion are often illustrated through Jewish subjects such as the rebirth of Israel, is said to be the first to translate concepts of abstract painting into sculpture. Jo Davidson, whose activity centered in Paris, sculpted busts of many outstanding personalities.

As revealed in Avram Kampf's *Contemporary Synagogue Art*, congregations in the United States have been attempting to utilize

Temple Mount Sinai (exterior), El Paso (Texas). Architect Sidney Eisenshtat's Temple Mount Sinai, El Paso, Texas, soars out to its desert setting and to the hills beyond. The site becomes an integral part of the artistic expression. Photo Julius Schulman, *Contemporary Synagogue Art*.

contemporary art forms to add to the beauty of their new buildings and to 'awaken an intrinsically religious feeling'. Boris Aronson, Ilya Schor, A. Raymond Katz, Nathaniel Katz, Abraham Rattner and Adolf Gottlieb are a few of the many artists who have designed stained glass and sculpture, doors and pulpits, to aid Jews to 'worship the Lord in the beauty of holiness'.

Jewish architects who have designed synagogue buildings include Erich Mendelsohn, Fritz Nathan and Percival Goodman; of these, Goodman has best achieved total synthesis between art and architecture on the one hand and the specific needs and functions of the sanctuary on the other.

Today

The six million Jews in America today constitute 3 per cent of the American population. Almost all live in the large urban centers. They belong almost entirely to the middle class. Increasingly they are concentrated in the professions. Education remains a top priority, with some three out of every four Jews of college age on campus. The dream of the immigrant has been realized. His sons are not in a shop or factory, but in an office or laboratory, his grandchildren in college classrooms. Almost all professions are fully open to the Jew. Settlement houses have become community centers. Synagogues are architectural landmarks on the American landscape and have taken their place in American religious life. The community remains divided into the three religious groupings, Orthodox, Conservative, Reform, but most congregants view these as institutional distinctions rather than as religious schisms. Although there is no overall American Jewish representative body, American Jewry is largely united in sentiment. Common concerns and joint efforts unite, where institutional differences and organizational competitiveness tend to divide.

The American Jew has entered the cultural life in all its aspects, has made important contributions and exerts signal influence. Initially, the Jewish participation and contribution was in the field of entertainment. More recently and increasingly it has been in the arts and literature. Jews are now prominent on university faculties. A good deal of American culture today has taken on a kind of Jewish coloration. Being Jewish is no handicap today in American cultural life or in American life in general. The Jews seem vividly, firmly and permanently incorporated into the American landscape.

But problems there are, and they are serious.

Sociologists point with concern to the low Jewish birthrate, a rate below the survival level. Religious leaders speak with alarm of the rising rate of intermarriage, particularly among the intellectually gifted and the economically favored. Integration is good and desirable. But at what point does integration become assimilation? In sum, the central question facing the American Jew is: can a minority group survive in a free and open democratic society? More pointedly, can Jew and Judaism survive and flourish in America?

The Jew has exerted vast energies and expended great sums in fashioning institutions to assure his survival and foster his faith, but the question of survival nevertheless remains. In a land torn by violence but aware of its potential and its dreams, Jewish survival is bound up with the future of other minorities who seek to flourish in America. The question asked, then, addresses itself not only to the Jew but also to his neighbors.

CHAPTER VIII

Israel Today

by Yaakov Tsur

At the turn of the century, Palestine—the present State of Israel —was of only secondary importance in the broader complex of Jewish life. A mere fifty thousand Jews lived in this impoverished, far-away province of the crumbling Ottoman empire. Most of them were concentrated in Jerusalem and in the other holy cities: Hebron, Tiberias, Safed. There were, certainly, already some tangible signs of a national revival: a thin network of agricultural settlements spread over the whole country, from Metullah in the north, to Ruhama on the Negev border. Palestinian Jews, however, did not represent, either quantitatively, or in any other form, an important factor in the general structure of Jewry— except for the militants of the new movement which, a short while previously, had styled itself 'Zionism'. At that time, as now, world Jewry numbered approximately thirteen million; but then, the overwhelming majority (more than nine million) lived in Europe, being mostly concentrated in the two giant empires of Eastern Europe, the Russian and the Austro-Hungarian.

Seventy years later, at the end of a period which witnessed the

First Zionist Congress in Basle, 1897. Theodor Herzl delivering the opening speech at the First Zionist Congress. The Viennese journalist and playwright Herzl was the founder of the modern political Zionist movement. He convened a gathering of representatives of Zionist groups from throughout the world in 1897 in Basle at which the basic program for the Zionist movement was adopted. To Herzl's right is the philosopher Max Nordau, also one of the leaders of the Zionist movement. Central Zionist Archives, Jerusalem.

horrors and destructions of two world wars, the State of Israel has revived Jewish independence lost in 70 A.D. With its two and a half million inhabitants it constitutes today the third largest Jewish community in the world and is outnumbered only by those of the US and possibly the USSR. Over 17 per cent of the Jewish world population lives in Israel.

The rise of Israel coincides with a total change in the face of Jewish dispersion. The communities of Eastern Europe which once constituted the very heart of Judaism have disappeared, wiped out by the Holocaust or cut off from the outside world by an impenetrable wall. Conversely, a new dispersion has come into being, spreading from Canada in the north, to Argentina and Australia in the southern hemisphere. Territorial and cultural cohesion which, in former times, had been the mainstay of Jewish survival, exists no more. On the other hand, the struggles, misfortunes and achievements of the Jewish State focus the permanent attention of this Diaspora and constitute a source of constant inspiration.

To a modern observer, the idea of Israel conjures up pictures of a Middle East on the brink of war and evokes the tragic clash between Arab and Jewish nationalisms. Discerning historians, however, had long previously pointed out that the present state of affairs is the outcome of a slow process, the origins of which are to be found in nineteenth-century liberal Europe. No one could then foresee the overwhelming changes that were to come over the world following the tragic pistol shot at Sarajevo in the summer of 1914. And certainly no one was concerned over the fate in store for millions of human beings condemned to lead lives of second-class citizens on the periphery of enlightened Europe. The only people who thought about the fate of the Jews were the Jews themselves.

THE BIRTH OF ZIONISM

The idea of Zionism took shape against the dismal grey backdrop of the seemingly endless misery in which the Jewish masses were sunk, apparently without hope of redemption. They were oppressed by an autocratic regime and forcibly crammed into the immense ghetto formed by the southern and western provinces of tsarist Russia, which included, at that time, the Russian-held part of Poland. Beyond the Austrian border, the Jewish population lived in the squalor of former Polish Galicia; alternatively, across the river Dniester, they eked out a miserable living in Rumania, a comparatively new kingdom which shared with its Russian neighbor a common hostile and contemptuous attitude toward the Jews.

The Jewish masses were mainly concentrated in small towns, the *stetl,* where they led a wretched existence behind the protective barrier of their religion. But the Haskalah, the lay doctrine of liberal enlightenment promoted by emancipated German Jewry, had already made breaches in the ghetto wall. Overcoming legal restrictions and the reluctance of their families, who were terrified at the mere thought of innovation, increasingly large groups left the houses of their fathers to go abroad and quench their thirst

at the sources of Science, especially in German and Swiss universities. Although they spoke Yiddish, their *langue savante* was Hebrew which they had been taught in the *heder* and in the *yeshivah* of their youth. As the 19th century drew to a close, thousands of them had already acquired a command of Russian, sometimes of German, which enabled them to associate with their emancipated brothers over the frontiers.

On their return, this new educated élite passionately absorbed the ideas which had begun to agitate Russia since the liberal reign of Alexander II. Jewish newspapers and literary reviews unleashed a crusade against Jewish obscurantism and the exclusive domination of rabbis. They were in favor of merging the Jewish masses into the great Russian nation. As far as censorship allowed them, the young Jewish intellectuals preached emancipation of the Jews, the abolition of restrictive laws and equality of rights with the other nationalities that went to make up the Russian empire.

It was in this environment, completely devoted to the idea of progress, freedom, equality and human brotherhood, dreaming of a cosmopolitan society in which the Jews, like the others, would have the rights and prerogatives of a free people, that the movement advocating the taking of practical steps to implement a return to Palestine was born. This was an unexpected turn, and not in keeping with the popular ideas of the period. It was the result of bitter disillusionment, of a sudden and tragic awakening from the sweet daydream entertained by progressive circles in the 19th century, which seemed so fraught with promise.

The 'Lovers of Zion' movement (*Hovevei Zion*) came into being around 1881. It was in that year that for the first time since the beginning of the century, a wave of pogroms swept over the 'Pale of Settlement'. In one fell swoop, all the illusions of liberal Jewry were destroyed including those of Jewish youths who had given their souls to the revolutionary ideals of the time and had possessed a seemingly unshakable faith in the humanitarian virtues of the Russian people. In their eyes, once they had overtly shown the moral beauty of Judaism to their non-Jewish environment, they would without further ado be admitted to their rightful place in this great civilization. Now, suddenly, without warning, the *muzhik,* idealized by Turgeniev and Tolstoy, glorified by the poetic fervor of Nekrassov, the idyllic peasant of the great poets slaughtered thousands of innocent Jews, men, women and children, whose only crime was to be different.

Liberal Russian opinion stood silently by; not a word was uttered in condemnation of these dastardly acts. Worse still, among the revolutionary circles, which were quietly preparing their revolt against absolutist power, pogroms were considered mere symptoms of the decay of the hated regime. As these fateful events were taking place, one of the theoreticians of the revolutionary movement is reported to have said: 'Jewish blood is the oil that lubricates the wheels of revolution'.

In the face of bitter reality, the ideology of assimilation lost a good deal of its appeal. From now on, the question which Jewish youth asked itself was: 'Is it only our religion that separates us from the Russian people? Is it not legitimate for us to live a free life according to our own customs, and follow our national destiny?' The answer was contained in the tragic revelation that they had just lived through. A Jewish national doctrine came into being. This was clearly formulated in a frank and penetrating pamphlet written in German and published in Odessa under the title *Auto-Emancipation*. Its author, Judah L. Pinsker, a middle-aged physician who was far from being a dreamer, soon became the head of the 'Lovers of Zion' movement which began to propagate itself in the towns and villages of Eastern Europe. In the meantime, a small group of university students who had joined the movement from the very beginning decided to get down to concrete action and formed a society which set out to prepare the return of the Jews to Palestine by promoting the reconstruction of their new homeland. The first group of pioneers belonging to the *Bilu* movement, as it was called, landed at Jaffa in 1882. This was the first stage in a chain reaction that was to culminate with the creation of a Jewish state in Palestine.

THE ZIONIST MOVEMENT

'Auto-Emancipation', or more simply 'self-liberation', is the keyword to this agitated period of the 1880s. The Jewish people, whether looked upon as a nation or as a demographic and cultural entity, had to wage its own battle and thereby decide its own fate. Fifteen years later, Theodor Herzl, with his astonishing intuitive capacity, his creative imagination and an acute sense of organization, was to give final shape to this theory.

Unlike the 'Lovers of Zion', Herzl came of emancipated Jewry and was steeped in Western culture. He created a Zionist organization the aims of which were expounded at the Basle Zionist Congress in 1897. The 'Lovers of Zion' became, then, Zionists and the movement took on an essentially political character. From then on, the Jewish problem was brought forcibly to the attention of world opinion. Anti-Semitism was no longer condemned as a passing ephemeral aberration of misled public opinion, but as the logical consequence of the abnormal, unbearable situation of the world Jewish masses. The doctrine expounded was the following: 'The Jews are a people. They are different from the others in their way of life and their ways of thought. They are heirs to a common heritage, to a great civilization which belongs to them alone. But everywhere they are a minority, dispersed throughout the world. This causes their very existence to be unnatural and distorted. They do not constitute a normal society because the conditions of national life are refused them. Their very qualities, stemming as they do from a long process of forced adjustment, doom them to remain a foreign body in the midst of their European environment. Although they are a people, they lack the main element that makes a nation: a territory in which they, like the other nations, might organize their life according to their own image of themselves. The only territory to which they have a natural right must be the cradle of their own culture—and no other—the land to which they are bound by their past, by their tongue and by the civilization which

they gave to the world and to which they have remained faithful for nineteen centuries: the Land of Israel.'

The dream of a return to the Holy Land was, of course, nothing new: the longing for the lost homeland was deeply rooted in Jewish tradition. The constant expectation of divine redemption, the faith in the coming of the Messiah and the restoration of former glory are an essential part of the Jewish faith. These themes are present in all the pages of the prayer-book which a pious Jew reads with complete devotion three times a day. In the same way, the nature festivals, in whichever clime Jews celebrate them, remain closely related to the four seasons of the lost paradise in the Land of Israel. Throughout the centuries, all the mystical revivals that the Jews experienced and all the scourges that were visited upon them, from the darkest periods of the Middle Ages to the beginning of modern times, were accompanied by messianic movements that promised a miraculous return to the Holy Land. If such movements never actually brought about a true national revolt, this is to be attributed to the very conditions of Jewish existence which was subjected to relentless oppression.

This metamorphosis of religious dogma into an ideology of national revival, essentially non-religious in character, at first raised the fierce opposition of the ultra-Orthodox circles of world Jewry. Their opposition was not without some effect on the subsequent history of Palestine and, to some extent, on that of the State of Israel. The movement was also bound to encounter the opposition of the Jewish upper class, which was numerically important and powerful in the emancipated communities of the West. This upper class categorically rejected a doctrine which stressed the particular character of the Jew for it saw a panacea in the total assimilation and adjustment of the Jews to their environment. Later, the movement found another irreconcilable adversary in the Jewish Socialists of the *Bund* (which at the time enjoyed vast popularity in Russia and Poland) who accused Zionism of being a retrograde movement, preaching a backward and reactionary brand of nationalism and diverting the Jewish proletariat from the more essential task of class struggle.

The Zionist movement, which was to change the face of world Jewry, was thus from the outset up against hostility and slander and stood in isolation. For a long period, it had to face its detractors with the only weapon it had at hand: its faith in the righteousness of its cause and in the correctness of its historical analysis of Jewish past and present. But the isolation and the bitterness that followed only succeeded in whetting the movement's thirst for action.

This national awakening must be put in the context of other contemporary doctrines of national awakening abroad at the same time which were based on a longing for independence and a return of lost freedom. It had a different inspiration from the modern nationalistic currents in which the independence of the new nations was based on the domination of a territory and on demographic unity. Like the nationalist movements in the Balkans, especially in Greece, Bulgaria and Serbia, which strongly influenced it, Zionism was surrounded with a romantic aura, with the nostalgia of a lost Golden Age. The young Jew turned away from his unhappy present to contemplate his remote past, bathed in its distant glory. The nineteen intervening centuries of exile had no appeal to him because, beyond their rich literary heritage, he could not avoid thinking of the accompanying suffering, persecution, and humiliation. The Bible nourished his dream of liberty. Not only did it appeal to him as divine revelation; it was also the written record of an age when the Jews lived free on their own land, like the other nations of the world. It was in the familiar pages of his Bible, which he had studied in his youth and which he now discovered in a new light, that he found the lost kingdom he longed for and would some day link to the future kingdom of his dreams.

THE HEBREW REVIVAL

Long before the Bible had become the inspiration behind the national revival, its language, its poetic style, its imagery and landscapes had nourished the writings of a multitude of writers,

The Western Wall, c. 1900. The Western Wall is one of the last surviving walls of the Herodian Temple compound. The bottom layers of stones are from the original Temple times, the upper layers of a later period. The wall reaches down very deep, twenty or so layers. The top part was added in the 19th century to stop stones being thrown over it. On the other side is the courtyard of the Mosque of Omar. Central Zionist Archives, Jerusalem.

novelists and poets. In the course of their everyday life, ghetto Jews seldom read the Bible, with the exception of those extracts included in the prayer-book and in the weekly portion read on the Sabbath. The Talmud, that gigantic creation of Jewish thinking during the first centuries of exile, was more central to their spiritual life. Rabbinic style, shaped by centuries of religious studies and casuistics, dominated epistolar and intellectual exchanges. And now, suddenly, without warning, the young emancipated rebels, reacting violently against the restrictive traditional teaching of the synagogue, turned toward the light of ancient sources.

Love of Zion, the famous novel by Abraham Mapu, written in a romantic style and drawing upon the purity of biblical language, revived the idealized picture of Judeans during the period of the Kings. In the same way, the nostalgic poems of Micha Joseph Lebenson and the heroic epics of Judah Leib Gordon, the prince of poets of the Haskalah period, gave new life to the Hebrew language and made it the perfect symbol of this renewal which the youth of that time so ardently longed for. All three writers shared the brilliant expectations of a generation that burned to shake loose its shackles.

However, Hebrew had always, in fact, remained the medium of Jewish literary creation. From Russia to Galicia, from Italy to Morocco, it was used as a *lingua franca* in scholarly and business letters and transactions. Because it was the language of the Bible, however, it had been kept in a sort of bondage; people wrote and read it but did not speak it in their everyday lives. In Eastern Europe, the vernacular was Yiddish, while Judeo-Spanish or Ladino was the idiom of Sephardi communities dispersed over the immense Ottoman empire after their exodus from Spain. The awakening of Jewish national consciousness implied, almost simultaneously, endeavors to turn Hebrew into a living language. This was done timidly at first, then more and more systematically. The language of the Bible thus became a national language; it was to become the basis and unique quality of Israel culture and of its influence throughout the Jewish world.

At about the same time that the idea of the return to Zion was gaining favor among the Russian Jews, Eliezer Ben-Yehuda wrote a sensational article in which he suggested turning Hebrew into a living language and thereby ensuring the unity of the Jewish people. As a young student in Paris, he used to consort with Bulgarian, Czech, and Serbian revolutionaries and dream with them of the rebirth of national cultures. Resolved to put his ideas into practice, he settled in Jerusalem with his family, with the intention of devoting himself to a revival of Hebrew.

Hebrew was actually already used at that time, as a vernacular, among the pious circles of the Holy City. Jerusalem was probably the only place in the whole of the Jewish world where Jews from Western and Eastern countries had the opportunity to meet. A never-ending stream of Jews flowed toward Jerusalem and constantly increased its Jewish population. They massed in the narrow streets of the old city and in the first quarters built outside the walls, representing all the different sectors of the dispersion. Emissaries were sent by institutions of sacred learning in Jerusalem, Hebron, and Safed to the remotest corners of the

Jewish world to whom they brought the message of Zion. Clad in the traditional garb of their communities, they would speak Hebrew with the Jews they met in the course of their travels.

This beehive of Jerusalem Jewry was a miniature model of the future Israel society. Down the narrow, dingy streets leading to the Western Wall, a picturesque crowd ebbed and flowed: Persian Jews who spoke their old Judeo-Persian dialect; Jews from North Africa talking in Judeo-Arabic or Judeo-Berber; Ashkenazi children, shouting in all the various accents of Eastern European Yiddish; rabbis from Salonika or Izmir discussing in Judeo-Spanish; bearded Kurds conversing in an old Aramaic dialect of which they alone knew the secret; and Bukharians in colorful dress went about their daily business using an idiom derived from one of the numerous vernaculars of Central Asia.

More and more frequently, these communities used Hebrew as a common language in their dealings' with each other and thus, Hebrew increasingly acquired the qualities of a spoken language. Moreover, Hebrew sounded more natural when spoken by Oriental Jews who had continued to use it in the course of their travels within the immense Ottoman empire. This probably explains why Sephardi pronunciation prevailed over Ashkenazi and became the accepted phonetics of current modern Hebrew.

But Ben-Yehuda, who was soon joined by a circle of young disciples, set himself a higher, long-term task. In his mind, Jewish revival and the creation of a new Jewish society could not take place unless Hebrew became not only a *lingua franca* but also the mother tongue of the new generation. He began speaking Hebrew at home and with his friends. He taught it to his children. Soon his example was followed by schoolteachers resolved to teach 'living Hebrew' without translating it first into the mother tongue of the pupils, a method which was fairly revolutionary at that time.

In everyday use, the language gradually became simpler and more versatile. It shed the rigidity of its former 'bookishness', that it had acquired as a result of drawing on the elevated style of the Bible. Everyday life demanded an exact terminology that would allow it to designate technical things. Such a terminology was created either by resorting to the inexhaustible talmudic literature, or the philosophical works of the Middle Ages, or by using analogies with other Semitic tongues, especially Arabic.

The result was a flood of neologisms which were often rejected by the European purists, for, at that time, Europe still remained the main center of Hebrew literature. If the younger generation of writers was prepared to give up the purity of biblical style in favor of a more flexible and concise tongue derived from the logical and wonderful simplicity of the Mishnah, the new terminology and bizarre coinages of the Jerusalem linguists were

See illustration page 303.

rejected by connoisseurs who ridiculed them. Some of the new terms that were naïve and sometimes artificial have, indeed, completely vanished; but most of the new coinages have survived and added to the richness of modern spoken and written Hebrew.

The first generation of Jews whose mother tongue was Hebrew was brought up by an admirable generation of school-teachers in Jerusalem, Jaffa, and in the new agricultural settlements of the coastal plain and the Galilee Hills. Young women teachers brought to the country by new waves of immigration, who adhered to the theories of Pestalozzi and Froebel, opened the first kindergarten in which young children got used to the sound of Hebrew. Nevertheless, the schools created by the Alliance Israélite Universelle kept teaching in French, those of the Hilfsverein propagated German, while the Anglo-Jewish Association of London taught in English. In secondary school programs, however, subjects related to Hebrew study played an increasingly important part. Furthermore the children spoke Hebrew among themselves.

On the eve of World War I, a few secondary schools already taught in Hebrew. The first among these was the Herzlia school in Tel Aviv, the construction of which was responsible for the creation of the first Jewish city in 1909. It was followed by other schools in Jerusalem and in Haifa, as well as by teachers' training colleges capable of supplying the teachers who, so far, had come from abroad.

In 1913, after a general strike of teachers and pupils at the German Hilfsverein, Hebrew was finally established as a teaching language—a demonstration of popular feeling that caused a great

Pioneers, pre-1914. A typical group of young pioneers of the pre-World War I Second Aliyah (wave of immigration). The members of *Ha-Shomer* (The Watchmen) defense organization carry rifles and some wear Bedouin *Keffieh* headdress. Many of Israel's leaders today are to be found among those who came with the Second Aliyah. Central Zionist Archives, Jerusalem.

stir in the whole Jewish world. The cause of this strike was the establishment by the German-Jewish association of an Institute of Higher Polytechnical Studies on the slope of Mount Carmel in Haifa. After prolonged discussions, the governing board of the school had decided that the teaching language of the Institute should be German, Hebrew being thought unsuitable for the teaching of technical and mathematical sciences. This led to the immediate resignation of all the representatives of Russian Zionism on the committee whose example was followed by all the teachers and pupils of the Hilfsverein schools throughout the country. Thousands of pupils left their classes. A general boycott was decided against those schools using German as a teaching language. The strikers (teachers and pupils) opened temporary schools in private buildings, with Hebrew as a teaching language. This strike had the enthusiastic character of a popular rebellion although the immediate issue at stake was the education of a few thousand children of a rather small community.

After the war, when Palestine Jewry was about to enter the new period of the National Home with universally recognized rights, the position of Hebrew as a national language was no longer in jeopardy. Soon it was recognized as one of the official tongues of the Mandate and became the medium of communication of modern Israel society.

THE RETURN TO ZION

It is customary to divide the formative years of Israel into five distinct periods corresponding to the five waves of immigration (called *Aliyah* or plural, *Aliyot*). These waves represent clear-cut periods, each of which had its own character and contributed in its own way to the evolution of the image of Palestinian society before the birth of the Jewish state. When the first Jewish pioneer set foot on the Holy Land, he intended to settle there and cultivate its soil. At that time, the idea of returning to the land was much in the air and had already caused some young Jerusalem and Safed Jews to leave the shelter of the walls of their Holy Cities and acquire land in the open plains and hills where they created villages and lived off the land.

In this way the village of Petah Tikvah was created among the swamps of the coastal plain which, at that time, bordered the site of the future Tel Aviv. Soon afterward, it was followed by Rosh Pinnah in the Galilee Hills and by Rishon le Zion and Gederah, founded by the *Biluim,* those pioneers of the 1880s. Nobody could conceive of a Jewish Homeland that was not an agricultural homeland, so that the aim was to change the Jew and have him return to the biblical idea of 'every man under his vine and under his fig-tree'.

These idealistic farmers had nothing in common with the peasant class. They were the sons of quiet middle-class towns-people from Russia or Rumania, students who had left their universities to engage upon a bizarre adventure; university students who had never handled a spade or hitched up a mule-cart. They knew nothing about the rainfall and the soil properties of their new country. They had never suspected that it had been devastated by centuries of destruction. However, they clung to their work which they regarded as a sacred mission. Their aim was to change the social structure of the Jewish nation and to recreate the missing peasant class. They also hoped that through their endeavors they would be able to dominate the land which, they felt, was theirs by right. Soon, however, they were beset by poverty and loneliness. The First Aliyah gradually lost its impetus, in spite of a short comeback in 1890. These proud pioneers had to have recourse to the philanthropic aid of a generous donor: Baron Edmond de Rothschild of Paris, a man of visionary imagination, who became their protector. In return, they had to accept direct administration and the inconvenience it implied. Strikes and revolts occasionally broke out. The more prosperous of the settlers hired Arab labor and became gentlemen-farmers who merely administered their plantations while the Arab hands did the hard work. Faced by reality, the generous impulse of the first period gave way; the idealism of their own early pioneering was forgotten.

However, these forefathers of Jewish agricultural reconstruction who, at the turn of the century, numbered barely five thousand, played a decisive role in the evolution of the national revival. Beyond the seas, Jewish public opinion became aware of the existence of a new type of Jew who was bound to the soil and led a peasant life. In Odessa and Warsaw, poets sang with nostalgia of the Jewish villages, of the cornfields and vineyards in the Land of Israel. Hayyim N. Bialik, who was to become the king of Hebrew poets, became known through his poem *To the Bird* in which he spoke of the beauty of the sunny fields that illuminated the gloom of his exile. At the same time, literary reviews in Russia received from Palestine the first naïve stories describing in idyllic tones the life of Jewish farmers driving their plows in the ground of the distant homeland.

It was there, in small lonely villages, at the far end of winding dusty paths, that the seeds of a new way of life were sown; a way of life that was truly Jewish, even though this term was completely different from its former meaning. Nothing, indeed, seemed farther removed from life in the *stetl* or the traditional Russian ghetto. In schools, Jewish children in a natural way learnt a Hebrew that was becoming more and more a living language. Life on the land and in the open gave birth to a proud, strong race that felt bound to the country which, only yesterday, had been unknown to their parents. From an early age, Jewish boys practiced riding and shooting. They rode further and further into the empty plains and barren hills.

As a result of their close contact with the land, the Bible acquired a new significance. The Arab names of localities were often recognized as biblical Hebrew names. The fauna and flora of the Scriptures became overnight a concrete reality.

In the villages, such as Rishon le-Zion, Rehovot, Rosh Pinnah and Zikhron Yaakov, a new way of life came into being. Young men and women used to gather in the village barn during the warm summer nights and sing Jewish songs. At first, it was Russian or Ukrainian ones that they had heard from their parents; but soon Hebrew words crept into—and were adapted to—the familiar tunes or to the Oriental melodies which they heard from their Arab neighbors. Thus, Naphtali Imber, an itinerant poet who was to die in poverty in the New York East Side, adapted new words to a popular East European melody that he called *Ha-Tikvah* (Hope). This song became the national anthem of the Zionist movement and later the national anthem of the State of Israel.

It was in these *moshavot* or 'colonies' as they were called in the vocabulary of the time, that the first popular orchestras and choirs (which were often organized by amateur schoolteachers) came into being. It was there that the first circulating libraries and the first people's clubs were established. But these villages also served as experimental laboratories for the young agronomists who had gone to study abroad in foreign universities. They made a great many experiments and published the results in the early journals appearing in Jerusalem and Jaffa.

Thus, as the years passed, a tiny New World grew among the vineyards and orange groves of the sandy Judean plains.

THE SECOND ALIYAH

The meteor-like career of Theodor Herzl, whose Zionist mission began in 1896 and ended with his premature death in 1904, completely changed the context of Zionist action in Europe. The idea of a national Jewish revival which until then had been popular with only a few scattered groups who felt the urge to support the struggle of their brothers in Palestine now infected the masses. Zionism became an ideological issue which in the feverish atmosphere of the time was passionately discussed. Even influential circles of emancipated Jewry were won over to this idea, especially in Germany and Austria, but also in Great Britain and in the United States. The outside world, for its part, did not remain indifferent: Herzl began negotiating with British statesmen, with the German Kaiser, and even with the inaccessible ministers of the tsar. The idea of a return of the Jews to Palestine was seriously discussed by European governments although these negotiations did not lead to any concrete political results.

After Herzl's death, the World Zionist Organization, disillusioned by its political setbacks, decided to create its own financial institutions in order to speed up the development projects of the Jews in Palestine. The Jewish National Fund came into being to provide the financial means of buying the land, as did a bank for the encouragement of economic initiatives, called the Jewish Colonial Trust. It opened branches in Jaffa, Jerusalem and Beirut, under the name of the Anglo-Palestinian Company. A few years later, a society for land development was created. Its Palestinian office was directed by a young economist of German birth, Dr. Arthur Ruppin, who soon became the soul of Zionist agricultural efforts. Although these institutions had few means, they represented the embryo of an administrative body as well as an organization to which newcomers could turn for aid.

Another characteristic of this period was that the young immigrants were motivated by a clearly defined ideal, and not by vague longings like those who came with the preceding *aliyot*. To them, this was the beginning in Palestine of a new Jewish society which foreshadowed the autonomous territory planned by the Basle Zionist Program of 1897. This program actually spoke of a 'home', a transitory stage before total independence which was not to be expected until the Ottoman empire had reached the last stages of its disintegration.

The number of immigrants that came to Palestine between 1906 and 1914 is estimated at about twenty thousand. Many of them were discouraged and disenchanted and went back to their home countries, while others emigrated overseas. However, this handful of men left its mark on the future development of the country. From their ranks came the leaders that created the Jewish State and a great many of the statesmen who formed its political élite when it came into existence (among them, three prime ministers: David Ben-Gurion, Moshe Sharett and Levi Eshkol, and two of its future presidents, Yitzhak Ben-Zvi and Zalman Shazar).

They were young men, the oldest among them being scarcely over twenty, and came from mostly poor or middle class families of Russian Jewry. Others came from the masses of Jewish youth that stagnated in Russian towns, waiting endlessly for changes that would grant them the right to study. Sometimes their families had provided them with the money for their passage on Russian ships carrying *muzhiks* and monks on pilgrimage to the Holy Land. But, in the majority of cases, they came without asking their father's blessing and paid their fare out of their own pocket or with borrowed money. As often as not, they landed in Palestine with no more than a bundle containing a change of clothing.

The Second Aliyah came straight from the whirlpool of the 1905 Russian Revolution. It bore the scars of its ideological struggle and of its bitter defeat, and those that came had witnessed shameful pogroms and had had the same bitter experience as their older brethren of the 1881 generation. They had watched the Russian people, for whom they had been ready to give their lives, slaughtering, looting, and raping in the Jewish streets of Bialystok, Kishinev and Kiev. They were deeply shaken and felt that they belonged to a people which had let itself be massacred without even attempting to defend itself. In their new homeland, they meant to create a new society and a new kind of Jewish life and were determined never again to put their fate into the hands of alien protectors.

Austerity and devotion to work were the characteristics of this wave of immigrants and for a long time these ideals continued to inspire Palestinian society. They scattered round the less prosperous villages of Galilee and volunteered for the hardest work: plowing the barren hill slopes like Beduin, for mere board and lodging. They were determined to create a Jewish working class; they themselves would therefore be the initiators and flagbearers of this new class. Physical work was the basis of their ideology and they found their theoretician in the person of a middle-aged, pious Jew, Aharon D. Gordon, the one exception among this group of young men. He had left his European home town and given up an easy job and the small fortune he had there in order to wander from village to village, an eternal optimist who preached to his younger comrades the theory of the purifying value of work. According to Gordon, creating a Jewish working class and teaching Jews to admire physical work were the only means of redeeming the Jewish people and working for its rebirth. Tolstoy's theories of renunciation and his cult of simplicity were the *leitmotifs* of the interminable discussions that took place in the huts or in the tents of the workers. For these pioneers, the 'religion of work', as people started calling it, was the path to the creation of a new Jewish society.

The young workers lived in small groups that scattered among the villages. They were often distrusted by the farmers who misunderstood them and accordingly they developed a strong sense of cooperation among themselves. Toward the end of this period, some of them, out of discouragement, went to the P.I.C.A., the society for land colonization which had succeeded the Rothschild administration. They were given farms, for the most part in Lower Galilee. Others continued to work as farmhands, either on plantations or on the experimental farms which had been created by the Zionist authorities.

At that period, a great decisive event took place. It is difficult to say whether it was a natural development or a consequence of ideological planning, but in 1909, following a strike in one of the experimental farms, a small group of farmhands was granted the right by the Palestinian office of the Zionist Organization to settle in the Jordan Valley on the basis of common responsibility and common lease of the land. The first communal settlement, the *kevutzah* of Deganiah was founded, thus initiating the era of the collectivist movement with its *kibbutzim* which, in turn, gave Israel society its specific character.

Not long before the outbreak of World War I, the labor leaders had decided to encourage the immigration of a small community of Jews who led an obscure existence in the southernmost corner of Arabia. This ancient branch of Oriental Jewry had been living for many centuries in a primitive kingdom where they had suffered persecutions and humiliations from their Muslim masters. Although they were completely cut off from the centers of Judaism, the Yemenite Jews had remained true to their ancestral faith and had kept the traditions of Judaism. They had also preserved their holy language, Hebrew, which they transmitted from generation to generation, and spoke in the course of their everyday lives.

An emissary of the workers' movement, disguised as a rabbi succeeded in entering Yemen at the risk of his life. He wandered on foot from one village to another telling the wonderstruck Jews about the miracle of the return to Zion. Everywhere he raised messianic hopes, and families, sometimes whole communities, set out for the Promised Land. They crossed deserts on foot, eventually reaching Aden from where, after a great many tribulations, they sailed for Jaffa. Soon these swarthy Jews, with their goatees and sidelocks, appeared in Judean villages and in the poorer districts of Jaffa and Jerusalem.

With their arrival, Hebrew gained in popularity because Yemen Jews spoke the holy tongue fluently while the vernaculars of European Jewry were completely unknown to them. Thus Hebrew became the necessary means of communication of labor circles that, otherwise, had little or no contact with the Oriental communities of Jerusalem.

Underpopulated and badly governed by the corrupt and lethargic Ottoman administration, Palestine was far from being a safe country. Brigandage was a normal and an almost officially recognized phenomenon. Beduin 'razzias' were frequent and did not spare the Jewish villages. According to custom the Jewish farmers employed the prospective robbers as watchmen over their cattle and crops. The thought that they depended on Arabs and on the Turkish police for their security was unbearable to the new elements that came with the Second Aliyah, who were forever haunted by the pogroms they had witnessed and the defenselessness and passivity of the Jewish victims. Many of them had organized units of self-defense armed with revolvers or with knives in their native towns and villages and these had often succeeded in saving whole communities. Unable, then, to accept that in their new homeland the Jews had to resort to foreign protection, they created a semi-clandestine organization, *Ha-Shomer* (The Watchman), that took in hand the protection of Jewish villages. It was organized as a secret order whose members were subject to strict discipline. Armed with rifles and wearing Beduin *keffieh* headdresses, they rode purebred mares and stood watch during the night around the basalt walls that surrounded Galilee villages. They not only drove the thieves away but sometimes chased them as far as their camps beyond the Jordan river. Taken aback by this unexpected turn of events, the Arabs began to respect these fearless riders. *Ha-Shomer* became a legendary corps that fired the imaginations of young people. Their feats evoked the admiration and longing of young Zionists in Eastern European countries.

The creation of *Ha-Shomer* is an important stage in the history of Jewish Palestine. Self-defense became a basic principle and similar groups were formed in the older settlements. When World War I broke out, the oppressive measures of the Turkish government became unbearable and another secret organization came into being in Zikhron Yaakov, in Samaria. This was *Nili,* set up to help the British armies take Palestine. Contact was made at an early date with British intelligence in Cairo, but the spy ring was clumsily organized and the number of its agents was too small. It was soon discovered by the Turks and wiped out. Nevertheless, it played an important role in establishing the first contacts between Palestine Jewry and Great Britain.

Ha-Shomer can be regarded as the forerunner of the underground army which made Israel's independence possible. It was this unshakable resolution never to be unprepared in case of surprise attack, and never to rely on the good will of the authorities for protection that led to the creation of the *Haganah,* the secret defense force. The same principle also inspired the formation of regiments of Jewish volunteers that fought in the ranks of the Allies during the two World Wars.

This was an important stage. Although they remained numerically weak, the Palestinian Jews from then on acquired a specific national physiognomy. Instead of being resigned to their fate or fleeing from it, they felt they were capable of taking their future into their own hands. The same spirit of initiative and taste for innovation soon came to infect urban development which had begun to expand before the outbreak of World War I. In Jerusalem, the majority of the population was Orthodox Jews who gave the city its very special character. New districts now began to rise outside the walls of the Old City. The number of modern schools constantly increased; the short-lived 'gazettes' were superseded by a modern daily press; banking institutions sprung up. Haifa, which according to Theodor Herzl's prophetic vision was to become the country's main industrial center, reached the first stage of its development with the building of the first modern districts on the slopes of Mount Carmel.

But it was principally in Jaffa that the newcomers concentrated. For the wave of immigration was made up not only of pioneers bent on tilling the soil, but also a large number of families who had been won over to the Zionist ideal or who merely wanted their children to receive a Hebrew education. They came at a period when the country was far from thriving. Yet enterprising men succeeded in setting up shops and even developing small industry. They were followed by young schoolteachers who took up their lodgings in the neighborhood of the Hebrew schools. Young Hebrew writers began to cater for a new reading public; intellectuals were drawn to Jaffa by its picturesque and stimulating atmosphere. Besides these, a new class of civil servants appeared in the city, as a consequence of the Palestinian Office's decision to establish its headquarters in Jaffa.

But the narrow, foul-smelling streets of the Arab city of Jaffa were not always to the taste of the new citizens accustomed to European housing conditions. Thus in 1909, a large plot of land was bought in the nearby dunes, reaching down as far as the sea coast. Presently, a new garden-city sprang up from the sandy dunes around the new high school (incidentally, this was to be the first secondary school in the world in which the teaching was entirely in Hebrew).

This new district was called Tel Aviv (an attempt to render in biblical Hebrew the title of Herzl's prophetic novel *Altneuland*). This large city with its gardens, its wide streets and modern buildings was entirely built by Jewish workers—something that at the time was absolutely novel. From its very beginning, it had an autonomous local council and was inhabited and administered exclusively by Jews. Its schools were attended by young people who had come to Palestine from all the corners of Russia. Young workers, who landed in the port of Jaffa, had no trouble finding employment there in building houses or streets. Long before Zion had become a reality, Tel Aviv was already 'the Gate to Zion'.

In this small society, intellectual life was very intense. It had many publishing houses, magazines and weeklies, which, although up against great financial difficulties, attracted a circle of assiduous readers and kept Hebrew literary life in Palestine and abroad alive and flourishing. They opened their columns to Hebrew poets

The Tribe of Dan, stained-glass window by Chagall. One of the stained-glass windows by Marc Chagall in the synagogue of the Hadassah Hospital, En Kerem, Jerusalem. This comes from a series of twelve depicting the twelve tribes. The inscription on top is from Genesis 49:16. Photo Sandak Inc., New York.

David, tapestry by Chagall. Part of the tapestry triptych by Marc Chagall in the main hall of the Knesset, Jerusalem. Chagall made his reputation as one of the initiators of the Surrealist school. His use of color and wild fantasy give his work its particular quality, quite apart from his superb technical mastery. Photo Harris, Jerusalem.

Moses, tapestry by Chagall. Part of the tapestry triptych by Marc Chagall (1887-) in the main hall of the Knesset (Israel's parliament), Jerusalem. Chagall left Russia in 1922 and settled in Paris but his work nevertheless has drawn much inspiration from scenes of life among the East European Hasidim and village communities near his native Vitebsk. Photo Harris, Jerusalem.

Over:

Independence day poster. For the twentieth anniversary of the foundation of the ▶ State of Israel, this independence day poster by Koppel Gorban, representing the *menorah* and the lions of Judah is a powerful evocation of the young nation with a long history. Photo Harris.

כותל יעקב.89

and novelists and soon Palestinians began to take great interest in the new Hebrew literature.

But the man who influenced the readers of this time more than any other was Joseph Hayyim Brenner, a writer of some reputation abroad who had come to settle in Tel Aviv. Brenner was an original writer and a rebel who had left London, where he had edited a small literary review, and had come to Palestine despite his misgivings. The helplessness of the Russian Jews on the one hand had driven him to despair, but on the other he also rejected the rootlessness of the young intellectuals and artists whom he describes in his novels. Palestine appealed to him despite the fact that he was disgusted by its oppressively provincial atmosphere. The small Palestinian working class listened to him, although he

constantly attacked its shortcomings and its false poses; at the same time he condemned the hypocrisy and ineffectiveness of Zionist leaders abroad. He put all the ardor of his faith and all the bitterness of his tormented soul into his stories, which told of the blind gropings, illusions, and mistakes of a world struggling to come to life. He was to die shortly after his arrival, knifed by an Arab during the bloody clashes of May 1921.

THE JEWISH NATIONAL HOME

The Great War almost put an end to the fragile structure which the pioneers of Israel had so painfully set up. The oppression of

Tel Aviv — early days, 1909. The first inhabitants-to-be of Tel Aviv visit the site of the future city as the building plots for the first houses are distributed. Tel Aviv, named after the Hebrew translation of Theodor Herzl's *Altneuland* started as a suburb of Jaffa. Within a few years these sand dunes had become a thriving little town. By now Tel Aviv is the hub of a conurbation of 388,000 inhabitants. Central Zionist Archives, Jerusalem.

Jewish soldiers in World War I. Soldiers of the first Jewish battalions of the British Army during World War I march to their barracks in the Southern Plain. At first, the British allowed only the Zion Mule Corps to be formed; despite opposition from various quarters, they decided in 1917, however, to raise a Jewish battalion, and in fact three (one coming from America and one from the liberated areas of South Palestine) were formed, comprising some 5,000 men. They participated in a number of campaigns against the Turkish army and in the crossing of the Jordan. Central Zionist Archives, Jerusalem.

the Turkish military regime, the deportations of foreign citizens, the famines and epidemics, took a heavy toll of the Jewish population. But when General Allenby made his triumphal entry into Jerusalem and British administration took over from the tyrannical Turkish rulers, new horizons opened before the Jewish inhabitants of Palestine. The future was full of promise. The 1917 Balfour Declaration recognized the historical bond between the Jewish people and Palestine, and the name of Great Britain was linked with the creation of a Jewish National Home in Palestine. This recognition became an international obligation when the British Mandate over Palestine was ratified by the League of Nations. Jewish battalions formed in Great Britain and in the United States had helped the British troops liberate the land, and volunteers from Palestine had joined the British army under their own blue and white flag, among them several distinguished leaders of the *Yishuv,* the Jewish community. A Zionist Commission, which had been given wide powers by the British government, arrived in the country, headed by Chaim Weizmann,

the man really behind the Balfour Declaration. Weizmann was to hold the reins of the Zionist government during the coming thirty years.

A dream had become reality. There was every reason to think that the sufferings and the sacrifices of two generations of pioneers had not been in vain. But the painful awakening was not long in coming. Palestinian Jews soon realized that a National Home was not a state. British administration, first military, then civilian, was far from convinced of the value of British commitment toward Zionism. It was pervaded with pan-Arab and pan-Islamic ideas nurtured by influential circles connected with the British embassy in Cairo.

The Arab world was in ferment. The creation of semi-independent states in Syria, Lebanon and Iraq, and the support given to pro-Arab circles in the British administration encouraged active opposition among the Arab population of Palestine. As early as 1920, riots broke out in Jerusalem. These outbreaks of hatred, fanned by unrelenting religious and racialist agitation, very soon became chronic, and caused the Palestine Jews to close their ranks for active defense and be in a permanent state of readiness.

The enthusiasm had been short-lived. Now, the Jewish community realized that the British Mandate, far from putting an end to its difficulties, was only the beginning of a long struggle on two fronts: on the one hand, against the reserved attitude of the mandatory administration; on the other, against the increasing hostility of Arab nationalists.

There were, however, yet further difficulties to be faced. The toll on the Jewish population in World War I had been high and Palestine's Jewish community needed to grow to strengthen the fragile structure now in place. Worse still was the question of Russia; it was there that the Zionist ideal was born and from there came the first waves of immigration to Palestine. Furthermore the financial contributions that enabled the Palestinian Jewish community to survive came largely from Russian Zionists. Now, quite suddenly and unexpectedly, Russian Jewry was cut off from the rest of the world. Toward the end of the 1920s, an 'iron curtain', the first of its kind in modern times, had fallen over millions of Russian Jews. At first, the February revolution of 1917 had been enthusiastically followed by the Jews who shared in the general elation of the newly won liberty of the Russians. At that time, the Jewish national revival experienced a renewal of popularity. The Balfour Declaration was seen by the Jewish masses as a messianic event. Zionism which, at the outset had been the doctrine of restricted circles, now became a mass movement with tens of thousands of young followers. A new pioneer organization came into existence called *He-Halutz* (the Pioneer),

which was headed by Captain Joseph Trumpeldor, a war hero who had lost an arm in the Russo-Japanese war and was to find a hero's death in defending an outpost in the Galilee Hills against Arab aggressors. Groups of young pioneers set out to join their brothers in the Land of Israel.

But these great hopes were shattered by the attitude of the new regime in Moscow. As the Soviet regime grew stronger, its attitude toward Zionism became more and more intolerant. The Jewish Communists had played an important part in the Revolution. They came for the most part from the Bund, the Socialist party that had always been bitterly hostile to Zionism. These militants now became the most active persecutors of their Zionist opponents. Hebrew papers and Hebrew schools were closed. Zionist circles were forced underground and their militants began to fill the Russian prisons and the Siberian camps.

Worse still, the borders were closed, shutting off three million Russian Jews from Palestine. At the beginning of the 1920s, certain isolated groups still succeeded in escaping, and prisoners deported to Siberia were sometimes allowed to exchange their prison terms for an emigration visa to Palestine, but as the years passed, these forms of escape became increasingly rare; Russian Jewry was now beyond reach.

THE THIRD AND FOURTH ALIYOT

The time was ripe for the Third Aliyah, the first mass immigration to Palestine. Ships cast anchor off Jaffa and crowded trains arrived from Egypt. They were loaded with Zionist families who

Third Aliyah, 1920-3. Pioneers of the Third Aliyah (1920-3) engaged in agricultural work near a new settlement. The wooden huts served as housing in the early days of the settlements in the Jezreel Valley. Much of the work was in draining swamps and the pioneers suffered terribly from malaria and other diseases. Central Zionist Archives, Jerusalem.

at the last moment had succeeded in leaving a Russia in the throes of civil war. Among the new arrivals were a number of Hebrew writers, most belonging to the Odessa school. But the great majority of the new immigrants were young pioneers, members of the new *He-Halutz* movement who had been infected with the enthusiasm of East European Jewish youths. Russian *halutzim* left their country via all imaginable routes: the Caucasian mountains, Persia, even Siberia and the Far East. Legally or illegally, they crossed the Polish or Rumanian borders where they were joined by thousands of young members of local organizations. They then made their way in organized groups to Trieste and Constanza whence they sailed for Palestine.

These young men were exultant with new ideas gleaned from the storm of the Revolution or from the ideological agitation which shook postwar Europe. They were apostles of renewal. Their aim was to live in *kibbutzim* and most of them could not imagine their future except in terms of collective action. Others preferred the *moshavim,* the cooperative villages which were being created for the first time. They launched themselves into the political turmoil of Palestinian Jewry which they inspired with a new ardor.

The Zionist authorities who had encouraged this movement were now overwhelmed by the task facing them: the country had barely emerged from the war and everything had to be rebuilt—with no money on hand. Russian Jewry could no longer be reached and America had not yet taken over, so that vital financial contributions from abroad simply failed to come. This money was desperately needed to create farming settlements and to develop the cities. The meager budgets of the Zionist institutions were hardly sufficient to maintain welcoming centers for the immigrants and the essential services, especially schools, which were now compelled to expand drastically under the demographic pressure of the new *aliyah.* But the most urgent task was to find work for the masses of newcomers. At first this was provided by public works undertaken by the mandatory administration to fill the vacuum left by the Ottoman powers. Groups of immigrants in this way found an occupation building roads. Government wages, though very low, were sufficient for the needs of the Arab workers, but inadequate to meet those of the new immigrants. However, the Jewish workers joined together and created collective companies. Living in tents, underpaid and underfed, they pitched their camps in every corner of the land and started building roads or breaking up stones for the paving. At night, after the day's exhausting work under the scorching sun of Palestinian summers, these camps resounded with songs and with the rhythms of the *Hora,* the Balkan folk-dance that became the national dance of Israel. The tents were the scene of passionate discussions, clashes between members of different parties; groups were formed and dissolved all the time.

The *Histadrut*—the Labor Federation created by the political parties in 1920—was strengthened by this wave of new immigrants. It played an increasingly important part in promoting the initiatives taken by the workers of the new *aliyah.* The enormous influence of this Labor Federation on the political life and economic structure of the country dates from that time.

Characteristic of this first postwar period was the purchase of a large expanse of land in the Jezreel Valley. From then on, the systematic agricultural settlement of the Jews in Palestine struck deep roots. This valley which people grew accustomed to call the *Emek* (the Valley) had been the granary of ancient Israel. In its present abandoned state, it was a desolate expanse of fallow land interspersed with swamps. The purchase of this valley was made by the Jewish National Fund, the agricultural fund of the Zionist Organization, which bought it from an Arab family in Beirut.

The valley became the center of Zionist agricultural efforts. All the different forms of settlements were represented there, ranging from the *kibbutzim* (or from their smaller models named *kevutzot*) to the *moshavim.* The *Emek* became the symbol of the new era. Owing to the lack of financial means, life in the new villages was a permanent struggle against poverty. The young farmers barely had enough to eat and their miserable huts were damp with rain during the rainy season. For all these hardships, the glamor of the *Emek* inspired thousands of would-be pioneers who ardently awaited their turn to come and settle in Palestine. Agricultural expansion in the valley was a model for future agricultural development for it was a testing-ground for agricultural theory and practice. It was there that the *kibbutz* and the *moshav* became crystallized institutions.

Simultaneously, the political direction of the Jewish community changed. The new wave of immigration with its organized groups, its insistence on economic planning and its ideal of fast economic growth and social justice, took over from the traditional élite of the prewar period. Conversely, the men from the Second Aliyah merged into the working class and integrated into the unions side by side with the new politicians that the new wave had brought to the fore.

As often happened in the history of Palestinian society, the Third Aliyah period was brought to a close by an economic crisis which did not, however, last very long. In 1924, a new type of immigrant, totally different from the preceding ones, appeared on the Palestinian scene. This new wave arrived from Poland, the European country with the most Jews.

The Fourth Aliyah was mixed in character: young enthusiastic pioneers rubbed shoulders with middle-class families. Small shopkeepers from Warsaw or from the provincial towns, businessmen, factory owners and artisans, all came together. These people had brought their children with them as well as their furniture, their stocks of merchandise or their work tools. In Jaffa harbor, small family chests replaced the bundles of clothing of former times.

A period of prosperity began. Hundreds of houses sprang up overnight on the sandy beaches of Tel Aviv. The price of plots soared in the cities. Industry, which so far had been practically non-existent in the economic structure of Palestine, was introduced into the country. Capital streamed in and unemployment was no longer a nightmare haunting workers. Apparently the Jewish National Home had overcome the dangerous period of its infancy and could look forward to a bright future.

In April 1925, the dream of Chaim Weizmann (President of the Zionist Organization who was also a chemist of international eminence) at last came true: on top of Mount Scopus, he presided over the opening ceremony of the first Hebrew university in the world. Zionism seemed to be on its way to success. Speeches were delivered by Lord Balfour, Lord Allenby, and by representatives of the foremost universities in the world. This forgotten corner of the Orient again became a center of interest for international scientific circles. The Jewish population was constantly on the increase. Tel Aviv was growing into a big city. In the agricultural domain, citrus-growing was in full swing. Everything seemed to be headed for success. But this period of euphoria was short-lived. In Poland, new restrictive measures were taken against the Jews, which represented a severe blow to the Palestinian economy and, what with land speculation as well, a financial crisis rapidly ensued. Several years later, this crisis worsened with the terrible crash on the New York Stock Exchange. Many immigrants returned to their former homelands. A long period of stagnation and unemployment followed, with all the political repercussions that such a crisis usually implies.

Thus the Fourth Aliyah, which had been so full of promise, eventually proved, in fact, a failure. It nevertheless left an enduring mark on the economy of the country. From that period on dates systematic town planning and development, as well as the first timid beginnings of Israel's industry which was later to become one of the fundamental elements of the economy. At the same time, many middle-class immigrants took to citrus-growing in the Sharon Valley, north of Tel Aviv, which presently became a densely populated zone, and even today the effects of this new direction taken by agriculture are to be felt: citrus-growing holds an important place in Israel's exports.

But, first and foremost, this wave of immigration proved to the world that Palestine was not only a center of attraction for young idealists ready for every sacrifice, but that it was also a shelter for the persecuted Jewish masses. The new immigrants of the Fourth Aliyah, peaceful families from small Polish towns, foreshadowed the 'rescue operations' to come.

REFUGEES FROM GERMANY

As far back as the early 1930s, there were discernible signs of the storm gathering over Europe. In Eastern European countries, anti-Semitism grew worse and racial discrimination became a principle of government. Hitler at that moment came to power. In one of the most enlightened countries in the world, hatred for the Jews was not only accepted as legitimate, it was made compulsory at all levels of political life. The indifference of the world and the cowardice of public opinion which was increasingly paralyzed by its desire for peace at all costs encouraged Nazi cruelty. But as long as the gates remained open, the European Jews sought to escape. First, there was the exodus from Germany, followed by that from Austria and Czechoslovakia. The roads of Europe began to fill with long columns of refugees.

Countries that could have opened their borders to the thousands of Jews who looked for a haven remained hermetically closed. The Evian Conference (which remains a sinister memory in world history) was convened to find a solution to this intolerable situation, but ended as a macaber farce. The Jewish refugees were not wanted. Living in perpetual fear, German Jews ran from one closed border to another. They raised their eyes toward Palestine. But at that time, access to the Holy Land was strictly limited. The Jewish Agency tried every possible means and a number of entrance visas were eventually obtained. Tens of thousands of Central European Jews crowded into the country. From 1933 till the outbreak of World War II, Jews in the Diaspora no longer had any illusions: even in such countries where Jews led a free existence and had a certain influence on the economic and political life of the nation, they were unable to change the attitude of their governments. The only country where, despite the mandatory administration, the Jews had the right to raise their voices and could successfully demand admittance for their persecuted brothers, was Palestine. In Palestine, the Jews could afford to ignore the official policy and did not hesitate to violate laws which, in their eyes, were iniquitous, in order to rescue the European Jews. As early as 1934, the first clandestine refugee ships began arriving in Palestine despite the close watch maintained by British patrol boats. Young *Haganah* fighters guided them from the coast and later took charge of the passengers.

The Jewish masses of the threatened countries of Europe looked toward this last haven. Political discussions had by now come to a stop, for there was no longer any point in bandying arguments for or against a Jewish national ideology. The racist threat menaced the whole Jewish people and Palestine was the only ray of light in the universal gloom.

The arrival of the German Jews of the Fifth Aliyah, the last before the outbreak of World War II, brought a completely new type of immigrant into the country. Although the contribution of German Jewry to the movement had been far from negligible, only a small minority had adhered to Zionism. As a rule, the German Jews were among the most assimilated in Europe. They had obtained Emancipation around the middle of the 19th century and had quickly merged into the life of the country with whose culture they had completely identified themselves.

The blow to the German Jews was heart-breaking, as, in many cases, they had been genuine German patriots that racialist laws had turned overnight into outcasts, whatever their social position or political opinions. Nevertheless, in spite of this dreadful trauma, the reaction of German Jewry did not fall short of its long tradition. The refugees who set out for Palestine engaged upon their new life with energy and determination. Although they were far less steeped in Jewish knowledge and tradition than their East European brothers of the preceding *aliyot,* they brought into the Israel melting pot new qualities which considerably enriched it and profoundly marked its character.

As soon as they had set foot in the land, they did their utmost to adjust themselves rapidly to their new and totally unfamiliar environment. They set aside for the time being their university degrees and professional experience and accepted any kind of work. This was a time when doctors raised chickens and lawyers became taxidrivers, when opera singers went to work on *kibbutzim.* The German immigrants also had a hard time learning their new and mysterious language, Hebrew, of which they had not had the slightest notion. Progressively, they managed to tear themselves loose from German culture in which they had been so steeped.

They introduced unfamiliar habits into Palestinian society and to some degree shattered the austerity which the Second Aliyah had imposed upon the country. These new immigrants had been accustomed to a high standard of comfort. They introduced modern architecture, habits of cleanliness and order into the appearance of the cities, a taste for luxurious window dressing and suchlike improvements. Palestine, which up to then had borne the stamp of the East European ghetto, took a step toward being more 'European'.

The coming of the German Jews had a lasting effect on the planning of the economy as well as on industrial development, science and art. The research institutes of the Hebrew University opened their doors to a great number of distinguished scientists from Germany, Austria and Czechoslovakia. After the anti-Semitic turn taken by the Mussolini regime, they were joined by scientists from the Jewish élite of Italy.

During World War II, Jewish Palestine happened to be part of one of the decisive fronts. As it was cut off from European harbors it had to mobilize all its scientific and industrial resources to contribute to the Allied war effort. This was made possible by the changes which had taken place in its economy during the years that had preceded the outbreak of the war. At the same time, war emphasized the progressive character of Israel society, its capacity for new initiative, and its Western bias.

DEVELOPMENT OF JEWISH AUTONOMY

Before attaining political independence, Jewish Palestinian society had almost acquired *de facto* autonomy. This achievement was a consequence of the specific conditions in Palestine and of the policy of the British administration compelling the Jews to create their own institutions and administrative services.

With a few exceptions, British rule in Palestine presented all the characteristics of a colonial regime. The civil servants of the Mandate considered it their duty to ensure that the services functioned properly. But, when it came to developing the country, they showed an utter lack of imagination. Their first care was the welfare of the Arab population who fitted better into their concept of 'natives'. The Jews they considered pretentious and restless romantics, pursuing an aim which seemed to them totally unreal. Moreover, at a very early stage, they saw the rapid progress of the Jewish National Home as a threat to British policy in the Middle East based, as it was, on winning the support of the Arab world.

The only solution left for the Zionist Executive and the National Jewish Council which democratically represented the Jews of Palestine, was to create their own executive institutions and establish a parallel administrative system, and thanks to the self-discipline of the Jewish population, they eventually succeeded in doing so. An independent educational system thus came into being. In a very short time, this parallel schooling system was attended by the majority of the Jewish children, though at that time education had not been made compulsory. Pedagogical methods constantly improved and kindergarten, elementary and secondary schools were set up in all the important settlements. Modern medical services, hospitals and social security won the battle against endemic diseases (such as malaria, which had been one of the main scourges of the country and had taken a heavy toll on the first pioneer settlements).

The executive institutions took advantage of this new liberty to emphasize the Jewish character of their administration. The *Histadrut* and its *kibbutzim* and *moshavim* constituted a 'ready-made' network for overt or clandestine action.

The creation of an independent economy was encouraged by the permanent Arab threat which forced the Jews into unrelenting vigilance, a vigilance made further necessary by the restrictive steps taken by the authorities to limit immigration and the purchase of land from the Arabs.

CONFLICT WITH THE ARABS

After the 1920 and 1921 disturbances in Jerusalem and Jaffa, the year 1929 saw new massacres of Jews by fanatical Arab crowds. Many were slaughtered in Hebron and Safed, although the *Haganah,* the self-defense organization, with its old rifles and rusty pistols, succeeded in protecting many isolated Jewish quarters. These riots were a warning which the *Haganah* never forgot. It systematically set out to purchase weapons and train men. In April 1936, new Arab rioting broke out. This new period of disturbances lasted almost three years and security became a crucial problem for the Jews.

This period of great danger in which thousands of defenders were killed (as well as many innocent victims), had a decisive effect on the formation of the nation. The Arab revolt spread quickly; it had won the support of the Nazi-Fascist axis which, in anticipation of the coming war, sought to infiltrate into the Middle East. It was encouraged in this aim by armed bands which crossed into the country from the neighboring Arab states with impunity. The British reaction was slow and weak. The Supreme Arab Committee, led by the Jerusalem Mufti, Hadj Amin el-Husseini (who a few years later proclaimed himself the friend and agent of the Berlin regime) led a general strike against the Jews and a total boycott of Jewish life. Isolated Jewish settlements and Jewish quarters situated near the Arab districts of towns with a mixed population were subjected to constant attacks. The lines of communication between cities were cut, buses were attacked by armed gangs. The Jewish population lived in an atmosphere of siege. One of the inevitable consequences of such a situation was the final separation between Jewish and Arab economies. Arab workers left their jobs on the plantations and were replaced by Jewish manpower while Arab products were withdrawn from the Jewish markets, causing Jewish agricultural production to improve in quantity and quality.

This was no longer rioting; this was war, on the issue of which depended the survival or total annihilation of the whole Jewish

Palmah soldiers. A group of *Palmah* (Shock Companies) soldiers attacking an Arab village during the Israel War of Independence (1948), followed by a few primitive armored cars. No uniform was worn until the companies were integrated into the Israel Defense Army. Originally formed to assist the British against the Germans, it continued to exist as an underground, permanently mobilized, force. Its units were dispersed throughout Palestinian labor settlements and their time was divided between work and training. Central Zionist Archives, Jerusalem.

community. But the nation rose in arms against its attackers. The *Haganah* mobilized all available men while the majority of the women and schoolchildren stood by ready for any emergency. Weapons which had been secretly purchased or had been made in clandestine factories piled up in their caches. Not a single village was allowed to remain isolated and a system of convoys kept the roads open. Presently, Jewish units left their purely defensive role and began attacking the concentrations of armed Arab bands.

It soon became necessary to organize regular troops. The *Palmah* (abbreviation of *Paluggot mahatz*—'assault units') was therefore formed. The young soldiers received a hard military training in camps which were usually located in *kibbutzim*. Their time was spent in cultivating the fields, training, and taking part in military actions. This élite corps was mainly composed of young people born in Palestine; most of the top people in Israel's army today, men who later achieved fame during the wars forced upon their country, emerged from this hard school of war. This is the case of Moshe Dayan, Yigal Allon, Yitzhak Rabin and many others. But the *Palmah* also bred a multitude of writers, poets and administrators who played a leading role after the independence of the country.

This period also saw the creation of dissenting organizations: first came the *Irgun Tzevai Leumi,* followed by the *Lohame Herut Yisrael* (also known as the Stern group). Both movements grew out of the Revisionist Zionist Party, an activist and overtly anti-British group, founded by Vladimir Jabotinsky. These groups did not recognize the authority of the *Haganah* and were in favor of direct offensive action both against the Arabs and the British administration.

This split with the underground organizations considerably hindered the unity of action of the Jewish community which could only be sporadically maintained. Under the leadership of David Ben-Gurion, the *Haganah* prepared to become a regular army, while, during the last years of the Mandate, bold terrorist actions committed by the dissenting groups drew the attention of world opinion to the situation in Palestine and helped to precipitate the withdrawal of the British.

The government of Great Britain did not resist the pressure of Arab terrorism very long. Its policy toward the Jews, which had always been reserved, became openly hostile. It made public its decision to restrict the number of Jews in Palestine in order to keep the Jewish community from becoming the majority since, at the outbreak of World War II, there were about half a million Jews and one million Arabs in Palestine. While the Arab revolt exhausted itself, the Jews had to face a new struggle. They now had to fight for their right to open the gates to the refugees and to settle on the lands which they had legally purchased from their former Arab owners.

Creating new villages in remote areas became a heroic feat. It had been decided from the very beginning of the Arab disturbances that settlements were to be established on every plot of land owned by Jews, even if it meant isolation in the midst of territories which were practically under the control of Arab bands. In order to keep the surprise element on their sides, the builders adhered to the so-called 'Tower and Stockade' system. Prefabricated elements were brought to the site of the future settlement and put together in the course of a day. The village consisted of a wooden palisade, a watchtower, and a few wooden huts. The epic of the 'Tower and Stockade' period reached its climax with the simultaneous creation, during one autumn night, of eleven settlements in the Negev desert.

WORLD WAR II

The events of the tragic years 1939 to 1949, the decade which preceded the birth of the State of Israel, are still vivid memories to many. War; the invasion of Poland; the last and desperate efforts to save the Jewish refugees that flocked to Balkan harbors and Danubian ports; then the hermetic closing of the gates; the invasion of Western Europe; the Nazi butchers masters of the fate of millions of Jews; the lightning thrust of Rommel's armies to the suburbs of Alexandria; the threat hanging over Palestine and the British plans for withdrawal. Mercifully, the El Alamein victory crushed the Nazi menace to the Middle East. Then there began to emerge the first incomplete rumors of horrors in ghettos and death camps. Following these events, the revolts broke out in ghettos and desperate efforts were made to help the Jewish partisans. The Jews now felt their terrible isolation and world indifference; the horrible truth concerning the fate of six million European Jews came out ... and, at last, peace, that came too late....

When the guns fell silent, there remained, however, the tremendous hope of saving the survivors, of welcoming to Palestine the pitiful remnants of the once prosperous communities of European Jewry. But what bitterness when, months after the end of the war, hundreds of thousands of 'displaced persons', ('D.Ps' as they were called), were still kept in German camps to serve the ends of a brutal policy and prevented from joining their brothers in Palestine. Then came open revolt and its repression. Dozens of refugee ships defied the might of the British fleet in the Mediterranean, highlighted by the tragedy of the *Exodus* in 1947. Argument raged in the United Nations until the resolution of November 29 1947, advocating the creation of a Jewish state in Palestine. The Arabs issued threats, but failed to prevent the proclamation of the State of Israel on May 14 1948. Israel found itself invaded by seven Arab armies. Bloody battles of the Independence War took place against tremendous odds, ending in the victory of the Jewish State. The first Truce Agreements were then signed and the new state entered into the family of nations.

From the very start of World War II, the Palestine Jews had spontaneously offered their services to Great Britain to contribute to the struggle of the Allies against the Germans who were the sworn enemies of the Jewish people. Tens of thousands of men volunteered for the Palestinian Jewish units of the British armies once the Jewish authorities had managed to overcome the prolonged hesitations of the British government, wary of Arab reactions. This success was largely due to the tenaciousness

David Ben-Gurion (1886-). David Ben-Gurion who led the struggle for the State during and after World War II and who became Israel's first Prime Minister and Minister of Defense. Born in Plonsk (Poland), he joined the Zionist movement at an early date and settled in Israel in 1906, since when he has played an active role in a multitude of different spheres. Government Press Office, Tel Aviv.

people spoke the holy tongue, enjoyed complete freedom, and led Jewish lives. The Palestinians, for their part, discovered a distinctly and deeply Jewish world in which the remembrance of Zion was alive; a world both very close to them and at the same time very different, utterly unlike the Europe from which they and their parents derived their Jewish heritage. This encounter marked the reuniting of the two branches of Judaism which had been separated by centuries of parallel development; a reuniting which had already been prepared by the recent history of Palestine. During their stay in the countries of the Orient as well as in Libya, Tunisia, and Iraq, the soldiers organized courses for the Jewish population. Emissaries were sent from Palestine under the cover of the Jewish units, whose task was to constitute the nuclei of a pioneer youth movement

These seeds were not long in bearing fruit: when the State of Israel came into being (at a period when life in Muslim countries

Chaim Weizmann (1874-1952). Chaim Weizmann, president of the Zionist organization, who became first president of the State of Israel. Born at Motel near Pinsk, he moved to England where he was largely responsible for winning the support of England's leaders and obtaining the Balfour Declaration. Government Press Office, Tel Aviv.

of Chaim Weizmann and to the indefatigable activity of Moshe Sharett, later to became the first Foreign Minister of Israel. Over thirty thousand Palestinian Jewish volunteers took part in the Desert War and in the operations in Greece and Ethiopia. Subsequently, a Jewish brigade helped in the invasion of Italy, Austria, Germany, Holland and Belgium.

As they proceeded along the North African coast, the Palestinian soldiers came into contact for the first time with the Jewish communities of Cyrenaica, Tripolitania and Tunisia. Other units, especially the engineers and the signal corps, as well as specialists in public works directing projects for the army, associated with Syrian, Iraqi, and Iranian Jews.

The encounter between Oriental Jews and the young Palestinian soldiers who came to them as liberators in the ranks of the British army had a tremendous effect on both groups. For the first time, Oriental Jews became really aware of the existence of a Jewish political center established in the land of Israel, where

had become unbearable) masses of Oriental Jews left the lands they had lived in for hundreds, sometimes even for thousands, of years. Syrian Jews had only to cross the mountains which served as northern border to the State. The majority of Iraq's Jews who had suffered terribly during the 1941 Nazi coup of Rashid Ali Keilani, were brought to Israel a few years after Independence, an exodus made possible through the intervention of the great European powers. In the following years, the majority of Tunisian, Moroccan, and Egyptian Jews came to settle in Israel. Mere vestiges of a once densely populated Diaspora were left in Islamic countries, after centuries of enslavement and decadence.

The encounter between the Palestinian brigade and refugees from the death camps in Europe was infinitely more tragic. These men and women had just emerged from long years of torture in the ghettos and concentration camps. Suddenly, before these skeletal figures loomed the unimaginable and unimagined sight of uniformed Jews of all grades and ranks, proudly sporting the Shield of David on their sleeves. For the Palestinians, it was a heart-breaking experience. Here they found their lost brothers, survivors from their own families whom they had given up prematurely for dead, neighbors from their native European towns and villages whose Jewish streets were now plunged in the everlasting silence of death.

'Illegal' immigration boat. An 'illegal' immigration boat arrives somewhere off the coast of Palestine. The passengers disembark with the help of a rope thrown into the sea by hundreds of volunteers coming from neighboring settlements. During the later part of the Mandate, the British authorities severely limited Jewish immigration to Palestine. Tension ran high as this was the Nazi- and immediately post-Nazi period when many Jews were struggling to get to Palestine. To get round the immigration quotas, 'illegal' immigration was organized which brought immigrants to Palestine without the knowledge of the British authorities. Those captured were deported to internment camps in Cyprus and elsewhere. Central Zionist Archives, Jerusalem.

These Palestinian units were largely responsible for rescuing the *Sheerit Ha-Pletah* (The Last Remnants), a biblical term used to designate the survivors of the death camps. It was they who organized, with the complicity of superior authorities in the Allied armies, the sending of the 'D.Ps' across chaotic postwar Europe, toward harbors in Italy, France, and Greece. There, the men in charge of the clandestine *aliyah* crowded them into dilapidated boats bound for the coast of Palestine. Many of these vessels were caught by the British patrol boats and their pas-

sengers put into camps in Palestine or in Cyprus. But, despite the repressive measures, the stream of immigrants kept flowing.

The annihilation of European Jewry left an indelible mark on the people of Israel, including the younger generations and Oriental Jews who had not lived through the same experience. Later the capture and trial of Adolf Eichmann was to give further intensity to their feelings. The young Israelis were proud of the act of justice accomplished by their State and realized how imperishable for them was the memory of this exterminated world.

Maabarah (tent camps), post-1948. New immigrants arriving at a *Maabarah* (transit immigration camp). From its establishment Israel received a mass immigration and many Jews from all parts of the world welcomed the foundation of a Jewish State, and went there in their hundreds of thousands. Especially during the early years of the State, it proved impossible to provide immediate housing for all the newcomers and tents, tin huts, and wooden barracks were put up throughout the country to house the immigrants until some more permanent home could be built. Central Zionist Archives, Jerusalem.

Haifa. The city of Haifa has been built up the slopes of Mount Carmel. The area became a major industrial zone partly as a result of the extensive port and harbor facilities in the nearby Kishon river. The view here is of the lower city in the neighborhood of the port. The residential quarters are built on the slopes and on the top of Mount Carmel. Photo Harris, Jerusalem.

THE INGATHERING OF THE EXILES

Because of its heterogeneous composition, the Israel nation is, demographically, like a tapestry, and woven with the multiple threads of the various Jewish communities dispersed throughout the world, whether now extinct or still alive in some remote corner. It was the first time in the course of Israel's 'long march' that such an 'Ingathering of the Exiles'—*Kibbutz Galuyyot*—had been achieved.

At the turn of the third decade of its existence, Israel had a Jewish population of almost two and a half millions (apart from 400,000 Muslims, Christians and Druze). Between 1882 and its independence, nearly 600,000 Jews came as immigrants; this figure doubled in the first twenty years following the creation of the State. During the latter period, the majority of the immigrants (about 700,000) came from Asian and African countries where the population was largely Muslim; the remainder (about 600,000) came from America and Europe, especially from countries beyond the Iron Curtain and from the European refugee camps.

But this very general statistical data can only give an abstract picture of the situation. In concrete terms, this meant that Israel had to absorb whole communities which, as a result of this emigration from their homelands, simply disappeared from the map of the Jewish dispersion. Such is the case of the Oriental communities as well as the remnants of formerly prosperous and influential groups of European Jewry. There remain practically no Jews in Yemen, Libya, Syria, Iraq, and Egypt any longer.

The North African communities have decreased by nine-tenths. The majority of Balkan Jews, especially the Bulgarian Jews, and the remnants of Greek and Yugoslav Jewry, have been absorbed into Israel. The exodus from Rumania brought hundreds of thousands of Jews to the country. Most of the survivors from Poland are now living in Israel; so, too, are tens of thousands of German, Austrian and Czech Jews. More recently and remarkably, Jews have begun to arrive from Soviet Russia.

Tel Aviv. Founded in 1909, the city developed rapidly under the British Mandate, mainly as Arab riots forced the Jews to abandon Jaffa. On the eve of Independence, Jaffa was abandoned and the two cities united in 1949 under the name Tel Aviv-Jaffa. The city houses Israel's main theaters and newspapers, and is the hub of national life. Shown here is the central part of Tel Aviv, seen from the air. In the foreground, left, Dizengoff Circle, main entertainment center of the city, named after the city's first mayor. On the seashore, the Dan Hotel, the first big hotel built in Tel Aviv. Government Press Office, Tel Aviv.

It is not an easy task to define the respective share of each of these communities in the building of the nation. As the years go by and new generations born or raised in the country take over, a new type of Jew has come to the fore. This is the native Israeli, the *sabra,* completely free from the outlandish heritage of the older generation and from their idiosyncrasies and national particularisms; for the older generation had absorbed so many elements from its non-Jewish environment that, until today, numerous communities have kept their own individual ways of life. These older people are bound together by their customs, by common memories and by the sentimental or linguistic contacts which they have maintained. Though it is too early to define the new type of Jew created in the Israeli melting pot, a general

Modern Israel coins. After the 1948 War of Independence, Israel's coinage remained denominationally the same as under the British Mandate (copper and nickel coinage up to 100 *perutot*), as well as 25 and 250 *perutot* nickel coins; 1,000 *perutot* = £I 1. In 1960, the *perutah* was abandoned in favour of the *agorah* (100 *agorot* = £I 1) and a new coinage adopted.

a) 25 *agorot* coin (reverse)
   Three-stringed lyre, inspired from silver dinars and bronze coins of the Bar Kokhba revolt.
b) 5 *agorot* coin (reverse)
   Three ripe pomegranates as a motif appear on coins of the Bar Kokhba revolt (132-5 A.D.).
c) 10 *agorot* coin (reverse)
   Seven-branched palm-tree, symbol of Judea in ancient times.
d) 1 *agorah* coin
   Three ears of barley, as on the ancient coins of Agrippa I (10 B.C.-44 A.D.)
All the coins are inscribed in Hebrew and Arabic. Photo Goldberg, Jerusalem, Israel Government Coins and Medals Corporation Ltd.

Postmarks, postage stamps. Israel's postage stamps are much sought after for their striking graphic qualities and vividness. Philatelic Service, Tel Aviv.
a) stamp commemorating the 400th anniversary of the publication of *Shulhan Arukh,* the authoritative code of Jewish Law, by Joseph Caro in 1565.
b) Stamp commemorating the Eighth Maccabiah World Jewish Sport Rally. The torches are carried from Modiin, the burial place of the ancient Maccabees.
c) Stamp commemorating the 20th anniversary of Israel's independence.
d) Stamp commemorating the 1969 national stamp exhibition and showing a carving above the Lion Gate (St. Stephen's Gate) in Jerusalem.
e) From a series of stamps representing Israel's main items of export.

appreciation of the share of each community in the building of the nation can at least be attempted.

The general direction and ideological trend was given by East European Jews (Russian, Polish, and Rumanian). Even today, the men who hold political power come largely from these countries (although many of them arrived before World War I). Immediately behind, comes the group of those born in the country, some of whom grew up on *kibbutzim* or *moshavim.* These men also form the majority in the leadership of the *Histadrut* (Israel Labor Federation) and of the *kibbutz* movements whose influence goes far beyond its rather restricted numerical importance. At the level of government administration, a field of foremost importance in the modern era of economic planning, the largest and most influential group is that of the *sabras.* The *sabras* also hold dominant positions in the army and in the defense ministry where, on David Ben-Gurion's insistence, young leadership has always been stressed. Officers retire from active service at a relatively early age and are then available as the executive class for the administration and the economy.

We have already mentioned the changes in structure introduced by the immigrants from Eastern Europe, Austria, and Czechoslovakia. The influence of these immigrants is still ubiquitous in the field of science (although the *sabras* are increasingly numerous there, especially in the provinces of nuclear and exact sciences) and art, particularly music. The banking sector of the economy also profited greatly from their contribution. In the field of literature, Hungarian Jews followed the tradition of their country of origin, contributing much to the development of humor and satire. Bulgarian Jewry gave many actors and directors to the Israel stage. The merchant navy was largely created through the initiative of Greek Jews, especially from Salonika

Hadassah Hospital. Hadassah Hospital and Medical School of the Hebrew University of Jerusalem built on a hill facing En Kerem in the south-western outskirts of the city. The hospital replaced that on Mount Scopus which was inaccessible between 1948 and 1967. Photo Harris, Jerusalem.

Meah Shearim. Main center of the extreme Orthodox Jewish community in the new city of Jerusalem, and the Jews here continue to lead an ultra-religious life. The notice in front is a warning to women not to dress immodestly (which would include the wearing of short sleeves). Photo Harris, Jerusalem.

where, for many decades, Jews practically controlled all the activities of this Balkan harbor, either as workers in the shipyards or as shipowners. The medical profession owes a great debt to the small but very active wave of immigration from South America.

Apart from the group of Sephardi Jews long established in the Holy Land, who quickly merged in the general stream, the first important group of Oriental Jews to settle in Eretz Israel were the Yemenites. They deeply influenced Israel society, for they clung to their original customs and introduced Oriental

themes into the folklore and music of Jewish Palestine which thus lost their exclusively Slavonic character. Very noteworthy is the fact that the first popular girl singers were for the most part of Yemenite origin.

Like the Sephardi Jews of Jerusalem, Iraqi Jews played an active role in developing the financial system of the country and its network of banks. The Egyptians, who came from a cosmopolitan environment, were quickly absorbed by the administration, the banks, and the municipalities.

It is still too early to give any final appreciation of the role

of the North African Jewish masses, one of the latest to come. Their élite, though numerically fairly small, contributed to expanding French cultural influence, which was further strengthened when Israel and France struck closer links of friendship. This mass of Jews from the Orient, North Africa, Iraq, Iran, and Yemen, also constituted the backbone of agricultural expansion at a time when the State had just come into existence, and hundreds of villages and small towns sprang up everywhere, from the borders of Upper Galilee to the outskirts of the Negev desert. These settlements owe their present prosperity largely to the Oriental immigrants and to their capacity for adjusting quickly to a totally new kind of work. Abruptly transplanted into a completely new environment, these families of newcomers overcame their initial setbacks with rare tenaciousness and became surprisingly successful.

Thanks to these successive layers of immigrants and to the varied influences of their respective communities, Israel was able to develop a unique culture, bearing little resemblance to that of the first pioneers. Today, the merging of the various elements is accelerated by the pursuit of a common aim and by the continuance of a mortal threat beyond the borders, a threat forcing Israel to live in a constant state of alert.

RELIGION IN ISRAEL

Is the national identity of the Israeli based on national consciousness or on his common religion? Since Israel's creation, this problem has never ceased to haunt the young state. The first law passed by the Israel parliament was the 'Law of the Return' which grants free entry into the country to every Jew wishing to settle there. But who is to be considered a Jew? Anyone who is conscious of being Jewish or someone whose Jewish identity is defined by the religious laws based on the Halakhah (the talmudic code)? How should the State be ruled? According to a modern legislation established by the elected bodies, or according to the religious code which had ruled the Jewish communities in ancient times?

A sensational verdict was returned by Israel's Supreme Court in the case of a Roman Catholic priest, Brother Daniel, who, on the grounds of his Jewish origin, claimed the status of Jew and the benefit of the 'Law of the Return'. The judgment did not enter into the definition of a Jew but established that a man who converts to another faith can no longer be regarded as Jewish. Of course, this case did not for a moment question the legitimacy of the fundamental assumption, accepted by all, according to which every citizen of the state, whether Christian, Muslim, or Druze, is entitled to enjoy full rights as well as

Torah breastplate, Jerusalem, 1945. Modern silver Torah breastplate, showing Tables of the Law. Jerusalem, Israel Museum, 148/190.

◄ *The Western Wall today*. Since 1967 the Western Wall has again become a focus for Jews all over the world. A piazza has been laid out front of the wall and considerable excavations carried out along the sides. Photo Harris, Jerusalem.

freedom of religion. Yet public opinion continues to be frequently agitated by discussions, controversies and further legal cases concerning the character of the state, and whether it should be secular or religious. A *de facto* situation has been accepted by the majority of the nation, with the exception of a small group of religious fanatics concentrated in Jerusalem.

Initially, Jewish Orthodox circles violently opposed Zionism. At the end of the 19th century, Jerusalem rabbis pronounced the anathema against Hebrew schools and Hebrew newspapers and against the ideals of the new immigrants. Enlightened rabbis in Central Europe as well as Hasidic Russian and Polish rabbis fought a long battle against those who sought to reconstitute a

Excavation, Southern Wall. Archaeological excavation at the Southern Wall of the Temple area in Jerusalem. The area being dug up by workmen was, in Temple times, a street along which were stalls where sacrificial animals could be purchased. The excavations over a wide area have given a clear picture of the approaches to the Temple and the routes by which the pilgrims entered its gates. Photo Harris, Jerusalem.

Jewish state by profane means. However, an opposite tendency also emerged in the circles of Orthodox Jewry. Leading rabbinical authorities were among those who initiated and founded the 'Return to Palestine' movement. Later, a Zionist religious party was constituted in the ranks of the Zionist Organization. This movement actively fought the predominant anticlerical tendencies but became a positive factor both in propagating the Zionist ideal and in promoting practical work in the Land of Israel. When mass immigration brought to the country thousands of Orthodox Jews from Eastern Europe and North Africa, religious influence over Israel society became stronger. It was further encouraged by systematic religious education and by the founding of religious youth movements.

Indifference toward religion, if not outright distrust, was the

Roman theater at Caesarea. Caesarea dates from the 1st century B.C. and was also an important center under the Crusaders; it has recently achieved new importance as a holiday resort when excavations revealed the full scope of the theater. It has today Israel's only golf course. Openair concerts and theatrical performances are periodically held in the theater, that had lain for centuries buried in the sand dunes. Photo Harris, Jerusalem.

Gasoline station near Avdat. Roadhouse near the ruins of the ancient Nabatean city of Avdat (central Negev plain), first built in the 1st century A.D. and destroyed in the 7th. The ruins, excavated and reconstructed, include Byzantine baths, a Roman camp, burial caves and churches. They can be seen on the hill behind the gasoline station, built by Nachum Zolotov. Photo J. Zafrir.

characteristic of young pioneers of the Second and Third Aliyot which respectively preceded and followed World War I. For them, Zionism was essentially a movement of national rebirth, a means to solve the problem of Jewish existence. They were the standard-bearers of social progress and individual liberty. They rejected the requirements of Orthodox Jewry and refused to put religious observance above everything.

In its essence, Zionism was basically a movement of return to the national past. Although it reflected the Orthodox conception of Judaism, it found its inspiration and its historical consciousness in Jewish tradition. Its main source of inspiration was the Bible. Biblical studies became a central subject, not only in Orthodox schools but in all the secular schools. A further source of inspiration was the Talmud and its legends.

The Israel way of life, though not subservient to the dictates of strict Orthodoxy, keeps traditional Jewish customs. The Sabbath came to be accepted as the national weekly holiday. Certain Jewish festivals returned to their original status of nature festivals or feasts commemorating historical events. Thus, Zionism and the new Palestine are largely responsible for the new significance of the *Hanukkah* festival, not only as the Festival of Lights but also as the feast commemorating the heroic victory of Judah the Maccabee over the Hellenistic oppressors.

In the same way *Lag ba-Omer* was given its true character of a festival commemorating the Bar Kokhba rebellion against the Romans (132-5 A.D.). Passover regained its character as a Spring festival, Pentecost (*Shavuot* or *Weeks*) was again regarded as the celebration of harvesting. The 15th of the month of *Shevat,* an almost forgotten festival was again the 'New Year of the

Trees' in order to glorify the plantation of new forests. The traditional customs of ancient Israel again found their natural ambiance.

In a different field, biblical interpretation and the study of the Jewish past underwent considerable development with the rebirth of Israel. Until then, biblical exegesis had been the almost exclusive province of non-Jewish researchers. Confronted by the topography of the Bible, living on the very site of the biblical drama, the scholars of Israel often superseded foreign researchers reconstructing the historical truth.

Yehezkel Kaufmann was the initiator of a new approach to the evolution of the Mosaic religion and modern Israel interpretation of the biblical past is largely due to him. His doctrine was continued and completed by his numerous disciples. The study of the Bible infected all classes and almost became a national hobby. Circles of biblical studies sprang up everywhere while congresses and biblical quizzes drew large audiences.

In the same way, the passion for archaeology, another characteristic of the Israelis, must be attributed to their nostalgia for the remote past and to their secret longing to bridge the tremendous historical gap that, for centuries, separated the people of Israel from its land. New archaeological discoveries thus elicit enthusiastic reactions throughout the country. Hundreds of volunteers often participate in the excavations: soldiers and members of the *kibbutzim* often become amateur archaeologists. After

Hechal Shlomo, Jerusalem. Hechal Shlomo in Jerusalem is the seat of the Chief ▶ Rabbinate and headquarters of other religious institutions. Photo Harris, Jerusalem.

325

326

the discovery of the Dead Sea Scrolls, the interest in archaeology became even more widespread and even specialized archaeological congresses arouse the interest of the man in the street.

For the circles of Orthodox Jewry, Israel has also become an important center of research and study of talmudic and rabbinic literature. The destruction of East European Jewry and the forced liquidation of the Oriental Diaspora have contributed to make Israel practically the greatest center of Jewish religious studies.

The great *yeshivot* (religious academies) of Poland and Lithuania have been reconstituted there. Prayer-books, new editions of the Talmud and other sacred works are printed in Israel and distributed all over the Jewish world.

The fundamental dichotomy between the two basic conceptions of Judaism still exists but the differences between Orthodox and secular elements are often made less acute through identity of opinion on the great political problems facing the State. The

Synagogue at Hebrew University, Jerusalem. The striking synagogue of the Hebrew University on the campus at Givat Ram, Western Jerusalem. Architect: Heinz Rau. Photo Harris, Jerusalem.

Synagogue at Hebrew University (interior), Jerusalem. The synagogue is raised from the ground, as can be seen from the exterior view (previous illustration); the ceiling is completely covered, and there are no windows so that the interior is lit solely from daylight entering from below. Photo Harris, Jerusalem.

mutual intolerance of the two groups that marked the early stages of the creation of the new society in Eretz Israel gradually abated. Avraham Yitzhak Kook, chief rabbi of Palestine during the first years of the Mandate, largely contributed to this development. He constantly preached mutual respect and insisted on priority being given to national interest over all else. The appearance of a religious working class, and above all, the formation in the thirties of religious *kibbutzim* and *moshavim,* helped promote systematic cooperation between secular and religious elements. As the years passed, interest in Jewish traditions and Jewish thought began to preoccupy the young generations. A general tendency to return to spiritual values as well as the desire to find new forms of contact with Judaism and Jews is discernible. This has been further stimulated by the demonstrations of solidarity with Israel throughout the large communities of the Diaspora during the Six Day War in June 1967.

THE NEW LITERATURE

Before Palestine became Israel, Jerusalem and Tel Aviv were already on their way to becoming the main centers of Hebrew literary life in the world. A fateful turn of events speeded up this process: from 1920 onward, literary creation in the Hebrew language was no longer possible in Russia, where it had matured. Similarly, Jewish life in Poland was on the wane between the two world wars, until its complete annihilation in Nazi crematoria. With the disappearance of this Jewish world another great Jewish vernacular also came close to extinction. Yiddish, which for centuries had been the language of East European Jewry and had recently waged a desperate war against the cultural supremacy of Hebrew, now lay in its death throes under the debris of the world in which it had come into existence. Once Europe had vanished from the picture, the Diaspora of western countries

Hebrew University campus, Western Jerusalem. The Hebrew University was founded on Mount Scopus in 1925, on the hill overlooking Jerusalem. Access was barred between 1948 and 1967 and during that period a second campus was created in Western Jerusalem. At the end can be seen the National Library; in the far left-hand corner, the Shrine of the Book, part of the Israel Museum, that houses the Dead Sea Scrolls. In 1972, seventeen thousand students attended the University. Photo Harris, Jerusalem.

which was linguistically assimilated, had no need for a specifically Jewish tongue. The Yiddish papers and reviews which are now left are not very numerous and the last paper written in Judeo-Spanish (outside Israel) disappeared when the Salonika ghetto was razed to the ground.

There was no doubt that the future of Hebrew literature was linked with Israel, where it lost its exclusive status of a literary language and found its natural reading public for whom Hebrew was the only medium of culture and thought. Although numeri-

cally restricted, this environment had the advantage of direct contact with the readers. The tongue was constantly enriched and became more flexible. The new generations spoke Hebrew, thought in Hebrew and, for the most part, read only Hebrew.

For a long time, the poets and novelists who had settled in Palestine continued to weave the threads of their literary work around life in, or characters from, the Old World. Hayyim N. Bialik and Saul Tschernikhovski, the two main poets of that time, continued to sing of their youth and bygone days. The novelists

described Russia, their youth in the *stetl,* the small Jewish communities and so on. They had some difficulty in adapting their palette to the unfamiliar colors of their new lives.

But new themes soon began to appear in Hebrew writing. Yehudah Burla and several other writers revealed the strange, little-known world of the Oriental Sephardi Jews. Later, Hayyim Hazaz, one of the best stylists of modern Hebrew prose, who had become known through his descriptions of his native Ukraine, discovered the mysterious and fascinating world of the Yemenite Jews. Avraham Kabak wrote a historical novel around the tragic figure of Solomon Molkho, the Jewish mystic martyred in the 16th century. At the end of his life, Kabak wrote the most successful of his novels, *The Narrow Path,* a historical evocation of Jesus.

Young writers looked for a new style and started exploring the hidden treasures of old Hebrew literature. The master of Hebrew prose, whose influence has been great on novelists and story-tellers ever since, was Nobel prizewinner Shemuel Agnon. His style, that skillfully blends elements from the Bible and talmudic literature, the symbolism of his descriptions, the graphic conciseness of his prose, left their mark on all the new literary movements in Israel. Though he mostly described the world of his native Galicia, *Temol Shilshom* (Only Yesterday) is a monumental description of Palestine at the time of the Second Aliyah.

Shemuel J. Agnon (1888-1970), winner of the Nobel prize for literature (1966), novelist and story writer, one of the most distinguished representatives of modern Hebrew literature. Born in Galicia, Agnon settled in Palestine in 1909, but spent twelve years in Germany. His writings deal largely with life in Galicia, though their scope is universal. He wrote in an original style of Hebrew, skilfully blending elements of talmudic and biblical literature. Government Press Office, Tel Aviv.

In the wake of the Third Aliyah, echoes of the literary revolution shaking the world after World War I brought about a revolt against Hebrew classicism. It was led by the poet Avraham Shlonsky, an innovator in the field of language and a virtuoso of the new Hebrew style. A multitude of disciplines joined him; the most important of them was Natan Alterman who, at a time when the Jewish population of Palestine was fighting for its very existence, helped in no small way to sustain the morale of the *Yishuv* and the courage of its young fighters with his poems revolving around topical themes.

From then on, Hebrew poetry acquired a new rhythm. Literary prose shed the successive historical layers, especially from the Bible, which had bogged it down. As with all new nations, poetry was the first province of literature to express the true character of the new society. The novel still had some difficulty in adjusting to the new reality. Yet, the hard life of the first pioneers, the famines, the constant struggle against Arab attackers, the sleepless nights in isolated villages, the atmosphere of siege and bloodshed, found their expression in the stories of that time.

The War of Independence caused the appearance of a new current known as the 'Palmah Generation'. For the first time, literature was in the hands of young writers who had been born and raised in Israel. This generation had not known the past from which its fathers had fled. To them Zionism was a remote ideal, for they had struck natural roots in their own land and did not need ideological justification in order to feel bound to it. They had been raised amid constant dangers. Before they had even reached manhood they had to drill with guns and grenades. It was they who won the War of Independence, using improvised weapons in pitiless battles, often in isolated groups in the midst of their enemies, sometimes alone. In these battles, many lost their comrades (the war took a toll of 7,000 of a population of 500,000). They emerged from it with a feeling of infinite sadness, a sadness pervading many of the literary works which appeared just after the war, and which finds its most typical expression in the great novel by S. Izhar, *Yemei Tsiklag* (The Days of Ziklag), telling of the actions and thoughts of a small group of fighters encircled on the top of a hill and doomed to certain death. Though not easy to read, this novel soon became very popular with the young generation whose feelings it expressed. Moshe Shamir followed the same line and produced a number of stories concerning life on the *kibbutz*. However, his reputation as a writer mainly rests on his historical novel *King of Flesh and Blood* which centers around the life of Alexander Yannai, one of the last kings of the Hasmonean dynasty.

The Knesset chandelier. Bronze *menorah* (seven-branched candelabrum) symbol of the State of Israel opposite the Knesset entrance, sculpted by the British-Jewish sculptor Benno Elkan. The *menorah* is decorated with scenes from Jewish history and was given to the Knesset by British parliamentarians.

331

Yad Va-Shem memorial hall (exterior), Jerusalem. A memorial and study center on Memorial Hill adjoining Mount Herzl, dedicated to the 6,000,000 Jews who perished in Nazi Europe. The main memorial hall is built of Galilee stones and concrete; the big stones for the lower part of the building and the plain concrete top were chosen for their gaunt impact. Photo Anatol Lewkowicz, Jerusalem.

Later, the young Hebrew literature opened its gates to the influence of literary currents in Europe and America. With the creation of the State, contacts with the outside world became more frequent, the taste for foreign languages spread and led to experiments in new and easier forms of expression. The avant-garde schools in America with their tendency to indulge in introspection, even to the point of sickness, have left their mark on Israel literature.

ISRAEL ART

The search for original expression and the will to keep abreast of the intellectual currents agitating the modern world have made themselves felt in the other branches of culture and art — more even than in the field of literature. Hebrew literature represented only the continuation of a long tradition, but this was not the case of painting, music, and theater where everything had to be started from scratch.

In 1906 an artist, a former professor at the Sofia Academy of Art, settled in Jerusalem and set out purposefully to create an authentic Palestinian art. Boris Schatz founded a school of arts and crafts which he called 'Bezalel', after the artist, who, according to biblical tradition, had decorated the Tabernacle in the wilderness. He created a style which was long identified with Israel's artistic production. He also discovered the artistic genius of the Yemenites and encouraged them to produce fine metal objects decorated with silver and copper filigree, after Damascene models, but representing specifically Jewish symbols. A whole generation of young painters came out of his school. Some engaged in experiments and found their own original style, while others kept to decorative painting.

After World War I, a number of Jewish artists arrived in Palestine, especially in Jerusalem to which they were attracted by the fame of the Bezalel school. Some came with the British army, in the uniforms of the Jewish Legion. At the beginning of the 1920s, an exhibition, sponsored by the British governor of Jerusalem, opened in the vaulted rooms of the Citadel of David, in the walls of the old city. This marked the beginning of genuine Israel painting.

In the following years, a number of Palestinian painters who had not found in the country an atmosphere favorable to artistic creation left their jobs, their *kibbutzim,* or their working camps,

Yad Va-Shem Memorial Hall (interior), Jerusalem. To the left, the Eternal Flame. On the ground, plaques bearing the names of the death camps: Maidanek, Auschwitz, Mauthausen, and others. Ashes of the victims are buried underneath. Photo Anatol Lewkowicz, Jerusalem.

and went to study in Paris, under the direction of the famous masters of that time. As a result, the influence of the Paris school is still very strong in Israel art.

At first, the artists tried to give plastic expression to the ideas of their environment. However, in the field of painting (as in the field of art in general), these experiments proved unsuccessful because of the very character of that ideology, which resisted artistic representation.

Before abstract art came onto the Israel art scene, landscape was the main genre of all the different schools that sought to capture the harsh quality of Oriental light. Later, the artists endeavored to capture the spirit of antique Hebrew and Canaanite models, especially in sculpture and the graphic arts.

At the end of the forties, an exhibition called *Ofakim Hadashim*

(New Horizons) took place in Tel Aviv, which showed the impact of modern expressionist art and of abstract painting. As the population of the country increased, the number of those interested in art grew. Israel art now exhibits all the different trends current in modern painting, and the work of its artists is increasingly appreciated abroad. Dozens of galleries appeared in the country's main cities. A deserted Arab village, Ein Hod, near Haifa, was turned into an artists' colony. Similarly, the old quarter of the kabbalists, in the Galilean town of Safed was restored as a residential area for artists and soon became a center of attraction for art dealers and collectors. Most representative and sought after today are perhaps Reuven Rubin, Moshe Mokady, Mordekhai Levanon, Jakob Steinhardt, Mordekhai Ardon, Marcel Jancu, and Avigdor Arikha.

Music Making

In this sphere, as in other aspects of culture, the artists have striven for, and to some extent achieved, a synthesis based on strong European training and influences, more exotic elements introduced by Jews emanating from Arab and Oriental lands, and the traditions of the Land of Israel itself. Jews that had never been aware of it discovered the beauty of the Sephardi liturgy and of the ancient Judeo-Spanish *romanzo*. The Yemenites brought all their collection of haunting melodies. And thus, from this mixture, the Israel song was born.

Symphonic musical activity began in earnest as early as 1936,

White from 80° to 180° by Buki Swartz. In the Billy Rose Art Garden, at the Israel Museum, Jerusalem. The museum was opened in 1965 and now consists of the Bezalel Museum, the Samuel Bronfman Biblical and Archaeological Museum, the Shrine of the Book, the Youth wing, and the Billy Rose Garden of Modern Sculpture, donated by the famous American entertainer. Photo Harris, Jerusalem.

'*Capriccio*' *by Sorel Etrog.* The Billy Rose Art Garden at the Israel Museum was designed by Isamo Noguchi, and its architecture follows the flowing lines of the Jerusalem landscape. The garden houses interesting specimens of modern sculpture. In the foreground Sorel Etrog's *Capriccio*. On the left Ezra Orion's *Sculpture* and on the right Picasso's *Profile*. In the background, sculptures by Vasarely, Karl Appel, Ossip Zadkine. Photo Harris, Jerusalem.

when the violinist Bronislaw Hubermann decided to create the Palestine Symphony (later the Israel Philharmonic) Orchestra. This was to provide employment for Jewish artists who had been expelled from German orchestras by the Nazi decrees. Previously, there had been numerous attempts at forming chamber orchestras and the few conservatories had already produced several young musicians who were later to achieve fame. The creation of the Philharmonic Orchestra was the starting signal for considerable development of Israel's musical life. The greatest conductors and the masters of modern music came to Israel concert halls and Toscanini himself directed the Philharmonic Orchestra during its opening concerts. This national orchestra also played a role in the

The John F. Kennedy Memorial outside Jerusalem. Built by the Jewish National Fund, in the center of a forest planted by US Jews in memory of President Kennedy. The building represents a truncated tree and has the same number of pillars as the US states. Architect: D. Reznik. Photo Werner Braun, Jerusalem.

historical events that agitated the State. During World War II, it gave concerts for the Palestinian soldiers in camps on the Egyptian front; it played in Eilat, after the liberation of the town; for the Israel Defense Forces during the Sinai Campaign; and in the amphitheater on Mount Scopus after the unification of Jerusalem. The Philharmonic Orchestra was invited to many foreign countries where it received a highly enthusiastic welcome.

Numerous other orchestras also rose to prominence, notably the Radio Orchestra and the Chamber Orchestra. Promising composers have begun writing authentic Israel music and expressing the national character of the country in modern musical idiom. The works of Menahem Avidom, Paul Ben-Haim, Ödön Partos (to name only a few) are frequently played abroad and a group of younger composers and conductors has achieved a reputation in the musical world.

See illustration page 304.

When Israel society was in its infancy, there were already timid attempts at theatrical activity. Amateur groups performed in the Jaffa schools and in the larger settlements. After World War I, a few professional groups appeared. But real theatrical life did not begin until the arrival of the Ha-Bimah Company in Palestine. This theater, the first professional Hebrew-speaking theater in the world, was created in Moscow in 1918, during the Revolution. This experiment at producing a play in a language that was not spoken at such a period, appeared somewhat incongruous. The initiative was due to a handful of young and passionate actors determined to realize their ideal whatever difficulties they had to face. A genial director, the Armenian Vakhtangov (a disciple of Stanislavsky, founder of Moscow's Art Theater) was won over to the idea. The enthusiasm for novelties and experiments which characterized the first months of the October revolution set a propitious mood. The first Hebrew theater in the world thus came into being in Moscow. When it staged S. An-Ski's *The Dibbuk,* a play based on Jewish folklore, it achieved immediate international fame.

But it soon became obvious that the Ha-Bimah Company could no longer pursue its artistic activities in Moscow where

Caesarea concert. A concert in the annual Israel Music and Theater Festival. Music enjoys enormous popularity in Israel today, with a process of amalgamation between musics of the different origins and generations. The elder generation brought composers and performers — some of the world's very greatest — with a rich European tradition; the middle seeks a stance between the music of Europe and the Orient, whilst the youngest composers try to base the language of their music on the inflections of Hebrew. Government Press Office, Tel Aviv.

hostility toward Hebrew culture became increasingly apparent. After a short stay in America and a tour of Europe, the theater settled in Tel Aviv in the late 1920s. Its chief problem there was the question of repertoire for, at that time, Hebrew dramatic literature was very restricted. This state of affairs compelled the theater to fall back upon translations of classical plays with biblical subjects and on adaptations from Yiddish comedies and dramas. Later, however, classics of the international stage were produced. Its fame abroad, which glamorized it in the eyes of the Israel public, and its team of first-class actors succeeded in satisfying and maintaining the interest of a wide audience.

At about the same time, another theater, Ohel (The Tent), which was set up and maintained by the *Histadrut* (Labor Federation) opened its doors in Tel Aviv. Its company of talented artists came for the most part from the working class and many of its members had been among the masons who built Tel Aviv.

In the following years, new theatrical companies came into being. The most famous among these are the Cameri (Chamber Theater) in Tel Aviv and the Haifa Municipal Theater. These new theaters usually reacted against the taste for 'classicism' and the influence of the Russian theater which characterized the Ha-Bimah. Israel's theatrical life continues to be very intense. Many

Zionist Congress in Jerusalem. Festive opening of the 27th Zionist Congress in Jerusalem (June 1968). Since 1951 (the Twenty-Third Congress) Zionist Congresses are held in the capital of Israel. The congress is being addressed by Dr. Nachum Goldmann, and seated on his left is President Shazar of Israel. Central Zionist Archives, Jerusalem.

338

original Hebrew plays have been very successful although no indigenous style has yet been born.

ISRAEL AND WORLD JEWRY

This intense intellectual life which we have tried, however schematically, to describe here, reflects a feverish urge to create, as quickly as possible, as if the artists intended to fill the vacuum left by centuries when they were unable to create independently. However, this constant pursuit of originality and tendency to return to the sources do not mean that Israel has acquired the cultural leadership of the Jewish world. Translations of Israel books frequently sell well abroad, Israel actors often achieve fame outside Israel, and Israel orchestras are greeted by storms of applause, but Jewish masses in the West continue to live in the cultural environment of their native countries, without these achievements leaving a deep influence. Seen in a historical perspective, the State of Israel is still far from holding the central position in the world of Jewish thought and culture as was the case with talmudic or gaonic Babylon, or Spain during its Golden Age, or Champagne at the time of Rashi.

The Knesset, Jerusalem (exterior view). Israel's single-chamber parliament. The Knesset was built with money left by James de Rothschild. With 120 members, the building was inaugurated in 1966. The view here is from the Israel Museum. Government Press Office, Tel Aviv.

Unlike the authority of these ancient centers of world Judaism, Israel's authority is not unchallenged. In those remote periods, Jewish life completely centered on the religious principles and on the philosophy of Judaism, whereas modern Western Jews, whatever the strength of their Jewish feelings, are primarily interested in the intellectual life of the countries they live in. It is not, therefore, so much the cultural glamor of the Jewish State,

as the very fact of its existence which has made its impact on the traditional basis of Jewish life.

It is not difficult to imagine what the fate of the Jewish people would have been in this tragic century, had the State of Israel not come into being. World Jewry stood on the brink of an abyss. The Nazi Holocaust had deprived it of its most active centers and of the communities that had been the most faithful to the values

The Knesset, Jerusalem (interior view). Government members sit round the table in the center. There is a portrait of Theodor Herzl on the wall at the back. Photo Hillel Burger.

Wall in Knesset chamber by Danny Caravan (detail). Photo Hillel Burger.

and traditions of Judaism. On the other hand, the newly acquired independence of Arab and North African nations was accompanied by eruptions of Muslim religious fanaticism and intolerance. Without the State of Israel, no trace would be left today of this ancient and individual world. Without the new state, millions of survivors, scattered through dozens of strange countries in complete isolation from their sources and without their traditions would never have been able to reconstruct their authentic way of life.

Without Israel, world Jewry would be represented by the great centers in the American continent, with the United States community in the leading position. But even there, the process of assimilation, which is in any case very strong, would have been bound to intensify to the point of endangering the existence of the Jewish community as a separate entity. As one modern thinker has put it: 'The hatred of the environment endangers the physical existence of the Jew while toleration endangers Judaism'. This is even more true when Jewish communities stray from their religious traditions or lack the centers that would ensure their cohesion.

The reality of Israel, its political, spiritual and security problems as well as the extraordinary achievements of its pioneers and the heroism of its soldiers, are a source of daily concern and of pride for millions of Jews all over the world. Russian Jewry, as has now been shown, sees in Israel a symbol of hope and a promise of survival.

One of the specific signs of the present revival of Judaism in Western countries is the extension of the school network which, for all its shortcomings, gives a Jewish and Hebrew education to an increasing number of young people, an unprecedented development since the opening of the ghetto gates. This education is based primarily on the teaching of modern Hebrew as it is spoken in Israel (besides the traditional Jewish subjects). The schoolteachers are trained in Israel's teacher training colleges or teach according to Israel methods; textbooks are composed of excerpts from modern Israel literature and the songs learned are Israel songs. 'Shalom' has become the normal form of greeting. In meetings between Jewish youngsters, girls and boys can be seen wearing Israel costumes and dancing the *Hora*.

A new style of Jewish identification has come into being. In the remotest corners of the dispersion, the Jews have their own flag: that of the Zionist movement which is also the national flag of Israel. When anti-Semitism reappears and incidents occur, no Jew tries to stand by and ignore the offense: Israel's courage is there as a constant reminder.

Public life revolves around Israel. Charitable institutions and

Africans in Israel. Students from developing countries in Africa study at the Hebrew University and other institutions of higher learning in Israel. In addition, many Israelis have visited Africa for extended periods in the framework of the government's technical assistance programs. Photo Harris, Jerusalem.

women's organizations do all they can to help Israel. Jewish students, when they are not drawn toward the leftist ideologies which are the fashion in Western universities, turn to the only alternative: Israel, for the Return to Zion represents a genuine and positive element of that change which youth seeks.

The unity of world Jewry and mutual responsibility concerning the fate of the various branches of Judaism are all expressed in the common concern for Israel. When a community is in danger, the Jews are no longer content simply to appeal to the conscience of the world. They demand the right of the persecuted community to join their brothers in Israel. To everybody, this appears as the most natural and sensible solution. Though only 17 per cent of the world Jewish population actually lives in Israel, the Jewish State has thus become the universally recognized center of international Jewry.

The deep concern of all Jews for Israel comes out clearly whenever a danger threatens the Jewish State. Never did this solidarity express itself more strongly than at the time of the May 1967 crisis which led to the Six Day War. With the threats of destruction hanging over them brandished by the Arab leaders who boasted of the coming victory and promised extermination of the citizens of Israel, the Jews of all Western countries, who had lost their confidence in the capacity and will of the Great Powers to find a peaceful solution to the crisis and doubted the genuineness of their determination to go to the rescue of the Jewish State, were not prepared to accept this time again the role of passive and powerless onlookers, unable to prevent the disaster about to befall their brethren. They were no longer prepared to stand by and do nothing. This determination brought about the completely unanimous stand of world Jewry in defense of Israel. It was an unprecedented manifestation. Thousands of volunteers set out for Israel and tried to get there before the outbreak of the war. Whole communities mobilized their resources in order to help the State.

Then came the first news of Israel's victories. When, after a few days, the sound of the *shophar* was heard before the Western Wall, in the very center of a reunited and liberated Jerusalem, a messianic wind swept over the Diaspora. Feelings of relief and pride, the intoxication of unexpected victory, immense emotion welled up in men and women who, the day before, had been struck with the premonition of impending catastrophe.

Israel is the product of a hard struggle, of the patient progress through time, and relentless work of three generations of builders whom nothing would divert from their final aim. When Israel came into being, the friends of the young state wondered what new message the young nation was going to give the world. Twenty years later, this question is still without an answer. A message is not something made to order. And yet, does it not verge on the miraculous that a young nation, isolated on its glorious but barren land, doomed by circumstances to live in a constant state of alert, should have turned the scales of Jewish history and aroused new hopes and expectations for an ancient civilization that stood on the brink of an abyss?

We have traveled far through space and time in the pages of this book. Our authors have applied themselves to discerning the Jewish spirit and its specific expressions in vastly varying contexts. It has sometimes been difficult to see the wood for the trees—but the wood is there, in fact a majestic, monumental forest. And—to change the metaphor—if we pick out the major strands, we find them woven into the overall pattern of Jewish civilization.

The many special manifestations evident through Jewish history are rooted in the vision of the Fathers of the Jewish People which has served as the inspiration of their descendants throughout the ages. First of course was the vision of the One God. Scholars of Bible and of comparative religion may dispute as to whether this was a sudden revelation or a gradual development, but the origin is irrelevant. Whatever its genesis, the purity of its conception and its implications became the lodestar of Jewish life. The great values of Judaism all flowed from this supreme vision.

It was this uncompromising monotheism which inspired the great ideals of the prophets that have informed Jewish life under all conditions. The natural corollary of the fatherhood of God is the brotherhood of man, proclaimed already by the biblical prophets and the attainment of which is a constant objective of Jewish endeavor. This is the basis for the universalistic aspect of Judaism. Unfortunately the outside world has too often stifled the possibilities for the Jew to give full vent to this side of his spirit. For this reason it has been important in these pages to indicate the external forces that have all too forcibly molded so much of Jewish life and stinted natural developments. But this side of the Jew has refused to be quenched. The vision can be detected even despite the grimmest restrictions and persecutions, and it bursts forth most visibly and irrepressibly in the humanitarianism that characterizes so much of Jewish life and thought. It has led Jews and Judaism to the liberal tradition where they have played so vital a role.

Pure monotheism implies not only human brotherhood but also human dignity. All men being in the image of God, they inherit an innate dignity which calls for recognition and respect. The Jew sees man as the subject, not the object, of history. He has himself known only too well the pain of humiliation. One of his achievements has been the maintenance of his own dignity in the face of heart-rending trials and provocations. Others under similar circumstances have become animals; the Jew has stubbornly clung to his culture and tradition and demonstrated that civilization need not be a veneer but can become so deeply ingrained as to defy the most outrageous challenges. And this

surely is one of the most striking lessons to be learnt from these pages, illustrated in the constant reiteration of the triumph of the spirit, evidenced for example by the unceasing cultural creativity or humane social structure maintained even in the degradation of the ghetto or in face of the callous deprivations that were so regularly the Jewish lot.

It is true that at the same time there has been a particularistic tradition in Jewish life. Its origins have been traced back to priestly circles but it has been nurtured by the external hostility to Jews and Judaism which inevitably turned the Jews in on themselves. Generally misunderstood from outside, it led to distorted pictures which reinforced the hatred, contempt, or mockery directed at the Jews, and this in turn only led to greater Jewish introspection. But even so the Jew knew that this image was a misrepresentation. He was criticized for his belief that Israel was a chosen people. There were times when the chosen people idea developed strong exclusivist overtones among the Jews but this was their escape from the horrors to which they were subject, from which they looked forward to the realization of their ideal to a time when their sufferings would no longer be in vain but would bring reward to them. But through them, all mankind would benefit. And the traditional view of the election of Israel was not a narrow exclusivism. On the contrary it imposed high moral duties and the Jew saw himself as the privileged bearer of the Divine vision—but the vision was open for all to behold and to accept. In fact the Jewish doctrine was far more tolerant than that of other faiths. 'Righteous men of all nations,' taught the rabbis, 'have a place in the world to come.' Salvation was not restricted to any one community.

And here is one of the cruxes of the Jewish condition. Faith as such was not enough. Indeed the very formulation of dogmas was a late development in Judaism and was only embarked upon to emulate external parallels. For the Jew the basis of his religion was action. Judaism was a way of life. This, too, had its particularistic side in the observance of the Commandments and the many special customs. The Law was basic and the respect for and veneration of Halakhah became a hallmark of the Jews. It engendered the discipline of Jewish society, which played such an important role in Jewish history and was one of the values communicated by the Jews to Western civilization. It sharpened the Jewish mind and in modern times conditioned the Jew for his prominence in the juridical profession.

But the universalistic application of the practical side of Jewish ideals has been one of the golden threads of Jewish life. One of the ringing messages of the Bible is that of social justice. From a modern viewpoint some of the provisions may appear primitive, but put in its own setting it remains a great document. It has only to be compared with other codes of its period for one to realize how progressive and forward-looking it is. And throughout the ages the Jews have applied that same spirit to their own situation and have always remained a few steps ahead of others. This has expressed itself in many ways. One recurring theme in this book has been the democracy of Jewish life. The Jews were one of the early democratic communities and their internal life has been conducted in a democratic spirit. It is therefore natural that Jews have been among the pioneers of democracy in general society and their inspiration can be detected in its development in countries such as England, the US and France where the founding fathers of democratic government were steeped in, and profoundly influenced by, Hebraic thought. It is therefore no accident that Jews have played a disproportionate role in the struggle for human rights. Here the Jew has been conditioned both by his long tradition and by the bitterness of his own experience as a perennial victim of social injustice.

A further basic ideal that we have seen emerge is the primacy of learning. The Jewish ideal is the scholar. The real leader is the sage versed in rabbinic lore who can draw on his knowledge for inspiration and guidance. Through him, the Law is personified. And the practical result is the predominant role of education in Jewish life. From the Babylonian academy to the Lithuanian *yeshivah,* from the Yemenite *heder* to the American day-school, education has been the keynote. When the surrounding society was boorish and ignorant, the Jew was literate and educated. Here, too, he has played a key role in handing down the vision of universal education and knowledge as the birthright of every individual. And when the Jew was admitted into non-Jewish society, he quickly shone by virtue of this tradition of literacy alongside the other qualities brought from his heritage, as well as a keen sensitivity, partly developed as a reaction to the negative factors which had forged so much of his history.

Ethics and morality have characterized Jewish life and this has been focused in the intimacy and healthy fabric of its family life. This is all part of the Jewish concept of Holiness which is another key to understanding the Jewish spirit. It is the result of their special relationship to God and was expressed biblically in the notion of the covenant—the acceptance of mutual obligations with God adopting Israel (together with all who would undertake the same obligations as Israel) while Israel agreed to a way of life embodying Holiness. Holiness permeates the life of the Jew. It is the reason for his acceptance of 'the yoke of the Commandments' which govern his every step and action. Some of the Commandments can be explained and accepted rationally, some not. But the Jew—at any rate traditionally—did not mind. It was the discipline of the holy life that was his special mission. Not only was he part of a Holy people but the Holy people had been granted a Holy land and the Holy land contained a Holy city. And apart from the people as a whole, the unit of Holiness was the family. The position of the woman in the Jewish world, it is true, retained many aspects of the Oriental attitude which had affected Judaism; but in the home her role was sanctified. And Jewish family life continued to be a model of its kind throughout

the centuries when it could serve as an example and inspiration to others. It is only recently that the Jewish family—like so many other traditional Jewish ideals—is being seriously challenged. The danger to Jewish *mores* stems from the challenge of assimilation and acculturation which threaten to achieve what all the oppression, persecution and discrimination could not succeed in doing.

Beyond the family, the reader will have detected the emergence of the sense of community. Indeed from earliest times the Jews have lived as a community. Their prayers, for example, are uttered not in the singular but in the plural; their confession reads not 'I have sinned' but 'We have sinned'. Worship ideally is a communal act and the Jew went three times a day to the synagogue which was not only a place for communal prayer but the center for study, fellowship and communal activity. Its very informality provides a key to the Jewish character; religion was not a remote expression of respect but an act of communal participation, an acknowledgment not only of gratitude to God but of devotion to the Jewish way of life and membership of the Jewish people.

And there is a further characteristic which should be recorded—and that is the Jewish belief in the dignity of labor. Circumstances forced Jews into an unnatural occupational structure but they have always retained their respect for labor bequeathed by the Bible. And whenever they have had the opportunity they have eagerly become working men—from the ancient talmudic rabbis who earned their living by the sweat of their brows, to the craftsmen of the medieval Mediterranean areas and of Eastern Europe, and the agriculturalists of modern times in Russia and Argentina and today's Israel. And to working men elsewhere the Jews have bequeathed the great boon of the Sabbath day's rest.

As we have followed the story of the Jewish people, its unique spirit has been manifested in a myriad ways. Details which perhaps appeared unimportant and irrelevant acquire their own significance when seen in their full perspective. The Jewish spirit can be detected in the way Jews lived, in their attitudes, in their writings, in the occupations they pursued, in their participation in the lives of the lands to which they were scattered, and in their many contributions to world culture, both creatively in every sphere of human endeavor, and as transmitters and catalysts. And in their determination to live according to their own lights, whatever the pressures put upon them, they have given an example of nonconformity and an insistence on maintaining their minority views and beliefs at all costs.

The special features we have described came to the fore in connection with the two cataclysmic events of recent Jewish history. The very fact of the Holocaust can be seen as a tribute to the potency of the Jewish spirit. It is a universal tragedy that Hitler succeeded as he did—but his attitude revealed a correct understanding that the Jews embodied everything to which he was opposed. Judaism represented the very antithesis of his insane paganism, of his degradation of man, of his wild attempt at the glorification of a group of 'supermen' on the basis of race rather than spirit. This would have been fought by Jews and by all who had inherited the Judaic spirit even if they had not been singled out as the major victims. And the behavior of the Jew in that period reflected their tradition—not only the desperate revolts but the study classes in the Warsaw ghetto, the orchestral and operatic performances in the Theresienstadt concentration camp, the synagogues established under the most bestial conditions, and the song sung by the tragic victims as they were herded into the gas chambers... 'I believe with perfect faith that the Messiah will come... even though he tarry, I still believe he will come.'

And most recently in the State of Israel, for which Jews have yearned, dreamed and prayed at every possible opportunity over the centuries. We are here at the outset of a new development in the Jewish spirit, the future of which is not clear. Inevitably under the new sociological circumstances, the new Israeli is not the same as the Diaspora Jew in many respects. But the bonds remain fundamental. They are different branches of the same tree and although they may appear at some levels to be growing away from each other, the trunk and roots remain common to both. The Israeli springs from the same Jewish tradition and is in fact more profoundly imbued in it than most of the Jews elsewhere in the world. And though the expression may differ, his way of life is influenced and directed by the same major traits as we have outlined above. There is, for example, the feeling for the brotherhood of man (witness the many contributions made by Israel to the development of the welfare of African states); there is the stress on democracy (unparalleled anywhere in or near the Middle East); there is the awareness of social justice, dignity of labor, and a feeling for community (most outstanding in the growth of the collective way of life, e.g. in the *kibbutz*); there is the stress on education (expressed not so much in its traditional forms as in impressive institutions of higher learning); and there is the flowering of cultural activities of the most intensive quantity and sometimes of notable quality. The signs are unmistakeable. They are the same as those that have distinguished the Jewish people throughout its checkered history, and which are still basic to Jewish living, in its various vicissitudes, throughout the world.

And underlying all these manifestations is one other fundamental—Jewish optimism. As we have seen, Jews have refused to give way or despair under the most gruelling situations. They have not given in or gone under but have continued to plan for the future—confident that eventually the world will be a better place and that they have still a unique contribution to make in that direction.

Geoffrey Wigoder

BIBLIOGRAPHY

(This list is confined to complete works in English).

General Works dealing with Jewish Spirit and Civilization

The Legacy of Israel; planned by I. Abrahams and edited by E.R. Bevan and C. Singer (Oxford, 1948)

Great Ages and Ideas of the Jewish People; edited by L.W. Schwarz (New York, 1956)

The Jewish Contribution to Civilization; by J. Jacobs (Philadelphia, 1919)

The Jewish Contribution to Civilization; by C. Roth (London, 1956)

Jewish Thought as a Factor in Civilization; by L. Roth (Unesco, 1954)

Jewish Influence in Modern Thought; by A.A. Roback (Cambridge, 1929)

The Jews: Their History, Culture and Religion; edited by L. Finkelstein (New York, 1961)

The Hebrew Impact on Western Civilization; edited by D. Runes (New York, 1951)

General Reference Works

Encyclopaedia Judaica; edited by C. Roth and G. Wigoder (Jerusalem, 1971)

Jewish Encyclopedia; edited by I. Singer (New York, 1901-6; reprinted 1963)

New Standard Jewish Encyclopedia; edited by C. Roth and G. Wigoder (New York, 1970)

Encyclopedia of the Jewish Religion; edited by R.J.Z. Werblowsky and G. Wigoder (New York, 1966)

Jewish History

History of the Jews; by H. Graetz (Philadelphia, 1956)

A Social and Religious History of the Jews; by S. Baron (Philadelphia, 1952 ff.)

A History of the Jewish People; by M. Margolis and A. Marx (Philadelphia, 1947)

A Short History of the Jewish People; by C. Roth (London, 1970)

A History of the Jews; by S. Grayzel (Philadelphia, 1968)

The Course of Modern Jewish History; by H.L. Sachar (New York, 1963)

The Jewish Community; by S. Baron (Philadelphia, 1942)

Jewish Life in the Middle Ages; by I. Abrahams (Philadelphia, 1932)

Judaism and Jewish Thought

Judaism; by I. Epstein (London, 1960)

Judaism: A Portrait; by L. Roth (London, 1960)

The Essence of Judaism; by L. Baeck (New York, 1967)

The Evolution of Jewish Thought; by J.B. Agus (New York, 1960)

The Wisdom of Israel; by L. Browne (London, 1960)

Judaism; edited by A. Hertzberg (New York, 1961)

A History of Medieval Jewish Philosophy; by I. Husik (Philadelphia, 1916)

Philosophies of Judaism; by J. Guttmann (New York, 1964)

Major Trends in Jewish Mysticism; by G. Scholem (New York, 1946)

The Arts and Sciences

A History of Jewish Literature; by M. Waxman (New York, 1960)

Modern Hebrew Literature; by S. Halkin (New York, 1950)

The Story of Yiddish Literature; by A.A. Roback (New York, 1940)

Jewish Music; by A.Z. Idelsohn (New York, 1929)

Music of the Jews; by M. Rothmuller (London, 1953)

Jewish Art; edited by C. Roth (New York, 1961; new edition, 1971)

A History of Jewish Art; by F. Landsberger (Cincinnati, 1956)

The Architecture of the European Synagogue; by R. Wischnitzer (Philadelphia, 1964)

Jewish Costume; by A. Rubens (London, 1967)

A History of Jewish Crafts and Guilds; by M. Wischnitzer (New York, 1965)

The Jew in Science; by L. Gershenfeld (Philadelphia, 1934)

The Jews and Medicine; by H. Friedenwald (New York, 1967)

Ancient Near East

The Religion of Israel; by Y. Kauffmann (New York, 1960)

The Archaeology of Palestine; by W.F. Albright (London, 1960)

Hellenistic Civilization and the Jews; by V. Tcherikover (Philadelphia, 1959)

Hellenism; by N. Bentwich (Philadelphia, 1919)

Judaism in the First Centuries of the Christian Era; by G.F. Moore (Harvard, 1927)

Everyman's Talmud; by A. Cohen (London, 1949)

A Rabbinic Anthology; edited by C.G. Montefiore and H. Loewe (London, 1938)

The Legends of the Jews; by L. Ginsberg (Philadelphia, 1946)

Byzantium

The Jews in the Byzantine Empire; by J. Starr (New York, 1939)

Byzantine Jewry; by A. Scharf (London, 1971)

Muslim Lands

Jews and Arabs; by S.D. Goitein (New York, 1955)

Judaism and Islam; by E.I.J. Rosenthal (New York, 1961)

Between East and West; by A. Chouraqui (Philadelphia, 1968)

Spain

A History of the Jews in Christian Spain; by Y.F. Baer (Philadelphia, 1961-6)

The Jews in Spain; by A.A. Neuman (Philadelphia, 1942)

Marranos

A History of the Marranos; by C. Roth (New York, 1959)

Italy

The History of the Jews in Italy; by C. Roth (Philadelphia, 1946)

The Jews of Ancient Rome; by H.J. Leon (Philadelphia, 1960)

The Jews in the Renaissance; by C. Roth (Philadelphia, 1960)

The Makers of Hebrew Books in Italy; by D.W. Amram (Philadelphia, 1909)

England and its former dependencies

A History of the Jews in England; by A.M. Hyamson (London, 1928)

A History of the Jews in England; by C. Roth (Oxford, 1964)

Social History of the Jews in England, 1850-1950; by V.D. Lipman (London, 1954)

The Jews in the Literature of England; by M.F. Modder (New York, 1966)

The Jews in South Africa; edited by L. Hotz and G. Saron (London, 1956)

Germany and Austria

The Jews of Germany; by M. Lowenthal (Philadelphia, 1944)

The Jews of Austria; edited by J. Fraenkel (London, 1968)

Eastern Europe

History of the Jews in Russia and Poland; by S. Dubnow (Philadelphia, 1916-20)

The Jews in Russia; by L. Greenberg (New Haven, 1965)

The Jews in the Soviet Union; by S.M. Schwarz (New York, 1951)

The Jews in Soviet Russia since 1917; edited by L. Kochan (Oxford, 1970)

Jews of Czechoslovakia (Philadelphia, 1968-71)

The Golden Tradition; edited by L. Dawidowicz (New York, 1967)

Life is with People; by E. Herzog and M. Zborowski (New York, 1962)

Hasidic Anthology; edited by L.I. Newman (New York, 1934)

North America

Jewish Experience in America; edited A.J. Karp (New York, 1969)

Early American Jewry; edited by J. Marcus (Philadelphia, 1951-3)

The Jews in America; by R. Learsi (Cleveland, 1954)

The American Jew; edited by O. Janowsky (New York, 1942)

The American Jew: A Reappraisal; edited by O. Janowsky (Philadelphia, 1964)

The History of the Jews in Canada; by B.G. Sack (Montreal, 1945)

Latin America

Jews in Latin America; by J. Beller (New York, 1969)

Jews in Colonial Brazil; by A. Wiznitzer (New York, 1960)

History of the Jews in the Netherlands Antilles; by I.S. Emmanuel (Cincinnati, 1970)

Zionism and Israel

The Zionist Idea; by J. Heller (New York, 1949)

The Zionist Idea; edited by A. Hertzberg (Philadelphia, 1966)

The Zionist Movement; by I. Cohen (London, 1945)

A History of the Holy Land; edited by M. Avi-Yonah (London, 1969)

A History of Palestine from 135 A.D. to Modern Times (London, 1949)

The Jews in their Land; edited by D. Ben-Gurion (London, 1966)

GLOSSARY

Aggadah
(adjective: aggadic)
The narrative and homiletical section of the Oral Law (Talmud and Midrash).

Aliyah
Immigration to the Land of Israel; in modern times, specific waves of immigration (First Aliyah, Second Aliyah, etc.)

Amora
(pl. amoraim)
Jewish rabbinical authorities between the period of the compilation of the Mishnah and the completion of the Talmud.

Ashkenazi
Jews adhering to the culture and ritual that was developed in Central Europe and eventually carried especially to Eastern Europe and to Western Europe and the Americas.

Bar Mitzvah
Ceremony at which a boy, on his thirteenth birthday, is recognized as an adult and assumes responsibility for observing the Commandments. The corresponding ceremony for girls (aged 12 years and a day) is called Bat Mitzvah.

Bet Din
Jewish religious law court.

Bet Midrash
Place of assembly for study or prayer.

Converso
Jew who embraced Christianity under pressure but remained at heart faithful to Judaism (also called Marrano).

Dayyan
Religious judge.

Dhimmi
Person in Muslim land accorded protected status and allowed to retain his religion.

Exilarch
Head of the Babylonian Jewish community.

Gaon
Head of the Babylonian (and other) academies.

Gemara
Exposition of the Mishnah; the Mishnah together with the Gemara comprise the Talmud.

Genizah
Depository for worn-out, sacred books; especially, the Cairo Genizah, discovered at the end of the 19th century, containing a wealth of documents from the Middle Ages.

Haggadah
Home ritual recited on the eve of Passover.

Halakhah
(adjective: halakhic)
The legal sections of the Oral Law.

Halutz
An agricultural pioneer in modern Israel.

Hasidism
(adjective: hasidic)
Pietistic movement. One such movement flourished in medieval Germany but the best-known one was founded in East Europe in the late 18th century.

Haskalah
Enlightenment movement through which the Jews of Central and Eastern Europe encountered the world of general European culture.

Havdalah
Service at the conclusion of the Sabbath.

Hazzan
Cantor in the synagogue service.

Heder
School (often a single room) for teaching Jewish religion.

Kabbalah
Jewish mystical lore.

Kashrut
Regulations governing dietary laws.

Karaites
Sect rejecting talmudic authority and basing itself solely on the Bible.

Kibbutz
Collective settlement in Israel.

Kiddush
Sanctification of Sabbaths and festivals.

Marrano
Forced convert; see Converso.

Masorah
Body of tradition governing the punctuation and reading of the Hebrew Bible.

Midrash	Exegetical interpretation of the Bible.
Mishnah (adjective: mishnaic)	Codification of the Oral Law carried out in the 3rd century A.D.
Moshav	Cooperative settlement in Israel.
Nagid (pl. Negidim)	Head of the Jewish community in Egypt and in certain other countries (generally Muslim lands).
Nasi (pl. nesi'im)	Title used by president of Sanhedrin and head of Palestinian Jewish community; also used by Jewish communal heads in other countries.
Pale of Settlement	Territories in tsarist Russia where Jewish residence was permitted.
Patriarch	Nasi (q.v.)
Piyyut	Liturgical poem.
Rabbinites	Normative Jews who accepted rabbinic tradition (as opposed to Karaites).
Sabbetaian	Followers of the 17th century pseudo-Messiah, Shabbetai Tzevi.
Sephardi	Jews living in Spain or descendants of those expelled from the Iberian peninsula at the end of the 15th century (as contrasted with Ashkenazim).
Stetl	Small community in East Europe.
Takkanot	Rabbinical or communal regulation.
Tallit	Prayer shawl.
Talmud	Name of the two major compilations of Jewish Law (Palestinian or Jerusalem Talmud; Babylonian Talmud) comprising the Mishnah and discussions on the Mishnah (Gemara).
Tanna (pl. tannaim)	Rabbinical authority quoted in the Mishnah.
Torah	The Pentateuch; the entire body of Jewish religious teaching.
Tosafot	Explanatory glosses on Rashi's commentary on the Talmud; the rabbis who compiled these glosses were known as tosafists.
Tzaddik	Hasidic rabbi.
Yeshivah (pl. yeshivot)	Talmudic academy; Jewish traditional school.
Yishuv	Modern Jewish settlement in the land of Israel; a place of Jewish settlement in Israel; a Jewish settlement-group.